Worklife Balance

Worklife Balance

The Agency and Capabilities Gap

Edited by Barbara Hobson

OXFORD
UNIVERSITY PRESS

OXFORD
UNIVERSITY PRESS

Great Clarendon Street, Oxford, OX2 6DP,
United Kingdom

Oxford University Press is a department of the University of Oxford.
It furthers the University's objective of excellence in research, scholarship,
and education by publishing worldwide. Oxford is a registered trade mark of
Oxford University Press in the UK and in certain other countries

First published 2014
First published in paperback 2015

Published in the United States of America by Oxford University Press
198 Madison Avenue, New York, NY 10016, United States of America

British Library Cataloguing in Publication Data
Data available

Library of Congress Cataloging in Publication Data
Data available

ISBN 978–0–19–968113–6 (Hbk.)
ISBN 978–0–19–874371–2 (Pbk.)

Acknowledgements

First, I want to acknowledge the excellent team of researchers who were involved in the making of this book; over the last four years we have met and grappled with how to develop models that fit our approach to the capabilities framework and then apply them in our research on gender, social policy and employment. This bore fruit in the innovative ways in which the capabilities approach has been integrated throughout the chapters in this book. Denis Bouget and Bruno Palier, coordinators for the FP6, Network of Excellence, Reconciling Work and Welfare (RECWOWE), were crucial for the evolution of this book. They brought us together along with a vast network of outstanding researchers. The cross-cutting dimensions of this book are mirrored in the four overlapping strands in the RECWOWE project: flexibility and security, family, work and welfare regimes, quality of jobs, and the future of welfare.

Our capabilities survey was initially conducted in two cities, Stockholm and Budapest. It was a collaborative effort; Judit Takács stood at the helm of the Budapest team. Then the dedicated group of Japanese scholars, led by Mieko Takahashi, took the initiative to get funding for the project and replicate the survey in Osaka. Their important contribution extended the scope of this book beyond the European context. I also had a wonderful team of researchers in Stockholm. Special thanks go to my collaborator and colleague in the Sociological Department, Susanne Fahlén, whose contributions are innumerable: conceptual and empirical, including the unique coding system that she created for the capabilities survey and the elegant diagrams in the book. For his heroic contribution during the last year, I am indebted to Christopher Grönberg, my research assistant, for data analysis and for getting this book ready for publication. For their comments on the Introduction and Conclusion, I express my gratitude to Jane Lewis, Livia Oláh, and Sony Michel as well Sonja Drobnič, Colette Fagan, and Aleksandra Kanjuo-Mrčela from our team.

I want to underscore the important role of Adam Swallow, our editor at Oxford University Press for his support and enthusiasm for this book and his recognition of the value of this interdisciplinary endeavor. I also thank Aimee Wright for guiding the manuscript through the production process. Eleanor Rapier from Stockholm did an excellent job in the initial copyediting of several chapters. For her important contribution in copyediting a book with this complexity and with so many authors, we express our gratitude to Caroline McPherson from OUP. We also are grateful to the three anonymous reviewers who provided us with comments and caveats for revision of the book.

The research funding came from different sources, mainly the European Commission, FP6 Network of Excellence, RECWOWE, <http://recwowe.vitamib.com/>. Two researchers in this the book also were supported through a European Science Foundation Grant; myself, through the Swedish Research Council, and Laura Den Dulk through the Netherlands Foundation for Scientific Research. Some of the research and data used in this book was funded through the Fifth framework project, Gender, Parenthood, and the Changing European Workplace; Susan Lewis was the coordinator and others in this book were participants.

Contents

List of Figures

List of Tables

Notes on Contributors

Nevenka Černigoj Sadar, PhD in psychology, is a senior researcher at the Organisations and HR Research Centre Faculty of Social Sciences, University of Ljubljana. Her main areas of research are: changing life patterns, gender divisions in paid and unpaid work in relation to social policy measures, quality of life in various life spheres, and women at the labour market. She lectures on organizational behaviour at undergraduate level and on career management on a post-graduate programme and is a mentor to graduate and post-graduate students. She participated in several of Slovenian and international comparative projects.

Laura den Dulk is a sociologist working as an associate professor at Erasmus University Rotterdam, Department of Public Administration. Her main area of expertise is cross-national research regarding worklife policies in organizations in different welfare state regimes. Current research interests include the role of managers, worklife balance support in the public sector, worklife balance among self-employed, and the social quality in European workplaces. Her latest co-edited book is on quality of life and work in Europe: *Quality of Life and Work: Theory, Policy and Practice* (Palgrave, 2011). She is editor of the international journal, *Community, Work and Family*.

Sonja Drobnič is Professor of Sociology at University of Bremen, Germany. Her research interests include social inequalities in the household and in the labour market, social networks and social capital, issues in social stratification, and quality of life and work. She is co-editor of books published by Oxford University Press, Palgrave Macmillan, and Stanford University Press. Her work has been published in journals such as *American Sociological Review, Družboslovne razprave, European Sociological Review, Journal of Marriage and the Family, Journal of Managerial Psychology, Journal of Vocational Behavior, Revue française de sociologie, Social Indicators Research, Social Politics, Zeitschrift für Soziologie,* and others.

Anneke van Doorne-Huiskes is Emeritus Professor of Sociology, Erasmus University Rotterdam and Utrecht University, the Netherlands. Her major research interests lie in the areas of welfare states, labour market and gender, gender and organization, organizational culture, and worklife balance. She has been engaged in the international research project 'Transitions: Gender, Parenthood and the Changing European Workplace', co-ordinated by Professor Susan Lewis, MMU, UK (2003–06) and participated in 'Quality', an internationally comparative project on quality of life and work of European citizens, financed by the European Commission (2006–09). She represented the Netherlands in the EU-Network Family & Work (1995–2001) and participated in 'Defining Family Obligations in Europe: A Cross-national Research', coordinated by Professor Jane Millar, University of Bath, UK (1994–95). She was a visiting professor at the University of Bath, UK (January–April 1995) and chaired the Social and Behavioural Sciences Section of the Netherlands Organisation for Scientific Research (2001–06).

Colette Fagan is Professor of Sociology at the University of Manchester, UK. Her research and publications address employment and public policy with particular interests in gender inequalities and gender mainstreaming; working conditions and job quality; working time (and time use more broadly); and international comparative analysis. She participated in the EC FP6 Network of Excellence 'Reconciling Work and Welfare in Europe' (RECWOWE, 2007–11). She advises the European Commission on gender equality policy as a member of its academic Expert Group on Gender and Employment (EGGE) and has been an academic consultant to a number of policy-shaping bodies including the International Labour Office, the OECD, and Eurofound.

Susanne Fahlén, PhD in sociology, is a post-doctoral researcher at the Department of Sociology, Stockholm University, with a background in demography, cultural anthropology, and political science. Her research concerns gender, social policies, and worklife balance across Europe. She has published articles in *Social Politics, The ANNALS of the American Academy of Political and Social Science*, co-authored a chapter in *Regulating Family Responsibilities* (ed. J. Bridgeman, H. Keating, and C. Lind) with Barbara Hobson, and chapters in *Childbearing Intentions, Women's Employment and Work–Life Balance Policies in Contemporary Europe* (ed. L.Sz. Oláh and E. Fratczak) with Livia Sz. Oláh.

Sandra Groeneveld is Associate Professor at the Department of Public Administration, Erasmus University Rotterdam, the Netherlands. Her current research interests include human resource management in the public sector, diversity management, and representative bureaucracy. Her work has been published in international journals, such as *Public Management Review* and *Review of Public Personnel Administration*. Recently she co-edited the book *New Steering Concepts in Public Management* (Emerald) and a Dutch handbook on strategic HRM in the public sector. In addition, she conducts commissioned research on personnel management and diversity management.

Barbara Hobson holds a professor's chair in sociology, with a specialization in comparative gender studies at Stockholm University. She has published many books and articles on gender and welfare states concerning themes of gender and citizenship, men and social politics, and social movements and gender diversity in welfare states. Her recent publications have focused on sociological applications of the capabilities approach, including articles on fertility and fathers and worklife balance. Her current comparative project: 'Do Welfare Regimes Matter: Migrant Care/Domestic Workers in Spain and Sweden', builds upon these applications of the capabilities paradigm. For the past few years, she has been Strand Coordinator for the EC FP6 Network of Excellence 'Reconciling Work and Welfare in Europe'

(RECWOWE, 2007–11). She is founder and one of the current editors of *Social Politics* (Oxford University Press).

Saori Kamano received her PhD in sociology at Stanford University and is a senior researcher at the National Institute of Population and Social Security Research, Japan. Her research interests are in families, sexualities, and gender. Besides being involved in the National Fertility Survey, National Survey on Family in Japan, and related projects at the Institute, she does research on lesbians/lesbian couples and has published work in English on the process of forming 'couples' (*East Asian Sexualities*, Zed Books, 2008), housework division (*Women's Studies International Forum*, 2009), and experiences of being 'lesbian' couples in the Japanese context (*Transforming Japan*, Feminist Press, 2011).

Aleksandra Kanjuo Mrčela is Professor of Sociology of Work at the Faculty of Social Sciences, University of Ljubljana (FSS, UL). She is a senior researcher at the Organisations and HR Research Centre (FSS, UL) and has been involved in a number of Slovene and international research projects. Her teaching, research, and consultancy activities are in the fields of industrial relations, organization, women at the labour market, ownership changes, and post-privatization changes in Slovene companies. Since 2003 she has been the coordinator of the national centre for European Foundation for Living and Working Conditions (Dublin). She is a member of the Network of Experts on Employment and Gender Issues (EC).

Margarita León is a senior research fellow at the Institute of Government and Public Policies (IGOP) of the Universitat Autònoma Barcelona. From 2003 until 2010 she was a lecturer in European Social Policy (SSPSSR, University of Kent). She has been a Marie Curie post-doctoral fellow at the RSCAS, European University Institute in Florence, Italy. She holds a PhD at the London School of Economics (2000) and an MA in sociological research from the University of Essex (1995). She has co-edited with A.M. Guillén *The Spanish Welfare State in European Context* (Ashgate, 2011) and is now preparing the manuscript *The Transformation of Care in European Societies* (Palgrave Macmillan, 2013).

Suzan Lewis is Professor of Organisational Psychology at Middlesex University Business School, London. Her research focuses on work–personal life issues and workplace practice, culture, and change, in diverse national contexts. She has led many national and international research projects on these topics and has worked with employers and policy-makers on worklife issues in Europe, Asia, and North America. She has been a member of an EU expert group on women in science, engineering, and technology. Her publications include numerous articles and books. She is a founding editor of the international journal, *Community, Work and Family*.

Tomoko Matsuda is a professor of the Faculty of Sociology, Bukkyo University, Japan. She has been involved in several comparative studies between Japan and Sweden regarding impacts of state policies on families and gender relations. Her research interests include work/family issues, domestic labour, and the influence of power on negotiations and conflicts in families as well as in organizations.

Setsuko Onode is a professor of family sociology at Kyoto Kacho University, Japan. She is also part-time researcher of the Kyoto Human Rights Research Institute, Japan. She has studied housework division and childcare networks in Asian societies. She is currently working on research on Japanese men's attitudes and practice of housework and childcare from a gender perspective.

Bram Peper is Assistant Professor at the Department of Sociology and at the Department of Criminology, Erasmus University Rotterdam, the Netherlands. His main area of expertise is cross-national research regarding worklife policies and wellbeing in organizations. He is co-editor of a number of books: *Flexible Working, Organizational Change and the Integration of Work and Personal Life* (Edward Elgar, 2005), an introduction to sociology in Dutch (Pearson, 2010), and *Diversity, Standardization and Social Transformation* (Ashgate, 2011). Current research interests include worklife balance, the role of managers, wellbeing and boundary management in European workplaces. He participated in the EC research project: 'Gender, Parenthood and the Changing European Workplace: Young Adults Negotiating the Work–Family Boundary' (TRANSITIONS).

Janet Smithson is a qualitative social psychology researcher. She has worked on a variety of national and European funded research projects. Her main research interests include gender and discourse, worklife practices and policies, life course transitions, qualitative methodologies, and Internet-mediated discourse and communication. She is currently carrying out research on mediation and alternative dispute resolution. She teaches research methods for research and clinical doctorates in the School of Psychology, University of Exeter, UK.

Mieko Takahashi is Professor at the Graduate School of Language and Culture, Osaka University, Japan. She obtained her PhD in sociology from Stockholm University. Her main interests are the changing role of the family in society, and working parents and gender from a comparative perspective. She is leading a research project, 'Work Family Balance of Japanese Men in an Era of Globalization' funded by the Ministry of Education, Culture, Sports and Technology (MEXT), Japan. She has also been involved in international surveys on worklife balance conducted by the Research Institute of Economy, Trade & Industry as well as Cabinet Office of Japan.

Judit Takács holds a PhD in sociology and currently works as the Head of Department of Research on Theory and Methodology at the Institute of Sociology, Centre for Social Sciences, Hungarian Academy of Sciences. She has been country representative at the Network of Excellence RECWOWE (Reconciling Work and Welfare in Europe). Her research has been focused on gender issues and family practices, social exclusion/inclusion of LGBT people, AIDS prevention, and anti-discrimination and equal treatment policies. She has authored and co-authored several books and journal articles, including her book on *How to Put Equality into Practice?* (2007), a book chapter on 'Differential Modernization in Hungary' in *Families and Family Policies in Europe* (ed. L. Appleton and L. Hantrais, 2003) and an article on 'Agency and Capabilities to Achieve Work–Life Balance' (with B. Hobson and S. Fahlén, *Social Politics*, 2011).

Kyoko Yoshizumi is a professor of sociology at Otemon Gakuin University,Japan. She received a PhD in sociology from Osaka City University. She has published broadly around the Japanese marriage and family system and has conducted numerous studies on illegitimate children and unmarried couples. She has done research on custody litigation in Sweden and has published work in Japanese on this: *Joint Custody after Separation and Divorce—'The Child's Best Interest' in Custody Lawsuits in Sweden* (Sekaishisosha, 2013).

Pierre Walthery is Research Fellow in Social Statistics at the University of Manchester, UK. He is specialized in quantitative methods, in particular longitudinal data analysis and latent variable modelling, whilst his substantive work revolves around gender and economic inequality in their spatial context. His latest projects include examining regional differences in working time and employment transitions among mothers and, more recently, health inequalities. He has co-authored several book chapters and journal articles on worklife balance and job quality, working time flexibility, as well as a large number of research reports in comparative industrial relations. He has participated in the EC FP6 Network of Excellence 'Reconciling Work and Welfare in Europe' (RECWOWE).

1

Introduction: capabilities and agency for worklife balance—a multidimensional framework

Barbara Hobson

Across welfare societies we have seen the emergence of policies and norms for Worklife Balance (hereafter WLB) and the rising expectations among working parents to be able to participate in employment and care and to have more time for leisure, friends, and family life. Yet alongside the value placed on WLB and quality of life, there has been a growing intensity and pressure at workplaces and increasing numbers of insecure and precarious jobs, both of which produce a deepening sense of economic uncertainty in everyday life. The agency and capabilities gap,[1] the title of this book, mirrors these tensions in WLB within families, workplace organizations, and policy frameworks.

WLB has become a norm within European societies as shown by attitudinal studies (ESS ISSP: see Chapter 2) in which the majority of women and men maintain that WLB is a main priority when considering their choice of job or workplace (Hobson and Fahlén 2009). There is also convincing evidence that most European men would like to reduce their working hours, even if it meant an equivalent loss in hourly pay (see Chapter 2).

New rights and entitlements for WLB have been introduced in European societies over the last decades, including rights to reduce hours, flexibility in working times and workplaces, and rights to care leave. However there remains an agency and capabilities gap in the possibilities for utilizing these rights and policy options, which varies across countries and within them. The extent of this agency gap is dependent upon how these entitlements are built into different national policy frameworks, how they are mediated through firms/workplaces, and how they are translated into individual lives and households.

This book is an effort to develop a framework for analysing agency and capabilities for WLB in a complex and multilayered universe of constraints and possibilities and of rights and capabilities to exercise them, considering different institutional contexts across European and Asian societies (Japan). The framework is inspired by Amartya Sen's capabilities approach (Sen 1992, 1999), which offers theoretical space for capturing the growing divide between the aspirations of working parents for WLB and quality of life and the economic, social, and normative constraints that limit their possibilities for achieving it. It asks us to consider not only what individuals do but also what their possibilities are for choosing alternative ways of living, their 'opportunities to be and do' (Sen 1992). This book applies the theoretical insights and conceptual tools in the capabilities approach to rich empirical studies across West and Eastern European countries and Japan with multidimensional perspectives within firm, family, and policy contexts (see the application of our approach in endnote 1).

This introductory chapter begins with a general discussion of how our agency and capabilities approach relates to debates on the concept of WLB. I then turn to our main focus: WLB theorized and applied within the capabilities framework. I provide a conceptual map of what, why, and how we apply capabilities in our studies of WLB. First, I present the main concepts in the capabilities framework that are relevant to research on WLB. In the following sections I discuss *why* a capabilities framework offers new insights into the agency gap in WLB and highlight our theoretical and empirical innovations to the capabilities framework: (1) by developing an institutional framework and models that adapt Sen's general capabilities approach to WLB with a gender focus; (2) by incorporating the firm/work organizational level to studies of capabilities; (3) by integrating the experiential cognitive level of agency into a capabilities framework.

Worklife Balance: A Borderless Concept

Surveying the research on WLB, Guest (2002) maintains that there is neither a precise definition of worklife balance nor of its constituent parts: What is work? What is life (nonwork), and what is balance? Research on the borders between work and life or work and leisure emphasize the lack of boundaries between these spheres (Clark 2000; Guest 2002).

We have taken away the hyphen between work and life balance intentionally. In doing this, we want to underscore the permeability and blurring of boundaries in the different spheres of life: work, family, and leisure time for oneself. The most obvious example of vanishing borders between life domains is taking unfinished work home. Another important phenomenon is the spillover effect, which refers to the process by which a role performed and affective experiences in one life domain (e.g. work) influence experiences in another domain (e.g. family) (Staines 1980). This can be seen in the emotional baggage that parents bring home after a stressful day at work or when they carry family worries over to work. The spillover effect also results from employers' demands that employees be available and on call all the time, connected virtually to tasks and unable to switch off (Fagan 2004; Perrons et al. 2006).

The distinctions between work and nonwork have become less clear in the case of care. Volunteering, community or philanthropic work is referred to as work, though it is unpaid. More recently, welfare states have instituted policies that allow family members to receive payment for taking care of an elderly or disabled family member (Ungerson and Yeandle 2007), a task that was not remunerated in the past and was understood in terms of obligation: 'compulsory altruism'.

Examples of leisure activities linked to one's employment abound, for instance, a working lunch. In Japan, one of our case studies in this book, dinner and drinks with your boss and colleagues is built into the long working day. Hochschild's study (2001) provides another perspective on the invasiveness of paid work in people's lives—crowding out other activities and values (Gambles et al. 2007). Among Hochschild's study of professionals, few working parents questioned their long hours or took advantage of the chance for flexi-time, paternity leave, or other 'family-friendly' policies. The roles of home and work were reversed: work offered stimulation, guidance, and a sense of belonging, while home became the place where there was too much to do in too little time. The Slovenian case of a multinational IT company (Chapter 9 in this book) has many features of the 'new company town' in which employees praise the pleasant work environment despite the long hours of work; yet those who are parents—mothers more than fathers—feel cut off from the rest of their lives with a workload that is incompatible with family life.

The institutional focus and multidimensional approach within the capabilities framework and the research strategies we use enable us to capture the complexity and dynamic interplay between work and family; and how institutional contexts can promote or weaken the potentialities for WLB and quality of life. The dominant research terrain in WLB is the demands and resources approach, in which role demands from one domain compete with one another (the result being work–family conflict) (Voydanoff 2005; Drobnič 2011). Our conceptual framework for WLB is much broader and allows for nuanced comparisons across institutional settings (a point made by Drobnič and León in Chapter 5). It is a multilevel approach integrating the individual/ household, work organization, and policy levels. We assume that WLB tensions exist between partners, within firms, and in cross currents in policies.

We do not view WLB in terms of utility or as a tradeoff between time and money (Gambles et al. 2007). Nor do we presume that there is an optimal division of work, home, and leisure that would suit all working parents (Leitner and Wroblewksi 2006). WLB, situated within a capabilities framework, is a lens from which to view WLB alternatives, quality of life, and wellbeing. It is a framework for analysing access to rights and policies for WLB and the possibilities of making claims for them (the agency and capabilities gap). When applied across different institutional/normative contexts it is a framework for understanding the mechanisms that underlie agency inequalities for participating in different spheres of life. Finally, it is a framework that calls upon us to ask different questions: beyond outcomes (what individuals do), to processes; the constraints and the possibilities for change.

What are Capabilities: A Worklife Balance Perspective?

Sen defines capabilities as being able to achieve a range of functionings (Sen 1992, 1993). At first glance this seems technical and abstract, but it is a fairly simple notion: being able to function in activities/achievements that expand the opportunities of what you can do and who you can be (beings and doings in Sen's terms). Functionings can be very basic, such as having shelter, healthcare, and an education, as well as more complex aspects of wellbeing, such as having self-respect (Sen 1992), all of which are seen as achievements that increase wellbeing and quality of life. We have added WLB to the list of potential functionings for wellbeing, which has become more salient in advanced capitalist societies where two earner families are more prevalent, job demands and work intensity have increased, and time outside of work is seen as a precious and scarce resource.

Rather than a specified theory, Sen's capabilities approach is a framework of thought (Sen 1992; Robeyns 2005). Most generally, it is an evaluative space to assess wellbeing and quality of life and the freedom to pursue it. Deciding which capabilities matter is dependent upon what aspects of wellbeing are being evaluated and for whom. Martha Nussbaum (2003) affirms the need for a list of universal capabilities, which she ascertains are minimally necessary for a fully human life.[2] More relevant to our research is Sen's context-specific approach that leaves open the choice of functionings and capabilities. He acknowledges the fact there are contextual differences in what kinds of values are valued and that different evaluative spaces are needed for assessing the capabilities to achieve them. These can vary across different geographic, social, and political regions and are legitimated through democratic dialogue

(Sen 1992). WLB is a value that has emerged through dialogues on many levels: policy discourse and laws and guidelines for best practice at the transnational level and within national governments, mobilization of actors beneath and above the state, advocated by NGOs and epistemic communities. European Surveys suggest a broad consensus on the extent to which WLB has become a norm, a value to be achieved (see Hobson and Fahlén 2009; and see also Chapter 2 in this volume).[3]

Achieving a WLB allows one to engage in activities that are intrinsically valuable for most of us, embracing many aspects of our lives that reflect wellbeing and quality of life: being able to combine employment with caring for family members, having time to develop friends and social networks. Not just having employment, but having a work environment that is enriching, and an employment situation where employer and co-workers are sensitive to family needs and desires (family friendly).

The difference between functionings and capabilities is the difference between what we seek to achieve (functionings), and the possibilities we have of achieving them (capabilities). Agency freedoms are the opportunities we have to achieve the things that we value (Sen 1992). Within the context of WLB and better of quality of life, this entails greater control over one's time, less daily stress and overwork, and a greater sense of security and wellbeing.

Capabilities and functionings are often intertwined and hard to distinguish from one another (Sen 1992) since often the things a person manages to do are linked to our possibilities for achieving them and the potentialities for making choices (the blurring of means and ends). Without good health, we cannot function in our jobs; conversely a poor WLB can affect our health. However, given that the specific lens in this book focuses on gender and capabilities, it is important to make a distinction between means and ends in capabilities (Robeyns 2005). This allows us to address what the long term consequences for wellbeing and agency freedoms over the life course are. Consider this example relevant to WLB policies addressed in this book. A mother might exercise her right to reduced hours, a policy that allows her to continue employment during the early years of childrearing. Yet, without the rights to return to her former position, this strategy might result in loss of employment or having to take a job in which her skills and education are not utilized (Fagan 2004).

Sen makes a distinction between wellbeing freedom and agency freedom, yet these are often conjoined (Sen 1992, 1993). Without basic functionings for wellbeing, one rarely has the freedoms/opportunities to make choices. Yet Sen recognizes that the constraints on achieving the values that are important to us go beyond a poor economy, and that gender inequalities are not reducible to inequalities in means and income (Sen 1993).

Why Capabilities

A Gender Sensitive Framework

Gender has been a key dimension in the capabilities paradigm in Sen's and Nussbaum's conceptual framing of capabilities, and has been the basis for developing various gender sensitive human development indices, including the Gender Empowerment Index and Gender Inequality Index. Feminist economists have taken the lead in accentuating gender in the capabilities framework (Agarwarl et al. 2003). Robeyns (2003) proposes a list of capabilities for assessing gender inequalities, several of which are pertinent to capabilities for WLB: employment, care, and time autonomy. For Nussbaum (1999), care is a universal need.

One theme that pervades the research on gender and capabilities is the importance of the capabilities approach for addressing the multiple sources of gender inequality that lie outside the market, including the gendered patterns of care and the division of household labour (Nussbaum and Sen 1993; Sen 1993; Agarwal 1997; Iversen 2003; Lewis and Giuillari 2005).

Care as a Value

As Lewis and Giuillari maintain (2005: 241). the capabilities approach provides a means of valuing care. Social care can be seen as a functioning in relation to choices around care: who cares and how care is organized. Women in particular have often experienced little effective or genuine choice around care (Land and Rose 1985; Lewis and Giuillari 2005). For instance, in societies where the male breadwinner model is strong, the benefits and considerable tax incentives for mothers to be full-time housewives have inhibited the development of institutional solutions that would allow women a genuine choice not to be the primary caregivers (Lewis 2006). On the other hand, in the former Soviet regime countries, full-time employment of mothers and fathers with little flexibility in working hours resulted in endemic time poverty among mothers (Heinen and Wator 2006). Traditional norms around women's primary responsibilities in the home were not challenged.

The valuing of care has been put into focus within the policy engines at the EU level, within agendas for work-first and activation of men and women in the labour market (Dean et al. 2005). The genuine choice to care has been submerged in what Lewis (2001) has referred to as the adult worker model, which presumes all adults will be in the labour market without taking into account the division of unpaid labour and the organization of care (Daly 2011). Within the capabilities framework, care and WLB are ends in themselves, not means to increase labour force or other instrumental goals, such as increasing fertility.

Gendered Norms

Sen, in his seminal article, 'Gender and Cooperative Conflict' (1990), demonstrates how the power of norms in family and society circumscribes women's agency and wellbeing. In that article, Sen maintains that in traditional societies women may lack even a notion of their own personal welfare because their identities are so tied to the household needs of others (Sen 1990: 148–9). Iversen (2003) considers intra-household inequalities and the implicit gendered norms and power relations underpinning them as challenges for the capabilities paradigm. Agawarl (1997) argues that underlying women's weak sense of entitlement to make claims for men's involvement in household work are basic sets of values over what work is and how it is valued–and that unpaid housework and care work are considered unskilled (Agawarl 1997).[4]

How cultural norms and gendered hierarchies in the family operate to restrict agency has been a dominant theme in the gender research on the power dynamics in the family in industrialized societies (Hobson 1990; Bittman et al. 2003). They also resonate in our studies of WLB, seen in the weak capabilities of working mothers to make claims for more gender equality in the household despite their earning contributions to the family. The double shift in women's work and burnout are its products.

The cultural constructions of motherhood and fatherhood can privilege men in prioritizing their role as earners and releasing them from contributing to care and unpaid work in the household: their choices limit the freedoms of women's choices in earning and caring (Crompton et al. 2007). The constructions of masculinities and workplace norms can limit men's agency to make claims for care rights and more active caregiving in households (discussed in Chapters 8 and 9 in this book).

Undeniably, the power of gendered norms underpins agency inequalities for WLB. However, the capabilities approach we employ recognizes that norms are grounded in institutional landscapes and embedded in policy frameworks. These shape the pathways and boundaries of choice for women and men to achieve a WLB. Normative/institutional contexts shape not only what we choose, but also what we perceive as within the realm of the possible.

An Agency-Centred Framework

Two key concepts in Sen's capabilities approach are choice and agency. Agency is at the core of Sen's framework (freedoms), but agency freedom exists within a universe of constraints. Choice and agency are interlocked in the capabilities framework: what one would choose is bound up with the real opportunities to choose. Sen's capabilities framework poses a frontal challenge to utility and preference theories in which choice is decoupled from agency, which do not recognize that the one's choices/freedoms are bounded by what we perceive as possible: not in terms of utility but of capabilities, not in terms of preferences, but in terms of genuine choice.

The assumption in economic theory is that workers' preferred hours correspond to actual hours (Becker 1991); that the market offers jobs that offer an optimal WLB (Hogarth and Bosworth 2009). These utility models do not reflect the preferences of workers or the constraints that they face in market economies. Empirical research reveals a discrepancy between workers' preferences and their actual working hours (reduction from longer work to shorter hours and deficit in actual and preferred hours (Fagan 2004; Lee 2004)). Using this work–time divide, Hobson and Fahlén (2009) found that a significant proportion of workers with young children would choose to work somewhat less even if it meant a reduction in hourly pay. Moreover, for women workers the gap between preferred hours and jobs in the market is determined by forces outside the market, most notably care/reconciliation policies (Anxo et al. 2006).

The household economic model assumes a fit between preferences and efficiency in the division of paid and unpaid work: women are better at caring (domestic capital) and men get the best economic returns on their human capital. Utility models do not recognize two key features that are central to our approach to capabilities and WLB: (1) that institutional settings shape work/family options and preferences; and (2) that preferences are not static but shaped by shifts in economic opportunities and cultural values.

The capabilities approach asks us what the opportunities are to exercise 'real' choice. What would individuals actually *prefer* if they had the capability to take alternative paths or choose another way of life? Of course we can never know what men and women would actually choose if they were liberated from gender roles. There is strong evidence in gender research that our choices are constrained and are structured along gender lines (Folbre 1993; Orloff 2010). Agawarl (1997) maintains that women's overt compliance with social norms does not necessarily mean that they accept their legitimacy, but rather that it can reflect their lack of options.

Choice in WLB is multidimensional, involving relational and structural features that are complex, contingent, and contradictory (Hantrais and Ackers 2005; Crompton and Lyonette 2006). Viewed from Sen's capabilities framework, one could regard all the women in Hakim's (2006) three categories of women's preferences and lifestyles as adaptive—the work-oriented, home-oriented, and adaptive—reflecting their capabilities for making choices. Their

WLB 'preferences' are not merely an expression of values and lifestyles, but rather reflect strategies or moral rationalities (Duncan 2005) for family and employment and their perception of the options available to them. These parenting strategies are often made and remade over the life course (Fagan 2001; Kan 2007). They can reflect shifts in one's personal situation and labour market options, as well as the introduction of new policies (Ginn et al. 1996). The same dynamic and contextual approach can be applied to fathers and WLB preferences, in which agency inequalities for WLB reflect norm constraints at the societal level, demands and expectations at the workplace, and economic and social pressures at the household level. As Lewis (2009) argues, the capabilities for choice in caring and employment among women would need to exist in a universe of fair and adequate wages, generous family policies, and secure work and family situations, as well as redistribution of household tasks.

Choice has generated much debate in the capabilities framework (Peter 2003). Sen's oft quoted example, the choice between starving and fasting, presents two unambiguous situations, in which agency is explicit in the latter and agency inequalities in the former. The analysis of time poverty by Goodin et al. (2008) formulates a similar dichotomy between agency (discretionary time) and agency inequality (poverty/time poverty), but the issues of choice (freedoms) are not as clear-cut as they are in Sen's example.

Goodin et al. (2008) construct an objective measure of discretionary time, which is time capabilities in WLB (though they do not use that concept). It is based upon the country-level median hours an individual must be employed to receive an income above the poverty line; all time use above that is discretionary time. Their corresponding measure of unpaid housework (discretionary unpaid work) is the median hours devoted to such work in a given country.[5] Though highly sophisticated in its construction of measures, the basic reasoning about choice and time autonomy assumes that most individuals in advanced Western societies have the agency to determine their working hours, change jobs, and have control over their working lives.[6] The conclusion of the study is that time poverty is a matter of choice for most of us who are not poor, so you should not complain about not having enough time as this is a consequence of your own choices about how to use time. A measure that uses the medium level of income as a baseline for assessing WLB, however, does not offer much analytical purchase on the agency inequalities in WLB. It is not inclusive enough for an evaluative space for WLB and quality of life (Burchardt 2010).

The ILO studies on decent working times in Boulin et al. (2006) offer another perspective on capabilities and choice, suggesting that most workers cannot vote with their feet and find another job that allows more family and leisure time. This may be even less of an option for the majority of workers in a period of global economic crises, downturns, and rising unemployment. Burchardt (2008) notes that few perceive themselves as having much discretion in reorganizing their time. Subjective time pressure is real and affects health, wellbeing, and quality of life, an outcome that is underlined in the studies in this book. Drobníc's (2011) research on work–home conflict also offers evidence for this within the demands resource approach. Time poverty and actual poverty are often connected, as seen in the double shifts workers take on under weak and precarious economic conditions. The capabilities approach applied to worklife makes visible the normative as well as the structural constraints under which we make our choices.

Choice in Sen's capabilities approach is not open ended, agency freedoms are framed in terms of what people are actually able to do and to be. Genuine choice in capabilities is cast in terms of effective choice. Put another way, effective choice embraces our scope of alternatives, our (potential) freedoms to make a choice. Choices are limited by our natural abilities and disabilities and natural environments, but they also are bounded by the normative/institutional settings in which we live (Sen 1992); WLB is an exemplary case for capturing the complexities in choice and agency within welfare states undergoing change.

A Dynamic Institutional Analysis

According to Sen, people live and operate in world of institutions and our prospects depend on what institutions exist and how they function (Sen 1992); institutions and policies play a central role in a person's opportunities to be and do (Sen 1992; Bifuculo et al. 2010). Within the context of welfare state institutions, the capabilities approach offers a dynamic and agency-centred set of perspectives on the multidimensional aspects of welfare state change and their impact on WLB possibilities.

Path dependency is the mechanism employed to explain patterns of institutional development and stratification outcomes in welfare states, as well as the gendered logics of welfare states (i.e. the extent to which welfare states weaken or sustain the male breadwinner ideal) (Lewis 1997; Korpi 2000). However, in the current period of welfare state change, the regime configurations we have used to analyse gender dimensions are less stable (Lewis 2009; Daly 2011). With its dynamic agency-centred framework, the capabilities approach allows us to capture the shifting configurations in state/market/family relations (Esping-Andersen 1999), the new social risks emerging from welfare state restructuring, globalizing markets (Bonoli 2006), and the challenges for organizing care emerging from women's entry into employment, particularly mothers of young children (Knijn and Komter 2004).

Two general trends that characterize what Bonoli and Natali (2012) refer to as the 'new welfare state' are salient for understanding WLB and welfare regime configurations: the reorientation from income protection to promotion of labour force participation; and the use of social investment policies facilitating work and family life. Some welfare regime theorists highlight the convergences among welfare states fostered in neoliberal economies, seen in the retrenchment in welfare states and labour market deregulation (Streeck and Thelen 2005; Bonoli 2006). Others (e.g. Hall 2007) maintain that European economies are not moving toward one common neoliberal model, but that similar processes are adapted and negotiated within national architectures. This is evident in the responses or lack thereof to the shifts in gendered patterns of care and employment (Blossfeld and Drobnič 2001; Crompton et al. 2007). Lewis (2009) argues that while we have seen a marked change in policy instruments relating to family and work, policy-makers do not start with a clean slate (p. 21).

WLB research calls for a paradigm that allows for more dynamic agency-centred approaches to welfare state change and its gender dimensions. Gendered norms with respect to care obligations shape and have been shaped by institutional path dependencies in welfare states, as seen in the gendered construction of various policies around caring and earning (care regimes) (Anttonen and Sipilä 1996) and the cultural norms that underpin them (Pfau-Effinger 2005). There has been a perceptible shift in how care needs of individuals are met, organized, and financed in societies with the rising levels of women's paid labour and the social investment of states in childcare (Jenson 2012), alongside the expanding marketization/privatization and outsourcing of care services (Mahon et al. 2012).

The concept of care culture (Pfau Effinger 2005) or gender culture (Cousins and Tang 2004; Van der Lippe et al. 2006) is often used to explain differences in WLB policies across societies (Van der Lippe and Peters 2007). In analysing the agency and capabilities gap, one has to unpack concepts such as these: to begin with, we have to consider how gendered norms operate overtly and covertly in different sites—family, market, law, and policy. The assumption in gender cultures is that norms and values operate in a consistent way; policies and practices follow suit. Changes in patterns of women's work, family fluidity, and welfare states challenge this assumption. Norms and values can change with the emergence of new discourses and policies. As legal theorists of capabilities acknowledge, rights and entitlements can themselves seed new norms (Barnard et al. 2001). A dynamic and agency-centred approach necessitates research strategies that capture dimensions of persistence and fluidity and change in 'doing gender' in everyday lives.

Built into a capabilities approach are the possibilities for different scenarios and alternatives. Though men's share of household work has increased, most agree that the change in men's care/domestic work has not been commensurate with women's increase in paid work (Gershuny 2000; Lewis 2009). Despite new rights for parental and paternal leave for fathers, the statistics on men's take-up of parental leave do not show dramatic change (Ferrarini and Duvander 2010).

However, these statistics on take-up of policies do not capture the shifting norms and aspirations of a new generation of mothers and fathers (Crompton et al. 2007; Hobson and Fahlén 2009; Doucet 2009) for participating in employment and care. Sen's framework allows us to go beyond the outcomes of who does what and for how long in parenting and care and engage with the potentialities for change for WLB.

By focusing on agency inequalities we are highlighting the need for more dynamic models for comparative welfare state research: for process-oriented frameworks rather than the more conventional analysis of welfare regimes or gender regimes for analysing the dynamics of welfare state change (Bonoli and Natali 2012) and the gender patterns within them (Crompton et al. 2007; Daly 2011).

How Capabilities: Adapting and Applying the Capabilities Approach to WLB

Conversion Factors and Capabilities: A Multidimensional Model

The capabilities approach has been employed most often as a normative framework for evaluating and assessing institutional forms. Our purpose here is not to develop measurements or benchmarks for policy design, though institutions and policy are core components in our analysis of conversion factors for WLB. The institutional approach we take is framed around two questions using the capabilities approach: how are resources converted into agency for WLB and what are the capabilities for individuals to choose to do so? These questions lead toward the core of the capabilities framework: conversion factors can either promote or impede the opportunities to achieve (capabilities) (Fahlén 2012). They influence genuine choice, and have a significant effect on agency and agency inequalities in realizing a valued functioning (in our case WLB and quality of life). Sen constructed three categories (later called conversion factors, Robeyns 2005): (1) individual factors, abilities, and skills; (2) environmental factors, including physical surroundings and technological infrastructure; and (3) societal factors that encompass social norms, legal norms, and public policies. While maintaining the multidimensionality in the capabilities approach, we have adapted these categories and modified them to fit our evaluative space: capabilities for WLB in advanced capitalist societies across welfare regimes. Our model of conversion factors shaping capabilities includes (1) individual factors (situated agency); (2) institutional factors; and (3) societal/cultural factors. Our institutional and gender focus takes us beyond the notion of individual factors as endowments or abilities (Nussbaum 1993). We use the concept of situated agency, laying emphasis on its relational and social dimensions that include resources, skills, and human capital (often included in other models), as well as gender, class, age, and ethnicity. In addition we add a partner's resources and situation and family networks. The latter are facets of situated agency that are important for capabilities and WLB and its gendered dimensions. This may seem to represent a contradiction in a framework built around individual freedoms.[7] Yet although the individual is the 'moral unit' in which human agency is at the centre of the capabilities approach, Sen underscores that persons are not isolated atoms in the capabilities approach, but instead their options/opportunities greatly depend upon relations with others and what the state and other institutions do (Drèze and Sen 2002: 6; Robeyns 2003). In fact, Sen's institutionally embedded framework for agency and capabilities offers an implicit critique of methodological individualism that assumes that all explanations are referenced by individual actions (Hedström and Swedberg 1996; Fahlén 2012).

Institutions are central for capabilities and WLB, and we distinguish them from societal/cultural factors (norms and civil society actors shaping them). In much the same way that the choice of valuable functionings are context-dependent (Sen 1992), our choice of institutional factors that affect agency achievement in WLB is derived from the extensive contextualized research on welfare regimes and gender, states, and citizenship.[8] We accentuate the nestedness of capabilities, illustrating the interplay of institutional and societal/cultural factors (see Figure 1.1). We highlight the multidimensionality of conversion factors and capabilities and their complex intersections, particularly at the institutional level, encompassing welfare regime configurations and the work organizational culture in firms.

Taken together these different dimensions of conversion factors and capabilities shape the individual potential to achieve (what Sen (1992) refers as the capability set) and his/her agency freedoms for WLB, the opportunities to achieve a WLB and quality of life.

Situated Agency

Agency is always situated agency in the capabilities framework. We use this concept to emphasisze that the possibilities of individuals to convert resources into capabilities for WLB are interwoven with gender. Situated agency also allows space for incorporating intersections across social categories such as gender, age, class, ethnicity—a now taken for granted approach

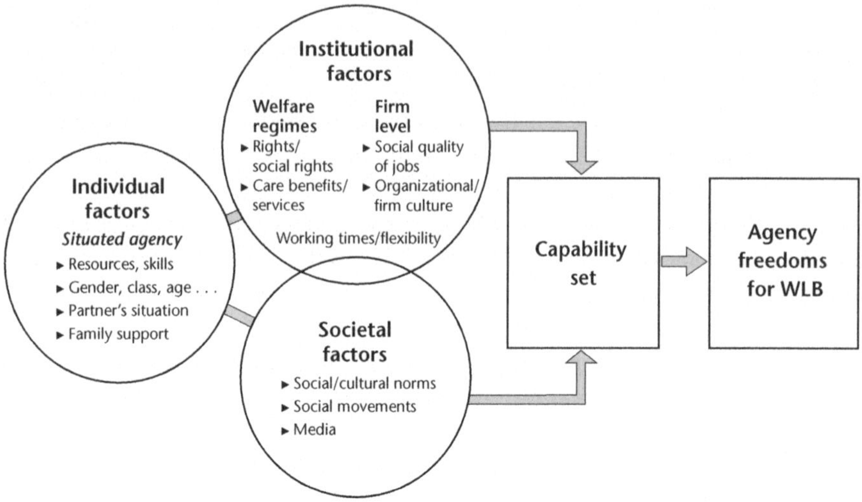

Figure 1.1 Capabilities and conversion factors

in research on gender inequalities (McCall 2005).[9] The research on WLB in this book lends support for consideration of differences in capabilities within gender categories. Our institutional approach to WLB makes the crucial distinction between abilities and capabilities more visible: those with less individual resources (both men and women), skills, and networks/social capital are more reliant on laws, policies that support WLB.

The gendering of conversion factors and capabilities in relational terms (Peter 2003) takes into account that what fathers do in terms of WLB affects mothers' capabilities and range of choices and vice versa. The skills and education of one partner has an influence on the agency/agency inequalities in WLB of the other. That women tend to earn less than men shapes the organization of care and domestic work in the household. Situated agency recognizes the power dimension in these negotiations (Iversen 2003).

The high correlation between education and egalitarianism in the family and men's contribution to care in the family (Blossfeld and Drobnič 2001) is another example of how these interactions shape capabilities. Situated agency acknowledges these relational sides of agency and agency inequalities (Peter 2003). Nevertheless, we depart from the household strategies approach (Wallace 2002), in which individual agency is not given theoretical space since the household is the unit of analysis.

Another dimension of the relational sides of agency, that has been less analysed or theorized within the capabilities framework, is the importance of networks (Stiglitz et al. 2009). Here again the interpendencies in agency are apparent. In WLB, family networks continue to play a significant role in providing care for children and the elderly, even in societies with substantial social care (Vabo and Szebehely 2102). Relatives taking on care responsibilities may be the only way that some parents (mainly mothers) gain the possibility of employment.[10] In Hungary, one of our case studies, parents can transfer their childcare benefit to a grandparent taking care of a child (noted in Chapter 3 in this book). Our Japanese study confirms the well-known pattern there: that having relatives is essential for women's possibilities of employment.

The Institutional Factors

Institutional factors lie at the centre of our model, reflecting their primacy for capabilities for WLB. The integration of social dimensions in Sen's framework has been recognized as an aspect of the capabilities approach that needs to be developed further (Evans 2002; Robeyns 2006; Bifulco et al. 2010). The complex institutional analysis, reflected in our research strategies and models, brings in new dimensions to the capabilities paradigm.

Within our multilayered model, at the institutional level, we recognize that capabilities for WLB exist beyond and beneath the state. For European societies, the EU has formulated frameworks for rights and policies in its various Directives: maternity and parental leave, reduced hours, limits weekly hours, and targets for childcare coverage. The agency gap in WLB can be tracked through the translation of rights and policies into the national institutional context: whether they are implemented or enforced.

Welfare Regime Configurations

As our model suggests, institutional characteristics of welfare regimes can enable or impede agency for WLB. How care is organized and who does the caring (care regime) continues to reflect differences in WLB capabilities across and within societies (Anttonen and Sipilä 1996; Daly and Lewis 2000), notwithstanding the increased social investment in childcare among conservative familialist welfare states and trends in privatization/marketization in Nordic welfare states (Mahon et al. 2012). Whether rights are social rights can enhance men's capabilities for care. As most benefits have a ceiling, raising the ceiling closer to wage replacement has been shown to increase men's possibilities of converting rights to care into WLB claims (Ferrarini and Duvander 2010). In fact, parental caring time can be seen as a redistributive resource within welfare states and a conversion factor for WLB: how care leave is compensated; how pension points are calibrated to cover leave; and more generally the level of resources/subsidies states and municipalities provide for services for children, the elderly, and the disabled. Gendered research on welfare states has led to the integration of this dimension into the welfare regime research (O'Connor et al. 1999; Williams et al. 1999; Daly and Lewis 2000).

Other dimensions of welfare states also reveal differences in capabilities for WLB. These include the degree of unionization and union coverage; the tolerance for informal and precarious employment and regulatory systems for employment health and safety; as well as laws protecting those who utilize WLB policies. All of these underlie the possibilities for working parents to claim rights for WLB.

Governance over market and firm practices vary across welfare regimes, expressed in terms of the degree of regulation over market structures (Hall and Soskice 2001). Nevertheless, even in most institutionalized welfare states, neoliberal deregulation has provided more space for firms to mediate WLB policies and practices (Lee and McCann 2006).

The Firm Level

With the new and expanding rights and policies for WLB that include male and female employees, the firm/work organization has become a mediator in granting or denying claims, an actor initiating new policies in flexible working schemes, and even a place where information is disseminated or withheld. The dominance of the firm in capabilities and agency for WLB is most visible in our Japanese case, where the firm has set the agenda of employment rights and responsibilities (Yamaguchi 2012) and where few employees are even aware of their rights (discussed in Chapter 4). Studies of the discretionary power of middle managers and human resource managerial staff show how entitlements are interpreted and claims at this level denied or granted in everyday practice, illustrating the ways in which the firm work organizational level is a conversion factor in WLB (developed in Chapters 8 and 9).

At the firm level, work organizational cultures operate in direct and indirect ways to reproduce gendered norms in WLB. Employees who are most valued are those who demonstrate loyalty to the firm: being present and being on call. This is most evident in Japanese firms, in which one cannot leave work until the boss does and in which there is an expectation that a full-time housewife sustains family life within the household (Chapter 4). In many workplaces, long working days are not necessarily a top-down effect, but have become part of work organizational cultures in which wages are often based on performance. In highly competitive work cultures the task determines the working day and allows for ever expanding demands on employees (Perrons et al. 2006; Hogarth and Bosworth 2009), a refrain that is repeated among respondents in the surveys and focus groups we interviewed for this book. The competitive atmosphere in firms, which has intensified in the global economy, can foster resentment among colleagues who have to pick up the slack for parents taking care leave: whether firms find replacements for employees on leave becomes a factor in the agency and capabilities gap for WLB.

Gendered norms operate in firms so that a mother's claims for WLB, care leave, and reduced hours, are supported to a greater degree than a father's. For working mothers, the penalties in wages and promotion or recruitment are underpinned by these gendered normative assumptions around care. The qualitative studies in this book show that fathers expect to experience penalties in pay and career trajectories when exercising their parental leave rights, as some previous studies suggest (Hobson et al. 2007). Masculine identities and gendered work cultures are intertwined (Perrons et al. 2006).

Working Times and Capabilities

The European Union's Working Time Directive (93/104/EC) has established a 48-hour upper limit to weekly hours and most member states have established a more stringent limit on weekly hours. (The UK has formally opted out of this.) Of course, this limit may or may not be applied in workplaces and does not relate to how many hours individuals are actual devoting to unpaid overtime work.

Working time patterns exist across countries, reaching up to 50 and 60 hours a week in Central Eastern European Countries (Fahlén and Hobson 2009), reflecting working time norms within countries, working time regimes. These regimes encompass legal contractual work limits set by governments or collective agreements, but also reflect norms in professions and within firms (Rubery 1998; Bruning and Plantenga 1999). Though working times vary across occupations, sectors, and individual contracts, there are gendered patterns in societies that reveal differences in the institutional context.

In some countries, full-time work is the norm for both men and women, and part-time work is not an available option for many working mothers. Not having this option often weakens women's capabilities for employment (highlighted in the Chapter 5 focusing on the German and Spanish cases). In European societies, women's working time regimes are on the average less than men's (Bruning and Plantenga 1999). Not to be forgotten in this context of working time regimes is the fact that if paid work and unpaid work are added together, women on average work longer hours than men (Aliaga 2006). Short, part-time, weekly hours exist in countries such as the Netherlands and the UK, in which working time patterns in certain feminized sectors of the labour market assume social norms and expectations about women's care responsibilities. Short, part-time work is also bound up with structural features in the labour market—jobs are organized around a temporary and flexible female workforce (Ginn et al. 1996). These jobs are characterized by weak agency and capabilities for WLB, a lack of fixed schedules, asocial hours, and may lack social benefits.

Lee and McCann (2006) employ a concept of working time capabilities that relates to policies for WLB implemented in workplaces. Various time options and policies exist in many workplaces to facilitate choice in working times: part-time work, flexi-time, compressed hours, staggering work, long days, home working, and many variants. Whether and to what extent these time options increase capabilities for WLB and quality of life is an open question addressed in in this book.

Flexibility in WLB demonstrates the complexity in assessing policies in terms of conversion factors in our capability set for WLB. Rights to reduce hours have allowed women to combine family and employment, yet whether this option weakens or strengthens capabilities for WLB over the life course varies in relation to state- and firm-level policies on the possibilities of switching from part-time to full-time work, the other way around, or both—full reversibility, which offers the most capabilities (elaborated in Fagan and Walthery, Chapter 7).

Of foremost significance with respect to flexibility is whether it is employee or employer driven. For the most part, flexibility has been driven largely by the efforts of enterprises to compete in the context of heightened market uncertainty and globalization, economic restructuring (highlighted in the chapter on Slovenia (Chapter 9)), and the increase in flexible jobs without flexicurity, i.e. jobs that lack social benefits (Clasen and Clegg 2006). This is a crucial distinction for WLB capabilities as it is critical for achieving WLB.

Flexible working times in scheduling and place of work that respond to employees' claims allow greater control in organizing family and employment, and employers have used flexible working time schemes to attract skilled workers and to keep them (discussed in Chapters 6 and 8). Yet, even in these kinds of jobs, in which flexibility in working times allows for autonomy and control over the pace of work, there is evidence that flexibility does not necessarily enhance WLB and quality of life (Lee and McCann 2006; Smith et al. 2008; Hobson and Fahlén 2009). One reason is that those with the most autonomy often hold positions of responsibility in work organizations that place high demands on them (Van Der Lippe 2007), and they often work some of the longest hours (Perrons et al. 2006). Drobnič (2011) underscores the fact that job control/autonomy have the reverse effect: increasing work–home interference rather than alleviating it. Time autonomy and flexibility for unskilled workers actually produce the weakest capabilities for WLB. Hobson et al. (Chapter 3, this volume) show that the precariousness of Hungarian self-employment, particularly among relatively low-skilled women, results in periods of working time deficits and working time overload. Although these women have flexibility in working time, they lack social benefits and often do not earn enough to support their families. Flexibility, when linked to precarious employment, reflects weak capabilities for WLB.

More generally, the tendency toward worker choice around working times can have the effect of deflecting broader institutional strategies for decent working times that would lead to a better quality of life (Deakin 2003; Lee and McCann 2006). Consider the cases of New Zealand and UK, both of which have adopted policies for flexibility and choice to promote WLB, but also allow firms working time opt outs from regulations limiting working hours. (Guest 2002; Lee and McCann 2006). Choice over working times and flexible schedules can widen the agency gap in WLB in a neoliberal institutional context in which self-regulation (Supiot 2001) can induce greater pressure on the employee to increase the productivity and profitability in firms.

Working time policies, however, can lead to enhanced capabilities for WLB. The possibility of organizing one's working time (flexibility) can be a capability for participating in earning and caring. Life course working time adjustments also have the potential to alter working patterns in relation to life stage and family needs. The studies in this book reveal the complexities in agencies and capabilities in achieving them.

Societal/Cultural Level

Gendering the capability set for WLB is implicit in the formulation of societal/cultural factors in our model, particularly the construction of norms around gender, care, and employment. Although family and friendship networks obviously shape norms and values, nonetheless, the media is a site for re-enforcing norms and challenging them. In Sweden, men's use of 'daddy leave' is front page news. From this perspective, gender equality discourse in political debates filtered through the media can enhance individuals' sense of entitlement, and hence agency, to make claims for WLB. The framing of gender equality and mobilizing around family-friendly policies at the European level and within welfare states placed WLB at the centre of debates. Men's groups in Japan were particularly important for putting men's care leave on the agenda in a society in which men's care had been conspicuously absent (Kimio 2003); their campaigns culminated in the 2007 Worklife Balance Charter. Evans refers to this as 'collective capabilities' (2002: 56).

This discursive level is an important dimension for the conversion of policies and entitlements into capabilities and agency freedoms for WLB (Olsson 2002; see also Chapter 3); and yet another set of analytical lenses in our capability set for understanding how gendered norms around mothering, parenting, and gender equality in the household shape agency and agency inequalities for WLB.

We emphasize that the cultural/normative layers of WLB are rooted in the institutional context and historical legacies (Crompton et al. 2007; Lewis 2009), and, as conversion factors, cannot be decoupled from other levels of analysis and sites for making claims, in the household, and at the firm workplace organizational level. As presented in our various studies and shown in our model of capabilities, the agency and capabilities gap in WLB has many dimensions and these are linked.

A crucial aspect of the agency and capabilities gap from the perspective of conversion factors is whether individuals view the state as a resource for solving societal problems (Svallfors 2011)—in our case worklife imbalances. Historical legacies and trajectories of welfare regimes have a profound effect on the extent to which individuals feel that they can rely on the state to regulate, deliver services, and implement laws preventing discrimination against those who use their formal rights. In two post-socialist regime countries analysed in chapters in this book, Hungary and Slovenia—both characterized by long working hours regimes and precarious work situations—there remains a deep scepticism about what states can do. This shapes working parents' sense of entitlement to make a claim for WLB, their perceptions about what can be challenged or might be improved, and their scope of alternatives for change (see Chapters 3, 4, and 9). At the other end of the spectrum are the Nordic countries, Sweden most notably, which appear unwavering in their belief that the state will deliver services, implement policies, and promote strategies to improve and support family-friendly policies (Svallfors 2011). The perceptions of what individuals expect from the state and where the responsibility for WLB lies reaches the cognitive level of agency and capabilities.

The Cognitive Dimensions of Capabilities

Implicit in the notions of choice and agency[11] are the cognitive aspects of the capabilities paradigm. The cognitive level of WLB is integrated in several analyses in this book that focus on the subjective experiential aspects of WLB; in Chapter 3 we present a model that illustrates how the cognitive sides of WLB are linked to the institutional/societal factors discussed above. We introduce two dimensions at the cognitive level of agency and choice that provide analytical purchase on the agency and capabilities gap: the sense of entitlement to make claims and the scope of alternatives to achieve a WLB. What one perceives as the scope of alternatives is bound up with our sense of entitlement to make claims for WLB. This sense of entitlement reflects not only what we can claim, but also our expectations about what is feasible and imaginable. It is embedded in different layers of the institutional normative context in societies mediated through firms and inlaid with gender (see Figure 3.1 in Chapter 3). The capabilities perspective differs from other cognitive approaches to WLB based upon subjective measures of satisfaction and challenges some of their assumptions.

SUBJECTIVE DEFINITIONS AND MEASURES OF WORKLIFE BALANCE

Much of the empirical research on WLB uses subjective measures: perceptions of conflict between work and home and measuring time stress and time strain (Milkie and Peltola 1999; Strandh and Nordenmark 2006). In psychological studies, WLB is defined in terms of 'satisfaction and good functioning at work and home with a minimum of role conflict' (Clark 2000: 751) or 'the extent to which an individual is equally engaged in—and equally satisfied with—his or her work role and family role' (Greenhaus et al. 2003: 513).

Seen from a capabilities perspective, research on subjective assessments of satisfaction is highly problematic as it does not take into account how expectations influence the perceptions of satisfaction and often masks gendered processes in the formation of these perceptions. Robeyns (2006) refers to a study by Clark (1997) comparing women's and men's job satisfaction, and makes the point that though the women had much poorer quality jobs and lower pay, they nevertheless expressed higher job satisfaction or utility, after controlling for their individual job characteristics. This is a reflection of their lower expectations. Sen's fundamental critique of measures of satisfaction has been gleaned from his studies of developing countries. A person who may be in a desperate situation can still claim to be contented, accept their lot, adapt to their circumstances (Sen 1992). Alternatively, high expectations regarding quality of life may shape perceptions of worklife stress, as seen in the cross-national study of work–family pressure by Van der Lippe et al. (2006). In the seven country comparison, Sweden emerges as the most time pressed, while the five Central European countries are at the other end of the spectrum, though in these countries fathers and mothers have some of the longest working hours. These examples offer an implicit challenge to the current vogue in social science research that measures happiness rather than wellbeing or agency and capabilities for quality of life. Our approach underscores the need for dimensions that capture the cognitive levels of quality of life that bring into focus how one's perceived scope of alternatives and expectations are context bound.

Challenges in Operationalizing in Capabilities

How to operationalize concepts such as agency inequalities and agency freedoms poses challenges for empirical studies with a capabilities approach (Robeyns 2006; Otto and Ziegler 2010). In this book we take up this challenge. Using our model of conversion factors and capabilities (Figure 1.1) as our point of departure, we assume that agency inequalities for working parents to achieve a WLB are multidimensional and vary across welfare states but also at the firm level and within individual families.

We are not suggesting that welfare state institutions or policies produce capabilities, but rather that they can expand the scope of alternatives for an individual's potential to achieve a desired functioning: his or her capability set (Sen 1992; Otto and Ziegler 2010). In our studies, WLB embraces many dimensions: the capabilities to participate in earning and in caring, the possibilities to organize one's time, to have time for family and leisure, to lead a less stressful and healthy life. Our concept of the agency and capabilities gap in WLB balance confronts how particular institutional settings can provide more opportunities for converting rights into capabilities for WLB or reinforcing existing agency inequalities.

How to operationalize freedoms (the possibilities to choose other alternatives) is another major challenge within the capabilities framework. Of course, freedoms are limited by outside forces that we cannot control, what Sen (1992) refers to as effective or substantive freedoms,[12] Nevertheless, the question remains: how can we know what an individual would choose if she is unable to imagine the alternatives and opportunities open to her? (This is presented as the counterfactual problem in analyses of choice (Sen 1992: 66–68; Comim et al. 2008)). One possibility that has been put forward is through the use of longitudinal studies,[13] a solution that does not overcome the contingent and dynamic aspects of individual lives and the agency and agency/inequalities for WLB that can be influenced by events such as global economic crises and recession, or structural changes, such as privitization and marketization of the care sector. Although we do not provide a methodological solution to this conundrum, the cognitive experiential dimensions in our analyses reach the perceptions of the scope of alternatives—both what is imagined as possible and the gendered dimensions of expectations and sense of entitlement that underlie the agency and capabilities gap.

Applications of the capabilities framework in data analysis, referred to as the practice of capabilities, poses other challenges (Robeyns 2005). Existing quantitative surveys have not been designed with functionings or capabilities in mind (Robeyns 2006). Quantitative measures are indirect measures of agency/agency inequalities. Qualitative studies do not often reach the institutional level and are rarely comparative. We use diverse methodologies and research strategies in our applications of the capabilities approach, which encompass agency inequalities in the scope of alternatives that produce the agency and capabilities gap in WLB: comparative quantitative analysis at the micro and macro level encompasses the institutional constraints shaping the scope of alternatives; comparative qualitative case studies and single case studies with focus groups engage with the subjective experiential level of capabilities. In particular, we have developed a semi-structured interview schedule specifically designed for a capabilities approach that was applied in three cities—Stockholm and Budapest (Chapter 3) and Japan (Chapter 4)—and which explores working parents' perceptions of what they would change and what barriers stand in the way of achieving a WLB.

The authors in this book operationalize agency and capabilities in innovative ways: (1) by embedding capabilities within different levels of analysis and sites for claims; (2) by introducing the firm as a conversion site for capabilities; and (3) by integrating the cognitive level of capabilities in ways that reveal how institutional/normative contexts shape the scope of alternatives and the perceptions of what is possible and imaginable, which can be seen as a key dimension in capabilities.

Structure of the Book

This book emerged from five years of meetings and workshops among the authors who were members of a large European Network of Excellence; RECWOWE: Reconciling Work and Welfare.

Worklife Balance: The Agency and Capabilities Gap is more than a series of case studies and a set of loosely connected chapters—true of many edited collections—as we share a common theoretical framework and set of conceptual tools that are applied throughout the book. The gender aspects of capabilities for WLB are explored in all chapters; we highlight the agency gap in WLB among men/fathers.

Using capabilities as a point of departure, all the studies have a multilevel and multidimensional approach, presumptive of their interactions and dependencies, though they focus on different sites for WLB claims: the individual/household and firm. The structure of the book of the book is divided into two sections to reflect this.

Part I starts from the individual/household level of agency and capabilities for WLB, considering different aspects of institutional context: policy frameworks, workplace organizational cultures, and societal norms. Part II concentrates on agency and capabilities at the firm level, including the implementation of policies within firms, the role of managers within specific workplace organizational cultures, and the employee perspective. Both sections include a presentation of the research areas within a capabilities framework: Chapter 2 addresses policies, norms, and practices; and Chapter 6 concentrates on the firm level and work organizational cultures across different welfare regimes.

Notes

1. Throughout this book agency is coupled with capabilities, which reflects our sociological perspectives on agency as interacting with structures (Sewell 1992), and Sen's dynamic approach to individual agency, the possibilities to be and do. Our concept of the agency and capabilities gap specifically refers to working parents' possibilities for claiming and exercising rights in different institutional and societal/normative contexts. Hence, when we use the shorthand of 'the agency gap' or 'agency' in worklife balance, agency and capabilities are implied. We use agency and capabilities when we are discussing specific policies and aspects of the agency gap in WLB and inequalities for WLB. Sen's concept of (agency) freedoms is used in our analyses in a more general sense, as possibilities for alternatives that would enhance WLB and quality of life. In our model, agency freedoms are operationalised as the opportunities to make choices that derive from the capability set (which include individual, institutional, and societal resources: see Figure 1.1), the end result of converting capabilities into agency.
2. Nussbuam's list consists of ten central capabilities: life; bodily health; bodily integrity; senses; imagination and thought; emotions; practical reason; affiliation; play; and control over one's environment (2003, pp. 33–34).
3. Alkire (2008) maintains that empirical evidence can demonstrate consensus and legitimacy for choosing values to be achieved (functionings).
4. Sen (1990) refers to these undervalued contributions of women in households as a 'perceived contribution response'.
5. There are implicit gendered assumptions in these calculations since when women increase their paid work, they tend to decrease their unpaid work, whereas men who work fewer hours rarely increase their unpaid work. Hence this measure does not tell us much about the gendered dynamics in discretionary time.
6. The empirical evidence for this claim is very thin. Goodin et al. (2008) cite one panel study in Germany in which 45% of individuals who said that they wanted to work fewer hours in the 1987 wave did so seven years later.
7. The criticisms lodged against Sen's individualistic approach have failed to recognize the social embeddedness of his concept of agency (Robeyns 2003).
8. There is voluminous literature on gender and welfare regimes that has influenced our institutional-level dimensions on capabilities for WLB. Much of the discussion and agendas for research on gender, welfare states, work, and family has appeared in *Social Politics* over the last two decades. Also the multidimensional aspects of our capability set for WLB have been shaped by the publications and research discussions in the Network of Excellence, RECWOWE (Reconciling Work and Welfare), of which several authors in the book were participants.
9. Sen (1992) cautions against reducing individuals to social categories, but recognizes that individuals have multiple identities and different types of interactions that influence agency and freedoms: what individuals can be and do (Fahlén 2012).
10. A significant proportion of European families are dependent upon informal childcare provided by relatives or friends (Plantenga and Remery 2009).

11. Burchardt et al. (2012) use a cognitive approach and design in their project on identifying inequalities in autonomy through the Equality Measurement Framework
12. Implicit in the concept of freedoms is the idea of effective freedoms to choose the life we would like to lead (Sen 1992: 65). Sen claims that we would obviously choose to be free of epidemics or chronic hunger; these are dependent upon forces that we cannot control. In WLB the lines are more blurred and the question of how much we are dependent on outside forces is less clear.
13. Halleröd and Strandh (2010) suggest longitudinal studies for dealing with the counterfactual problem in an essay on measurements: see the report of FP 7: 'Final Comparative Report: A blueprint of capabilities for work and education'.

Bibliography

Agawarl, B. (1997). 'Bargaining' and Gender Relations: Within and Beyond the Household. *Feminist Economics* 2(1):1–51.

Agawarl, B., J. Humphries, and I. Robeyns (2003). Exploring the Challenges of Amartya Sen's Work and Ideas: An Introduction. *Feminist Economics*, 9(2–3): 3–12.

Aliaga, C. (2006). How is the Time of Women and Men Distributed in Europe? *Statistics in Focus, Population and Social Conditions*. Eurostat: 4/2006. European Communities. <http://epp.eurostat.ec.europa.eu/cache/ITY_OFFPUB/KS-NK-06-004/EN/KS-NK-06-004-EN>.

Alkire, S. (2008). Using the Capability Approach: Prospective and Evaluative Analyses, in F. Comim, M. Qizilbash, and S. Alkire (eds), *The Capability Approach: Concepts, Measures and Applications*, pp. 26–49. New York: Cambridge University Press.

Anttonen, A. and J. Sipilä (1996). European Social Care Services: Is It Possible To Identify Models? *Journal of European Social Policy*, 6(2):87–100.

Anxo, D., J-Y. Boulin, and C. Fagan (2006). Decent Working Time in a Life-Course Perspective, in J-Y. Boulin, M. Lallement, J.C. Messenger, and F. Michon (eds), *Decent Working Time: New Trends; New Issues*, pp. 93–122. Geneva: International Labour Office.

Barnard, C., S. Deakin, and R. Hobbs (2001). Capabilities and Rights: An Emerging Agenda for Social Policy? *Industrial Relations Journal*, 32(5):464–79.

Becker, G.S. (1991). *A Treatise on the Family*. Cambridge, MA: Harvard University Press.

Becker-Schmidt, R. (2002) (ed.). *Gender and Work in Transition: Globalisation in Western, Middle and Eastern Europe*. Opladen: Leske.

Bifulco, L., R. Monteleone, C. Mozzana, and I. Rolfini (2010). A Social Theory for the Capability Approach: Conversion Factors, Capabilities and Education. Final Comparative Report: A Blue-print of Capabilities for Work and Education, Collaborative Project, WorkAble—Making Capabilities Work (EU Framework Project 7) .

Bittman, M., P. England, L. Sayer, N. Folbre, and G. Matheson (2003). When Does Gender Trump Money? Bargaining and Time in Household Work. *American Journal of Sociology*, 109(1):186–214.

Blossfeld, H-P. and S. Drobnič (2001) (eds), *Career of Couples in Contemporary Societies: From Male Breadwinner to Dual-Earner Families*. New York: Oxford University Press.

Bonoli, G. (2006). New Social Risks and the Politics of Post-industrial Social Policies, in K. Armingeon and G. Boboli (eds), *The Politics of Post-Industrial Welfare States: Adapting Post-war Social Policies to New Social Risks*, pp. 3–26. New York: Routledge.

Bonoli, G. and D. Natali (2012) (eds), *The Politics of the New Welfare State*. Oxford: Oxford University Press.

Boulin, J-Y., M. Lallement, J.C. Messenger, and F. Michon (2006) (eds), *Decent Working Time: New trends; New Issues*. Geneva: International Labour Office.

Bruning, G. and J. Plantenga (1999). Parental Leave and Equal Opportunities: Experiences in Eight European Countries. *Journal of European Social Policy*, 9:195–209.

Burchardt, T. (2008). Time and Income Poverty. Centre for Analysis of Social Exclusion CASE report 57. London: London School of Economics.

Burchardt, T. (2010). Time, Income and Substantive Freedom: A Capability Approach. *Time and Society*, 19(13):31–344.

Burchardt, T., H. Holder, and P. Vizard (2012). Identifying Inequalities in Autonomy through the Equality Measurement Framework. *Social Indicators Research*, 106(1):1–25.

Clark, A.E. (1997). Job Satisfaction and Gender: Why are Women so Happy at Work? *Labour Economics*, 4(4):341–72.

Clark, S.C. (2000). Work/Family Border Theory: A New Theory of Work/Family Balance. *Human Relations*, 53(6):747–70.

Clasen, J. and D. Clegg (2006). Beyond Activation Reforming European Unemployment Protection Systems in Post-industrial Labour Markets. *European Societies*, 8(4): 527–53.

Comim, F., M. Qizilbash, and S. Alkire (2008) (eds), *The Capability Approach: Concepts, Measures and Applications*. New York: Cambridge University Press.

Cousins, C. and N. Tang (2004). Working Time and Work and Family Conflict in the Netherlands, Sweden and the UK. *Work, Employment and Society*, 18(3):531–49.

Crompton, R., S. Lewis, and C. Lyonette (2007) (eds), *Women, Men, Work and Family in Europe*. Basingstoke: Palgrave Macmillan.

Daly, M. and J. Lewis (2000). The Concept of Social Care and the Analysis of Contemporary Welfare States. *The British Journal of Sociology*, 51(2):281–98.

Daly, M. (2011). What Adult Worker Model? A Critical Look at Recent Social Policy Reform in Europe from a Gender and Family Perspective. *Social Politics*, 18(1):1–23.

Deakin, S. (2003). Social Rights and the Market: An Evolutionary Perspective, in B. Burchell, S. Deakin, J. Michie, and J. Rubery (eds), *Systems of Production: Markets, Organizations and Performance*, pp. 74–88. London: Routledge.

Dean, H., J-M. Bonvin, P. Vielle, and N. Faraque (2005). Developing Capabilities and Rights in Welfare-work Policies. *European Societies*, 7(1):3–126.

Doucet, A. (2009). Dad and Baby in the First Year: Gendered Responsibilities and Embodiment. *The Annals of the American Academy of Political and Social Science*, 624(1):78–98.

Drèze, J. and A. Sen (2002). *India: Development and Participation*. Oxford: Oxford University Press.

Drobnič, S. (2011). Introduction: Job Quality and Work–Life Balance, in S. Drobnič and A.M. Guillén (eds), *Work–Life Balance in Europe: The Role of Job Quality*, pp. 1–16. Houndmills: Palgrave Macmillan.

Duncan, S. (2005). Mothering, Class and Rationality. *The Sociological Review*, 53(1):50–76.

Esping-Andersen, G. (1999). *Social Foundations of Post Industrial Economics*. New York: Oxford University Press.

Evans, P. (2002). Collective Capabilities, Culture, and Amartya Sen's Development as Freedom. *Studies in Comparative International Development*, Summer 37(2):54–60.

Fagan, C. (2001). Time, Money and the Gender Order: Work Orientations and Working-Time Preferences in Britain. *Gender, Work and Organization*, 8(3):239–66.

Fagan, C. (2004). 'Gender and Working-Time in Industrialized Countries: Practices and Preferences', in J. Messenger (ed.) *Finding the Balance: Working-Time and Workers' Needs and Preferences in Industrialized Countries*, pp. 108–46. London: Routledge/Institute for Labour Studies of the International Labour Organisation.

Fahlén, S. (2012). *Facets of Work–Life Balance across Europe: How the Interplay of Institutional Contexts, Work Arrangements and Individual Resources Affect Capabilities for Having a Family, and for Being Involved in Family Life*. Stockholm: Acta Universitatis Stockholmiensis, Stockholm University.

Ferrarini, T. and A-Z. Duvander (2010). Earner-Carer Model at the Crossroads: Reforms and Outcomes of Sweden's Family Policy in Comparative Perspective. *International Journal of Health Services*, 40(3):373–98.

Folbre, N. (1993). Guys Don't Do That: Gender Coalitions and Social Norms. Paper presented at the meetings of the American Economics Association, Anaheim.

Gambles, R., S. Lewis, and R. Rapoport (2007). Evolutions and Approaches to Equitable Division of Paid Work and Care in Three European Countries: A Multi-level Challenge, in R. Crompton, S. Lewis, and C. Lyonette (eds), *Women, Men, Work and Family in Europe*. New York: Palgrave Macmillan.

Gershuny, J. (2000). *Changing Times: Work and Leisure in Post-Industrial Society*. New York: Oxford University Press.

Ginn, J., S. Arber, J. Brannen, A. Dale, S. Dex, P. Elias, P. Moss, J.P. Ceridwen Roberts, and J. Rubery (1996). Feminist Fallacies: A Reply to Hakim on Women's Employment. *The British Journal of Sociology*, 47(1):167–74.

Goodin, R., J.F. Rice, A. Parpo, and L. Eriksson (2008). *Discretionary Time: A New Measure of Freedom*. Cambridge: Cambridge University Press.

Greenhaus, J.H., K.M. Collin, and J.D. Shaw (2003). The Relation between Work–Family Balance and Quality of Life. *Journal of Vocational Behavior*, 63(3):510–31.

Guest, D.E. (2002). Perspectives on the Study of Work–Life Balance. *Social Science Information*, 42(2):255–79.

Hakim, C. (2006). Women, Careers, and Work-life Preferences. *British Journal of Guidance & Counselling*, 34(3):279–94.

Hall, P. and D. Soskice (2001). *Varieties of Capitalism: The Institutional Foundations of Comparative Advantage*. Oxford: Oxford University Press

Hall, P. A. (2007) The Evolution of Varieties of Capitalism in Europe, in B. Hancké, M. Rhodes, and M. Thatcher (eds), *Beyond Varieties of Capitalism: Conflict, Contradiction and Complementarities in the European Economy*, pp. 41–82. Oxford/New York: Oxford University Press.

Halleröd, B. and M. Strandh (2010). Measuring Capabilities—Possibilities and Obstacles. Final Comparative Report: A Blue-print of Capabilities for Work and Education, Collaborative Project, WorkAble—Making Capabilities Work (EU Framework Project 7).

Hantrais, L. and P. Ackers (2005). Women's Choices in Europe: Striking the Work–Life Balance. *European Journal of Industrial Relations*, 11(2):197–212

Hedström, P. and R. Swedberg (1996). Rational Choice, Empirical Research, and the Sociological Tradition. *European Sociological Review*, 12(2):127–46.

Heinen, J. and M. Wator (2006). Child Care in Poland Before, During, and After the Transition: Still a Women's Business. *Social Politics*, 13(2):189–216.

Hobson, B. (1990). No Exit, No Voice: Women's Economic Dependency and the Welfare State. *Acta Sociologica*, 33(3):235–50.

Hobson, B. and S. Fahlén (2009). Competing Scenarios for European Fathers: Applying Sen's Capabilities and Agency Framework to Work Family Balance. *The Annals of the American Academy of Political and Social Science*, 624(1):214–33.

Hobson, B., A-Z. Duvander, and K. Halldén (2007). Men and Women's Agency and Capabilities to Create a Worklife Balance in Diverse and Changing Institutional Contexts, in J. Lewis (ed.), *Children, Changing Families and Welfare State Change*, pp. 267–96. Cheltenham: Edward Elgar.

Hochschild, A.R. (2001). *The Time Bind: When Work Becomes Home and Home Becomes Work* (second edition). New York: Henry Holt and Company, LLC.

Hogarth, T. and D. Bosworth (2009). Future Horizons for Work–Life Balance. Beyond Current Horizons. Institute for Employment Research, University of Warwick. <http://www.beyondcurrenthorizons.org.uk>.

Iversen, V. (2003). Intra-household Inequality: A Challenge for the Capability Approach? *Feminist Economics*, 9:93–116.

Jenson, J. (2012). A New Politics for the Social Investment Perspective: Objectives, Instruments, and Areas of Interventions in Welfare Regimes, in G. Bonoli and D. Natali (eds), *The Politics of the New Welfare State*, pp. 21–44. Oxford: Oxford University Press

Kan, M.Y. (2007). Work Orientation and Wives' Employment Careers: An Evaluation of Hakim's Preference Theory. *Work and Occupations*, 34(4):45–66.

Kimio, I. (2003). *Questioning* 'Gender Equality'—*Modern Japanese Society and Gender Politics*. Tokyo: Impact Publishing House.

Knijn, T. and A. Komter (eds) (2004). *Solidarity Between the Sexes and the Generations: Transformations in Europe*. Cheltenham: Edward Elgar Publishing Limited.

Korpi, W. (2000). Faces of Inequality: Gender, Class, and Patterns of Inequalities in Different Types of Welfare States. *Social Politics*, 7(2):127–91.

Land, H. and H. Rose (1985). Compulsory Altruism for Some or an Altruistic Society for All?, in P. Bean, J. Ferris, and D. Whynes (eds), *In Defence of Welfare*, pp. 74–96. London: Tavistock.

Lee, S. (2004). Working-Hour Gaps: Trends and Issues, in J. Messenger (ed.), *Working-Time and Workers' Needs and Preferences in Industrialized Countries: Finding the Balance*, pp. 29–59. London: Routledge/Institute for Labour Studies of the International Labour Organisation.

Lee, S. and D. McCann (2006). Working Time Capability: Towards Realizing Individual Choice, in J-Y. Boulin, M. Lallement, J.C. Messenger, and F. Michon (eds), *Decent Working Time: New Trends; New Issues*, pp. 65–82. Geneva: International Labour Office.

Leitner, A. and A Wroblewski (2006). Welfare State and Work–Life Balance. *European Societies*, 8(2): 295–317.

Lewis, J. (1997). Gender and Welfare Regimes: Further Thoughts. *Social Politics*, 4:160–77.

Lewis. J. (2001). The Decline of the Male-Breadwinner Model: Implications for Work and Care. *Social Politics*, 8(2): 152–69.

Lewis, J. (2006). Work/Family Reconciliation, Equal Opportunities and Social Policies: The Interpretation of Policy Trajectories at the EU Level and the Meaning of Gender Equality. *Journal of European Public Policy*, 13(3):420–37.

Lewis. J. (2009). *Work–Family Balance and Gender Policy*. Cheltenham: Edward Alger.

Lewis, J. and Giullari, S. (2005). The Adult Worker Model Family, Gender Equality and Care: The Search for New Policy Principles and the Possibilities and Problems of a Capabilities Approach. *Economy and Society*, 34(1):76–104.

Mahon, R., A. Anttonen, C. Bergqvist, D. Brennan, and B. Hobson (2012). Convergent Care Regimes? Childcare Arrangements in Australia, Canada, Finland and Sweden. *Journal of European Social Policy*, 22(4):419–31.

McCall, L. (2005). The Complexity of Intersectionality. *Signs: Journal of Women in Culture and Society*, 30(3):1771–800.

Milkie, M.A. and P. Peltola (1999). Playing All the Roles: Gender and the Work–Family Balancing Act. *Journal of Marriage and the Family*, 61(2):476–90.

Nussbaum, M (1999) *Sex and Social Justice*. New York: Oxford University Press.

Nussbaum, M. (2003) Capabilities and Fundamental Entitlements: Sen and Social Justice. *Feminist Economics*, 9(2/3): 33–59.

Nussbaum, M. and A. Sen (1993). Introduction, in M. Nussbaum and A. Sen (eds), *The Quality of Life*, pp. 1–6. Oxford: Clarendon Press

O'Connor, J., A.S. Orloff, and S. Shaver (1999). *States, Markets, Families: Gender, Liberalism and Social Policy in Australia, Canada, Great Britain and the United States*. New York: Cambridge University Press.

Olsson, K. (2002). Recognizing Gender, Redistributing Labor. *Social Politics*, 9(3):380–410.

Orloff, A. (2010). Gender, in F.G. Castles, S. Leibfried, J. Lewis, H. Obinger, and C. Pierson (eds), The *Oxford Handbook of Comparative Welfare States*, pp. 252–64. Oxford and New York: Oxford University Press.

Otto, H-U. and H. Ziegler (2010). Theoretical Framework and Methodology of Capability Acquisition—A Final Report. Final Comparative Report: A Blue-print of Capabilities for Work and Education, Collaborative Project, WorkAble—Making Capabilities Work.

Perrons, D., C. Fagan, L. McDowell, K. Ray, and K. Ward (2006) (eds), *Gender Divisions and Working Time in the New Economy: Changing Patterns of Work, Care and Public Policy in Europe and North America*. Cheltenham: Edward Elgar.

Peter, F. (2003). Gender and the Foundations of Social Choice: The Role of Situated Agency. *Feminist Economics*, 9(2/3):13–32.

Pfau-Effinger, B. (2005). Culture and Welfare State Policies: Reflections on a Complex Interaction. *Social Policy*, 34(1):1–18.

Plantenga, J. and C. Remery (2009) (eds), The Provision of Childcare Services: A Comparative Review of 30 European Countries. European Commission's Expert Group on Gender and Employment Issues (EGGE). European Commission, Luxemburg: Directorate-General for Employment, Social Affairs and Equal Opportunities/Office for Official Publications of the European Communities.

Robeyns, I. (2003). Sen's Capability Approach and Gender Inequality: Selecting Relevant Capabilities. *Feminist Economics*, 9(2/3):61–92.

Robeyns, I. (2005). The Capability Approach: A Theoretical Survey. *Journal of Human Development*, 6(1):93–114.

Robeyns, I. (2006). The Capability Approach in Practice. *The Journal of Political Philosophy*, 14(3):351–76.

Rubery, J., M. Smith, and C. Fagan (1998). National Working-Time Regimes and Equal Opportunities. *Feminist Economics*, 4(1):71–101.

Sen, A. (1990). Gender and Cooperative Conflicts, in I. Tinker (ed.) *Persistent Inequalities: Women and World Development*, pp. 123–49. New York: Oxford University Press.

Sen, A. (1992). *Inequality Re-examined*. Cambridge, MA: Harvard University Press.

Sen, A. (1993). Capability and Well-being, in M. Nussbaum and A. Sen (eds), *The Quality of Life*, pp. 30–53. Oxford: Clarendon Press.

Sen, A. (1999). *Development as Freedom*. Oxford: Oxford University Press.

Sewell, W. (1992). A Theory of Structure: Duality, Agency and Transformation. *AJS*, 98(1):1–29.

Smith, M., B. Burchell, and C. Fagan (2008). Job Quality in Europe. *Industrial Relations Journal*, 39(6):586–603.

Staines, G. (1980). Spillover Versus Compensation: A Review of the Literature on the Relationship between Work and Nonwork. *Human Relations*, 33(2): 111–29

Stiglitz, J.E., A. Sen, and J-P. Fitoussi (2009). Report by the Commission on the Measurement of Economic Performance and Social Progress. <http://www.stiglitz-sen-fitoussi.fr/documents/rapport_anglais.pdf>.

Strandh, M. and M. Nordenmark (2006). The Interference of Paid Work with Household Demands in Different Social Policy Contexts. *British Journal of Sociology*, 57(4):597–617.

Streeck, W. and K. Thelen (2005). Introduction: Institutional Change in Advanced Political Economies, in T. Streeck (ed.), *Beyond Continuity. Institutional Change in Advanced Political Economies*, pp. 1–39. Oxford: Oxford University Press.

Supiot, A. (2001). *Beyond Employment: Changes in Work and the Future of Labour Law in Europe*. Oxford: Oxford University Press.

Svallfors, S. (2011). A Bedrock of Support? Trends in Welfare State Attitudes in Sweden, 2001–2010. *Social Policy Administration*, 45(7):806–25.

Ungerson, C. and S. Yeandle (2007). Conclusion: Dilemmas, Contradictions and Change, in C. Ungerson and S. Yeandle (eds), *Cash-for-Care: Systems in Developed Welfare States*, pp. 32–59. London: Palgrave.

Van der Lippe, T and P. Peters (2007). *Competing Claims in Work and Family Life.* Cheltenham: Edward Elgar.

Voydanoff, P. (2005). Work Demands and Work-to-Family and Family-to-Work Conflict: Direct and Indirect Relationships. *Journal of Family Issues,* 26(6):707–26.

Wallace, C. (2002). Household Strategies: Their Conceptual Relevance and Analytical Scope in Social Research. *Sociology,* 36(2):275–92.

Williams, F.J. Popay and A. Oakley (1999) (eds), *Welfare Research: A Critical Review.* London: UCL Press.

Yamaguchi, K. (2012). <http://www.rieti.go.jp/en/papers/contribution/yamaguchi/06.html>.

Part I

The Individual/Household and the Agency and Capabilities Gap: Policy Frameworks, Norms, and Work Organizational Cultures

2

The agency gap: policies, norms, and working time capabilities across welfare states

Susanne Fahlén

Introduction

This chapter confronts the agency and capabilities gap in worklife balance (WLB) from two perspectives. First, it explores the interrelation between policies, aimed at promoting WLB and their implementation and outcomes, and gendered norms regarding work and care across 11 European countries and Japan. Second, it examines the agency and capabilities gap in attitudes regarding WLB priorities and *working time capabilities* (Lee and McCann 2006), mirrored in the differences between actual paid working hours and how many hours one would choose to work, whether it meant a loss or a gain in pay.

Work demands have intensified in recent decades (Burchell and Fagan 2004), making the fulfilment of home and family responsibilities while simultaneously engaging in gainful employment an even greater challenge for many individuals in Europe and other industrialized societies. WLB has therefore become an important concern on the EU political agenda and among academics, as a normative value as well as an indicator of quality of life (Guest 2002; Hobson and Fahlén 2009a, b). In this book we conceive WLB as a *functioning*, that is a valued achievement (Chapter 1). By taking policies and norms into account we can show how these factors interplay with individuals' life situation possibilities to make alternative choices (Sen 1992, 1993; Agarwal et al. 2003; Robeyns 2003; Hobson and Fahlén 2009b). In addition, gendered working time norms can also be linked to institutional contexts (Anxo et al. 2007b). In some countries full-time work is the norm for both men and women, while in other countries mothers are expected to work only part-time. This reflects both gendered and contextual variations in working time capabilities (Lee and McCann 2006), a concept closely related to the workplace implementations of WLB policies and the agency and capabilities gap in practices, and potential choices if other options were available.

Using contextual data from OECD regarding policies and outcomes, and attitudinal data from the 2008 European Values Study (EVS), the 2002 International Social Survey Programme (ISSP), the 2005 World Values Study (WVS), and the most recent data from the European Social Survey (ESS), Round 5 (2010), I examine the interrelation between policies, norms, and practices. This analysis covers 12 countries, representing different welfare regime configurations (Esping-Andersen 1990; Korpi 2000), working time regimes (Rubery et al. 1998; Mutari and Figart 2001), and care regimes (Anttonen and Sipilä 1996; Gornick et al. 1997; Bettio and Plantenga 2004). The countries are the Czech Republic (CZ), Denmark (DK), Finland (FI), Germany (DE), Hungary (HU), Japan (JP), the Netherlands (NL), Poland (PL), Slovenia (SI), Spain (ES), Sweden (SW), and the United Kingdom (UK) (see Chapters 1 and 6 for a more detailed discussion of welfare regimes). In the analysis of WLB norms and working time capabilities I use ESS Round 5 data on individuals in 11 European countries (Japan is not included in this data set) who are between 20–58 years of age, living with a partner and with at least one child under 13 in the household; a total of 3,353 individuals (1,703 women and 1,650 men).

The first section discusses various policy measures aimed at increasing the capabilities to combine work and home responsibilities, and considers the outcome of these policies in terms of take-up of the policy entitlements. The second section discusses the role of norms in work and family life. The third section focuses on the agency and capabilities gap in attitudes regarding WLB priorities, and what alternative working time situation a person would choose within the framework of working time capabilities in the 11 European countries.

Worklife Balance Policies: National Implementations and Practices

As discussed in the introductory chapter, individual capabilities for WLB are shaped at various levels of the society: the institutional/societal level, the workplace level (see also Chapter 6), and the individual/household level. Hence institutional factors (rights and laws) and societal factors (gender norms) are two key components for understanding individuals' capabilities for WLB. The integration of the institutional and the social dimensions enables us to analyse how agency and agency inequalities operate within different layers of the national contexts in which people make decisions regarding work and family life. The various national level structures of rights regarding work–family reconciliation policies, and gender norms related to work and family life, can be regarded as conversion factors as they constitute opportunities and constraints that shape and affect people's capabilities to combine both these life spheres. People's experiences of their roles as earners and parents are thus influenced by the support they get from the state and from their employers, which varies across countries (Perrons et al. 2006).

Policy strategies to enhance people's WLB in the EU have mainly addressed parental leave, part-time work, and childcare provision (see Directive 92/24/EEC; Directive 96/34/EC; Directive 97/81/EC; Directive 2010/18/EU; European Council 2002),with the objective of promoting gender equality in the labour market by supporting women to enter paid work. Hence, the policies are targeted towards increasing women's paid work and legitimizing flexible working conditions, rather than actively increasing men's share of unpaid care work (Stratigaki 2004). However, in the last decade we have seen more policy discussions on policies that effectively would encourage men to share leave provisions and caring responsibilities (Brodolini and Fagan 2010; European Commission 2010a, b). The outcomes of these policies are nevertheless highly gendered; women continue to bear the main responsibility for childcare, taking more parental leave, and working part-time or withdrawing from the labour market when they become mothers. At the same time, fathers in many countries have limited capabilities to exercise their rights to parental leave (four months stipulated by the Directive 2010/18/EU), or to employ the right to reduce their working hours, given the low or non-existent income replacement level, both alternatives would have a negative impact on the household economy. In Japan, similar policies have been implemented to promote gender equality, or more specifically to enable women to continue their working career after marriage and childbirth, in order to protect women from discrimination and prohibit the unfair treatment of pregnant women and mothers. Japan's falling birth rates in recent years have also added explicit pro-natalist objectives to these policies, as they not only support childbearing but also childrearing by both men and women (Fukunda 2003; see also Chapter 4).

Regardless of the underlying objectives, these policies can either enable or hinder men and women's capabilities to be both earner and carers, depending on the implementation of such policies. Lewis and Smithson (2001) argue that an individual's sense of entitlement for WLB at the workplace level is closely related to the extent of such support at the institutional level (see also Chapters 1 and 3). However, to be fully effective it is not enough to merely introduce WLB policies; they need to be integrated into the organizational culture at the workplace level (see chapters in Part 2) to enhance parents' capabilities to exercise their rights.

Parental Leave

Leave systems across the selected countries show vast dissimilarities with regard to duration and payment levels (see Moss and Korintus 2008; OECD 2010a). To facilitate a comparison of the systems, entitlement to paid leave can be measured as the *full-time equivalent of paid leave* (FTE).[1] The Nordic countries, Slovenia, the Czech Republic, and Hungary have the most generous leave systems (accounting for the total FTE of paid leave), while the Netherlands, Spain, and the UK mainly provide paid maternity leave (OECD 2010a). In Japan, the total FTE of paid leave approximates the levels of Germany and Poland (OECD 2010a). With regard to fathers, only Sweden, Finland, and Slovenia have a statutory paternity leave of more than one month (part of the parental leave in Sweden) (Moss and Korintus 2008), although Germany did introduce a 'fathers' quota' in 2007 (Moss and Korintus 2008).The available information on leave benefit take-up indicates that it is mainly women who use their leave rights, but the extent to which the right is exercised varies across the selected countries (Moss 2010).[2] Nearly all eligible mothers make use of the *maternity leave* (parental leave in Sweden). However the take-up in Japan is lower compared with the European countries (see Chapter 4). Take-up of *parental leave* is low or on part-time basis where the parental leave is unpaid or the replacement levels are relatively low (for instance in Germany, the Netherlands, and the UK). Higher take-up rates of parental leave are found in countries with more generous benefits, such as the Nordic countries, Slovenia, the Czech Republic, and Hungary (Moss 2010). Still, it is mainly mothers who make use of parental leave, and their capabilities to exercise their leave entitlement are closely linked to the benefit level.

Parental leave within the EU and in Japan is gender neutral (see Directive 96/34/EC; Kanno 2007), which implicitly recognizes that parenting includes men's right to be active fathers. However, fathers are more likely to exercise their rights if some of the leave is earmarked for fathers, as in Sweden, Norway, and more recently Germany (Moss and Korintus 2008; Reich 2010). Where no such quota exists, fathers' take-up is low in EU countries (Moss 2010), and very low in Japan, which has not been exposed to the same EU discourse on fathers' involvement with family responsibilities (see Chapter 4).

Childcare

The ability to combine family responsibilities with gainful employment is not achieved only by the provision of parental leave systems, but also by the availability and affordability of childcare arrangements. To remove disincentives for female labour force participation, after the Barcelona summit in 2002 the European Council set a goal that by 2010 the Member States should provide childcare for at least 90% of children between 3 and school age, and for at least 33% of the children under 3 (European Council 2002: 12). In 2008 only ten of the EU27 had reached the target for the youngest children, and only nine the target for the older ones (OECD 2012a).[3]

Across the 12 selected countries, the accessibility and affordability of childcare services varies widely: from being a social right with highly subsidized fees in the Nordic countries, to fairly costly childcare in the Netherlands, the UK, Spain, and Japan (OECD 2010b). In the CEE countries, the costs are comparatively low, yet the demand greatly exceeds the supply of childcare for the youngest children, with the exception of Slovenia (Plantenga and Remery 2005, 2009; OECD 2010b). In 2008, the enrolment rate for the youngest children was lowest in Germany (17.8%), the Czech Republic (8.6%), Hungary (4.2%), and Poland (6.8%), while the enrolment was above 45% in Denmark, Sweden, and the Netherlands, and about 28% in Japan (OECD 2012a). The low rates in the Czech Republic, Hungary, and Poland are closely linked to parental leave systems that encourage women to exit the labour market for a relatively long period of time after having children (Saxonberg and Sirovátka 2006). Denmark, the UK, Spain, and Japan had an enrolment rate of about 90% for children aged 3–5 years, while the lowest enrolment rates for preschool children were found in the Netherlands and Poland (OECD 2012a). Not only the availability of childcare but also the hours of attendance affect women's capabilities to combine work with care responsibilities. The average weekly hours of childcare attendance for the youngest children is highest in the Nordic countries (33–34 hours a week), Slovenia (36 hours a week), Hungary (30 hours a week), and Poland (35 hours a week), and lowest in the Netherlands (19 hours a week), the UK (16 hours a week), and the Czech Republic (16 hours a week) (OECD 2012a). The general tendency is that scarcity and high costs of childcare services for young children corresponds to fewer hours of attendance per week.

Parental leave and childcare services are not only policy instruments to increase parents' ability to combine work and family life, they are also measures for increasing female labour force participation and women's capacity to remain in the labour market after having children; a goal set by the Lisbon Treaty in 2000, which stated that 60% of the women were to be employed by 2010 (European Council 2000). This level has been reached in all 11 European countries as well as in Japan, when considering the overall employment rate for women aged 25–54 (OECD 2012b). For mothers with young children (0–2 years), however, the employment rate is below 60% in most of the selected countries, except for Denmark, the Netherlands, and Sweden, and even below 30% in the Czech Republic, Hungary, and Japan (OECD 2012b). This can be linked to the length of parental leave and the lack of childcare facilities for the youngest children, which constrain women's capabilities to combine work and childcare responsibilities. The maternal employment rates for women with preschool children (3–5 years) are over 60% in most countries, except for the UK, the Czech Republic, Hungary, and Japan (OECD 2012b). This suggests that mothers in these countries have weaker capabilities to re-enter the labour market. In other countries, a high maternal employment rate tends to coincide with a large proportion of part-time working women.

Part-time Work

As discussed in the first section, working hours are an important factor for WLB, that is, the more hours spent at work, the fewer hours left for the family and other activities. Part-time work is one among other working time arrangements considered to improve employees' WLB, but can have a negative impact on WLB if it is not the workers' own choice (Anxo et al. 2007b). Within the EU, the directive on part-time work (Directive 97/81/EC) proposes that an employer as far as possible should consider workers' requests to transfer from full-time to part-time work as well as from part-time to full-time work. The reversibility between full-time and part-time enables employees to adjust their working hours to different life stages. The regulation and implementation of part-time work varies across the countries (Anxo et al. 2007b; see also Chapter 7), but in most European countries the part-time directive is implemented as the *right to request* part-time. The extent of this right varies, as does the employer's grounds for refusing this request and the right to return to full-time hours (ILO 2007; OECD 2010c). Furthermore, in all 11 European countries, parents with small children can request or apply for reduced working hours together with part-time parental leave (Moss and Korintus 2008; see also Chapter 7). This is also the case in Japan, where reduced working hours and flexi-time is provided through the parental leave system, allowing parents to take part-time parental leave (Fukunda 2003).

Refusal of the request to work part-time relates to whether part-time work is a legal entitlement or just a right to request (see Chapter 7). Entitlements to work part-time, with an automatic reversion to full-time, are stronger in Finland, Sweden, Germany, the Netherlands, Slovenia, and Japan (OECD 2010c), whereas for part-timers in the UK, Spain, the Czech Republic, and Hungary there is no automatic right to revert to full-time (OECD 2010c). These differences illuminate agency inequalities among women across the selected countries with regard to capabilities to make claims for part-time work at their workplace. In Japan, for example, entitlements at the policy level are rarely requested at the workplace level (see Chapter 4).

Part-time work is clearly gendered in practice, as it is mainly women who work reduced hours. The proportion of women (aged 25–54) who in 2010 worked 30 hours or less a week in the selected countries, ranges from less than 7% in Slovenia, the Czech Republic, and Hungary, to more than 35% in Germany, the Netherlands, and the UK (OECD.Stat 2012). The proportion of women who worked 30 hours or less per week in Japan was close to 30%.

The proportion of men working part-time is much smaller, ranging from less than 2% in the Czech Republic and Hungary to about 7% in the Netherlands (OECD.Stat 2012). The gender differences in part-time work can be explained by women's main care responsibilities and the potential childcare problems they may encounter. For some women, part-time work might be a preferred alternative selected from a range of other forms of childcare or working arrangements, while for others it may be a constrained decision, especially if other childcare services or options are limited, expensive, or socially undesirable (Fagan 2004). The decision to work part-time might thus not be an individual choice, but rather the result of a lack of institutional support for working mothers. Although part-time work has been important for mothers' capabilities to combine work and family life, it is double-edged. Part-time does allow many women to be in paid work, who otherwise could not while having young children, but the cost of this solution is high in terms of limited job opportunities and promotion prospects and the negative effects on women's short-term and lifetime earnings and social protection coverage (Fagan et al. 2001).

As discussed in this section, the institutional settings described provide various more or less supportive conditions in terms of parents', and particularly women's, capability to be both earners and carers, while the incentives for more active fathering can be regarded as quite weak in most countries. As a result, the outcomes of the work–family and working time policies are highly gendered, as it most often is the women who adjust their working hours to fit the family needs (Perrons et al. 2006).

The next issue addressed is to what extent gender norms and attitudes regarding work and family life map onto practices across different countries.

Social Norms Regarding Work and Family Roles

Countries not only vary in the way that the work–care nexus is institutionalized in terms of social policies (e.g. Lewis 1992; Orloff 1993; Korpi 2000), but also with regard to gender norms concerning work and care, which both shape and are shaped by the policy framework (Anttonen and Sipilä 1996; Gregory

Table 2.1 Norms regarding fathers and mothers in 11 European countries and Japan: proportions agree/strongly agree with the statements

	DK	FI	SW	DE	NL	UK	ES	SI	CZ	HU	PL	JP
Men should have more right to job than women when jobs are scarce (1)	4.8	9.6	5.0	12.8	13.5	17.2	14.8	16.7	27.7	53.3	53.3	27.1
A man's job is to earn money; a woman's job is to look after the home and family (2)	12.5	11.6	7.6	20.1	12.4	19.4	24.3	29.1	46.8	39.1	44.6	31.0
A preschool child is likely to suffer if the mother works (3)	8.9	18.3	17.9	47.1	39.9	34.6	45.8	35.7	39.7	54.4	59.1	29.4
Woman should be prepared to cut down on paid work for sake of family (1)	15.4	22.1	18.4	44.7	27.5	41.5	45.3	43.3	49.8	54.2	55.4	-
Family life suffers when the woman has a full-time job (2)	28	21	25	40	43	36	54	53	44	53	40	32.4

Sources: Calculated from (1) ESS 2010; for Japan WVS 2005 (2) ISSP 2002 (3) EVS 2008; for Japan ISSP 2002.

and Milner 2009). The question is whether this interplay between policies and gender norms is also reflected in people's attitudes regarding work and care?

Across the 12 countries we find a vast acceptance of women's equal rights to employment (Table 2.1). Less than one-third of the population aged 18 and above agreed with the statement that men should have employment priority when jobs are scarce, Hungary and Poland being the exception. Weakest support for the male breadwinner norm is found in the Nordic countries and the Netherlands, where only 13% or less agree that a man's job is to earn money and the woman's job is to take care of the home and the family. These are also countries with relatively high maternal employment rates. Strongest support for the gendered division of paid and unpaid work is found in the CEE countries and Japan, where 31–45% support the male earner and female carer norm (Table 2.1). The CEE countries are countries with lower maternal employment rates, a low supply of childcare for the youngest children, and low part-time work rates, while Japan has intermediate part-time work rates and relatively expensive childcare.

Gender equality within the family does not have the same support; significant proportions agree with the statement that a woman should reduce her working hours for the sake of the family. Over 40% in all countries, except for the Nordic countries and the Netherlands, agree with this statement, and one-third in Japan think that family life will suffer if the woman works full-time (Table 2.1). A similar pattern is found regarding gender norms concerning childcare, as 35–59% believe that a preschool child will suffer if the mother works. Again, the Nordic countries stand out as the least traditional in regard to gender norms, where less than 20% agree with this statement, and Japan is positioned in between the Nordic countries and the other European countries (Table 2.1).

In general, fewer traditional gender norms are found in the Nordic countries, where both policies and norms encourage equal division of earning and caring responsibilities. The most traditional gender norms are found in the Czech Republic, Hungary, and Poland; countries with a relatively long and generous FTE of paid maternal/parental leave, but a low provision of childcare. In Germany, the Netherlands, the UK, and Spain we find a strong support for women to cut down on paid work for the sake of the family, while attitudes regarding traditional gender roles on women's rights to work are less prevalent. These are countries with unpaid or short FTE of paid parental leave and intermediate levels of childcare provision (Germany and the Netherlands), or expensive childcare provision (the UK and Spain), mainly on a part-time basis. This is also mirrored in the relatively high proportion of short part-time working women (that is less than 30 hours a week), except in Spain, with an overall low employment rate for mothers of preschoolers. Gender norms in Japan do not deviate to any great extent relative to the European countries, but are positioned somewhere in the middle both in regard to work–family reconciliation policies, and gender norms.

The relationships between policies, practices, and norms are rather complex in countries such as Germany, the Netherlands, and the UK. In other countries, such as the Nordic ones, there is a clear fit between polices and norms supportive of working mothers and women's practices in terms of high labour force participation, whereas in the Czech Republic, Hungary, Poland, Spain, and Japan there is an agency gap between policies and norms and the capability to be both earner and carer. Nevertheless, this section has shown that men and women to a great extent adjust their practices to the existing policies and norms of their society. The agency and capabilities gap in WLB is also related to people's practices in actual working hours versus how many hours they would choose to work if other alternatives were available. In the previous section, I focused on the capabilities to use policies that allow for participation in both earning and caring, in the following section, I consider WLB and working time capabilities.

Worklife Balance and Working Time Capabilities

WLB has received considerable attention in the European public debates and research (see Anxo et al. 2007a, b; European Commission 2008, 2010a, 2010b; Giaccone and Colleoni 2009). The relationship between WLB and quality of life has been reported in several Eurofound publications (see Fagan 2003; Eurofound 2004, 2009; Kotowska et al. 2010). This suggests that WLB has become a leading norm in EU countries. We also find a strong consensus on WLB as a value to be achieved, reflected in the fact that not only women (aged 20–58 years) but also the vast majority of men place importance on the ability to combine work and family life, though this is slightly less the case in the Czech Republic (Figure 2.1).

In the WLB research terrain there is great consensus that long working hours are associated with a low level of WLB or a high degree of work–family conflict (Milkie and Peltola 1999; Grzywacz and Marks 2000; Hill et al. 2001; Frone 2003; Burchell and Fagan 2004; Dilworth 2004; Strandh and Nordenmark 2006; Van der Lippe et al. 2006; Lyonette and Clark 2009; McGinnity and Calvert 2009; Steiber 2009; Drobnič et al. 2010; Chung 2011; Drobnič and Guillén 2011; Fagan and Walthery 2011; Salmi and Lammi-Taskula 2011).[4] Several studies have also revealed that inflexible work schedules, shift-work,

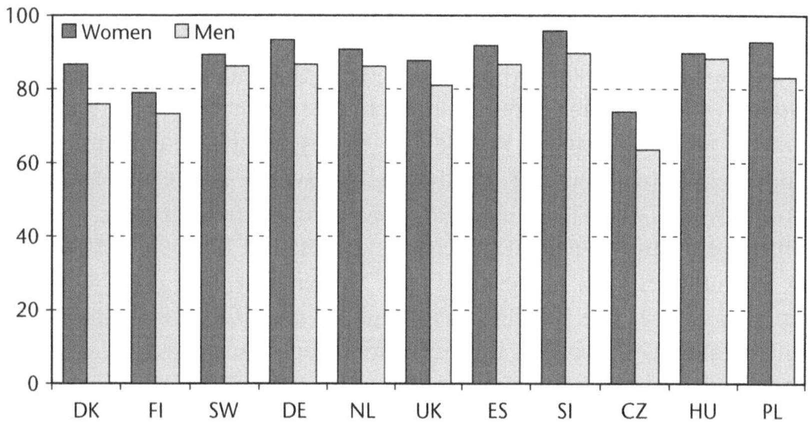

CZ=the Czech Republic ES=Spain NL=the Netherlands SW=Sweden

DE=Germany FI=Finland PL=Poland UK=United Kingdom

DK=Denmark HU=Hungary SI=Slovenia

Figure 2.1 Proportions stating that it is important/very important, when choosing a job, that the work allows them to combine work and family life

Note: Men and women aged 20–58 years (weight by design).

Source: Calculated from ESS (2010).

and overtime at short notice increase work–family conflict (e.g. Voydanoff 2005; Crompton and Lyonette 2006; Gallie and Russel 2009).

As shown above; the amount of working hours in paid work and the allocation of working hours have proved to be important components for achieving WLB (see also Chapter 1). However, working time is highly gendered, as seen in the previous section, and previous research shows that fathers spend longer hours in paid work than men in general, while typically mothers spend less time in paid work, even if they are full-time employed (Anxo and Boulin 2006). If paid work and unpaid work are added together, women on average work longer hours than men (Eurostat 2004; Aliaga 2006). These working patterns are consistent across Europe, yet the extent of these gender differences varies both within and between countries (Messenger 2004; Aliaga 2006; Anxo and Boulin 2006). Institutional regulations and gender norms shape men's and women's expectations and aspirations concerning WLB (Hobson and Fahlén 2009b). The differences between people's aspirations (as seen in attitudes regarding WLB) and their practices is a way of gauging the agency and capabilities gap for WLB (see Chapter 1), which is particularly apparent when considering the high proportion of working parents who value WLB (Figure 2.1) and the proportion of mothers and fathers working more than 40 hours a week (Figure 2.2). Over 55% of the fathers in Germany, the UK, Spain, Slovenia, the Czech Republic, and

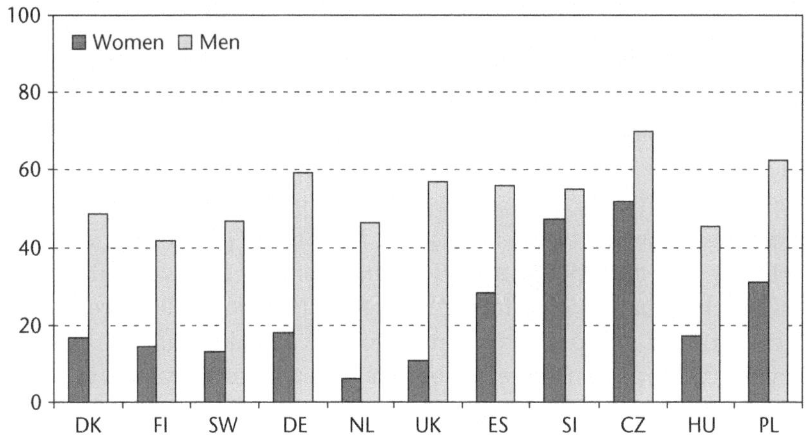

CZ=the Czech Republic ES=Spain NL=the Netherlands SW=Sweden
DE=Germany FI=Finland PL=Poland UK=United Kingdom
DK=Denmark HU=Hungary SI=Slovenia

Figure 2.2 Proportions of mothers and fathers working more than 40 hours a week

Note: Men and women aged 20–58 years, living in a relationship and with at least one child younger than 13 years in the household (weight by design).

Source: Calculated from ESS (2010).

Poland work more than 40 hours a week, and a significant proportion of fathers in the Nordic countries, with the most family-friendly policies for fathers, also work long hours (42–49%). In general, women tend to work less than 40 hours a week. However, close to 30% or more of the women in Spain, Slovenia, the Czech Republic, and Poland work over 40 hours. Long hours are least frequent among mothers in the Netherlands, where the vast majority of the women work part-time. It is quite clear that for a large proportion of women in some countries, for instance Spain, Slovenia, and Poland, gender norms (as seen in Table 2.1) and WLB ideals (Figure 2.1) are at odds with actual practices.

Considering working times, aspirations do not always go hand in hand with practices, and as working time is highly gendered it is important to disentangle to what extent actual working hours reflect needs and real choice (Anxo et al. 2004). In economic theory it is often assumed that employees' actual working hours correspond to their needs and preferences, but for many this is not the case (Lee 2004). In fact, desired working hours are limited to a large extent by perceived economic constraints and the person's sense of risk and security related to the their overall wellbeing. Bielenski et al. (2002) argue that the amount of hours a person would like to work reflects a compromise between what is desirable and what is feasible. This suggests that genuine choice is constrained and bounded by what we perceive as possible.

Several studies have revealed a working hour gap between actual working hours and the preferred number of hours, especially for those who work very long or very short hours (see Fagan 2004; Lee 2004; Lee and McCann 2006), and in their analysis Lee and McCann (2006) conclude that working time capabilities are more limited for these groups.

The ESS data enable a cross-European comparison between men's and women's actual working hours and what hours they would choose, even if this means a proportional decrease or increase in pay. This is an indicator of what Lee and McCann (2006) label working time capabilities. This is not purely a matter of preference; but reflects opportunities, constraints, and conditioned choice. It is an indicator of capabilities (Sen 1992, 1993; Robeyns 2003) and can therefore be regarded as capability hours. The gap between actual and capability hours can reflect agency inequalities in WLB capabilities (Hobson and Fahlén 2009a).

Across all countries and by gender, we can observe that average capability hours are less than the actual weekly hours, except for fathers in Hungary and Poland (Figure 2.3). Looking at fathers, the average capability hours are 3–9 hours less than the actual working hours, while the gap is less than 1 hour in Hungary and Poland, suggesting greater agency inequalities in these two countries. We assume that when fathers in Hungary and Poland say that they would like to work as many as 46–47 hours a week, if it means an increase in pay, they are revealing more about the economic constraints in their lives

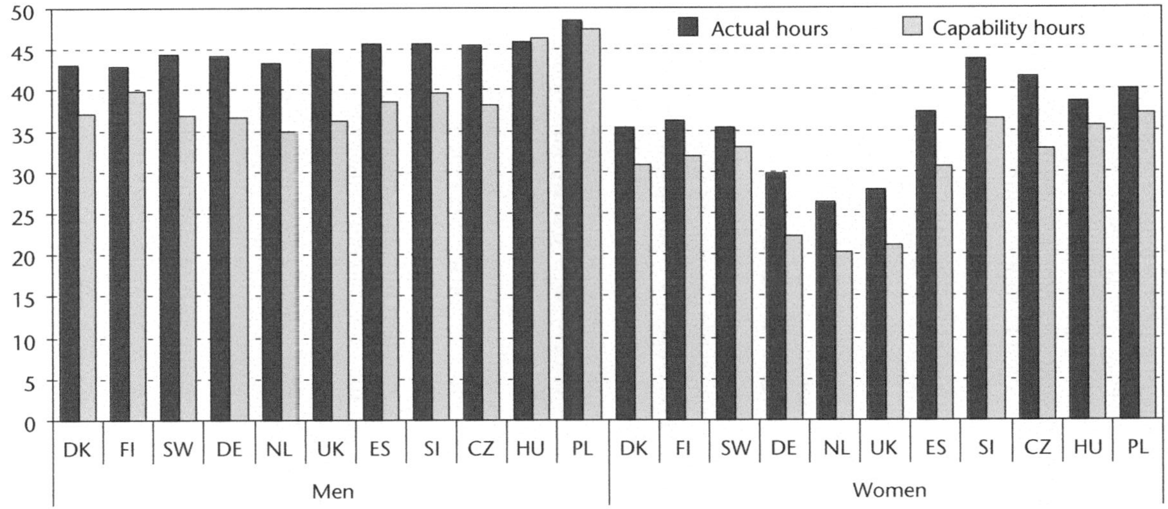

CZ=the Czech Republic ES=Spain NL=the Netherlands UK=United Kingdom

DE=Germany FI=Finland SI=Slovenia PL=Poland

DK=Denmark HU=Hungary SW=Sweden

Figure 2.3 Average actual weekly working hours (overtime include) and average capability hours

Note: Men and women aged 20–58 years, living in a relationship with at least one child younger than 13 years in the household (weight by design).

Source: Calculated from ESS (2010).

than expressing a strong desire to work as many hours as they do. Not to be forgotten is the fact that the vast majority of the men in these two countries state that the ability to combine work and family life is an important factor when choosing a job. This clearly indicates an agency and capabilities gap to achieve WLB as they cannot even imagine reducing their working hours.

Fathers in the Nordic countries, Germany, and the Netherlands work the shortest average hours and would reduce their hours substantially below 40 hours a week, except for fathers in Finland. Fathers in the UK have among the longest average working hours of the West European countries and would choose to reduce their working time up to 9, even if it means a loss of pay. This indicates another side of the agency and capabilities gap. Even if men are able to conceive of an hour reduction, they may encounter difficulty in realizing it, especially if their partner is at home full-time or works part-time. Their capabilities for WLB and effective choice regarding working hours may be constrained by their main breadwinner situation.

Considering mothers, in light of their care responsibilities, we are not surprised by the fact that they have much lower average actual hours than the fathers (Figure 2.3), having adjusted their working hours to fit their care responsibilities. We can also observe that mothers on average would like to work shorter hours than fathers, even if it means a loss of pay, consistent with the findings of Lee and McCann (2006). Still, we find a similar pattern in Hungary and Poland as for the fathers, that is, no major difference between actual working hours and capability hours despite the fact that their average working hours are the fourth and the fifth highest among the 11 European countries. As for the fathers, we can assume that this foremost reflects economic constraints rather than a true desire for long hours, especially considering the gender norms: that mothers should reduce their working hours for the sake of the children and the family (see Table 2.1). Mothers in Slovenia and the Czech Republic have the highest average working hours (42–44 hours a week). It is also here that we find among the largest gaps between actual and capability hours. Given the gender norms and difficulties in finding a part-time job (reflected in the low part-time rates), this indicates an agency gap for WLB due to limited options and alternatives.

A relatively small gap between actual hours and capability hours is found in the Nordic countries (2–4.5 hours), with average working hours of 35–36 hours a week. This result should not surprise us, given the fact that these countries have relatively strong policy support for working mothers, terms of available and affordable childcare, the right to reduce working hours and full reversibility to full-time hours, and less traditional gender norms. These institutional resources clearly increase women's agency to achieve WLB.

Mothers in Germany, the Netherlands, and the UK have on average the shortest hours (26–30 hours a week), though the gap between actual hours and capability hours is still relatively wide (6–7.5 hours). These are countries with relatively large proportions of part-time working mothers, so the result may reflect aspirations and gender norms related to motherhood and expectations that mothers should work less.

When the capability hours are divided by categories of the mother's actual working hours, an interaction between actual and capability hours becomes clearer (Figure 2.4). Across the selected countries we can observe a working hours deficit among mothers who work shorter hours, as a high proportion of these women would like to increase their working hours; and a working hours surplus among mothers who work long hours, reflected in the high proportion of these mothers who want a reduction, even if it means a loss of pay—a result consistent with Lee and McCann's (2006) study of working time capabilities. These results suggest that long working hours constrain a mother's capabilities to achieve WLB, which is especially evident in the CEE countries where mothers seem to have the least capabilities to achieve WLB. Many parents in these countries, except for Slovenia, perceive their future as uncertain due to insecure jobs and economic situation, and may not have the alternative of reducing their working hours so as to have more time for the family (Hobson and Oláh 2006; Hobson and Fahlén 2009a). The result regarding capability hours also suggests that part-time work is not always the preferred work situation for the mothers, as suggested by Fagan (2004). This is especially evident in Germany, the Netherlands, and the UK; countries where mothers may encounter social constraints, such as gender norms related to motherhood, and less assessable and/or affordable childcare (see Chapter 5).

Concluding Remarks

In this chapter I have examined the agency and capabilities gap from two perspectives; the interrelation between policies aimed at promoting WLB, their implementation, and outcomes, and the agency and capabilities gap in attitudes regarding WLB priorities and working time capabilities.

The implementation of WLB policies aimed at increasing women and mens' capabilities to achieve WLB, and gender norms regarding work and care, vary across Europe and in Japan. It is clear that individuals' capabilities for WLB are shaped by policies and norms, reflected in the take-up of parental leave, maternal employment, and part-time work. However, the agency and capabilities gap, especially for women to combine earning and caring, is greater in institutional contexts where there is both a lack of policies to support working mothers and traditional gender norms. In such contexts women's capabilities to make real choices regarding work and care are constrained. If we consider fathers' agency and capabilities to participate in care,

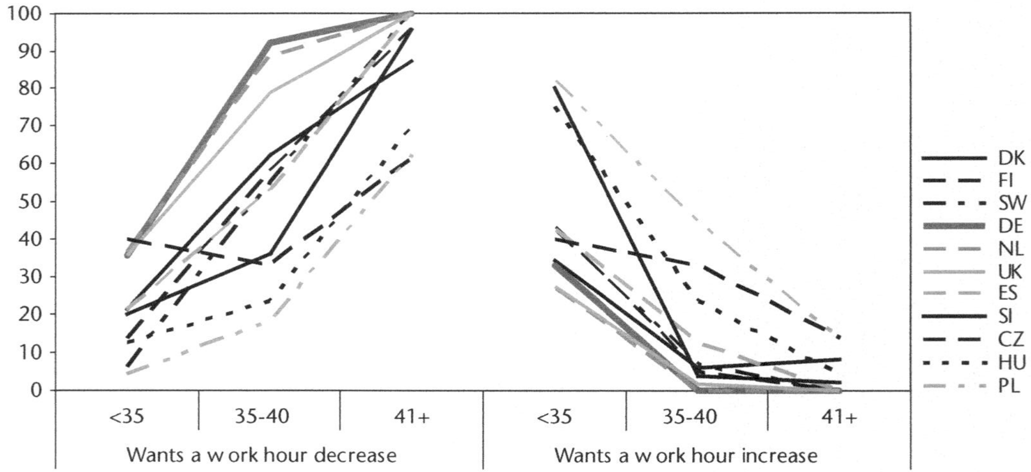

CZ=the Czech Republic ES=Spain NL=the Netherlands PL=Poland

DE=Germany FI=Finland SI=Slovenia UK=United Kingdom

DK=Denmark HU=Hungary SW=Sweden

Figure 2.4 Interactions between actual working hours and capability hours

Note: Women aged 20–58 years, living in a relationship with at least one child younger than 13 years in the household (weight by design).

Source: Calculated from ESS (2010).

and those policy contexts in which fatherhood is supported by specific policies and norms, they have a greater scope of alternatives for achieving WLB.

Previous studies have revealed that working hours are an important factor for an individual's capabilities to achieve WLB. Yet, there exists a significant agency and capabilities gap between the desire and practices across the 11 European countries, which is revealed in terms of time; the differences between actual working hours and capability hours, that is, the number of hours one would choose even if it means a loss or gain in pay. The latter reflects opportunities and constraints related to a person's sense of risk and security, and the gap between actual and capability hours can be interpreted as a lack of agency. The agency and capabilities gap in working time capabilities is largest for those women who either work more than 40 hours a week or less than 35 hours a week, suggesting that genuine choice regarding working hours lies beyond the perceived scope of alternatives for these women.

The results underscore that time is a relevant dimension in the capability set for understanding capabilities and agency for WLB. However, we should take into account that capability hours can be an adaptation that to a large extent is shaped by a range of social and institutional factors, for instance gender norms concerning work and care, available daycare services, and inadequate institutional supports for WLB balance, as well as household factors such as the partner's working arrangements. Nevertheless, the cross-national comparisons highlight the importance of taking into account how an individual's practices are embedded in an institutional context, in terms of policies, regulations, and norms. These shape men and women's expectations, aspirations, and capabilities to achieve WLB. Furthermore, the analysis has shown the importance of not only looking at what people are doing, but also at what they would like to be able choose; an analytical strategy for revealing agency inequalities.

Notes

1. The FTE of paid leave can be described as the duration of paid leave if it were paid at 100% of last earnings, calculated as follows: FTE = Duration of leave in weeks*payment (as a percentage of average wage) received by the claimant (see OECD 2010a).
2. Information on leave benefit take-up is irregular and inconsistent across Europe, which makes systematic cross-national comparison difficult (Moss 2010).
3. Countries who had reached the target of 33% for the youngest children in 2008: Belgium, Denmark, France, Luxembourg, the Netherlands, Portugal, Slovenia, Spain, Sweden, the UK. Countries who had reached the target of 90% for older children: Belgium, Denmark, France, Germany, Italy, Malta, Spain, Sweden, the UK (OECD 2012a).
4. Researchers have referred to the topic as work–family balance, work life balance, or work–family conflict, and sometimes these concepts are used interchangeably.

References

Agarwal, B., J. Humphries, and I. Robeyns (2003). Exploring the Challenges of Amartya Sen's Work and Ideas: An Introduction. *Feminist Economics*, 9(2/3):3–12.

Aliaga, C. (2006). How is the Time of Women and Men Distributed in Europe? *Statistics in Focus, Population and Social Conditions* 4/2006. European Communities Luxemburg: Office for Official Publications of the European Communities.

Anttonen, A. and J. Sipilä (1996). European Social Care Services: Is it Possible to Identify Models? *Journal of European Social Policy*, 6(2):87–100.

Anxo, D., C. Fagan, D. McCann, S. Lee, and J.C. Messenger (2004). Introduction: Working Time in Industrialized Countries, in J.C. Messenger (ed.), *Working Time and Workers' Preferences in Industrialized Countries: Finding the Balance*, pp. 1–9. International Labour Office. London: Routledge.

Anxo, D. and J-Y. Boulin (2006) (eds), Working Time Options Over the Life Course: New Work Patterns and Company Strategies. European Foundation for the Improvement of Living and Working Conditions. Luxembourg: Office for Official Publications of the European Communities.

Anxo, D., C. Fagan, M. Smith, M-T. Letablier, and C. Perraudin (2007a). Parental Leave in European Companies. Establishment Survey on Working Time 2004–2005. European Foundation for the Improvement of Living and Working Conditions. Luxembourg: Office for Official Publications of the European Communities.

Anxo, D., C. Fagan, M. Smith, M-T. Letablier, and C. Perraudin (2007b). Part-time Work in European Companies. Establishment Survey on Working Time 2004–2005. European Foundation for the Improvement of Living and Working Conditions. Luxembourg: Office for Official Publications of the European Communities.

Bettio, F. and J. Plantenga (2004). Comparing Care Regimes in Europe. *Feminist Economics*, 10(1):85–113.

Bielenski, H., G. Bosch, and A. Wagner (2002). Working Time Preferences in Sixteen European Countries. European Foundation for the Improvement of Living and Working Conditions. Luxembourg: Office for Official Publications of the European Communities.

Brodolini, F.G. and C. Fagan (2010). Analysis Note: Men and Gender Equality Tackling Gender Segregated Family Roles and Social Care Jobs. European Commission, Employment, Social Affairs and Equal Opportunities. Brussels: European Commission.

Burchell, B. and C. Fagan (2004). Gender and the Intensification of Work: Evidence from the European Working Condition Surveys. *Eastern Economic Journal*, 30(4):627–42.

Chung, H. (2011). Work Family Conflict Across 28 European Countries: A Multi-level Approach, in S. Drobnič and A. M. Guillén (eds), *Work–Life Balance in Europe: The Role of Job Quality*, pp. 42–68. Basingstoke: Palgrave Macmillan.

Crompton, R. and C. Lyonette (2006). Work–Life 'Balance' in Europe. *Acta Sociologica*, 49:379–93.

Dilworth, J. E. (2004). Predictors of Negative Spillover from Family to Work. *Journal of Family Issues*, 25(2):241–61.

Directive 2010/18/EU. Council Directive 2010/18/EU of March 8, 2010 Implementing the Revised Framework Agreement on Parental Leave Concluded by BUSINESSEUROPE, UEAPME, CEEP, and ETUC, and repealing Directive 96/34/EC.

Directive 96/34/EC. Council Directive 96/34/EC of June 3, 1996 on the Framework Agreement on Parental Leave Concluded by UNICE, CEEP, and the ETUC.

Directive 97/81/EC. Council Directive 97/81/EC of December 15, 1997, Concerning the Framework Agreement on Part-time Work Concluded by UNICE, CEEP, and the ETUC.

Drobnič, S. and A.M. Guillén (2011). Tensions Between Work and Home: Job Quality and Working Conditions in the Institutional Contexts of Germany and Spain. *Social Politics*, 18(2):232–68.

Drobnič, S., B. Beham, and P. Präg (2010). Good Job, Good Life? Working Conditions and Quality of Life in Europe. *Social Indicators Research*, 99(2):205–25.

Esping-Andersen, G. (1990) *The Three Worlds of Welfare Capitalism*. Cambridge: Polity Press.

Eurofound (2004). Quality of Life in Europe—Résumé. Dublin: European Foundation for the Improvement of Living and Working Conditions.

Eurofound (2009). Childcare Services in Europe. Foundation Findings. Dublin: European Foundation for the Improvement of Living and Working Conditions.

European Commission (2008). Report from the Commission to the Council, the European Parliament, the European Economic and Social Committee and the Committee of Regions. A Better Work–Life Balance: Stronger Support for Reconciling Professional, Private and Family Life. COM(2008) 635 final. Brussels: European Commission.

European Commission (2010a). Opinion on: The Future of Gender Equality Policy after 2010 and on the Priorities for a Possible Future Framework for Equality between Women and Men. Advisory Committee on Equal Opportunities for Women and Men. Brussels: European Commission.

European Commission (2010b). Opinion on: On Flexible and Part-time Working Arrangements and the Gender Dimension of the Labour Market. Advisory Committee on Equal Opportunities for Women and Men. Brussels: European Commission.

European Council (2000). Presidency Conclusions. Lisbon European Council, 23 and 24 March 2000. Online publication. <http://www.consilium.europa.eu/uedocs/cms_data/docs/pressdata/en/ec/00100-r1.en0.htm> [2011-05-24].

European Council (2002). Presidency Conclusions. Barcelona European Council, 15 and 16 March 2002. SN 100/1/02 REV 1. Online publication. <http:// www.consilium.europa.eu/uedocs/cms_data/docs/pressdata/en/ec/71025.pdf> [2009-10-06].

Eurostat (2004). How Europeans Spend Their Time: Everyday Life of Women and Men 1998–2002. Luxembourg: Office for Official Publications of the European Communities.

Fagan, C. (2003). Working-Time Preferences and Work–Life Balance in the EU: Some Policy Considerations for Enhancing the Quality of Life. European Foundation for the Improvement of Living and Working Conditions. Dublin: European Foundation for the Improvement of Living and Working Conditions.

Fagan, C. (2004). Gender and Working-Time in Industrialized Countries, in J.C. Messenger (ed.) *Working-time and Workers' Needs and Preferences in Industrialized Countries: Finding the Balance*, pp. 108–46. London: Routledge/Institute for Labour Studies of the International Labour Organisation.

Fagan, C and P. Walthery (2011). Job Quality and the Perceived Work–Life Balance Fit between Work Hours and Personal Commitments: A Comparison of Parents and

Older Workers in Europe, in S. Drobnič and A.M. Guillén (eds), *Work–Life Balance in Europe: The Role of Job Quality*, pp. 69–94. Basingstoke: Palgrave Macmillan.

Fagan, C., T. Warren, and I. McAllister (2001). Gender, Employment and Working Time Preferences in Europe. European Foundation for the Improvement of Living and Working Conditions. Luxembourg: Office for Official Publications of the European Communities.

Frone, M. R. (2003). Work–Family Balance, in J. Campbell Quick and L.E. Tetrick (eds), *Handbook of Occupational Health Psychology*, pp. 143–62. Washington, DC: American Psychological Association.

Fukunda, N. (2003) Comparing Family-Friendly Policies in Japan and Europe: Are We in the Same or in a Different League? *Journal of Population and Social Security*, Supplement, 1:31–45.

Gallie, D. and H. Russel (2009). Work–Family Conflict and Working Conditions in Western Europe. *Social Indicators Research*, 93(3):445–67.

Giaccone, M. and E. Colleoni (2009). Annual Review of Working Conditions in the EU 2008–2009. European Foundation for the Improvement of Living and Working Conditions. Luxembourg: Office for Official Publications of the European Communities

Gornick, J., M. Meyers, and K. Ross (1997) Supporting the Employment of Mothers: Policy Variation across Fourteen Welfare States. *Journal of European Social Policy*, 7(1):45–70.

Gregory, A. and S. Milner (2009). Editorial: Work–Life Balance. A Matter of Choice? *Gender, Work and Organization*, 16(1):1–13.

Grzywacz, J.G. and N.F. Marks (2000). Reconceptualizing the Work–Family Interface: An Ecological Perspective on the Correlates of Positive and Negative Spillover Between Work and Family. *Journal of Occupational Health Psychology*, 5(1):111–26.

Guest, D.E. (2002). Perspectives on the Study of Work–Life Balance. *Social Science Information*, 42(2):255–79.

Hill, J.E., A.J. Hawkins, M. Ferris, and M. Weitzman (2001). Finding an Extra Day a Week: The Positive Influence of Perceived Job Flexibility on Work and Family Life Balance. *Family Relations*, 50(1):49–58.

Hobson, B. and S. Fahlén (2009a). Competing Scenarios for European Fathers: Applying Sen's Capabilities and Agency Framework to Work Family Balance. *The Annals of the American Academy of Political and Social Science*, 624(1): 214–33.

Hobson, B. and S. Fahlén (2009b). Applying Sen's Capabilities Framework within a European Context: Theoretical and Empirical Challenges. REC-WP 03/2009. Working Papers on Reconciliation of Work and Welfare in Europe. Edinburgh: RECWOWE Publication, Dissemination and Dialogue Center.

Hobson, B. and L. Sz. Oláh (2006). Birthstrikes? Agency and Capabilities in the Reconciliation of Employment and Family. *Journal of Marriage and the Family Review*, 39(3/4):197–227.

ILO (2007) Working Time and Work Organizations. Working Time Database. <http://www.ilo.org/travaildatabase/servlet/workingtime> [2009-09-10].

Kanno, T. (2007) Act on the Welfare of Workers Who Take Care of Children or Other Family Members, Including Child Care and Family Care Leave. The Japan Institute for Labour Policy and Training. Online publication <http://www.jil.go.jp/english/JLR/.../JLR15_kanno.pdf> [2012-12-03].

Korpi, W. (2000). Faces of Inequality: Gender, Class, and Patterns of Inequalities in Different Types of Welfare States. *Social Politics*, 7(2):127–91.

Kotowska, I., A. Matysiak, M. Styrc, A. Pailhé, A. Solaz, and F. Vignoli (2010). Family Life and Work. Second European Quality of Life Survey. Luxembourg: Office for Official Publications of the European Communities.

Lee, S. (2004). Working-Hour Gaps: Trends and Issues, in J.C. Messenger (ed.), *Working Time and Workers' Preferences in Industrialized Countries: Finding the Balance*, pp. 10–59. International Labour Office. London: Routledge.

Lee, S. and D. McCann (2006). Working Time Capability: Towards Realizing Individual Choice, in J-Y. Boulin, M. Lallement, J.C. Messenger, and F. Michon (eds), *Decent Working Time: New Trends; New Issues*, pp. 65–82. Geneva: International Labour Office.

Lewis, J. (1992) Gender and the Development of Welfare Regimes. *Journal of European Social Policy*, 2(3):159–73.

Lewis, S. and L. Smithson (2001). Sense of Entitlement to Support for the Reconciliation of Employment and Family Life. *Human Relations*, 54:1455–81.

Lyonette, C. and M. Clark (2009). *Unsocial Hours Unsocial Families?* Cambridge: Relationships Foundation.

McGinnity, F. and E. Calvert (2009). Work–Life Conflict and Social Inequality in Western Europe. *Social Indicators Research*, 94:489–508.

Messenger, J.C. (ed.) (2004). *Working Time and Workers' Preferences in Industrialized Countries: Finding the Balance*. International Labour Office. London: Routledge.

Milkie, M.A. and P. Peltola (1999). Playing All the Roles: Gender and the Work–Family Balancing Act. *Journal of Marriage and the Family*, 61(2):476–90.

Mutari, E. and D.M. Figart (2001). Europe at a Crossroads: Harmonization, Liberalization, and the Gender of Work Time. *Social Politics*, 8(1):36–64.

Moss, P. (ed.) (2010). International Review of Leave Policies and Related Research 2010. Employment Relation Research Series No. 115. London: Department for Business Innovation and Skills.

Moss, P. and M. Korintus (2008) (eds), International Review of Leave Policies and Related Research 2008. Employment Relation Research Series No. 100. London: Department for Business Enterprise and Regulatory Reform.

OECD (2009b). Usual Working Hours per Week by Gender, 2007. <http://www.oecd.org/els/social/family/database> [2010-10-21].

OECD (2010a). Key Characteristics of Parental Leave Systems. OECD Family Database, 2006/07. <http://www.oecd.org/els/social/family/database> [2010-06-29].

OECD (2010b). Childcare Support. Family Database, 2004. <http://www.oecd.org/els/social/family/database> [2011-03-21].

OECD (2010c). *Employment Outlook 2010. Moving Beyond the Job Crisis*. Paris: OECD Publishing.

OECD (2012a). Enrolment in Day-care and Pre-schools. Family Database, 2008. <http://www.oecd.org/els/social/family/database> [2012-02-7].

OECD (2012b). Maternal Employment Rates 2009. <http://www.oecd.org/els/social/family/database> [2012-08-16].

OECD.Stat (2012). Incidence of FTPT Employment—Common Definition. <http://stats.oecd.org/> [2012-12-02].

Orloff, A. (1993) Gender and the Social Rights of Citizenship: The Comparative Analysis of Gender Relations and Welfare States. *American Sociological Review*, 58(3):303–28.

Perrons, D., L. McDowell, C. Fagan, K. Ray, and K. Ward (2006) Introduction: Work, Life and Time in the New Economy, in D. Perrons, L. McDowell, C. Fagan, K. Ray, and K. Ward (eds), *Gender Division and Working Time in the New Economy*, pp. 1–15. Cheltenham: Edward Elgar Publishing Limited.

Plantenga, J. and C. Remery (2005) (eds), Reconciliation of Work and Private Life: A Comparative Review of Thirty European Countries. European Commission, Luxemburg: Directorate-General for Employment, Social Affairs and Equal Opportunities.

Plantenga, J. and C. Remery (2009) (eds), The Provision of Childcare Services: A Comparative Review of Thirty European Countries. European Commission's Expert Group on Gender and Employment Issues (EGGE). Luxembourg: Office for Official Publications of the European Communities.

Reich, N. (2010). Who Cares? Determinants of the Fathers' Use of Parental Leave in Germany. HWWI Research Paper 1–31. Hamburg Institute of International Economics. Hamburg: Hamburg Institute of International Economics.

Robeyns, I. (2003) Sen's Capability Approach and Gender Inequality: Selecting Relevant Capabilities. *Feminist Economics*, 9(2/3):61–92.

Rubery, J., M. Smith, and C. Fagan (1998) National Working-Time Regimes and Equal Opportunities. *Feminist Economics*, 4(1):71–101.

Salmi, M. and J. Lammi-Taskula (2011). Job Quality, Work–Family Tensions and Well-being: The Finnish Case, in S, Drobnič and A.M, Guillén (eds), *Work–Life Balance in Europe. The Role of Job Quality*, pp. 120–46. Basingstoke: Palgrave Macmillan.

Saxonberg, S. and T. Sirovátka (2006). Failing Family Policy in Post-communist Central Europe. *Journal of Comparative Policy Analysis: Research and Practice*, 8(2):185–202.

Sen, A. (1992) *Inequality Re-examined*. Cambridge, MA: Harvard University Press.

Sen, A. (1993) Capability and Well-being, in M. Nussbaum and A. Sen (eds), *The Quality of Life*, pp. 30–53. Oxford: Clarendon Press.

Steiber, N. (2009). Reported Levels of Time-based and Strain-based Conflict Between Work and Family Roles in Europe: A Multilevel Approach. *Social Indicators Research*, 93(3):469–88.

Strandh, M. and M. Nordenmark (2006). The Interference of Paid Work with Household Demands in Different Social Policy Contexts. *British Journal of Sociology*, 57(4):597–617.

Stratigaki, M. (2004). The Cooptation of Gender Concepts in EU Policies: The Case of Reconciliation of Work of Family. *Social Politics*, 11(1):30–56.

Van der Lippe, T., A. Jager, and T. Kops (2006). Combination Pressure: The Paid Work–Family Balance of Men and Women in European Countries. *Acta Sociologica*, 49:303–19.

Voydanoff, P. (2005). Work Demands and Work-to-Family and Family-to-Work Conflict: Direct and Indirect Relationships. *Journal of Family Issues*, 26(6):707–26.

3

A sense of entitlement? Agency and capabilities in Sweden and Hungary

Barbara Hobson, Susanne Fahlén, and Judit Takács

Introduction

Many scholars are engaged with worklife balance (WLB hereafter) and its importance for quality of life. An expanding literature has emerged with cross-national comparisons addressing the time pressures and difficulties individuals experience when trying to accommodate the demands of both home and the workplace (Perrons et al. 2006; Van der Lippe and Peters 2007; Drobnič and Guillén 2011). Some focus on job resources and the quality of jobs, workplace policies, and their effects on WLB (Lewis et al. 2009 and Bäck-Wiklund et al. 2011). Others focus on reconciliation policies in different welfare regimes and their effects on WLB practices (Leitner and Wroblewski 2006). There is growing recognition of the complexity in explaining the patterns of WLB across societies, what Crompton and Lyonette (2006) refer to as the 'work–family articulation', encompassing the structural (national social policies and regulations) and the relational (people's attitudes and practices embedded in the cultural normative context). Understanding how the agency and capabilities gap in WLB capabilities operates in different societies necessitates models for capturing these different levels and dimensions and their interactions, and strategies that reveal processes underlying agency inequalities for achieving WLB.

Sen's multidimensional agency-centred approach provides conceptual tools for analysing the agency and capabilities gap across societies. The model of conversion and capabilities that we have adapted to WLB (see Figure 1.1, Chapter 1) offers a framework for comparative analysis: considering the policy, firm, and household levels as sites for making claims for WLB and how agency inequalities are situated within these different layers of institutional and normative context. In this chapter we apply a capabilities framework for WLB to agency inequalities of mothers and fathers with young children in two institutional contexts (Hungary and Sweden) with differences in working time regimes and divergent gendered discourses around parenting norms. These differences shape expectations and perceptions of the constraints and possibilities to make claims for WLB, and capabilities for making alternative choices for a better quality of life. We have designed a survey tailored to the capability approach that enables us to reach the subjective-experiential layers of agency/agency inequalities. This cognitive dimension in capabilities is important for understanding not only what one does or would like to do, but also the perceptions of the scope of alternatives; what is seen as feasible or within the realm of the possible. The sense of entitlement for making claims in our analysis is a dimension that offers conceptual leverage for explaining differences in the agency and capabilities gap across these two societies as well as differences within them. This level of analysis is introduced in our model below (see Figure 3.1).

The chapter is divided into three parts. The first presents the cognitive model; the second provides a brief summary of the institutional features of our two cases: Sweden and Hungary; followed by a brief presentation of the research design. The rest of the chapter is devoted to analysis of the subjective-experiential perceptions of working parents derived from the capabilities survey, concluding with a discussion of how agency/agency inequalities for WLB among working parents reflect different institutional normative contexts.

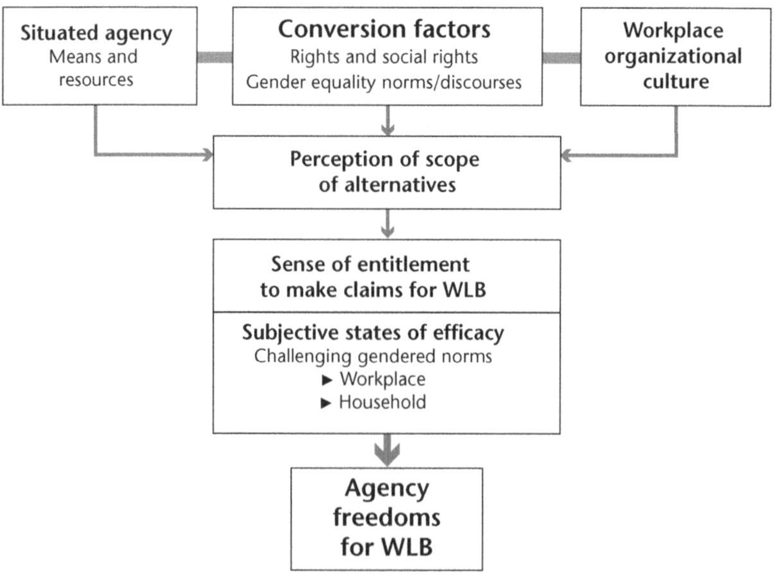

Figure 3.1 Converting entitlements into a sense of entitlement

A Model of the Theoretical Framework

The model below provides a framework for analysing the agency and capabilities gap for WLB across several dimensions. It builds upon the multilevel dimensional structure elaborated in Figure 1.1 (Chapter 1), but our focus in this chapter is on the conversion of rights and policies into claims for WLB, the different sites where claims are made, and the normative and institutional constraints and opportunities for exercising them.

As Figure 3.1 shows, conversion factors bracket both situated agency and workplace organizational cultures. In our survey, these conversion factors include specific policies at the state and firm level that legitimate a sense of entitlement to make claims for care leave and for flexibility in times and place of work. Regarding care leave, not just the rights themselves but also whether these are social rights are critical for converting entitlements into capabilities for WLB (Deakin 2003).

The workplace firm level is where claims are mediated. A workplace organizational culture that reflects sensitivity to WLB acts as conversion factor for WLB claims (see Chapter 8). In our survey, workplace organizational culture can generate its own norms on work performance that weaken capabilities for WLB, even within societies that are considered family friendly, such as Sweden.

Gender equality discourses and norms in themselves can be seen as conversion factors enhancing a sense of entitlement to claims for WLB. Men's care work has been the subject of government campaigns and media coverage, promoting active fatherhood (Hobson 2002; Brandth and Kvande 2009). Gender equality discourses empower men to confront their bosses for care leave and women to ask their partners to do more. How policies are discursively framed affects the cognitive level of agency. If care leave is anchored in a discourse of gender equality and fathers' rights to care, it makes it easier to challenge gendered norms in the workplace and household. Alternatively, if care leave is cast only in terms of activating mother's labour force, or child wellbeing (Daly 2011), fathers' sense of entitlement is weakened, particularly in societies where care is considered to be the primary responsibility of mothers and breadwinning the obligation of men (see Chapter 4).

We highlight the *cognitive* facets of capabilities in this chapter, expressed in the perception of scope of alternatives and sense of entitlement to make claims for WLB and how these dimensions are linked to situated agency. For example, the scope of alternatives for WLB is connected to situated agency, mirrored in how individuals view their futures: those with the least skills and resources may not have access to secure jobs, may have experienced precariousness in employment or may expect to in the future. Workplace organizational cultures overtly, as well as covertly, limit the scope of alternatives and agency freedoms for WLB. The risk in making claims for WLB is often tacitly recognized by employees as a tradeoff between career and family priorities (see Chapters 8 and 9). Narratives of risk about penalties for those who make claims for WLB, including job loss and discriminatory treatment in pay and promotion, travel through work organizations, an aspect that we include in our survey.

Clearly the sense of entitlement to make claims for WLB is shaped by the perception of one's scope of alternatives. However, the sense of entitlement cuts through many layers of capabilities. Whether a policy has statutory backing increases a sense of entitlement (Lewis and Smithson 2001), yet even when these laws exist, employees may not have a sense of entitlement to ask for them in the workplace.[1] A sense of entitlement increases self-efficacy[2] to challenge gender norms around men's breadwinning and women's care that are taken for granted and persist in the household, workplace, and community. Within the context of WLB claims, the sense of entitlement to make a claim is the conceptual lynchpin connecting capabilities to agency for WLB.

Deakin (2003) and Browne et al. (2004), among others, address the question of how entitlements are converted into achievements. They recognize that the existence of laws and policies can indirectly lead toward a 'different ethos' or 'seed' new norms that can destabilize gendered norms and practices. In our analysis of capabilities within specific institutional contexts, we study how this seeding mechanism operates when laws become legitimized in a society and institutionally embedded so that they have an impact on norms in the workplace and household. Alternatively these seeds may fall onto barren ground where the normative and institutional environment does not foster a sense of entitlement and capabilities for WLB are weak.

These aspects of capabilities emerge from the questions in our survey that allow us to reach into the subjective experiential level of capabilities. This emphasis in the survey allows us to address different aspects of agency freedoms and agency inequalities: what alternatives a person would choose to improve his/her WLB. We ask specific questions on alternative scenarios for organizing WLB: what would lead to change and what stands in the way of achieving this?

Two Institutional Contexts

Hungary and Sweden are interesting comparative cases for WLB and capabilities. Both countries have had an institutionalized dual-earner family model for many decades. However, these dual-earner societies emerged from different socio-political contexts.

Hungary, like other Central Eastern European societies, followed a dual-earner family model. Even after the demise of the regime, Hungary continued generous state support for parental leave and affordable childcare. Yet traditional patterns of care and housework were not disturbed during the former regime and remain in place (Oláh 2003; Tang and Cousins 2005; Lewis et al. 2009).The foundational policies of the dual-earner model emerged in Sweden in the 1970s. Although increasing women's labour force was a rationale for a dual-earner family model, gender equality discourses and politics were key forces shaping the formation of policies (Hobson 2002).

These societies vary along dimensions that have been used as indicators of capabilities for WLB: labour force attachment, working times, and fertility (see Table 3.1 for the comparative statistics). Women in Sweden have higher labour force participation and more mothers of small children are employed compared to women in Hungary: more mothers in Sweden work part-time. Though there is little difference in the working hours set by collective agreements in the two countries, average actual weekly working hours in Hungary are significantly longer among men and women with small children than for parents in Sweden (Hobson and Fahlén 2009). Levels of unemployment should affect agency and capabilities to make claims for WLB, as joblessness generates a sense of risk and insecurity among working parents. In the year we conducted our survey, unemployment was higher in Hungary than Sweden and the difference between women was even greater. Finally, there are striking differences in the fertility rates in these two countries—Hungary has one of the lowest fertility levels in Europe and Sweden has among the highest. Uncertain economic futures, as well as long working time regimes (see Chapter 1) are some of the explanations for the low fertility rate in Hungary and other Central Eastern European countries (Hobson and Oláh 2006).

In comparing these two societies, we confront the agency and capabilities gap by focusing on specific policies: parental leave, flexible hours, and rights

Table 3.1 Contextual indicators for Hungary and Sweden

	Hungary	Sweden
Total fertility rate 2008 (1)	1.35	1.91
Female employment ratio, 25–49 years (2)	64.1	79.8
Maternal employment ratio, child 3–5 years (2)	53	81.3
Part-time as % of total female employment, 25–59 years (3)	5.1	37.1
Male unemployment (%), age 25–59 years (4)	6.8	4
Female unemployment (%), age 25–59 years (4)	7.2	4.5
Trade union density (5)	16.8	68.4
Collectively agreed weekly working hours (7)	40	37.5

Source: (1) Statistics Sweden (2009a) and KSH (2009). (2) OECD Family database (2007). (3) Eurostat 2008a. (4) Eurostat (2008b). (5) OECD (2012), data for Sweden from 2012 and from 2008 for Hungary. (5) Eurofound (2009).

to reduce hours; we analyse how working parents perceive the constraints in exercising these. We provide a multilayered lens for capturing these agency inequalities: seen from the construction of policies, the work organizational culture in firms, and the individual household situation; gendered norms permeate all these sites for WLB claims.

Methodological Approach and Research Design

Our qualitative survey was conducted in two capital cities, Budapest and Stockholm,[3] which are fairly similar in population size. We used three main selection criteria for participants: each had to be the parent of at least one child younger than 7, living as part of a couple, and having been employed during the previous year. The sample of 100 respondents in each city (50 women and 50 men aged 25–57 years), was stratified by firm size[4] and firm sector (public and private sectors), with equal proportions within each category for both cities. In our sample, we also sought to approximate the educational attainment levels in each city. Given the contextual differences in our two cities, there are variations in educational attainment, size of public and private work sectors, and the proportions of small, medium, and large firms. The Budapest sample has a larger proportion of individuals with low levels of education, while the Stockholm sample has a larger proportion with high levels of education. The public sector is much smaller in Budapest than in Stockholm and there are fewer small firms in Sweden than in Hungary, which was also reflected in our samples.[5]

The survey has a semi-structured design. We obtained socio-demographic data from a questionnaire sent prior to the face-to-face interviews. Specifically designed for an agency and capabilities approach, the survey considered many aspects of WLB, though in this chapter we focus on *employment* and the organization of *working times*, *parental leave*, *work environment*, and *workplace culture*.[6] We analyse the responses of parents concerning their use of parental leave and flexible working times. We also consider the respondents' assessments of their work organizational culture and family-friendly work environments, which reflect perceptions of agency and capabilities. Finally, we posed questions that directly address agency inequalities: what our respondents could ask for or would refuse to do regarding working times and what they would change.

Agency and Capabilities in Two Cities

In this section, we conduct comparisons across three policy areas: parental leave, flexible working hours, and more generally we consider differences in family-(un)friendly workplace practices. We analyse the cognitive aspects of the scope of alternatives embracing not only boundaries around choice and agency, but also what our respondents perceive as possibilities for change.

Parental Leave

We begin our analysis with parental leave, as this has been a crucial policy for enabling parents (particularly mothers) to combine employment with family. It has also been cast as a policy that can reduce inequalities in the family and labour market (Gornick and Meyers 2003; Hobson et al. 2006), specifically the proactive measures for fathers' leave. The exercise of parental leave rights is dependent on whether and how it is compensated and the strength of the laws and protections for job security. Beyond these basic rights, parental leave claims are nested within normative/societal and institutional contexts that shape the capabilities of mothers and fathers to use it. This differs markedly across the two societies.

Both Hungary and Sweden have relatively generous parental leave benefits linked to previous employment. However, in Hungary the national policy provisions on childcare leave allow for an exceptionally long period of three years, an income-related two-year benefit at 70% of income for two years, and a low flat-rate benefit[7] not tied to previous earnings. This is also available to those who wish to extend the benefit beyond the higher-level income-related benefit period up to another year beyond the two years. In the case of childcare allowance (GYES) there is the possibility of transferring leave entitlements to a grandparent, provided that the child is older than 1 year, and raised and cared for in the household of the parent.

The common pattern is that women take the entire three years of benefit, although there is a gap between the highly and less skilled. In one of our cases, a Hungarian woman was on leave for nine years (with three consecutive children). Highly skilled professional women are exceptional, and are more likely to take a very short leave (3–9 months), compared to those working in routine administrative jobs or blue-collar occupations (Plantenga and Remery 2005).

The three-year leave policy reinforces gender role expectations, as it assumes that mothers will take the leave (Neményi and Takács 2006), and reproduces the gender divide in care. It weakens the capabilities to return to the labour market after the long period of parental leave, especially for mothers with lower education and those living in smaller communities. According to one EU study, more than 75% of Hungarian parents on parental leave (mainly mothers) said that they planned to continue working after their leave was over. However, the actual return rate is less than 45% (Plantenga and Remery 2005; KSH 2006). There are various reasons for this, including firm closure or the termination of the former position and the creation of a new position that is unsuitable for the employee's skills (Spéder and Kamarás 2008). This outcome suggests that, while EU case law has strong protections against firing women who take maternity leave, these are not well-enforced in Hungary.

How some women in our sample used the benefit reveals the high levels of unemployment and precarious labour market. While in theory one of the most important functions of parental leave is to allow a parent to take a temporary leave from paid work activities, for lower educated women in our Budapest sample the three year flat-rate childcare allowance (GYES) functioned as a quasi-unemployment benefit. This reflects a broader pattern observed between 1993 and 2005 in Hungary, reflecting the rapidly increasing proportion of women without a previous employment, and who tend to be those with low levels of education (Bálint and Köllő 2008).

We also found instances in our sample of higher educated women using the flat-rate parental leave benefit as a stop gap measure between jobs. For example, one father reported that his partner with a high level education went on leave only for a couple of months:

> We spent a few months abroad before delivery, and she didn't have a job at home. She was receiving childcare allowance while trying to find a job. (father, 42, two children, IT specialist)

A college teacher in the public sector mentioned that she received childcare allowance for a year:

> I claimed it in both cases, because I was looking for a job in the meantime.

The virtually 'women only' use of parental leave found in our survey matches the national statistics (Moss and Korintus 2008). Out of 100 interviewees, we found only four fathers who had taken any leave. These fathers are the exception, and tended to have partners who earned more than them. This group also includes highly educated fathers with strong convictions regarding a father's active role in caring (Takács 2008).

The economic loss that would result from fathers taking leave is a factor for most Hungarian families, and we found instances in which mothers and fathers said that sharing was not an issue because the mother did not have a job. Nonetheless, one cannot ignore the undeniably powerful role of gendered assumptions in determining why so few men take any parental leave beyond the targeted father days after birth. The survey respondents (both men and women), irrespective of their education level, interpreted the organization of care and the gender divide in parental leave practices as natural, essentializing gender difference. Breastfeeding was repeatedly given as a reason why men should not take any of the leave.

These were typical responses:

> I am the mother. This is the best way to do it. I have the patience. (mother, 33, two children, medium ed., working in the private sector as a masseuse)

or

> A child primarily needs his/her mother at this age [i.e. in the first three years]. (mother, 45, one child, high education, working in the private sector as an economist)

while a father put it simply as

> I think it's a sort of a social tradition—we never considered that I should do it. (father, 36, one child, working as a public school teacher)

The gendered normative expectations in the workplace in Hungary were so taken for granted that the idea of fathers making a claim for parental leave appeared untenable. This was apparent in the account of one father who said the he and his wife had discussed the possibility.

> We had doubts considering the potential reactions at my workplace. For example, if I accepted a grant to do research abroad for a year, it would make sense at my workplace even if it would cause some problems, but surely it would be accepted. But going on childcare leave! I think they can't comprehend even the fact that my family and childcare duties limit my working capacities to some extent. (father, 39, one child, high education, lecturer)

Sweden has one of the most generous parental leave systems in Europe (see Gornick and Meyers 2003; Plantenga and Remery 2005), 390 days at about 80% of previous earnings, and 90 days at a flat-rate low benefit. A person with no previous earnings will receive the basic level for 480 days. The ceiling of income replacement is fairly high; a large proportion of high income parents, especially fathers, receive less than 80%. However, all state employees receive 90% replacement of their income, and many private large employers top-up their employees leave benefit to similar or higher levels (Hobson et al. 2006).

In theory a mother could be out of the labour force for a relatively long time, using a policy known as the 'speed premium' that enables mothers who have children close together to keep the higher level of benefit if the interval between the two births does not exceed 30 months (Hoem 1993). However, the most common pattern is to return to work for a short period after the first birth, often reducing hours, as a strategy for keeping one's foot in the workplace. Reintegration in employment has been the driving force of the parental leave policy in Sweden; it has enabled mothers to sustain a WLB over the life course in which motherhood embraces both caring and earning (Ferrarini and Duvander 2010).

The Swedish leave system is highly flexible. One can choose to take fewer days per week or even divide the days up to 1/8 of a day, with a proportional decrease in leave benefit. For mothers flexible use of the leave can be a strategy for extending their leave time. However, we found that highly educated women are less likely to take the extended leave than the middle and the less educated. About half the highly educated women in our survey took less than ten months of the leave. This flexibility facilitates the father's use of the leave, as he can take scattered days off, or shorter periods of leave, without interrupting his work routine. Yet this very flexibility in the leave may work against a change in redistribution of care and change in gender norms (Hobson et al. 2006).

On the one hand, the flexibility in the leave can encourage WLB strategies that result in the sharing of care and work responsibilities. For instance, five highly educated women in our sample opted for a part-time division of the leave with their husbands after the first few months. This allowed the father and mother to have a continuous work connection during the parental leave period.

The Swedish parental leave system is best known for the two non-transferable 'daddy months'. This entitlement has increased men's capabilities for claims for care. Since the daddy months were introduced, the father's share of parental leave has increased significantly. During the year of our survey, 84% of fathers took some of the leave before their child's 8th birthday and fathers' share of the leave reached 21.5%; recent figures show that the proportion of men's leave is now above 24% (Swedish Social Insurance Agency 2011).

The Stockholm sample shows a slightly higher proportion of fathers who use more of the leave than the national average: about one-third claim that they have taken more than the two daddy months. Fifteen percent of the fathers shared the leave fairly equally, defined here as 40/60%, compared to the national average of 8.7% (Ferrarini and Duvander 2010). These tended to be highly educated fathers, a result that is confirmed by other Swedish studies on parental leave (National Social Insurance Board 2003; Hobson et al. 2006).

When asked about the division of parental leave, most mothers and fathers interviewed said that they were satisfied with the way they divided the leave: this was especially true for women, even if they took almost all the parental leave, and this was also found in a national study of the Swedish insurance board done a few years earlier (National Social Insurance Board 2003). Still, even though the majority of fathers said that they agreed with the division of the parental leave, about one-third said that they would have liked to have taken more. This figure is higher than the Insurance Board study in which 20% of fathers made a similar claim (Hobson et al. 2006). Fathers in our study said that the main obstacle standing in the way of not taking more daddy leave is the household economy, that there is less of a reduction in household income when the mother, who usually earns less, stays at home; however workplace demands and career goals figure prominently in the reasons why men did not take more leave than the daddy months. Consider the case of a father who would have liked to have taken more leave, however, he was concerned about the effects on his work situation:

> I would absolutely have wanted to do that [take more parental leave], but if you look at a lot of jobs, many on parental leave are badly treated and overlooked at work. If I'd been away for 6 months with both children then I don't know if I would be here now. (father, 44, two children, managerial position in state administration)

Among those fathers who did not take their two months, we find fathers who showed ambivalence, and even appeared apologetic, yet maintained that they had little choice as the main breadwinner whose income was essential for maintaining the family's standard of living. For example, one father said:

> I haven't completely pulled my weight. There's also an economic side, we don't make ends meet when I'm on parental leave. We lose loads of money. So I've had a month with each child together with vacation so then you get more time off. . . . I have lots of 'daddy days' left. But we can't afford it. Sure I take days here and there but I'm not home for an extended period of time. (father, 38, two children, medium education, working as a superintendent of estate management, public sector)

This father, typical of many middle class families, is the main earner in his family, whose wife earns a much lower salary as a caretaker for elderly and works 75%).

In cross-national comparisons of traditional gender attitudes toward work and family, Sweden stands out as a society with one of the lowest proportions of persons holding such attitudes (Wall 2007; see also Chapter 2). To be sure, gender norms around earning and caring persist. These norms endow men with a sense of entitlement to assert their role as the primary earner, but also confer on women their sense of entitlement to make claims to be the main carer. For example, when asked what she would have said if her husband wanted more leave, one mother rejected this outright.

> No, not if he'd wanted to take half. I wanted to be home. We talked about it [how to divide the leave] and we were in complete agreement. (mother, 44, two children, medium education, working with purchasing in the public health sector)

We found very few cases of women feeling entitled to take all the leave (only six cases), three of which were women who did not want to return their former jobs. Nor did we find rationales for women taking all or most of the leave based upon naturalized gender roles of maternal care and bonding, in contrast to our parents in the Hungarian sample. This was true even among the few Stockholm fathers who did not take any leave. Their reasons were related to their job situation or economic factors, rather than the mother's natural role.

Several studies in Sweden and other countries show that highly educated fathers tend to take more parental leave than those with less education (Sundström and Duvander 2002). A recent study of Haas and Hwang (2009) maintains that there is a class effect;[8] working class men are less likely to be able to make claims for leave at their workplaces. In our survey, we do not find a class effect but a sector/job effect: private versus public; high skilled versus less skilled; flexible versus inflexible jobs.

Work organizational culture was a determining factor in men's claims for parental leave, consistent with the most comprehensive study of fathers' parental leave in Stockholm: Bygren and Duvander (2006) showed that the likelihood of fathers taking leave and the proportion of leave were dependent upon previous men's parental leave practices in the firm, after controlling for education, time in the firm, and firm size. This indicates that specific workplaces can be conversion sites for WLB claims, re-enforcing the sense of entitlement generated from the policy and discourse surrounding fatherhood and care (SOU 2005). Alternatively, an organizational culture in which the norms are unstated and unchallenged can weaken agency for WLB, as several of the fathers in our survey revealed in their reasons for why they did not exercise their full rights to parental leave.

The tensions in men's parental leave decisions express the agency and capabilities gap in WLB as well the potentialities for change: the push and pull of involvement in family and work; the expectations of bosses and workmates; and the perceived costs of alternative scenarios of taking more leave within the family economy. However, alongside these perceived constraints is a strong sense of entitlement among men for claiming their parental leave rights, a right that has been seeded in policy and practice.

Parental leave policy and practices in the two societies reveal profound differences in capabilities for mothers' WLB. These reflect policy formulae as well as labour market regulations in employment protections and security linked to leave policy, which reflect and shape gendered norms in parenting and care. The most striking differences between Hungary and Sweden are seen in the incentives and disincentives for women to re-enter the labour market and the pro-active policy for fathers in Sweden to use their parental leave rights. For Swedish women, the parental leave system not only facilitates continuous labour force attachment, but also reintegration into their jobs and work organizations. These policy outcomes interact with other capabilities in the welfare regime, such as high levels of employment and secure jobs. In contrast, the extended leave policy in Hungary and the precariousness in the labour market weaken women's capabilities to re-enter the labour market.

Flexibility

Flexible working hours (other than the right to work part-time) in terms of organizing one's schedule for family needs is not inscribed in EU law, but was rather put forward as an example of good practice to promote WLB (see EC 2008). One can distinguish between two dimensions in the EU policy framework: (1) external flexibility, in which the aim is to ease the hiring and firing of workers and use of more flexible contract arrangements; and (2) internal flexibility, geared towards achieving more flexible patterns within the work organization either to meet market fluctuations or the employer's need for flexibility (Lewis and Plomien 2009; Viebrock and Clasen 2009).[9] The crucial divide in flexibility and capabilities for WLB is whether it is employer driven to maximize productivity or employee drive to facilitate WLB (Purcell et al. 1999; Fagan 2004).

In comparative studies, Hungarian and Sweden appear at different ends of the spectrum regarding the level of flexibility and the extent to which they are characterized as firm-oriented or worker-oriented: Sweden exemplified the high flexibility/worker-oriented model; Hungary was placed in the low flexibility/firm-oriented category (Ramioul and Huys 2007). However, other factors need to be taken into account when considering within-country flexible work options: gender, education, job sector, and work structure; and whether the job is task or time dependent.

Although flexibility encompasses a range of situations, we operationalize flexibility as employee-driven, that is, whether individuals are able to organize their working time and/or rearrange their workday schedule to suit their family's needs. In the survey we asked a series of questions concerning the perceptions of flexibility at the workplace, as well as specific questions on the right to refuse extra working hours and asocial hours such as night and evening work. We also included a series of questions that related to the general work environment; whether their workplace was family friendly and, more specifically, whether they had personal experience or knowledge of particular instances of mistreatment at the workplace for those prioritizing family (what we refer to as narratives of risk). These questions allowed us to capture the extent to which workplace organizational cultures support or hinder agency and capabilities for WLB.

Considering our direct question on the *perceptions* of flexibility at the workplace for organizing time to fit family needs, we found very little difference between our Stockholm and Budapest parents: 77% of Stockholm parents and 75% of Budapest parents said that they were able to organize their time and workday according to their family's needs. Moreover, in both there were gender differences in working time flexibility.

In the Hungarian sample, more men than women said that their work situation was not flexible (19% and 32%, respectively). Men working in the public sector were the most dissatisfied, while both male and female respondents working in the private sector were satisfied with their work flexibility. This reflects the high proportion of self-employed Hungarians (20% in our sample), both those working in micro-enterprises and the significant levels of outsourced home-based work among the self-employed; more men than women in our sample were self-employed.[10]

The self-employed private entrepreneurs had the most opportunity to organize work schedules and had flexi-time, as these two examples suggest. One, a self-employed mother stated that:

> as an entrepreneur I am family friendly. However, conditions are determined by the clients—although it is not like you must comply with them. You may decide not to work for them next time. (mother, 40, two children, medium education, decorator)

The other, a father and a self-employed carpenter, declared:

> I think entrepreneurship is family friendly because I decide on my schedule and nobody tells me what to do and when, though financially it is not profitable. (father, 35, two children, medium education)

It is important to keep in mind that the category of 'self-employed' covers a range of employment situations, from small business entrepreneurs to irregular workers who depend on contract work from both private and public sector employers and may lack social benefits. For the latter group, particularly among women, what appears to be a tradeoff between security and flexibility does not reflect choice, but rather is the result of weak capabilities, as many are precarious workers who cannot be assured employment contracts. This is supported by our finding that most would prefer to work more hours if it meant a gain in hourly pay.

Among the parents in Stockholm, there was less of a gender difference in work flexibility, 20% of women and 26% of men say they lack flexibility in their work. When comparing men and women in different work sectors, we see the same pattern as in the Hungarian sample: men in the public sector have less flexibility compared to women; and women in the private sector have less flexibility than men. We also find that less educated and low income mothers and fathers have less flexibility than highly educated and high income parents.

Flexibility was widely accepted in Swedish firms; and the classic distinction between task- and time-oriented jobs mainly explained why some Swedish working parents said that they were unable to reorganize their schedule. Those who tended to have jobs that did not allow for any flexibility included bus drivers, restaurant workers, and nurses and care workers in both the public and the private sector. For example, one woman working in the private sector characterized her work situation as inflexible as she was responsible for someone's care; she had a specified time shift and had to remain with her client until her replacement arrived. A policeman in our survey also claimed that his work demands allowed for little or no flexibility in rearranging his work schedule.

> Everything is controlled by external events. The jobs that come in we have to do. All the time in between we have open cases and assignments that we plan out together and do, but when something happens we have to drop all that and leave to do those jobs. So it is very free, but sometimes very controlled. (father, 38, three children, high education)

Nevertheless, this same man had reduced his hours to 75% and maintained that he could leave work if there were family responsibilities that he had to attend to; he did not see his workplace as being family unfriendly.

> It is never a problem; the social things come first, and then work. . . . No one ever complains. There are never any angry glances in the workplace because you are leaving.

Highly educated working parents in Sweden have the most flexibility; the bottom line is getting the task done. One respondent describes his situation in terms of work cycles: there is overtime and undertime; sometimes he works a 40 hour week, sometimes 20 hours, and sometimes 60, and this can involve evenings and weekends. The sense of lack of boundaries and borderless working times resonated in responses among white-collar employees in the private sector. As one father explained:

> Talking about 40 hours doesn't seem relevant. I have a full-time job, but no idea really of how many hours I put in. It's more a job that has to be done. My bosses want me to get things done but then it's very much up to me how and when I want it done. (father, 34, three children, high education, working in the IT-sector)

A similar statement was made by another father:

> It is freedom with responsibility. Usually the responsibility bit is so big that you work much more than the others do. . . . With responsibility comes limited freedom unfortunately. (father, 37, one child, high education, working as a marketing director in the private sector)

The majority of our Stockholm respondents said that they could work from home (over 60%), and only slightly more women than men. Among these women we found greater reluctance to have work spill over into family time; for them, it meant working late in the evening after the children were asleep. There were several fathers who affirmed the value of being able to take work home and were encouraged to do so by their employers. Yet this opportunity was linked to being available and on call for extra work. Blue-collar workers or service workers suggested that they would like more flexibility in their jobs; as one father said:

> I can only trade in my lunch breaks. (father, 43, three children, low education, working as a nursing assistant in the public sector)

However, they were rarely asked to work overtime and were compensated if they did. These different takes on flexible work are echoed in scholarly debates about whether regulated and predictable work schedules lead to better WLB (Lee and McCann 2006; Perrons et al. 2006).

We asked our respondents if they could refuse to work extra hours, weekend nights, and evenings, questions that directly show capabilities and agency for WLB. Here we found some variation in our two cases. The vast majority of Swedish mothers and fathers (62 out of 87) said that they could refuse to work evenings, weekends, and overtime, and claimed that family reasons were nearly always considered a valid reason for doing so. We also found examples of men and women who said that this was an irrelevant question as their job was organized around finishing a task and the responsibility for getting the work done. Nevertheless, family responsibilities and family time are given special status in Sweden. Several of our respondents said that they were not even asked to work extra hours, as it was known that they had small children.

Intense working time regimes and expectations of commitment to the firm are mirrored in the responses of Budapest parents, mainly fathers. Typical of this group are the highly qualified fathers working for private companies of which they are partial owners. Consider this terse response of one such father:

> There is no such thing as overwork—there are only tasks to be completed. (father, 44, one child, high education, sales engineer)

Compare his response with that of a father in the Swedish sample who claimed that he felt that overtime was often part of the job, although he received generous overtime pay.

> I have never, in the 20 years that I have been here, had someone tell me that I need to work overtime. However, you know what needs to be done and you take your responsibility. So, no one needs to tell you that you should work overtime but rather it's something you do when it's necessary. (father, 40, two children, medium education, engineer in the private sector)

The question of whether they can refuse extra hours, or work on weekends or evenings, was not an issue for some Budapest respondents who claimed that would not say no to extra hours. These included less educated fathers with large families, typically working in the private sector. The primary concern was their economy; more work meant more money:

> I could say no but I rarely would, as extra money is always welcome. (father, 32, three children, low education, security guard)

In contrast, a mother with high education working as an advisor in the public sector appeared to have more choice. She asserted that time was more important for her than money:

> I am not getting paid for the extra hours. Extra work should mean extra money. If I would get extra money, and I still would not want to do it, I would bring up family reasons. I already have so little time to spend with my child. (mother, 41, one child, high education)

The Right to Reduce Working Hours

There were significant differences between our Budapest and Stockholm parents regarding their sense of entitlement to exercise their rights to reduce hours. Every parent in Sweden has had the right to reduce working hours until the child is 8 years old for several decades. About half (46.3%) of mothers with a child younger than 7 used this right (Statistics Sweden 2009b), about the same proportion we found in our Stockholm sample.

In Hungary, there is no statutory right for parents of young children to reduce hours. The Budapest parents considered the opportunity to reduce hours a sign of a family-friendly workplace. The Hungarian labour market is characterized by a very low level of part-time employment (see Table 3.1). A woman in our Hungarian sample who was an office worker claimed that it took six months to find a job that would allow her to work six hours a day.

> When they learned at the job interviews that I had a child, I was immediately dismissed. Working only six hours was out of the question. (mother, 33, one child, low education)

Similarly, a father working full-time as a journalist in a large private company revealed the difficulties in making claims for part-time work:

> You are not given a hard time if you have children. However, there is no opportunity to get transferred to a part-time job. (father, 42, one child, medium education)

The above examples on part-time work in Hungary illustrate that even though a right may be inscribed in EU law, it may not be become a statutory right in national law. This was a crucial difference in Sweden and Hungary around rights for part-time work: without a formal right, the capabilities to convert resources into claims are weaker. The real litmus test, however, is whether WLB policies are recognized in the daily practices of firms and work organizations; what the costs or penalties are for using parental rights or more broadly prioritizing family needs when there is conflict between them and work demands. Within this context the workplace is a crucial site for WLB, not only for mediating the exercise of rights but also for the very sense of entitlement to claim them.

Family-Friendly and -Unfriendly Practices

We asked a series of questions to capture perceptions of the family-friendly or -unfriendly character of the work environment. First we posed a general question about whether the respondents considered their workplace family friendly. Then we asked about specific instances of mistreatment and discrimination at workplaces. Our purpose was to examine parents' expectations around what a workplace should provide for its employees, obviously linked to their perceptions of their scope of alternatives for achieving WLB and a better quality of life. The capabilities framework recognizes that expectations and norms shape agency, what is possible and what can be imagined. This cognitive level comes into play when assessing one's work environment as friendly or unfriendly.

More than half of the Budapest respondents (54 out of 93) viewed their workplace as family friendly, while more than one-fifth (21 out of 93) said theirs was unfriendly. Three fathers in blue-collar jobs in the private sector claimed that they did not know what family friendliness meant. One of them, a semi-skilled construction worker explained:

> Well, I'm at a loss as to interpret this question. Obviously, one must support his/her family so working is a must. You have no choice. Well, I wouldn't mind to leave earlier sometimes. However, we don't have a say in this matter. (father, 26, one child, low education)

Beyond an inability to interpret the question, low expectations for achieving WLB were revealed in the responses of manual workers in Hungary with only a basic education. For them, being employed was seen as an asset in itself. WLB lay outside the possible or imaginable. This is illustrated in the response of this father, working as a repairman in a large Hungarian state-owned company. For him WLB was an individual problem to be solved by increasing his wage. Asked if his workplace was family friendly, he responded:

> Most of the employees are men. This is not an issue here. In fact, I do not know anything about it. I wish I could make the same money in fewer hours so I can spend more time with my family. (father, 38, one child, low education)

In the Stockholm sample, regardless of levels of education and skill, working parents understood the notion of a family-friendly workplace and were aware of their rights. WLB is an idea that has been featured in Swedish media and political debate. We found only one atypical father in our Swedish survey who was unaware of his parental rights, a truck driver with low education and with a large family, four children and two step-children.

The vast majority of the Swedish respondents (76%) perceived their workplace to be family friendly, and defined it in terms of specific policies and work organizational practices. Family friendliness was associated with flexibility: being able to work from home, having the ability to plan the workday, having flexible working hours, and being able to bring children to work if the childcare centre or school were not open. Another example given was the scheduling of meetings sensitive to parental needs, which meant no early mornings or late afternoons that would interfere with taking children to and from daycare or after-school care. In addition our respondents noted the pro-active family-friendly policy in some private sector firms that top-up the parental leave benefit to compensate for the 80% wage replacement. More generally, parents portrayed a family-friendly work culture as one in which their employers and workmates demonstrated understanding and support for parents on parental leave or those off from work caring for sick children.

Gender differences in the perceptions of workplace friendliness were primarily related to the work sector in our Stockholm sample. The public sector, predominantly female, is acknowledged as a gender-sensitive work environment, and many women move from private to public sector jobs after they have children (Hoem 1995). Therefore, it is not surprising that women in the public sector characterize their workplaces much more positively than those working in the private sector. Conversely, we found several mothers in the private sector who stated that their workplaces were 'unfriendly' and both men and women who maintained that that gender-role expectations in male-dominated firms worked against women. Among men who reported that their workplaces were family unfriendly, there were no differences between those working in public and private sector firms.

In the Budapest sample, this pattern is reversed. Respondents, especially women working in the private sector, found their workplace more family friendly than those working in the public sector. Once again this can be explained by the higher proportion of self-employment in Hungary compared to Sweden. The self-employed in our sample did not always work long hours or unsocial hours and some tended to work less than those not self-employed. In fact, the majority of self-employed women in our sample showed a working time capability deficit (Lee and McCann 2006) as they would have liked to work more hours. In this context working hours may be flexible, but may not reflect greater capabilities for WLB and better quality of life, given the high proportions of men and women who have irregular, precarious jobs.

In order to capture the penalties and risks involved in putting family first, we asked our respondents about their own experiences of mistreatment at the workplace, or whether they knew or had heard about others who faced discrimination in pay, job task, or promotion because of prioritizing family. These *narratives of risk* travel through organizations and act as warning signals to others.

Compared to Stockholm, more Budapest respondents brought up cases of mistreatment (slightly less than one-fifth), regardless of gender and work sector. Though relatively few in number, these cases of overt mistreatment allow us to see how disciplining of employees reproduces agency inequalities in WLB. For example, a mother working as a clerk for a multinational company in Hungary described the situation at her workplace:

> One of my colleagues had a sickly child. That multinational [company] would not stand for that. She was continually being called in. She wasn't sacked, but left. It was completely unfair. She did not know that she would bear a sick child. I have yet to see a man take a lot of time off for family reasons. It is always lumped on the woman. (mother, 33, one child, low education)

This blatant case of mistreatment involved a multinational corporation; more subtle forms of mistreatment were more commonplace.

For the most part, there seemed to be more tolerance for women to prioritize family needs, as care for children is still viewed as mainly women's responsibility in Hungary. In this context fathers' WLB claims at the workplace entailed greater risk, as this sales representative working in the public sector confided to her male colleague:

> They [i.e. other colleagues] thought that he was not telling the truth when he said that he needed time off for his family.

Another related the story of her husband who was told not to come back work after he had taken one day off because their child was ill.

> It was unfair and inhumane.

We found far fewer cases of mistreatment and discrimination among our Stockholm parents; only two out of ten cited their own experiences of being mistreated; the others had heard about instances of mistreatment. Second, we did not find important gender differences in work sectors, neither in first hand experiences of mistreatment nor knowledge about penalties for others prioritizing family. However, there were slightly more cases of women being treated unfairly. This reflects the fact that the majority of cases of discrimination involved parental leave.[11] Mothers tend to take much more of the leave than fathers, and private sector firms have difficulty finding replacements in work teams for parents who take more than a couple of months. The discriminatory processes that result from the gendered norms in workplaces around parental leave were made visible in this narrative by a male senior project leader working in a private company in Stockholm. He himself had taken parental leave and was actually sympathetic to the push and pull of family and job responsibilities. Yet, he admitted that, in the company, there is a different attitude toward men and women in job recruitment.

> If a 32 or 28 year-old girl walks in on the verge of pregnancy I know that there will be trouble involved in hiring a person like that. . . . The company probably has an official policy that it isn't a problem at all, but in a hiring situation I know that young women are mistreated. (father, 35, two children, high education)

His response is a classic example of how statistical discrimination can operate in societies with generous parental leave policies and high take-up rates by female workers (Mandel and Shalev 2009). The same respondent claimed that, although it is not official policy, he felt that it was not sustainable to hire women who will have kids:

> With travel and overtime project work, women with small children fail to deliver or quit.

A higher share of low income parents in the Stockholm sample, especially fathers, have experienced or knew about mistreatment in the workplace. In these cases, the mistreatment relates to the care of sick children and the redistribution of the workload among the colleagues, especially in the private sector. Colleagues, who felt forced to take on an extra workload, talked behind the parent's back or made comments that the person was away too often to take care of sick children. This illustrates tensions within the work organization that can occur when parents exercise their legal parental rights.

In many instances in our Stockholm sample, the discriminatory patterns are covert or understood, as exemplified by this father who felt his family involvement put him in a vulnerable position in the firm.

> There's a lot of talk behind the back. Partly it's been suggested that some people think that you're lying if you're home with sick children, or that there are some mean-spirited rumours. . . . An employer cannot treat some differently because of their family circumstances, that's against the law. But behind one's back talk goes on. (father, 28, three children, medium education, working in a public warehouse)

This example above suggests that overt cases of mistreatment are the tip of the iceberg in terms of work organizational cultures and the gendered norms within them. Nonetheless, they can tell us something about what is interpreted as mistreatment in the two societies and the contextual differences in perceptions of rights, as well as the importance of legal rights and protections for assessing capabilities. One difference we found in these narratives of mistreatment for prioritizing family was that, in Hungary, the outcome most often was losing one's job or not being called back.

For the most part, the accounts of discriminatory treatment in the Stockholm sample related to parental leave and pay rises. In these exceptional cases, the parents, two men and one woman, maintained that they were disadvantaged during wage negotiations since they were not at the workplace. The Swedish Parental Leave Act (SFS 1995: 584) should protect parents from wage discrimination during parental leave, as well as guaranteeing them the right to return to a similar position. Both men and women cited this law as giving them a sense of entitlement to make a claim for family, yet in some workplaces informal norms and expectations override this. We found only one instance in the Swedish sample in which taking up parental leave rights resulted in the loss of a job. This involved a father at a multinational corporation, employed on a project basis, who had to resign when he started his parental leave. Given the widespread support for father's rights in Sweden and the law underpinning the exercise of parental rights, it is not surprising that we did not find cases of open and explicit discrimination. More often the unstated norms and narratives of risk that run through organizations, particularly in competitive, high end private sector jobs, reproduce the agency inequalities for WLB for both women and men.

Considering workplace organizational cultures in the two societies, we find similarities in the Swedish and Budapest samples. In both cases workplace cultures can foster highly competitive environments that undermine agency and capabilities for WLB. Many mothers and fathers in our Swedish sample noted that flexibility in working times allowed for greater agency and capabilities in WLB, specifically mentioned was the possibility of taking work home. This allowed them to pick up their children from daycare early and work in the evenings. Excluding the self-employed, parents in Sweden appear to have more flexibility to organize their work schedules around family needs than in Hungary. This is mirrored in aggregate statistics on family-friendly working conditions in the degree to which the employee or employer sets working times. In 2007, a much higher proportion of employees in Sweden than Hungary had the ability to adapt working hours or choose between different schedules (46% compared to 17%), and 38% of employees in Sweden had working time entirely set by the company compared to 72% in Hungary (see Figure 3.2 below).

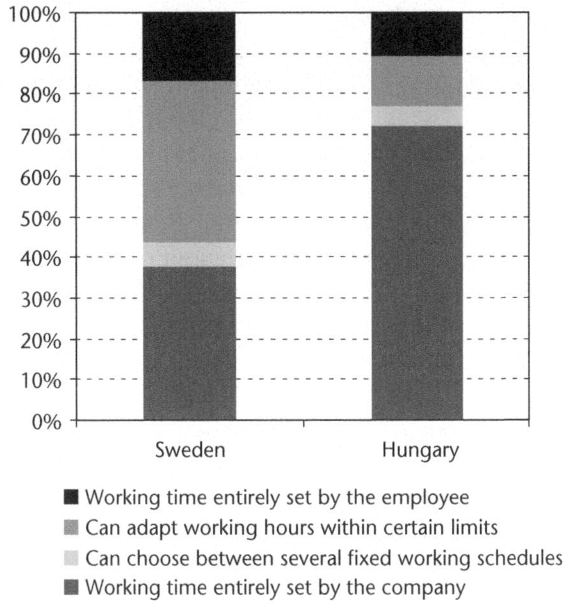

Figure 3.2 Family-friendly working conditions: proportion of employees having working time set by the employer or the employee.

Alternative Scenarios: Obstacles to Change

The essence of Sen's capabilities approach revolves around agency freedoms: what the capabilities for achieving alternative ways of living are (in our case WLB and quality of life). At the end of the survey, we devised questions that would allow to us to tap into the cognitive experiential layers of capabilities and contextualize agency and agency inequalities in the two societies. We asked questions about dream scenarios: what would enable them to achieve a better WLB, what they would change, and what were the obstacles that they would face. The responses reveal the scope of alternatives; the limits on what can even be imagined.

We started by asking our respondents what their scenarios for change were;[12] providing a list from which to select the most important factors that would result in a better WLB, including length of work days, flexibility of working hours, shorter distance to work, more relief from housework or childcare, better access to childcare, flexible hours at childcare, better economy, more time for themselves.[13] We then asked them to elaborate further on what were the circumstances and situations that inhibited a change in WLB.

When asked about the most important factors that would result in a better WLB, economic factors were cited most often among parents in the Budapest sample (42%; 23 women and 19 men) and had the greatest salience among the low and middle income households. In Stockholm, only ten respondents noted economy as the most important factor. For Stockholm parents, having more time was the overriding issue: 57 respondents claimed time (shorter work days, shorter distance to work, more time for themselves, and their own suggestions related to time) was the major factor that would lead toward a better WLB (30 women and 27 men); this was true for both middle and high income families, particularly mothers working full-time (more than 35 hours a week).

'Time for themselves' ranked highest for about one-fifth of parents in the Stockholm sample. Slightly more mothers than fathers expressed this desire, which cut across income levels. Researchers on mothers' working times refer to the exhaustion and pressure women experience as the time squeeze of the double burden women carry (Wiesmann et al. 2008).

Lack of time also stood in the way of improving Budapest parents' WLB and more so for men. This relates to men's long working time regimes in Hungary: more time meant 'shorter workdays' (19 out of 50 specified this). When we looked at responses in which they listed their three most important priorities, better economy appeared as the dominate concern for our Budapest parents, which is also evident in their presentation of the obstacles they would have to overcome in order to achieve a better WLB.

Few of our respondents considered flexibility as a main priority for achieving WLB, but it was still a factor for parents in Hungary, specifically those who were not self-employed highlighted lack of flexibility as an obstacle for achieving a WLB. This included reducing working hours, rigid work schedules, poor time-management skills and a work organizational culture that was insensitive to family needs. For Swedish parents, flexibility was not high on their list of things that would improve their WLB: rights to reduce hours when children are small have been in place for decades and flexibility in organizing schedules and working times has become the norm in many workplaces. Shorter days, rather than flexibility, was the way to achieve WLB for parents with young children in Sweden (Hobson et al 2006).

Contextualizing Economic Constraints in the Two Societies

Economy featured as an obstacle to achieving WLB in both samples, but its contextualized meaning reveals differences in capabilities for Swedish and Hungarian parents. Though having a better economy was not listed as top a priority for WLB for Stockholm parents, economy was interconnected to issues of time and underlay the possibilities of realizing an ideal balance between work and family life. In the Swedish sample, economic constraints not only involved families from lower and middle economic groups, but were just as likely to be experienced by parents in more secure and better economic circumstances. Here, economy was a question of maintaining their living standard. For example, one highly educated mother working in the private sector would have liked to reduce her hours, but framed the consequences for doing that in terms of 'economic scope'. A father, who claimed that he would like to reduce his working hours to have a better WLB, made a similar point in his elaboration of economic scope versus economic constraints. In his dream scenario he wanted to work between 9 pm and 3 am, and then have the rest of his time with his family. However, he did not imagine that he would be able to achieve this. When asked what prevented him from having a better WLB, he answered:

> A good balance, it's about money to a large extent. I wouldn't be able to go down a lot of working hours. But that's about priorities as well. We've chosen to have the car that we do, we've chosen to live here and do what we do and go on the holidays that we do. That money has to come from somewhere. That's the way it is. (father, 33, two children, high education, working as a project manager in the private sector)

In Budapest, financial circumstances were invoked again and again as the main obstacle standing in the way of achieving a better WLB, especially among those with basic and middling education, exemplified by this father:

> It is so hard nowadays to earn enough to cover the cost of living. (father, 32, three children, low education, working as a security guard in the private sector)

or even among those with a high school degree

> There is no choice: both of us must work in order to cover our living costs. (father, 35, three children, medium education, working as a courier in the private sector)

Budapest parents highlighted the increased level of stress within the family that resulted from the combination of economic pressures and long working hours. Here, economic poverty and low incomes are conjoined with time poverty, a combination that produces the weakest capabilities for WLB. This was most evident among the less educated, seen in this example of a mother who pointed out that

> Someone from the family has to work a daily 10–12 hours in order to make ends meet. But then the family cannot be together, and in the end the family will fall apart this way. (mother, 34, three children, low education, working in the private sector)

In light of the long working regimes for both men and women in the Hungarian sample, and the limited opportunities for part-time work among women, one would expect that time would be a top priority for WLB, though economic problems were the dominant concern for our Budapest parents.

About one out of four respondents referred to the lack of time as a hindrance to achieve a better WLB, and twice as many men as women claimed that more time was important for WLB. This difference in time stress is reflected in a study by Hobson and Fahlén (2011) in which 44% of fathers compared to 25% of mothers claimed that their work prevented them from giving time to their partner and family, a finding reflecting men's long working days; yet surveys, such as the European Social Survey, showed that most men would increase their hours slightly if it meant a loss in hourly pay (see Chapter 2).

In Hungary, time stress is reflected among full-time working mothers who also have nearly all the burden of housework and care; 13 out of 22 of the full-time working mothers said that they shouldered nearly all of the housework demands (compared to 9 out of 25 in the Swedish sample). Hungarian mothers lacked a sense of entitlement to makes claims for greater sharing of care and domestic work. Whereas Swedish mothers could ask their partners to do more, and men felt apologetic for not contributing more, in Hungary the double shift in working women's lives was taken for granted, underpinned by societal norms that released men from their responsibilities for domestic work. One mother in the Budapest sample claimed:

> There should be a family counselling service, where men could be convinced that there are no such things as women-only duties just because they were socialized this way at home. (mother, 30, one child, medium education, journalist in the private sector)

As many mothers in Sweden reduce their hours when children are small, the time squeeze is most felt by full-time working mothers, who used phrases like 'chasing time' or 'on the go all the time'. A mother provided a vivid narrative of her frantic life in which she claimed that she had no time for herself since her child was born:

> I almost never sit on the sofa during weekdays. It's horrible. I run around like a headless chicken, tidying and arranging, until I fall into bed. (mother, 47, one child, high education, full-time working lawyer in a governmental agency)

However, the respondents in the Stockholm sample did not frame time pressures around the men's lack of contribution, but rather within the overall time spent in unpaid work. Compared to the Hungarian case, we did not find the visible gender conflicts around the unequal division of housework among our Stockholm parents.[14] Only about five women in our Stockholm sample saw their pathway to achieving an ideal WLB scenario in terms of the division of housework and care; they said that they would like their husbands to take a larger share so that they could get more personal time. In fact, both women and men claimed that relief from housework was a priority for WLB, which they imagined would be improved by outsourcing, hiring someone else to do the work. At the time of the survey, only 24 persons hired someone to help with domestic work, which can be explained by a taboo against hiring others to do domestic work, reflected in our responses, but also by the choice of either hiring someone illegally or paying the high social costs included in the wage.[15] However, there has been dramatic rise in the hiring of domestic workers since the tax subsidy passed in the year of our survey (Skatteverket 2013).

Time was a scarce resource for working parents in both societies and this time deficit cut across differences in education, occupation, and social class. Women, more than men, experienced this to a greater degree. Parents in our Swedish survey described themselves as time pressed and the time squeeze in everyday life lay behind the scenarios for change that would lead to a better WLB and quality of life. In Hungary, time poverty is pervasive: the long working time regimes for both Hungarian men and women, and for women the additional burden of two work shifts; full-time paid work and unpaid work in the home. However, financial circumstances were invoked again and again as the obstacle standing in the way of change for a better WLB. Here, time poverty was conjoined with poverty

Discussion

Representing two ends of the spectrum of agency/agency inequalities in WLB, our comparative cases, Hungary and Sweden, underscore the importance of evaluating policies for WLB in terms of agency and capabilities for exercising them. Despite the grounding of WLB policies in EU law, men and women in Hungary face greater agency inequalities in making claims for WLB than parents in Sweden. Though parents in both countries are protected by law against job loss or discrimination after returning from care leave, in Sweden, the law is enforced, strengthened by union collective agreements that regulate dismissals. Perceptions of insecurity in jobs and precarious economic situations affect individual agency to make claims. There are marked differences between the two societies reflected in the responses of the interviewees in our survey and shown in previous analyses of ESS data (Hobson and Fahlén 2008). Over a third of fathers living in Hungary reported that they had difficulties living on their income, six times greater than Swedish fathers. These data also indicate that a much higher proportion of working parents in Hungary viewed their jobs as insecure and the greatest differences were among the mothers in the two countries.

In comparing the agency and capabilities gap in WLB in Hungary and Sweden, both dual-earner societies, we found similarities in the pressures fostered by competitive work environments and the experiences of the time deficit in WLB, the lack of time for family and leisure. Still, we found striking differences in the capabilities for WLB; reflecting differences in institutional resources (conversion factors), and the strength of traditional cultural/ societal norms limiting agency for claims for WLB in the workplace and household.

Gendered norms encased the perceived scope of alternatives for making change in WLB among working parents in both societies. In Sweden and Hungary, women still bear the main responsibility for care. Mothers in Sweden take the lion's share of the parental leave and a significant majority reduce hours when their children are small while few men use this option. Men's primary economic role in the family was a factor underlying the rationales for why leave was not shared more equally. Nevertheless, neither fathers nor mothers in our Swedish survey viewed care for children as naturalized. Gendered norms operated at the firm level, and the gendered effects mirrored the agency and capabilities for WLB expressed by working parents; workplace organizational culture and work demands were factors restraining the agency and capabilities of fathers in Sweden who claimed that they would have liked to have taken more parental leave. The gender role expectations in the private sector limited women's possibilities to find jobs in that sector and to retain them after starting a family. However, the widespread acceptance of flexibility in working schedules allowed for greater capabilities to organize family time—for instance to pick up their children from the daycare centre early.

In Hungary the normative barriers against fathers' claims for WLB policies appeared insurmountable: parental leave, in particular, was beyond the realm of the possible. Traditional norms around women's responsibilities for home and childrearing appeared deeply imprinted in the Hungarian landscape: both mothers and fathers expressed this naturalized view of motherhood and care and the three-year leave policy normalized this. At the workplace, long working days and a lack of sensitivity to family needs constrained both mothers' and fathers' WLB capabilities. The self-employed imposed long working time regimes on themselves.

The multidimensional approach in the capabilities framework provided a framework for understanding how norms are reproduced in multiple sites: in policies, in workplaces, and in families; and (2) how conversion factors, rights and social rights, and gender equality discourses, enhance capabilities for challenging them.

The cognitive level of agency and agency inequalities in our survey allowed us to explore capabilities from the perspective of the sense of entitlement to make claims. We found that parents in Sweden expressed a sense of entitlement to make claims and self-efficacy to exercise rights. They knew about their rights and invoked the specific anti-discrimination law and policies as the basis for them. The right to reduce hours in Sweden predated the EU directive by decades, and women have a strong sense of entitlement to this right and use it during early childrearing years. These examples illustrate how the seeding process operates, in which rights become embedded in institutions and daily practices. New norms surrounding family life filter into the workplace. The statements from Stockholm parents, that they were rarely even asked to do overtime or weekend work as their workmates and employers knew that they had small children, reflects this. Underpinning this sense of entitlement felt by Stockholm parents are strong conversion factors: rights supported by union organization and collective bargaining, but also buttressed by public discourse and debates on the importance of family-friendly workplaces.

In contrast, working parents in Hungary had both a weak sense of entitlement and low expectations about achieving a WLB. This is demonstrated in a recent survey of equal treatment awareness (EBH 2011) in which parents were asked to define what a family-friendly workplace would comprise: mothers with young children can keep employment; employees with sick children are not sacked; employees can go home if their children are sick; employees can go on sick leave if their children are sick; employees can go on vacation if their children are sick; vacation time can actually be used. These rights and protections are taken for granted in Swedish workplaces.

Underlying the agency inequalities in the exercise of policies and claims for WLB in Hungary, are the structural features of the economy and labour market, which were revealed in men and women's weak sense of entitlement and the narrow scope of alternatives they perceived for achieving a WLB. These include insecurity in jobs, unstable futures, and precarious economies. The possibilities for effective choice are diminished when individuals lack a sense of wellbeing (Sen 1992), which was evident in the responses of less educated fathers and mothers in Hungary. The reality for fathers in our Budapest sample with a low education was one in which just having a job and wage shaded out all other concerns. The existence of family-friendly policies, such as the ability to reduce hours, the rights to refuse hours, or claims for more flexible hours, were beyond their grasp. For mothers, the scope of alternatives and weak capabilities for WLB were reflected in their difficulties in re-entering employment after parental leave, the lack of possibilities of part-time work, and the long hours of working the double shift of paid and unpaid work.

Our survey ended in 2008, the year of the global financial crisis. In our survey we found profound differences in the agency and capabilities gap in WLB, both in the existence of rights and policies and the possibilities of exercising them, but even more broadly in WLB and quality of life. The gap appears to be widening between East and West Europe (Frey 2011; see Chapter 9) but also between Northern and Southern Europe (see Chapter 5) since the economic crises and recession.

Notes

1. Lewis and Smithson (2001) use the sense of entitlement to reflect how employees view support from the employer for reconciling employment with family—whether they are grounded in moral arguments, economic interests, or justice. Our agency-centred model places a sense of entitlement in relation to broader social/contextual variables and conversion factors.
2. Here we define self-efficacy as a person's belief in his or her ability to succeed in a particular situation (Bandura 1994).
3. The same survey was conducted in Osaka Japan (see Chapter 4).
4. The sample in Stockholm was drawn from the Statistical Central Bureau; in Budapest the personal data of respondents was provided by the Central Office for Administrative and Electronic Public Services for research purposes.
5. In both samples we selected equal proportions by firm size; small=1–19 employees; medium 20–249; and large over 250. The actual distributions are: in Sweden: small (14%), medium (34%), and large (52%); in Hungary: small (51%), medium (24%), and large (25%). The educational level was distributed as follows. Stockholm: compulsory level 8%, secondary level 40%, tertiary level 52%. Budapest: compulsory level 25%, secondary level 20%, and tertiary level 25%. The average number of children was 2.16 in the Stockholm sample and 1.68 in the Budapest sample.
6. The questionnaire also includes the division of household work, a social network component, and a social policy country-specific module.
7. The flat-rate benefit (GYES), is equal to the amount of the minimum old-age pension; parents can access this benefit even when the child is enrolled in a daycare facility.
8. Haas and Hwang (2009) interview managers of global companies who may not have records of employee practices.
9. Internal flexibility can be defined as overtime, flexi-time, part-time, temporary work, casual work, or sub-contracting (Viebrock and Clasen 2009).
10. In 2006 there were approximately 700,000 private enterprises officially registered in Hungary, 90% of which were micro-enterprises with a maximum of ten employees; 50% of all enterprises were noted as self-employed sole proprietors (KSH 2008).
11. The law itself protects against discrimination in the use of parental leave. Even in cases of downsizing, employers are not permitted to openly discriminate against

those who are on parental leave. Yet employers can argue that a worker on parental leave is redundant within the organization when downsizing.

12. For the most part, they wanted an equal split between spheres of family, work, and leisure.
13. We also included a category: their own suggestions, which in some cases replicated or further nuanced their answer.
14. This does not imply that there were not latent conflicts, as our section on household work reveals: one study, using our survey, found instances in which women would refer to specific examples of unfairness in household work even though they had answered in the affirmative that they thought the division was fair. See Livia Johannesson's unpublished Master's thesis, 2009.
15. The recent legislation providing families with a tax subsidy for household services has led to a dramatic rise in the outsourcing of household services since the survey year.

Bibliography

Bálint, M. and J. Köllő (2008). The Labour Supply Effect of Maternity Benefits, in K. Fazekas, Zs. Cseres-Gergely, and Á. Scharle (eds), *The Hungarian Labour Market: Review and Analysis*, pp. 53–71. Budapest: Institute of Economics, Hungarian Academy of Sciences (HAS) and Hungarian Employment Foundation <http://econ.core.hu/file/download/mt/4_infocus.pdf>.

Bandura, A. (1994). Self-efficacy, in V.S. Ramachaudran (ed.), *Encyclopedia of Human Behavior*, vol. 4, pp. 71–81. New York: Academic Press.

Brandth, B. and E. Kvande (2009). Gendered or Gender-Neutral Care Politics for Fathers? *The ANNALS of the American Academy of Political and Social Science*, 624(1):177–89.

Browne, J., S. Deakin, and F. Wilkinson (2004). Capabilities, Social Rights and European Market Integration, in R. Salais and R. Villeneuve (eds), *Europe and the Politics of Capabilities*, pp. 205–21. Cambridge: Cambridge University Press.

Bygren, M. and A-Z. Duvander (2006). Parents' Workplace Situations and Fathers' Parental Leave. *Journal of Marriage and the Family*, 68(May):363–72.

Bäck-Wiklund, M., T. van der Lippe, L. den Dulk, and A. Doorne-Huiskes (2011) (eds), *Quality of Life and Work in Europe*. Houndmills, Basingstoke: Palgrave Macmillan.

Crompton, R. and C. Lyonette (2006). Work–Life 'Balance' in Europe. *Acta Sociologica*, 49:379–93.

Daly, M. (2011). What Adult Worker Model? A Critical Look at Recent Social Policy Reform in Europe from a Gender and Family Perspective. *Social Politics*, 18(1): 1–23.

Deakin, S. (2003). Social Rights and the Market: An Evolutionary Perspective, in D. Burchell, S. Deakin, J. Michie, and J. Rubery (eds), *Systems of Production: Markets, Organizations and Performance*, pp. 74–88. London: Routledge.

EBH [Equal Treatment Authority] (2011) Az egyenlő bánásmóddal kapcsolatos jogtudatosság növekedésének mértéke—fókuszban a nők, a romák, a fogyatékos és az LMBT emberek. Kutatási zárójelentés. [The Extent of Equal Treatment Awareness—With Special Focus on Women, Roma, People with Disabilities, and LGBT people.

Research Report] Budapest: EBH <http://www.egyenlobanasmod.hu/tamop/data/MTA_1hullam.pdf> [2011-06-08].

EC (2008). A Better Worklife Balance: Stronger Support for Reconciling Professional, Private and Family Life. Report from the Commission to the Council, the European Parliament, The European Economic and Social Committee and the Committee of Regions. COM(2008) 635 final. Brussels: European Commission.

Eurofound (2009). EiroOnline, Country profiles <http://www.eurofound.europa.eu/eiro/country_index.htm> [2010-01-21].

Eurostat (2008a) Part-time Employment as a Percentage of the Total Employment for a Given Sex and Age Group (%). Database/Employment and Unemployment (LFS). <http://epp.eurostat.ec.europa.eu/portal/page/portal/employment_unemployment_lfs/data/database> [2010-01-13].

Eurostat (2008b). Database/Employment and unemployment (LFS). <http://epp.eurostat.ec.europa.eu/portal/page/portal/employment_unemployment_lfs/data/database> [2010-01-26].

Fagan, C. (2004). Gender and Working-Time in Industrialized Countries: Practices and Preferences, in J. Messenger (ed.) *Finding the Balance: Working-Time and Workers' Needs and Preferences in Industrialized Countries*, pp. 108–46. London: Routledge/Institute for Labour Studies of the International Labour Organisation.

Ferrarini, T. and A-Z. Duvander (2010). Earner-Carer Model at the Crossroads: Reforms and Outcomes of Sweden's Family Policy in Comparative Perspective. *International Journal of Health Services*, 40(3):373–98.

Frey M. (2011) Nők és férfiak a munkaerőpiacon, különös tekintettel a válságkezelés hatásaira. [Women and Men on the Labour Market—With Special Focus on the Effects of Crisis Management], in I. Nagy and T. Pongrácz (eds), *Szerepváltozások. Jelentés a nők és a férfiak helyzetéről 2011* [Changing Roles: Report on the Situation of Women and Men in Hungary 2011], pp. 17–48. Budapest: TÁRKI Zrt.—Nemzeti Erőforrás Minisztérium.

Gornick, J.C. and M.C. Meyers (2003). *Families that Work: Policies for Reconciling Parenthood and Employment*. New York: Russell Sage Foundation.

Hobson. B. (2002) (ed.). *Making Men into Fathers: Men, Masculinities and the Social Politics of Fatherhood*. Cambridge: Cambridge University Press.

Haas, L. and C.P. Hwang (2009). Is Fatherhood Becoming more Visible at Work? Trends in Corporate Support for Fathers Taking Parental Leave in Sweden. *Fathering*, 7(3):303–21.

Hobson, B. and L.Sz. Oláh (2006). Birthstrikes? Agency and Capabilities in the Reconciliation of Employment and Family. *Marriage and Family Review*, 39:197–227.

Hobson, B. and S. Fahlén (2009). Applying Sen's Capabilities Framework within a European Context: Theoretical and Empirical Challenges. REC-WP 03/2009. Working papers on Reconciliation of Work and Welfare in Europe. RECWOWE Publication, Dissemination and Dialogue Center, Edinburgh.

Hobson, B. and S. Fahlén (2011). Parent's Work–Life Balance: Beyond Responsibilities and Obligations to Agency and Capabilities, in J. Bridgeman, H. Keating, and C. Lind (eds), *Regulating Family Responsibilities*, pp. 21–46. Farnham: Ashgate Publishing Limited.

Hobson, B., A-Z. Duvander, and K. Halldén (2006). Men and Women's Agency and Capabilities to Create a Worklife Balance in Diverse and Changing Institutional Contexts, in J. Lewis (ed.) *Children, Changing Families and Welfare State Change*, pp. 267–96. Cheltenham: Edward Elgar.

Hoem, B. (1995). The Way to the Swedish Gender Segregated Labor Market, in K.O. Mason, and A-M. Jensen (eds), *Gender and Family Change in Industrialized Countries*, pp. 279–96. Oxford: Oxford University Press.

Hoem, J.M. (1993). Public Policy as the Fuel of Fertility: Effects of a Policy Reform on the Pace of Childbearing in Sweden in the 1980s. *Acta Sociologica*, 36(1):19–31.

KSH (Hungarian Central Statistical Office) (2006). Visszatérés a munkaerőpiacra gyermekvállalás után [Returning to the Labour Market after Having Children]. Budapest: KSH. <http://portal.ksh.hu/pls/ksh/docs/hun/xftp/idoszaki/pdf/visszamunkaero05.pdf> [2008-12-15].

KSH (Hungarian Central Statistical Office) (2008). Nők és férfiak Magyarországon 2007 [Women and Men in Hungary 2007]. Budapest: KSH-SzMM <http://portal.ksh.hu/pls/ksh/docs/hun/xftp/idoszaki/valldemog/valldemog06.pdf> [2009-04-07].

KSH (Hungarian Central Statistical Office) (2009). Total Fertility Rate in 2008 <http://portal.ksh.hu/pls/ksh/docs/eng/xstadat/xstadat_annual/tabl1_01ieb.html> [2009-04-23].

Lee, S. and D. McCann (2006). Working Time Capability: Towards Realizing Individual Choice, in J-Y. Boulin, M. Lallement, J.C. Messenger, and F. Michon (eds), *Working Time: New Trends, New Issues*, pp. 65–91. Geneva: International Labour Office.

Leitner, A. and A. Wroblewski (2006). Welfare State and Work–Life Balance. *European Societies*, 8(2): 295–317.

Lewis, J. and A. Plomien (2009). Flexicurity' as a Policy Strategy: The Implications for Gender Equality. *Economy and Society*, 38(3):433–459.

Lewis, S. and J. Smithson (2000). Sense of Entitlement to Support for the Reconciliation of Employment and Family Life. *Human Relations*, 54(11):1455–81.

Lewis, S., J. Brannen, and A. Nilsen (2009) (eds), *Work, Families and Organisations in Transition: European Perspectives*. Bristol: The Policy Press.

Mandel, H. and M. Shalev (2009). How Welfare States Shape the Gender Pay Gap: A Theoretical and Comparative Analysis. *Social Forces*, 87(4):1873–912.

Moss, P. and M. Korintus (2008) (eds), International Review of Leave Policies and Related Research 2008. Employment Relation Research Series No. 100. London: Department for Business Enterprise and Regulatory Reform.

National Social Insurance Board (2003). Social Insurance in Sweden 2003. Family Assets—Time and money. Stockholm: National Social Insurance Board.

Neményi, M. and J. Takács (2006). Changing Family—Changing Politics. *Review of Sociology of the Hungarian Sociological Association*, 12(2):37–63 <http://www.akademiai.com/content/g30u48884j735687/fulltext.pdf> [2007-02-01].

OECD (2012). Employment Outlook 2012. OECD Publishing. Online publication, <http://dx.doi.org/10.1787/empl_outlook-2012-en> [2012-11-12].

OECD Family database (2007). Maternal Employment <http://www.oecd.org/els/social/family> [2010-01-13].

Oláh, L.Sz. (2003). Gendering Fertility: Second Births in Sweden and Hungary. *Population Research and Policy Review*, 22(2):171–200.

Perrons, D., C. Fagan, L. McDowell, K. Ray, and K. Ward (2006) (eds), *Gender Divisions and Working Time in the New Economy: Changing Patterns of Work, Care and Public Policy in Europe and North America*. Cheltenham: Edward Elgar.

Plantenga, J. and C. Remery (2005). Reconciliation of Work and Private Life: A Comparative Review of Thirty European Countries. European Expert Group on Gender, Social Exclusion and Employment (EGGSIE). Luxembourg: Office for Official Publications of the European Communities.

Purcell, K., T. Hogarth, and C. Simms (1999). *Whose Flexibility? The Costs and Benefits of 'Non-standard' Working Arrangements and Contractual Relations*. York: York Publishing Services/Joseph Rowntree Foundation.

Ramioul, M. and R. Huys (2007). Comparative Analysis of Organisation Surveys in Europe: Literature Review of Secondary Analysis. Works report, HKU Leuven.

Sen, A. (1992). *Inequality Re-examined*. Oxford: Oxford University Press.

SFS (1995). 584, Parental Leave Act.

Skatteverket (2013) 'Intresset för rutavdrag ökar kraftigt', press release <http://www.skatteverket.se/omskatteverket/press/pressmeddelanden/riks/2013/2013/intressetforrutavdragokarkraftigt.5.2b543913a42158acf800025965.html> [2013-01-08].

SOU (2005). Makt att forma samhället och sitt eget liv—jämställdhetspolitiken mot nya mål. Slutbetänkande av Jämställdhetspolitiska utredningen. Statens Offentliga Utredningar. SOU 2005:66. Stockholm: Fritzes.

Spéder, Z. and F. Kamarás (2008). Hungary: Secular Fertility Decline with Distinct Period Fluctuations. *Demographic Research*, 19(18):599–664.

Statistics Sweden (2009a). Total Fertility Rate in 2008 <http://www.scb.se/Pages/TableAndChart____231102.aspx> [2009-04-23].

Statistics Sweden (2009b). Labour Market Statistics <http://www.ssd.scb.se/databaser/makro/start.asp> [2009-09-25].

Sundström, M. and A-Z. Duvander (2002). Gender Division of Childcare and the Sharing of Parental Leave among New Parents in Sweden. *European Sociological Review*, 18(4):433–47.

Swedish Social Insurance Agency (2011). Föräldrapenning/Statistikrapporter. Antal mottagare som uppburit ersättning, antal barn och antal nettodagar med fördelning efter ålder <http://www.forsakringskassan.se/omfk/statistik_och_analys/barn_och_familj/foraldrapenning> [2011-02-28].

Takács, J. (2008). Ha mosogatógép nem lenne, már elváltunk volna. Férfiak és nők otthoni munkamegosztáa európai összehasonlitásban [If there were No Dish-washer at Home, We would already have Gotten a Divorce . . . Sharing of Domestic Work Between Men and Women—A European Comparison], *Esély*, 19(6):51–73.

Tang, N. and C. Cousins (2005). Working Time, Gender and Family: An East–West European Comparison. *Gender, Work and Organization*, 12(6):527–50.

Van der Lippe, T. and P. Peters (2007). *Competing Claims in Work and Family Balance*. Cheltenham: Edward Elgar.

Viebrock, E. and J. Clasen (2009). Flexicurity—A State-of-the-Art Review. REC-WP 01/2009. Working Papers on the Reconciling Work and Welfare in Europe. Edinburgh: RECWOWE Publication, Dissemination and Dialogue Center.

Wall, K. (2007). Main Patterns in Attitudes to the Articulation between Work and Family Life: A Cross-National Analysis, in R. Crompton, S. Lewis, and C. Lyonette (eds), *Women, Men, Work and Family in Europe*, pp. 86–115. New York: Palgrave Macmillan.

Weismann, S.M., H. Boejie, A. Van Doorne Huiskes, and L. den Dulk (2008). 'Not Worth Mentioning?': The Implicit and Explicit Nature of Decision-making about the Division of Paid and Domestic Work. *Community, Work and Family*, 11(4): 341–63.

4

Worklife balance in Japan: new policies, old practices

Mieko Takahashi, Saori Kamano, Tomoko Matsuda, Setsuko Onode, and Kyoko Yoshizumi

Introduction

The Japanese national government, trade unions, and employer representatives concertedly drew up a 'Work–Life Balance Charter' in December 2007, calling for the harmonization of work and personal life in order to create a society that facilitates financial independence through work, allows time for a healthy and fulfilling life, and offers a variety of working and living patterns. Worklife balance (hereafter referred to as WLB) is touted as the way to achieve gender equality and reverse the longstanding low fertility rate in Japan. WLB-related measures have been developed to encompass all individuals, beyond categories of age, gender, and marital status, as a comprehensive strategy that spans public and private spheres. This provision of new incentives for women and men to achieve a better WLB was a break with past measures that paid very little attention to gender equality and quality of life with regard to reconciliation of work and family life.

However, the emergence of WLB-related policies, including leave arrangements and reduction of working hours, has not altered the core of the social structure premised upon the gender logic that defines 'men as earners and women as caretakers'. Indeed, Japan has been characterized in welfare regime typologies as the archetype of male breadwinner societies, structured around gender differences, male breadwinner norms and policies to support them (Takahashi 2003). Corporations likewise exemplify deep-rooted ideas of the gender division of labour. As a result, women are still forced to make a choice between working and childrearing, while men are expected to put in long working hours.

Japan appears to be a country with a wide agency and capabilities gap between policies and practices, and between entitlements and a sense of entitlement to make claims for WLB (Takahashi 2011a). To explore the sources and extent of the agency and capabilities gap, we use data from an original study on WLB. This was supplemented with data from national surveys (see endnotes 3 and 4). In this chapter, we ask three questions:

1) Have these reforms enhanced individuals' capabilities to make claims for WLB?
2) What are the barriers to be confronted in order to increase the sense of entitlement to make claims and exercise rights for WLB, including workplace organizational cultures and gendered norms that operate within the family and at the workplace?
3) What implications can be derived from our findings that might lead towards a better worklife balance for mothers and fathers?

First, the chapter presents the theoretical framework, particularly as it applies to the Japanese context, and describes the data used for our analysis. Second, we present the gendered patterns at work and in family life. We then turn to specific policies aimed at improving worklife balance among men and women and consider whether and how they are utilized and what the constraints and possibilities are for claiming them. In the final sections of the chapter, we focus on the agency and capabilities gap itself: what kind of worklife balance would parents choose and what do they perceive as the major obstacles inhibiting them from achieving it. In the conclusion, we will highlight the key findings and suggest possibilities for making changes. What kinds of reforms are needed to enhance the capabilities of men and women to achieve a better WLB?

The Capabilities Framework in the Japanese Context

The capabilities approach asks us to consider what people are able to accomplish by utilizing their existing resources—a process that Sen argues makes possible the combined total of one's being and doing (Sen 1985, 1992). Capabilities are both obstructed and facilitated through interaction with both individual and social/institutional factors. This capabilities framework applied to WLB is highly relevant to the Japanese case as the agency and capabilities gap is expressed in terms of lack of knowledge about policies, which in itself reflects workplace cultural norms as well as the normative societal constraints (particularly for men) that inhibit individuals from claiming their rights. In Japan, the firm is a central institutional factor shaping agency and capabilities, which makes it vital for understanding the gap in capabilities for WLB. We have adapted the model in Chapter 3 to illustrate this (see Figure 4.1 below).

To justify why the firm was placed at the nexus between conversion factors and agency achievements of WLB in the figure, we present general features of agency inequalities relating to the centrality of work in Japanese society. The work world is disproportionately significant; achieving a balance between work and home does not come naturally. It requires working parents with young children to draw on whatever resources are available to them. In a study on WLB in the Japanese private sector, Takeishi (2012) points outs that in order to realize the WLB of individual employees, it is more important to construct a managed workplace environment than to put forward relevant policies or company-level systems. In Japan, the workplace seems to operate as an implementer rather than a mediator of WLB-related policies. Workplace organizational culture features prominently in our analysis, particularly the long working hours regime, as well as aspects of the work culture that require employees to be present at work until others leave. Another relevant aspect of this, yet not explicit in the model, is reluctance and resistance to becoming a burden at the workplace, although sense of loyalty to the firm, especially among male white-collar employees, has been changing in the last two decades (Taga 2011). The inclination towards risk avoidance and protecting one's position in the firm remains strong among employees. In the Japanese labour market, a system in which a worker is able to advance their career by changing jobs

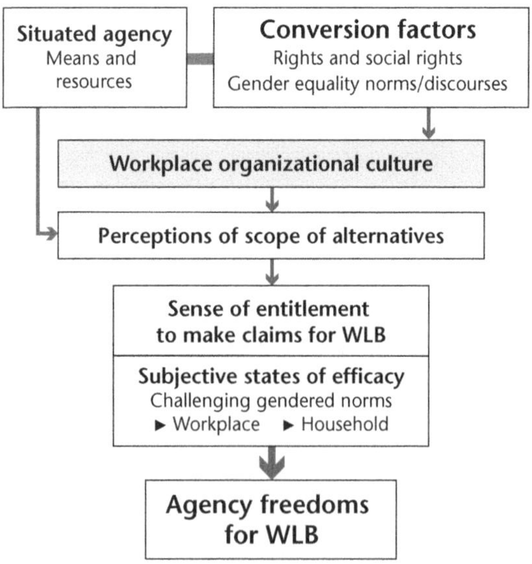

Figure 4.1 The workplace organization nexus in agency and worklife balance

has not been in place, as lifetime employment and automatic pay rises with age have long been common practice in companies. With the recent economic recession, people who are forced to change jobs as a result of organizational restructuring face downward career mobility and a reduction in income.[1] Such lack of flexibility in the Japanese labour market is one of the factors that constrain individual employees from realizing capabilities for WLB.

Combination of Data Sources

We used a combination of national surveys along with a capabilities survey that was specifically designed to capture the experiential subjective aspects of agency and agency inequalities for WLB. Our study is part of a collaborative undertaking in an international comparative research project of worklife balance analysis headed by Barbara Hobson (see the Introduction in this volume). To facilitate cross-national comparisons, we use the same framework to understand the mechanisms connecting policy, institutional norms and culture, and individual resources and constraints in the Japanese context. Our sampling and questionnaires are similar to those of the surveys conducted in Sweden and in Hungary. However, we slightly modified some questions to adapt to particularities of the Japanese case. Since the target of our study includes men and women in dual-working households, we added questions to explore factors that enable women with young children to work, as well as questions on the aforementioned reluctance and resistance to leave work early and/or take vacations. Using data collected from face-to-face interviews[2] with 104 employees (51 women and 53 men) from dual-earning nuclear families with preschool-aged children, conducted in the Osaka Metropolitan area between April and November 2010, we examine capabilities for WLB at the policy, workplace, and individual level. Our respondents are between the ages of 26–45 and the average number of children for the parents is 1.62. About 57% have a university or post-graduate degree (47% of the women and 66% of the men); 27% have vocational training, junior college, or technical college (35% of the women and 1% of the men). The majority work in the private sector (94% or the women and 79% of the men) and are regular employees (79%); 41% of the women and less than 2% of the men are non-regular employees (part-time, temporary employed, dispatch worker, non-regular staff). About 19% work in small companies (<30 employees), 20% work in middle-size companies (30–299 employees), 49% work in large companies (300+ employees), and about 14% are government employees.

In addition to the qualitative interview data, we also incorporate findings based on nationwide surveys on relevant issues, such as the International Opinion Survey on a Low Birth-rate Society conducted by the Cabinet Office of Japan, Director General for Policies on Cohesive Society (2011)[3] and the Work Life Balance Survey conducted by the Research Institute of Economy, Trade and Industry (RIETI hereafter).[4]

Gendered Patterns in Work and Family Life

Although there has been an increase in women's labour participation, working patterns are still distinctly different between the genders in Japan. While men's work patterns do not change dramatically throughout their life course, as indicated by the stable labour force participation rates for men aged 25 to 54 at around 95%, women's work patterns do vary. In 2010, the labour force participation rate of women in their late 20s was 77%; 10% lower at 68% for women in their 30s, but over 70% for women in their 40s (see Figure 4.2). The lower labour force participation rate for women in their 30s is attributed to women leaving the labour force while they have young children. Indeed, a more detailed examination of women's working patterns shows that they vary greatly depending upon whether the women have a spouse and/or children, as shown in Table 4.1, with a lower employment rate when married, having children, and having young children.[5] There is, in addition, a difference in the type of employment by marital and/or parental status among women: those who are married with children tend to be part-time/temporary workers and those never married tend to be full-time workers,[6] which indicates that responsibilities associated with family life have limited

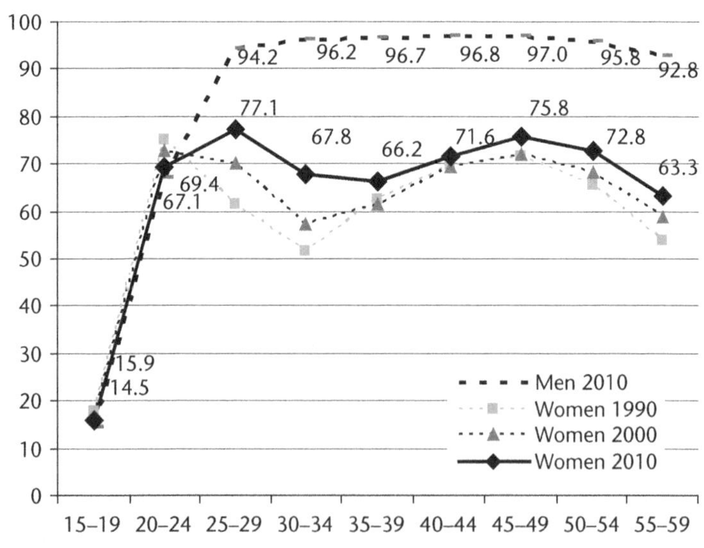

Figure 4.2 Employment rates by age group in Japan, 1990–2010

Table 4.1 Employment rate of women aged 30 to 34, by marital status and presence and ages of children (2007)

Total	Never Married	Married				
		All	No children	With children		
				All	Under 6 years old	Under 3 years old
63.5%	86.0%	49.5%	63.5%	44.0%	40.0%	33.6%

Source: Employment Status Survey 2007 (Ministry of Internal Affairs and Communications Statistics Bureau 2008b).

women from taking up full-time work (Ministry of Health, Labour and Welfare 2011b).

The labour market is such that women who temporarily leave their jobs have a difficult time utilizing their past job experience in order to re-enter the workforce. Among women who were working prior to becoming parents in 2005 to 2009, when the child was aged 46% were working full-time (of whom 41% used parental leave), 6.6% were working part-time, and 147% were unemployed (National Institute of Population and Social Security Research 2012). This pattern is also seen among our interviewees. This employment pattern reinforces disparities not only in wages but also in social security benefits, as many corporations actively recruit full-time housewives as part-time workers in order to cut costs on salaries by avoiding having to pay social security benefits. The assumption is that part-time workers will accept these conditions as the jobs allow them to take days off for family reasons. The difference between part-time/temporary workers and full-time regular workers lies not in the number of working hours but in working status. Part-time workers can work more than 35 hours a week and still remain part-time workers. Usually, they are not entitled to paid vacations and do not enjoy the same chances for promotion or have the same protection as full-time regular workers (Takahashi 2003).[7] At the same time, women who continue in full-time employment are compelled to either delay or forgo marriage and childbirth. This no-win situation is understood to be one of the reasons for delayed marriage as well as for the extremely low fertility rate (1.41 in 2012).

Gendered Division of Unpaid Work

Underlying the employment pattern for women is a gendered division of domestic work. In 2008, for dual-income households with a child under 3, women spent, on a daily basis, roughly six hours on housework and three hours taking care of children, whereas men spent only half an hour on housework and 45 minutes on their children. While the men's long hours at work is conventionally taken as an explanation for their low participation in unpaid work, the average amount of free time per day counters such an explanation: 3 hours and 10 minutes for married men as compared with 2 hours and 17 minutes for married women (Ministry of Internal Affairs and Communications Statistics Bureau 2008a).

This division of paid work and family responsibilities is undergirded by pervasive gendered norms. According to the Cabinet Office survey (see endnote 3), in response to a question on the most important roles of a father in a family, over 90% of both men and women chose 'working and earning a living', while only slightly over 40% of the same chose 'taking care of the children' (Takahashi 2011a). Consistent with widely accepted ideas, the majority of women interviewees in our study said that housework is 'mostly the wife's' responsibility (67%), and that earning money is 'mostly the husband's' responsibility (69%).

Among dual-working couples in Japan, extant studies consistently show that very few women engage their husbands in open communication to negotiate the division of household tasks (Takahashi 2003, Yoshizumi and Takahashi 2003, Matsuda 2004),[8] making it difficult to achieve the balance they actually desire. This was also true among many of our women interviewees.

For example, a woman who decided to work at weekends while her husband watches the children (a 40 year-old with 12 and 1 year-old children, high school graduate, sales staff, non-regular worker) said that she wished her husband would do her housework tasks more often, but that she found herself unable to tell him her feelings in this regard.

> If I asked him I think he would do it, but well, *he comes home late and all, and well, he does watch over the children for me on Saturdays and Sundays*, so I don't say anything. No, I've never mentioned it. (emphasis added)

With her husband performing only around 10% of household chores, she wants to ask him to take on a greater share, but has given up on the idea because she feels indebted to him for watching over the children at weekends, and because he comes home late.

These women's reluctance to negotiate housework division with their husbands and the latter's attitudes and longer hours of work all reflect adherence to the norm and practice of conventional gender roles, which are obstacles preventing these women from realizing their full potential.

Our analyses of dual-working households show that there are more inhibiting factors related to individual circumstances for women compared with men, which reflects widely diffused gender norms in the society. Women have no choice but to accept the double burden of housework and paid work in order to manage both work and family lives. However, they tend not to see it as a problem and generally accept their circumstances. In a society where becoming a full-time housewife is accepted as a way of life for married women, the social norm that family life is a woman's responsibility remains unchallenged.

Policies and their use

WLB policies in Japan can be understood as the merging of two parallel strands of policies; support for working women both at work and in the home, and policies related to the falling birth-rate (Matsuda 2012; see also Yamaguchi 2009). The first strand of policies goes back to the 1986 Equal Employment Opportunity Act for Men and Women, which stipulated that women were to be guaranteed a working environment free of gender-based discrimination and which would allow them to continue working through marriage and childbirth. The law underwent two revisions in 1999 and 2007, and was developed in order to promote gender-based equality in the workplace, including a ban on unfair treatment in case of pregnancy and childbirth and the establishment of maternal health-related measures.[9] This was followed by the passage of the Law on Parental Leave in 1994, offering balanced support for work and care of both children and the elderly. In 1999, the Basic Act for a Gender-Equal Society was passed, stipulating concrete plans to enable gender equality of participation in the workplace, communities, and at home.

The second strand of policies aimed at halting the country's persistently low fertility rate. A number of childrearing assistance measures were developed, including the 'Angel Plan' of 1994 and the ' Angel Plan' of 1999, which aimed at increasing childcare services.[10] The passing of the New Generation Childcare Policy Promotion Law in 2004 encouraged proactive measures on the part of corporations, including modifying existing working patterns for men as well as for women, and requiring corporations with more than 300 full-time employees to create action plans aimed at building work environments enabling a balance of work and childcare.

WLB policies today have emerged from these parallel strands. From the state's perspective, the aims of WLB policies are to raise the fertility rate, and to strengthen human resources that lead to greater competitiveness and productivity in companies in order to survive in the globalization era. Viewed this way, WLB policies are important not only to balance personal and work lives, but also are linked to the economic strength of the nation as a whole.

The specific policies/available to working parents based on the Child Care Leave Act discussed earlier are shown in Table 4.2. Workers have the right to request leave until the child is 1 year of age. This measure is important in the sense that fathers are also able to take parental leave, but unlike parental leave in countries like Sweden, fathers and mothers cannot alternate in taking the

Table 4.2 WLB related measures for workers who take care of children

Worker's rights	
Maternity leave	14 weeks, paid about 2/3 of salary
Parental leave	Until the child reaches 1 year of age, paid about 50% of salary. Extra 2 months if parents take leave together before the child turns 1. Extendable up to 1.5 years when a childcare facility is not available. If the father takes leave within 8 weeks from childbirth then returns to work, he may take leave once more
Sick/injured childcare leave	5 days per child under 6/year, max. 10 days, unpaid
Shortened working hours	6 hours/day until the child is 3, unpaid
Exemption from extra works	Until the child is 3
Limited legal extra working hours	24 hrs/week or 150 hrs/year until the child is 6
Employer efforts (until the child is 6 years of age)	
Flexi-time system	A system equivalent to parental leave
Advancement/postponement of the hours for starting/finishing work	
Establishment and operation of an on-site daycare centre for children	
Benefits equivalent to access to childcare centre	
A system equivalent to parental leave	

Source: Ministry of Health, Labour and Welfare HP. <http://www.mhlw.go.jp/english/wp/wp-hw4/dl/equal_employment_and_child_welfare/2011071905.pdf>.

leave or repeatedly take it. Compensation has increased slightly in recent years, but remains at only 50%. Besides parental leave, workers with small children have the right to reject overtime and working late evening hours, but it should be noted that it is generally very rare for workers, especially men, to actually utilize such rights. In addition, companies are not required to implement work policies that promote more flexible working arrangements, such as the flexi-time system. These are listed as official WLB policies, but their implementation is not mandatory and they are merely possible measures that companies can try to implement.

It should also be noted that while these measures appear to be 'gender neutral' (with the exception of maternity leave), there still exist governmental polices related to the family which are premised upon the continuation and stabilization of families based upon the strong male breadwinner model, including support for statutory share inheritances (1980), special tax reductions for part-time earners (1984), guarantee of basic pension for housewives (1985), implementation of gift taxes, and special income tax deductions for spouses (1985/87), all of which provide commensurate rewards for the role of a full-time housewife. These policies are built upon and further perpetuate the gendered working and family patterns of Japan.

As noted above, policies that enable people to manage both work and childrearing are being established in Japan, but the utilization rate is low and gender difference in utilization is also prominent in comparison with EU countries. Another recent phenomenon is the new image of men caring for their children as '*ikumen*' (a play on words combining '*ikuji*', or childrearing, and 'men'). In June 2010, the Ministry of Health, Labour and Welfare started an 'Ikumen Project' to promote men's participation in caring for their children. However, whether viewing it in a comparative perspective or on its own, there is low utilization of policies targeting both men and women for taking leave from work and changing working arrangements (Cabinet Office of Japan, Gender Equal Bureau 2011).

However, unlike such European countries as Sweden with high proportions of married women in the labour force, take-up rates for policies that support both women and men taking parental leave, including maternity leave, as well as measures supporting flexible work, are much lower in Japan (and even lower in Korea, where male breadwinner norms remain strong and the traditional gendered division of family and work responsibilities are firmly entrenched) (see Table 4.3).

With respect to parental leave, although more than 30% of men say that they would in fact like to take such leave (Ministry of Health, Labour and Welfare 2011a), they rarely do so. Indeed, according to the Ministry of Health, Labour and Welfare, only 1.4% of men took parental leave in 2010. In contrast, 84% of women who continued working throughout their pregnancy went on to take parental leave (Ministry of Health, Labour and Welfare 2011b). A study on full-time white-collar employees with children under 6 years of age reveals

Table 4.3 WLB related measures used: responses from females and males (2010)

	Japan		Korea		Sweden	
	Women	Men	Women	Men	Women	Men
Maternity leave	22.9	–	14.4	–	85.1	–
Paternal leave	–	4.4	–	2.3	–	77.1
Parental leave	17.0	4.8	6.3	5.8	75.2	74.0
Nursing leave for children	3.1	4.1	1.8	2.7	67.6	64.0
Shorter working hours	7.3	4.1	8.1	5.8	42.0	15.4
Teleworking, home-based work	2.7	0.7	3.3	1.2	18.4	24.7

Notes: The original question asked about past usage of childcare support policies, including usage of childcare facilities. For detailed information, see source.

Source: Takahashi 2011a, Figure 4–14A, 4–14B.

a similar pattern: 83.6% of women (out of a total of 312) utilized parental leave policies, while a mere 2.1% of men did so (out of a total of 1260). The percentage of those utilizing the policy of shorter working hours for childcare was even lower—only 32.4% of women and 0.6% of men used it (RIETI 2009 study, see endnote 4).

In our study of employed men and women, many of the measures involving changing one's way of working were infrequently used. We asked the respondents whether, and how well, they knew about the possibilities and whether they utilized the policies related to taking care of young children. Not surprisingly, women use these provisions more than men do: among the 26 women who continued working throughout their pregnancy and currently are full-time regular workers, the majority, 20 women, used parental leave and 18 used shortened working hours, and about half of them used sick/injured childcare leave and a late start and early finish system (14 and 13 women respectively).[11]

Male respondents rarely use these measures and provisions; only 13% (7 out of 51) have used sick/injured childcare leave, and no more than 2 persons used the late start and early finish system, restriction of late night work, or flexible time system. More men working in the public sector took sick/injured childcare leave (36%, 4 out of 11) as opposed to 13% (3 out of 40) among those in the private sector, but none in the public sector used other measures.[12] Clearly, while the implementation of worklife balance policies in Japan has shown some success with women, facilitating continued employment, it has yet to achieve comparable results for men with regard to participation in the family (Takahashi 2011a).

A structural reason for the low utilization rate of these policies is that many workplaces do not offer them. Here, firm size plays an important role. Generally, larger companies offer better WLB policies, and it is also easier for employees to use them.[13] In our interviews, shortened working hours was used by 30% of the women who had worked throughout their pregnancy and were currently working at firms with 300 or more employees, while the figure was 4% (1 person) for women in firms under 300 employees. Another reason for the low level of utilization of policies is lack of knowledge of them. Even if the policies were implemented within individual firms, it would be difficult to achieve worklife balance unless the idea of WLB infiltrates workplace culture, where knowledge of policies is shared and a sense of entitlement is developed among all employees.

In our study, except for the widely known parental leave, many had not heard of other policies. Among the full-time regular employees (30 women and 52 men) who were the main targets of such policies, only 37% of women and 44% of men had heard about the flexible time system, and 27% of women and 35% of men about the late start and early finish system. Further, only 13% of the full-time and 43% of the part-time working women had heard of parental leave for part-time workers. In some cases, knowledge does not directly connect to use of these policies, such as restriction of late night work; for example, there were only a few women who did not know about restriction of overtime work.

As is true of the use of these policies, knowledge also seems to vary by sector and firm size: 22% (9 out of 41) men in the private sector had not heard about sick/injured childcare leave while the figure was 9% (1 out of 11) for those in the public sector. Examining knowledge by firm size, among men in smaller firms of fewer than 30 employees, 4 out of 7 had not heard about shortened working hours as opposed to 8 out of 52 men overall.

It should be mentioned that while most of these policies are available both to men and to women, this knowledge is not necessarily shared, partly contributing to low usage of such policies by men. For example, even with respect to the most widely known parental leave, a 2007 workplace study showed that less than half of men and women knew that male employees could take parental leave (Tokyo Metropolitan Government Bureau of Industrial and Labour Affairs Employment Division 2007). Clearly, it may be inferred that given the low awareness regarding the array of available policies, the sense of entitlement to the right to use childcare policies is on the whole quite weak.

Parental Leave and Related Entitlements

A common explanation as to why it is mostly women who take parental leave is the arguably lower cost it incurs on women's career and income, given men's relative advantages in income and career progression. In the European context, this explanation assumes that individuals make rational choices not to take parental leave. However, in Japan, where the norms for taking such leaves for men have not been established, taking parental leave is not a viable option for men. Not taking parental leave is not the result of a rational decision making process, that 'if I take the leave, it will impact negatively on my career, and hence I should not take it'. Rather than seeing that men are 'opting out' of parental leave, it is more appropriate to say that they just do not take any action towards it. This is because they are reluctant to do anything different from their colleagues. Moreover, it is important to point out that the length of the (father's) parental leave that our interviewees are considering is short, about one week. In our interviews, 35 out of 49 men took regular paid leave (not parental leave) for a few days when their wives gave birth. In rare cases, a company gives a special leave for fathers for the wife's childbirth and some fathers took this leave, but again, it was less than a week.

Generally, policies related to WLB, including general paid leave, are not implemented strongly in Japanese workplaces. For example, the utilization rate of yearly paid vacation (an average of 17.9 days yearly per person) among employees aged 30 and above in private corporations remains at 48.1% (Ministry of Health, Labour and Welfare 2012). Moreover, many companies regard negatively their employees' taking of long vacations for the purpose of leisure or travel. As a result, many workers use their paid vacations when taking days off for illness.[14] Implementation of such policies constitutes an obstacle preventing employees' from achieving WLB.

In predominantly female workplaces, such as public service work and the care sector, it has become commonplace for women to utilize childcare policies. An elementary school teacher described taking parental leave as 'completely normal', and she took the leave without even negotiating directly with her employer (a 41 year-old university graduate with a 3 year-old child). In this case, the policies are available for women to use 'automatically', regardless of their intention to take the leave. In workplaces outside of these types of fields, however, it is not always easy for women to utilize such policies even if they may be aware of their existence.

An employee at a private corporation was a pioneer for continuing to work at a place where the norm was to quit following marriage. Still, she did not obtain parental leave.

> My workplace provides parental leave which is longer than required by law, but, well, how can I say it, it is just on paper. It is written down, but with not many people taking leave, it's pretty difficult for me to take parental leave after already having taken time off using maternity leave. (43 year-old junior college graduate with a 2 year-old child)

A mother who stopped working before giving birth to her child, taking a 2 year temporary leave of absence rather than parental leave and now working part-time, commented:

> Even though parental leave is a national policy, it is not possible to take it at my workplace. (37 year-old university graduate with a 3 year-old child)

Similarly, an employee at a design firm, who became a manager before giving birth and then took parental leave, commented with regard to the system of shorter working hours that:

> Even though there is a policy in this regard, not many people make use of it. (45 year-old university graduate with a 5 year-old child)

If the working atmosphere does not encourage the use of such measures and provisions, then many people do not take the initiative to try.

While it is generally easier for women to take paid leave for family-related matters than it is for men, in some workplaces it is still quite difficult. A part-time (30 hours a week) employee at a nursing home commented that she had

> not seen many [full-time women employees] utilize the leave policy. (31 year-old with children aged 7, 5, and 1, vocational education after high school)

In many workplaces, the policies are not implemented properly and it is difficult for employees to utilize their basic right to take leave. It will be seen in the next subsection that, for men, gendered expectations make it even more difficult to exercise rights.

Men who participate in childcare are violating entrenched gender norms and must constantly put up with the disapproval of others who do not want to understand why men would be engaged in this (Suemori 2010). In many cases, the struggles are located at the workplace, where a deep-rooted double standard exists in expectations towards fathers. In the RIETI survey, with regard to the statement, 'The general atmosphere is such that taking time off for family reasons such as parental or dependents leave is accepted, regardless of the person's gender or position in the company', 42% of women responded 'true' or 'basically true', while the percentage of men was eight points lower, at 34% (Takahashi 2011b).[15] This suggests that the idea that mothers as the main caretakers of children can be afforded consideration and assistance within the workplace on various levels, men who take parental or other leaves risk negative reactions from their superiors and colleagues.

For example, a 38 year-old section head (supervisor) at a major corporation (a university graduate with a 3 year-old and a 1 year-old) said that at his company, there is a gap making it is easy for women to take parental leave but no man in his company has ever done so. Although information sessions have been held in order to familiarize employees—including men—with the leave policies, he explained,

> but then, if one were to really take it, it's hard to tell if they'd welcome it or not. It would be something like, 'Are you really taking it'?

Similarly, an employee at a small-scale, half-governmental/half-private organization knew that men could take parental leave because it was part of the work of the organization to provide such information to private companies. However, if a man at his organization ever tried to actually avail himself of the leave, the response would probably be a negative one along the lines of 'don't you have a wife'? He also added that no male employees had ever taken parental leave or asked for a system of shorter working hours (31 year-old university graduate with a 9 year-old and a 2 year-old child).

As we have seen, policies for worklife balance have begun to be implemented by the Japanese government with increasing corporate awareness and the creation of supportive measures. At the same time, in reality, working men and women have generally not achieved WLB in terms of allocating time for work, for family and for self in ways they desire, and available measures, while still limited, are not utilized to their full extent. The attempted reforms have not enhanced individuals' agency and capabilities to make claims for WLB. In a later section, we will further explore this gap between the ideal and the actual practice by identifying the factors that facilitate or inhibit WLB capabilities.

Workplace Organizational Culture

In this section, we will explore what kind of barriers at the workplace confront working men and women in dual-earner households that inhibit their sense of entitlement for making claims and exercising rights for WLB. For women, one common strategy for achieving some sort of WLB is to find new employment accommodating their needs, where working hours can be structured around family-related needs and employees are able to prioritize their families. It seems that many of our interviewees working part-time had no other choice. A part-time office worker (junior college graduate) unhappy at not being able to use her work skills, as her current job was just a lot of miscellaneous duties, nevertheless stated;

> They are accommodating, however, and that's what is most important.

Other women also make similar points:

> 'I took a job here because of their flexibility, since I have small children, so I am able to easily come in late or leave work early depending on the situation at home. (part-time bookstore cashier, university graduate)
>
> I went for job interviews at many different places, and they asked me what I would do if I had to take a day off (due to a child's illness). Not many places will allow you to take a sudden day off, so I am grateful to my current employer for letting me do so when necessary. (part-time at a call centre, junior college education)

Taking an 'accommodating' or 'low demand' job is a practical move that helps women survive but does not enable achieving WLB because they are settling for jobs that do not fully use their skills and experiences and which are usually part-time.

Working Time Regimes

One important policy measure necessary for realizing WLB is reducing working hours. Although this was identified long ago as an important initiative at the national level, partly in order to reduce incidents of *karoshi* (death by overwork) (Kawahito 1998), many companies still routinely enforce the policy of overtime without pay. Average weekly working hours among women was 34.5 hours and among men 45.5 hours in 2008 (ILO, LABORSTA

Internet). Having a young child does not seem to make men reduce their working hours.

Among our interviewees, around 40% of men worked more than 50 hours a week and over three-quarters (77%) worked overtime. The practice has been institutionalized in Japanese workplaces across sectors and lines of business. There is not much difference in overtime whether one works in the public or in the private sector in our study.

When asked their reasons for working overtime, three-quarters of men answered that it was 'my own choice' instead of being ordered by a boss/superior (less than 20%) or because 'the workplace atmosphere encouraged it' (less than 10%). In a way, working overtime can be seen as a norm that has been internalized by each employee. At the same time, even though they may work overtime 'voluntarily', it might also be because they are expected to fulfil a particular work-related quota. When prompted as to the reason why this choice was made, a man responsible for accounting and server maintenance at a design firm answered,

> I can say no [to overtime work], but there is quota I have to fill, and [if I don't do it], the work just ends up accumulating. (32 year-old university graduate with a 4 year-old child)

Another 44 year-old male employee who is responsible for sales and operations (a university graduate with 12 and 5 year-old children) responded:

> Even if I am not asked to work overtime, well, there is work that I must get done, and if I don't finish it during the day, I have no choice but to either work overtime or do it the next day.

Embracing overtime work seems to indicate adherence to workplace norms that need to be considered independently from these men's desire for WLB, even though it is apparent that they constitute obstacles for men to reducing working hours for whatever reason.

Related to the expectation of working long hours, Japanese employees tend to feel resistance against leaving work before others do. The RIETI employee survey (see endnote 4) shows that among 1,432 men and 345 women who were employed with children under 7 years old, only 27% of men and 36% of women responded negatively to the statement, 'If other people are still in the office, it is difficult to leave even if I have finished my work', indicating that the majority of workers find it difficult to leave before others do. These feelings are shared by one-third of men and women in our interviews, who said that they felt uneasy about leaving before a superior or colleague. There are also variations by occupation and sector in how common such feelings are.

People who attempt to exercise their rights in Japan are frequently labelled 'selfish', while there is a strong tendency to regard those who practice silent endurance of difficult situations as 'virtuous'. Such ideologies apparently contribute to a weak sense of entitlement for claiming their rights, providing one explanation for the gap between WLB policy measures and the reality.

Fear of Becoming a Burden at the Workplace

We also identified a concern about burdening the workplace and sense of responsibility toward one's colleagues as elements that get in the way of men and women achieving WLB by utilizing various policies to adjust their work schedule to meet family needs.

One interviewee working in sales at a women's clothing store described his reason for not utilizing these policies as follows:

> [My colleagues] are also working, so I think it is absolutely wrong to put a further burden on them. Being thoughtful of others means not asking them to do extra tasks, but instead take care of your work on your own. I'd never do something to others that I wouldn't want done to me, so I don't plan to use the parental leave. (40 year-old father of children aged 9, 7, and 1, high school graduate)

Another father pointed out that in order to be able to utilize such policies, an important question is whether or not one is able to take leave without burdening others in the workplace. He explained,

> when this person is away, the company should make arrangements so that the work won't be left undone. If work would be shifted to another person if they took time off, this resulting burden would for sure stop them [from taking time off]. (38 year-old male accounting supervisor/section head, father of a 3 year-old and a 1 year-old, university graduate)

One reason women gave for not utilizing childcare support policies is so as not to 'cause an inconvenience at the workplace'. The employee at a private corporation (doing clerical work) described above (a 43 year-old with a 2 year-old child, junior college) utilized a flexi-time measure, arriving at and leaving work 20 minutes earlier than her normal schedule. She explained that she was utilizing this provision *in order not to be a burden on her company*. This woman knew a great deal more than other women about such policies, and her desire to continue working was strong. Moreover, she works for a large corporation that is implementing WLB-related initiatives. This notwithstanding, she does not attempt to exercise her rights since she does not want to 'burden her company'. The accepted working pattern within her immediate workplace surroundings is one that does not encompass a balanced work and home life, and she has adjusted to this concept.

In the private sector, it is rare for companies to hire a substitute worker to take the place of an employee on parental leave. In our interviews, too, no one mentioned that the workplace hired a substitute worker in case someone took parental leave. The feeling of becoming a burden by taking a leave, which is aggravated by such practices as not hiring substitutes, constitutes an inhibiting factor.

Fear of Being 'Left Behind'

For many men 'being successful at work' forms a core part of their gender identity. Among our interviewees as well, nearly half expressed a desire for some level of career advancement—some 'proactively' and others 'at the same rate as others' or felt that 'it does not hurt to have it'. For example, a salesman stated:

> [career advancement] is a normal thing. With children and a wife, it certainly can't hurt...and I think my wife agrees. (32 year-old with a 2 year-old child, vocational education after high school)

Men seem to fear being left behind, even while not having career advancement as the goal of their life.

> Well, uh, career advancement, umm, well, uh, I'd like to do so at the same rate as others. Yes. That...the...well, it's not like I want to rise to the top by kicking others down, but well, umm, considering my age, I'd like to achieve a certain position, truthfully speaking, yes. (39 year-old office worker section head with 13 and 4 year-old children, university graduate)

Given concerns for being left behind, however mild, men fear damaging their career by utilizing paid leave and parental leave policies, as well as altering their work plans due to family needs. The office worker mentioned above describes how a workplace atmosphere prioritizing work above all can work to prevent utilization of paid leave:

> The climate in the office is certainly not one that encourages us to utilize our paid leave. It's not like our boss is forbidding us from using it, but as a person in a management position, well, it's like we feel compelled to always be at the office. Therefore, well, we aren't in a position to take time off for our own personal reasons.

Such a work environment interacts with his interest in career advancement, preventing him from exercising his right to take paid leave for 'personal reasons' such as his family.

Some express a more direct fear of negatively affecting career chances and hesitate to adjust their work schedule for family-related matters due to fears of negatively impacting appraisals of their work.

> I could probably get permission to step out a little bit, but others won't like it. It's difficult because I'm concerned about how I'll be evaluated. There is one man who leaves early and passes the work to others, but I think it affects his evaluation.

(37 year-old sales office supervisor with a 4 year-old child, vocational education after high school)

Unlike in many European countries, career progression through changing jobs is not common. For Japanese workers, especially men, there is no exit option. If they leave a firm, they will rarely be employed at the same position in another. Such absence of labour market flexibility is likely to constrain individuals from exercising rights at work. A stronger framework for restricting punitive employee evaluations at the workplace could alleviate these concerns, especially for men, as well as strengthen the sense of entitlement for making work adjustments in favour of the family.

Facilitating for Worklife Balance

In this section we will discuss the different resources available to the parents in our survey for achieving worklife balance at the levels of the individual, including family networks, the firm, and society/the public discourse, where we focus on whether and how they transform these resources to achieve worklife balance or, in Sen's terminology, the conversion factors.

Family Network

For women in the workforce with preschool-aged children, having the support of extended family is essential, since husbands participate only minimally in housework and childcare (Ochiai 2008; Ochiai et al. 2008). While women tend to work fewer hours than men, the difference is not large enough to permit the smooth functioning of a household with small children. In areas with long waiting lists for daycare services, extended families—particularly those on the mother's side—provide necessary support. Even when children are lucky enough to get a slot in a local day nursery, care is still necessary outside their operating hours and when the children become sick. This role is fulfilled by the extended family, and without this support working women face great difficulties.

Among our female respondents, 65% reported receiving some sort of family support, and among those who returned to work after having children this figure was 74%. This assistance constitutes a critical element of their WLB and is often apparently more reliable than the assistance received from their husbands.

While support from parent(s) is often received in times of crisis, it also serves as an important resource on a daily basis. A 32 year-old civil servant with a 2 year-old and a 1 year-old (university graduate) found that the local day nursery was full at the end of her 11 month term of parental leave for her second child, and so she decided to leave her children with her mother. She believed that returning to work would give her higher priority at the nursery, and so she chose to do so while relying on her mother's support as a sort of 'bridge' until slots at the nursery opened up.

Siblings who live nearby can also be a support. A part-time care worker received assistance from her mother and her older sister, who often took the children to the nursery. The sisters also shared childcare duties with each on a regular basis (a 31 year-old with a 7 year-old, a 5 year-old and a 1 year-old, vocational education after high school). Working part-time and having a husband who often came home at midnight and was unavailable for helping out with household tasks, she relied fully upon the assistance from her family network.

Work Ability and Achievements

Being competent at work can also bring about the support of superiors and colleagues, making it easier to utilize relevant policies or to make special arrangements. Ability, therefore, can function indirectly as a conversion factor. A woman on parental leave to raise her second child (a 33 year-old university graduate with a 3 year-old child) considered quitting when she was pregnant with her first child, but changed her mind after her male boss said to her, 'Why don't you continue working'? There are few women in her workplace, and she is the first employee to have taken parental leave. Her boss pointed out to her that she was special in being granted the leave, saying, 'I'm only doing this because it's you', and 'even if any of the other girls asked, I probably wouldn't give it to them'. Her case of being allowed to continue working after taking leave, then, was an exceptional one because she was highly valued for her job performance.

Another female respondent working as a section chief at a retail store (a 33 year-old with a 3 year-old and a 1 year-old, high school education) returned to work following childbirth without taking parental leave. Although the workplace was one with long working hours and tight work schedules, she found herself having to reduce her working hours, and, 'surprisingly', to take days off for family reasons including caring for her sick child.

> The environment of my company is not one where it is easy to take days off...well, I guess that I was able to do so without raising eyebrows because of my position. It's not like everyone is able to take leave in my company.

With her position being an important one at the company, clearly her case represents an exception that applies to her and her alone.

Family-Friendly Firm Culture

While the percentage of women utilizing WLB assistance policies is higher than that of men, in many cases this is achievable only through support provided by superiors and colleagues. A specialist at a social welfare facility credited her boss for making it possible for her to continue working. While people had succeeded in taking parental leave in other branch offices, she was the first in her own department to do so.

> My boss at the time was a woman, and she herself had continued working throughout all her childcaring years, so I really felt that she was supporting me. [Had my boss been someone else] the situation would likely have been very different

she recounted, noting the important influence of her boss. She is now working 1 hour and 15 minutes less every day, which she similarly attributes to her present male boss helping her by researching available policies.

> My boss is male, but since he married young and worked while helping out with childcare at home, I think he has a lot of understanding [about my situation]. (33 year-old with a 5 year-old and a 1 year-old, university graduate)

An employee at a large corporate foods manufacturer (a 38 year-old with a 3 year-old and a 2 year-old, junior college graduate) was the first person in her department to have returned to work following a parental leave. Despite a demanding environment in terms of workplace performance, she reported that her colleagues supported her both during her pregnancy by telling her to take care of herself and asking when the baby was due, as well as currently, since she feels that the atmosphere is favourable toward her leaving work early.

More women are using policies aimed at providing assistance with childcare. On the other hand, workplaces where few utilize such provisions demonstrate a low sense of entitlement with regard to childcare measures on the part both of working mothers and of workplaces in general. For women who are hesitant about utilizing such measures, the support received from superiors and colleagues serves as the necessary push that brings the policies to life and enables them to be implemented in reality.

Awareness/Knowledge of Relevant Policies

If lack of knowledge and awareness prevent the use of various measures, we would expect that knowledge boosts their use. Awareness of policy in claiming rights is essential. In our interviews, having knowledge of sick/injured childcare leave, a male fire-fighter (public sector) (a 34 year-old university graduate with a 5 year-old) managed to exercise his right by educating his superior about the policies, asking him 'Did you know about this policy?' Having been provided information in this regard, his boss was willing to allow him time off using the sick/injured childcare leave when his child became ill.

Another male employee at a large insurance firm (a 32 year-old university graduate with a 2 year-old), after gaining knowledge about overtime regulation, used it to make his life better. Up until his child was 1 year and 10 months old, he worked 35 hours of overtime every month, returning home after 9 pm every night and experiencing hardship as a result.

Following the enactment of a law regulating the maximum number of overtime hours and utilizing his experiences in the legal field, he managed to convince his boss to let him make use of this policy.

What these fathers have achieved might partly be attributed to their personalities and persistence, but it is also clear that their becoming aware of relevant policies is a necessary factor, facilitating their sense of entitlement for the exercise of their rights.

Path-breakers

As we have seen, many fathers spend a great deal of time and energy at their work. In order for them to spend time with their families and engage in childcare, they are required to adopt strategies of consciously giving priority to their families with regard to their existing working styles and workplace (Suemori 2010).

This change in consciousness was shown by an accounting division head (a 38 year-old father of newborn twins and university graduate) who realized once his twins arrived that his 'participation (in childcare tasks) was an absolute necessity' and decided to utilize the strategy of finishing work early. While he had not previously worked an extreme amount of overtime, he had still felt uneasy about leaving before his subordinates. After the birth of their twins, however, he began leaving on time after his wife told him repeatedly that it would 'help her out to have him home earlier'. He explained that overtime work was wasted time, and so he became practical about the matter and decided to just leave at the end of the workday. 'It's now a given [at my workplace] that I will leave early because of my children', he explained, adding that he did not feel negatively judged for this reason, as his boss seemed to be 'satisfied as long as his work was done'.

The 32 year-old male employee at a large insurance firm with a 2 year-old mentioned earlier also explained that one reason he had become actively involved with childcare tasks was because his wife had begun having an emotional breakdown. 'In the past, I thought that men were only supposed to be the breadwinner', he said, adding that he had to change his views after his child was born and began attending a day nursery. He decided to throw away his male pride and change his views to one that envisioned both partners striving together for a balance between work and family life.

For another male respondent working in the personnel department at a university, his wife's severe distress was similarly a factor causing him to make the decision to change his working pattern. Working in the International Relations division, he routinely returned home after 10 pm. Realizing that something had to change, he made a direct appeal to be transferred to a section with less overtime. After half-threatening his boss that he would quit, he was transferred and was then able to get home by 6:30 pm. Despite reporting having only 10% job satisfaction at his new position, he stated that he did not regret the sacrifice on behalf of his family.

Regardless of the immediate cause leading to making a decision to prioritize family, the cases discussed here show that making the decision and acting on it has the potential for increasing capabilities to make claims for rights as path-breakers.

Another factor that seems to enhance men's WLB-related capabilities is improving work efficiency. Changing the mind set to envision a style of work allowing them to use a limited amount of time more efficiently can enable them to reprioritize work tasks and encourage better workdays (Sato 2008). One male respondent, a university personnel department employee (35 year-old, with a 4 year-old and a 2 year-old), spoke critically of long working hours and aimed for efficient work that would enable him to balance his job with childcare. He felt no uneasiness about the idea of leaving work earlier than his boss or colleagues, commenting that, 'those people who cannot finish their allotted work tasks within eight hours need to work harder'. He was skilful at his work, and also had a high level of self-confidence in this regard. He said that in order to gain understanding for his home situation among his superiors and colleagues, he consistently made a point of talking about his home life and his children. Each time he had to leave work early, he would tell everyone in his division the reason. As a personnel department employee, he said that he always reminded others, 'we have this policy, so you should use it', recognizing himself as something of a leader in terms of creating a working atmosphere in which it is easy for employees to balance their jobs and families. In this respondent's case, his efforts in making his needs for WLB understood by his peers and reminding others of relevant policies were rooted in his critical attitudes toward the typical way of working in Japan, which operated as facilitating factors towards exercising his rights and realizing WLB.

These apparently exceptional cases show a pattern; that when particular individuals are appreciated at work they can make use of WLB policies. Or, phrased differently, even in a workplace where no one makes use of these policies, exceptions are made for competent employees deemed indispensable by the company. Individual factors seem to convert into claims only when they involve these exceptional people and circumstances. However, these factors do not alter the institutional/normative constraints operating at the workplace and in society at large.

The Agency and Capabilities Gap: The WLB Ideal and Practice

The analyses so far have shown various factors militating against the achievement of WLB by working men and women. On an individual level, we therefore expect individuals to experience a gap between their actual balancing of work, family, and time for themselves, and their WLB ideal. To show and explore this gap, we compared the real and the ideal allocation of time between work, family, and self of our interviewees. Not surprisingly, our analysis shows a clear difference between the real and the ideal.

In the conducted interviews, we asked our respondents to state the ratio of time actually allocated to work, family, and self (own free time) in their current lives ('the reality') and how in the best circumstances they would want to allocate their time between work, family, and themselves ('the ideal'). The reported ratio of time currently allocated to the three spheres indicated their perception of their current life.[16]

In both real and ideal allocation, work occupied a more central place in men's than in women's lives. In reality, men allocate the largest proportion of their time to work (59%) and much less to home (30%), while the proportions allocated to work (44%) and home (45%) by women are almost the same. With regard to the ideal, men, on average, wished to allocate 48% of their time to work, 34% to home and 19% to themselves, while women wished for about 39% each to work and to home and the remaining 22% to themselves.[17]

To examine the gap between the reality and the ideal WLB in the three spheres, we looked at the difference between the real proportion and the ideal proportion in each of the three. If the real proportion is higher than that of the ideal, this indicates that the person wishes to 'reduce' the time allocation for that particular sphere. Likewise, if the real proportion is less than the ideal, the person is seen as wishing to 'increase' the time allocation. Figure 4.3 indicates the percentages of women and men who want to reduce, maintain, or increase the proportion of time allocated to each sphere. As Figure 4.3 shows, the majority of women and men want to reduce time for work (59 and 68%) and increase time for themselves (77 and 66%); but men and women

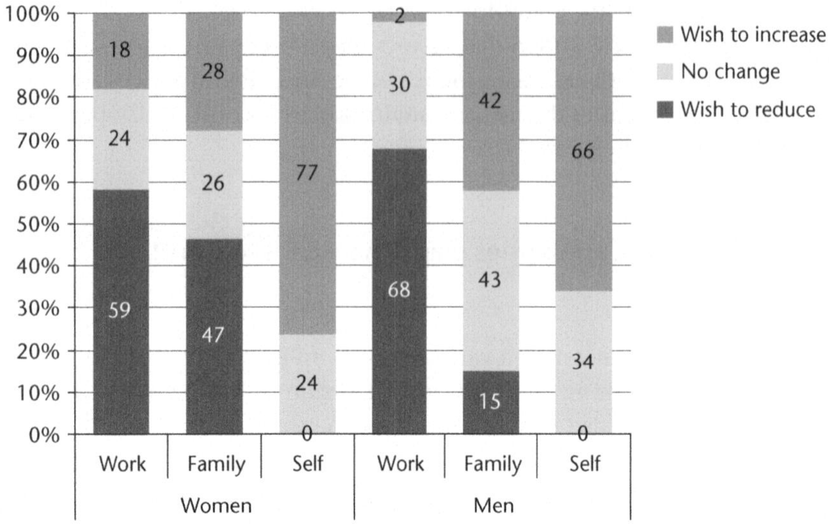

Figure 4.3 Gap between actual and ideal time allocation to work, family, and self

show a reverse pattern with respect to the family—47% of women want to reduce while 42% of men want to increase time for the family.

Our finding is consistent with the analysis of the Cabinet Office cross-national survey data. Compared with men and women in Sweden, the difference between stated ideal worklife balance and reality was largest for men in Japan, where work occupies a more central part of their life than they desire. By contrast, women in Japan, compared with both men and women in Sweden, are forced to devote more time to 'family life' than they wish (Takahashi 2011a).

It is possible that personal economic situation influences time allocation to work: one might want to work more if experiencing economic difficulties. Our analysis shows that economic considerations do affect individuals' inclination to adjust time allocated to work, but in a gendered manner. Reported economic difficulties dispose women to increase the proportion of time for work, but dispose men to decrease it: 31% of women who reported economic difficulties, but only 11% of those who did not, wanted to increase relative time allocated to work. Similarly, 40% of those reporting economic difficulties wanted to reduce relative time for work compared with 66% of those who did not. For men, by contrast, 86% reporting economic difficulties actually wished to allocate *less* of their time to work, while 56% of men who were not experiencing economic difficulties wished to do so.

At the same time, income per se might not be an incentive under any circumstances, as over 60% of both men and women said they wanted to keep their (absolute) current working hours even if income increased with more hours. There are men who desired to work more given an income increase (25%), and this pattern is more pronounced among those experiencing economic difficulties (over 40%), but no such tendency is found among women; only less than 20% would put in more hours even if there was more income.

The foregoing discussion suggests that, while economic difficulties might force women to work more, economic considerations are not the only factor in this regard. This is true also of men, who show a more complex and contradictory pattern. Working hours not only relate to income per se but also to chances of career trajectories and work hour norms. If, as suggested here, the weight allocated to work, whether absolutely or in relation to other spheres of life, is affected by a combination of factors—including economic circumstances, fulfilment and expectations about work, and gendered obligations towards work and family—we need to consider a multiplicity of factors to enhance capabilities to achieve WLB.

Enhancing Capabilities

In the previous section we examined the gap between WLB policies and their implementation among working parents and found strong workplace factors inhibiting men from realizing WLB. This was observed in the wider gap for men than for women between policy and implementation in the work sphere. If Japan maintains the present structure and ideology of work, any campaign for improving WLB would, especially for men, not be effective.

The majority of Japanese parents interviewed could not imagine an alternative scenario with regards to WLB. When the questions in the interview about workplace cultures and flexibility were directly asked, responses did not include that their workplaces prioritized work, that there was no flexibility, or that it was difficult to take days off. In a way, this could be interpreted as a sign that working parents have, unconsciously, given up on expecting more from their work lives and think that the workplace is supposed to be as it is.

In response to our interview question on what initiatives would be necessary to enable fathers to spend more time with their families, one-third of the men cited the *need for legal obligations and enforcement with regard to corporations*. For example:

> In order to reduce working hours, policies need to be implemented that make it obligatory to leave the office. There are policies targeting dual-working families, but it is presently not possible to use them. This would change, however, if

> there were obligations and enforcements in place. It's not enough to simply give approval when employees apply [to utilize these policies].
>
> If the government made it a legal obligation to take time off from work, it would have an effect. I think everyone else would do likewise.
>
> Companies need to be required to make available a variety of working styles. The fact that policies exist but are not utilized means that men are not changing their attitudes. In a sense, a system needs to be created wherein childcare for men is made obligatory.

For Japanese working parents, with a weak sense of entitlement, it might be necessary to construct an institutional setting that normalizes individuals' exercise of their rights for WLB by mandatory action enforced by the government to make companies and workplaces truly implement WLB policies in a non-gendered manner.

Conclusion

In this chapter, we have explored barriers in workplace organization and the socially endorsed gendered patterns that working parents need to overcome in order to increase their agency and capabilities to achieve WLB. We also identified resources at the individual, firm, and societal/discursive level that enhance their sense of entitlement to make claims and exercise rights for WLB. To conclude this chapter, we will highlight outstanding characteristics of WLB in Japan, and suggest directions for change.

Our analysis shows that the gap existing between WLB policies and actual practices is caused in large part by gendered working patterns that are legitimated in the public discourse and reproduced in workplace culture and practices.

Gendered expectations for men and women have normalized long working hours and work-centred lives for men, and coerced women to choose between work and childcare, in response to which many leave their jobs following childbirth and lead lives focused on housework and childcare. Such expectations are reinforced by gendered implementation of WLB policies at work: women were allowed more latitude in leaving early for a sick child or taking care of other family matters and therefore also made use of these policies more than men. One common strategy women use to balance work and childcare, besides relying on family networks, is to seek employment at a workplace that can accommodate their needs.[18] These practices, however, reinforce the expectation that the family, rather than work, is women's priority. Men, on the other hand, through self-censoring and out of consideration for others, did not make use of available policies as much. The utilization of

WLB policies on their part is perceived as causing problems for others. They are constrained, reluctant to 'stand out from the crowd', and do not even think of claiming their rights.

Our analysis also shows that cultural expectations, workplace culture, and policy implementation mutually reinforce each other. The feeling of becoming a burden at work is partly constructed by the workplace practice of not hiring substitute workers, and employees' fear of being left behind on the career ladder is partially created by the lack of guarantees against discrimination when prioritizing the family. On the other hand, while a supportive work culture is important for transforming awareness and knowledge of policies/rights into an actual increase in agency and capabilities, at times such support from colleagues and superiors can come about only if individuals are seen as extremely capable and hence, indispensable.

We reported signs of change in individuals utilizing their WLB rights. These included pioneering fathers who took the initiative to change their own consciousness regarding working patterns and to educate their superiors regarding WLB-related policies. However, it should be noted that the number of such individuals remains exceedingly small and that it was rather extreme situations, such as a wife's extreme distress or having twins, that actually transformed them into path-breakers.

Quite obviously, relying on exceptional individuals cannot be the path towards improving WLB for most working parents. On the basis of our analyses, we would suggest an increase in incentives for WLB, drawing up an agenda for a gender-equal family policy, and changing the current working time regime.

The first step toward increasing capabilities for WLB is arguably to create incentives for both women and men so that they can reconcile work and family life. In order for fathers to increase their sense of entitlement to make claims for family leave or self-development, the level of compensation must be increased and firms need to hire substitutes for employees on leave. Women's lack of agency and capabilities for WLB is implicit in the discrepancy between the small number of women who, in fact, wish to stay at home their whole life and the small number of women who continue or return to work after becoming mothers. The inability of mothers of small children to return to the same employment could be improved with job protection, guarantee of reduced working hours and increase in public daycare services.

The focus on 'self-responsibility' in recent policies addressing the declining fertility rate and calling for worklife balance, at the same time leaves untouched the gender division of labour and its resulting unfairly gendered labour structure. While these policies aim at providing support for dual-earner families, including public childcare and parental leave, fathers involved in childcare tasks and women continuing in employment are viewed as simply choosing one option among an array of possible life patterns. In this light, it is important to draw up an agenda for a gender equal family policy in Japan with the premise that the family is constituted of 'dual-earners/dual-caretakers' and that guarantees all parents the dual rights to both work and raise children.

The current working time regime is another area to address for WLB. Even if incentives for WLB were created at the workplace, these initiatives would not be effective if the firm and work organization were in a dominant position, as indicated by the long working hours. In workplace organizational cultures where workers lack mobility, capabilities and agency for WLB are weakened. With temporary staffing regulations becoming extremely lax due to the economic restructuring brought about by globalization and neo-liberalism, the number of non-regular workers in Japan has exploded, and previous systems of lifetime employment and pay increase by seniority continue to crumble. In order to fill the gap created by the reduced number of workers, full-time employees are in turn being subjected to severe performance-based payment structures and long working hours. Moreover, with managerial labour not being subject to working hour restrictions, laws targeting shorter working hours have been repealed, thus continuing the autonomous regulation of labour and management structures, under which labourers become 'personally responsible' for discretionary working patterns.

As a result, the provision of parental leave can be used only by the select few. Thus it becomes important that working hours are not left to company autonomous decisions, but are regulated and companies made subject to punitive measures as necessary. It is critical that companies be required to make alternative staffing arrangements so that no burden falls on others when workers avail themselves of existing WLB support policies. It is also urgent and important to promote measures that enable employees to work in a more flexible manner, such as the flexi-time system.

A recent OECD (2012) report presented the latest evidence indicating poor female labour market outcomes in Japan with regard to wages, achievement of high positions, entrepreneurial activity, and so on. The report attributed this to 'difficulties with reconciling work and family commitments'. It also noted that Japanese men spent the least amount of time in unpaid housework among OECD countries. The report is timely, corroborating our analysis here that the WLB policies in Japan are useful perhaps only to a very select minority of women with extremely high potential, leaving out the vast majority of women and practically all the men. Policies that leave untouched the masculine standard of working, in terms of commitment, working hours, and so on, will not go far towards enabling the achievement of WLB for the vast majority of working parents. Our suggestions directly address the pattern of employment, which has important implications not only for working parents, but also for the quality of life of individuals in a myriad ways.

Notes

1. The suicide of middle-aged men from depression triggered by being laid off and losing all hope in life has for a long time been receiving much attention as a serious social problem (Kawahito 1998).
2. The Japan-based research was conducted using a 2009–11 science research grant ('Grant-in-Aid for Scientific Research') (B) (general) (No. 21330116) 'Work–Life Balance and Father's Child Rearing: A Comparative Study of Japan, Sweden and the EU' (Principle Investigator: Mieko Takahashi). Cooperating with a research group headed by Barbara Hobson, we designed a questionnaire and a face-to-face interview schedule that allowed us to engage in a comparison with studies taking place in Sweden and Hungary.

   This research was based upon a combination of structured and semi-structured interviews, and we asked a research firm to locate respondents who fit our requirements. The firm utilized a list of possible candidates that had been compiled for use in postal mail- and web-based research, from which interview subjects were then solicited. An interview space was arranged, and individual interviews took place for an average of 2 hours each. Respondents were asked to fill out and return a questionnaire in advance via postal mail regarding their attributes and other basic information.

   It is important to note that the sample in this study is not representative of the population since we have selected mothers and fathers from dual-earner households. Many respondents were highly educated, white-collar workers in their 30s. They represented dual-working nuclear families of men and women from the Osaka Metropolitan area (Osaka, Hyogo, and Kyoto), although several respondents were women who were on parental leave at the time of the interviews, as well as several more who were the husbands of such women (Onode 2011).
3. The respective total numbers of respondents in the three countries noted in this paper are as follows (numbers in parentheses refer to the 2005 survey): 1,248 (1,115) in Japan, 1,005 (1,004) in Korea, and 1,001 (1,019) in Sweden.
4. Conducted between December 2009 and July 2010.The number of valid respondents in each country for both surveys is as follows: Japan (corporate (questionnaire) survey: 1,677 companies; employee (questionnaire) survey: 10,069 workers); England (corporate (telephone) survey: 202 companies; employee (Internet) survey: 979 workers); Netherlands and Sweden (corporate (telephone) survey: 100 companies); Germany (corporate (telephone) survey (conducted by Economic and Social Research Institute): 201 companies; personal (Internet) survey: 1,012 persons). For more information on these surveys, see Takeishi (2011, 2012).
5. According to OECD data, the percentage of women in Japan with children under the age of 3 who were in the workforce in 2008 was 29.8%—a dramatically lower figure than those from Western developed countries during the same year (for example, 54.0% in England, 55.2% in Germany, 75.0% in the Netherlands, and 71.9% in Sweden) (OECD database).

6. The 2007 Employment Status Survey showed that among those women who had never married, aged 25 to 44, 62% were full-time workers compared to 32% of those married with children less than 3 years of age. This was reversed for the part-time workers where married women with children less than 3 years of age counted for 49% compared to the never married at 15% (Ministry of Internal Affairs and Communications Statistics Bureau 2008b).
7. See Takahashi (2003) for a further description of part-time labor in Japan. Also, Rebick (2006) provides an overview of changes in the workplace and their impact on the family since the mid 1980s as the effect of the economic environment in early 1990s, including the growth of part-time employment especially for the young, efforts to improve women's position in the firm, and efforts to improve the worklife balance.
8. For more discussion, see Takahashi (2003), Yoshizumi and Takahashi (2003), and Matsuda (2004) who have applied Komter's (1989) argument on the three dimensions of power—manifest, latent, and hidden—in their study of Japanese dual-earner couples.
9. In addition to the existing comprehensive prohibition of discrimination against women with regard to measures including recruitment, employment, placement, and advancement, provisions were also added to forbid discrimination against men on both a direct and indirect level.

   Besides making the establishment of maternal health-related measures obligatory for women during pregnancy and after childbirth, offending corporations will also face sanctions in the form of their name being publicly announced.
10. See Roberts (2002) for a detailed explanation of the 'Angel Plan', including its background, related debates, and examples of programmes both at the national and the local level of the Angel Plan in which she participated herself. Her work also analyses the 'problem of a low-birthrate society' through examining media and scholarly publications.
11. Only one or two women out of 27 who went back to work after stopping (four of them are currently full-time regular workers) used these provisions and measures.
12. The Basic Survey of Gender Equality in Employment Management conducted in 2010 (Ministry of Health, Labour and Welfare 2011b) revealed that 83.7% of respondents had taken parental leave—more than twice the rate of the interviewees in the present study. This figure excludes women who quit their jobs before childbirth, however, and so when we consider that the majority of our interviewees had quit their jobs and found new employment, this figure is not particularly low.
13. The Ministry of Health, Labour and Welfare established a certification system in 2007 that grants certification (the 'Kurumin' certification logo) to companies that actively promote measures to create an environment in which men and women with young children can continue to work (based on Act for Measures to Support the Development of the Next Generation). The companies thus certified tend to be large corporations.
14. Many of our respondents also indicated likewise during interviews.

15. It is worthy of note that both in Japan and in Sweden a significant correlation exists between companies that have implemented worklife balance policies (flexi-time, working from home, etc.) and those that value equal treatment of male and female employees. In other words, those companies that are more likely than other firms in their field to value the capabilities of their employees regardless of gender are also more likely to implement worklife balance policies (Takahashi 2011b).
16. The ratio they reported is their perception of the reality, and hence, it would not necessarily correspond exactly with the number of hours worked, number of hours spent with their family, and so on.
17. This shows that men who are feeling the economic pinch want less time allocated to work. So, they are not making ends meet and yet do not want to increase working time to possibly bring in more income. This could indicate that they don't expect to bring in more income even if they work more, or that they do not want to work just to bring in more income. One interviewee who wanted to reduce his personal time was included in the 'keep/no change' group.
18. All but one man in our sample were regular employees, hence we did not consider the experiences of men working as part-time/temporary employees or the related issue of the 'working poor' in Japan. The issue of WLB needs to be examined from various angles and, needless to say, further research is necessary.

Bibliography

Cabinet Office of Japan, Director General for Policies on Cohesive Society (2011). *International Opinion Survey on a Low Birthrate Society. Reports of Survey Result*. Tokyo: Cabinet Office of Japan.

Cabinet Office of Japan, Gender Equal Bureau (2011). *White Paper on Gender Equality*. Tokyo: Cabinet Office of Japan.

International Labor Organisation, LABORSTA Internet <http://laborsta.ilo.org/> [2012-12-20].

Kawahito, H. (1998). *Karo jisatsu* [Suicide from overwork]. Tokyo: Iwanamishoten.

Komter, A. (1989). Hidden Power in Marriage. *Gender and Society*, 3(2); 187–216.

Matsuda, T. (2004). Division of Household Work in Dual Working Couples—Is the Traditional Pattern Changing? in Yoshizumi, K. (ed.), *Families and Partner Relationships: A Comparative Study of Sweden and Japan*, pp. 145–69. Tokyo: Aoki Shoten Publishing (in Japanese).

Matsuda, T. (2012). Toward a New Discourse of Work–Family Balance—Efficacy of Sen's Capability Approach. *Journal of the Faculty of Sociology*, 54: 85–100. Kyoto: Bukkyo University (in Japanese).

Ministry of Health, Labour and Welfare (Japan) (2011a). *The Status of Working Women*. Tokyo: Ministry of Health, Labour and Welfare.

Ministry of Health, Labour and Welfare (Japan) (2011b). Basic Survey of Gender Equality in Employment Management 2010 <http://www.mhlw.go.jp/stf/houdou/2r9852000001ihm5-att/2r9852000001iz9v.pdf > [2012-02-28].

Ministry of Health, Labour and Welfare (Japan) (2012). General Survey on Working Conditions 2011 <http://www.mhlw.go.jp/toukei/itiran/roudou/jikan/syurou/11/dl/gaikyou.pdf> [2012-02-24].

Ministry of Internal Affairs and Communications Statistics Bureau (2008a). <http://www.stat.go.jp/data/shakai/topics/topi30.htm> [2012-02-28].

Ministry of Internal Affairs and Communications Statistics Bureau (2008b). *Employment Status Survey 2007*. Tokyo: Ministry of Internal Affairs and Communications Statistics Bureau.

Ministry of Internal Affairs and Communications Statistics Bureau Home Page/Historical Data. Labour Force Survey Historical Data <http://www.stat.go.jp/data/roudou/longtime/zuhyou/lt03-02.xls> [2012-10-16].

National Institute of Population and Social Security Research (2012). *Report on the Fourteenth Japanese National Fertility Survey in 2010: Marriage Process and Fertility of Japanese Married Couples*. National Institute of Population and Social Security Research, Survey Series No. 29, 30 March 2012. Tokyo: National Institute of Population and Social Security Research.

Ochiai, E. (2008). Researching Gender and Childcare in Contemporary Asia, in E. Ochiai and B. Molony (eds), *Asia's New Mothers: Crafting Gender Roles and Childcare Networks in East and Southeast Asian Societies*, pp. 1–30. Folkestone: Global Oriental.

Ochiai, E. *et al*. (2008). Gender Roles and Childcare Networks in East and Southeast Asian Societies, in E. Ochiai and B. Molony (eds), *Asia's New Mothers: Crafting Gender Roles and Childcare Networks in East and Southeast Asian Societies*, pp. 31–70. Folkestone: Global Oriental.

OECD database <http://stats.oecd.org/Index.aspx> [2012-02-24].

OECD (2012). Closing the Gender Gap: ACT NOW JAPAN <http://www.oecd.org/gender/Closing%20the%20Gender%20Gap%20-%20Japan%20FINAL.pdf> [2013-06-17].

Onode, S. (2011). Fathers' Practices of Work–Family Balance in Double Income Families with Preschool Children: Analysis based on Sen's Capabilities Approach. *Bulletin of Kyoto Kacho University and Kacho College*, 56: 1–15 (in Japanese).

Rebick, M. (2006). Changes in the Workplace and their Impact on the Family, in M. Rebick and A. Takenaka (eds), *The Changing Japanese Family*, pp. 75–93. London: Routledge.

Roberts, G. S. (2002). Pinning Hopes on Angels: Reflections from an Aging Japan's Urban Landscape, in Richard Goodman (ed.), *Family and Social Policy in Japan: Anthropological Approaches*, pp. 54–91. Cambridge: Cambridge University Press.

Sato, H. (2008). Waaku raifu baransu to kigyoo ni yoru WLB shien [Work–Life Balance and Companies' Support for Work–Life Balance], in K. Yamaguchi and Y. Higuchi (eds), *Ronsoo Waaku raifu baransu* [Debate over Work–Life Balance], pp. 106–23. Tokyo: Nihon Keizai Shinbunsha.

Sen A. (1985) *Commodities and Capabilities*. Amsterdam: Elsevier Science Publishers B.V.

Sen A. (1992). *Inequality Reexamined*. Oxford: Oxford University Press.

Suemori, K. (2010). Shokuba kankyo to dansei no Waaku raifu baransu jendaa chitsujo ga yureugoku jouken [Workplace Environment and Men's Work–Life Balance—A

Condition for Shifting the Gender Order), in S. Matsuda et al. (eds), *Yuragu kosodate kiban: Shoushika shakai no genjo to konnan* [Shifting Bases for Childrearing: Situations and Difficulties of Low Birthrate Society), pp. 161–81. Tokyo: Keiso Shobo.

Taga, F. (2011) (ed.). *Yuragu Salaryman Seikatsu.* [An Uncertain Salaried Man's Life]. Kyoto: Mineruva Press.

Takahashi, M. (2003). *Gender Dimension in Family Life—A Comparative Study of Structural Constraints and Power in Sweden and Japan.* Stockholm: Almqvist and Wiksell International.

Takahashi, M. (2011a). Work Styles and Work–Life Balance, *International Opinion Survey on a Low Birthrate Society: Reports of Survey Result*, pp. 160–86. Tokyo: Cabinet Office of Japan, Director General for Policies on Cohesive Society.

Takahashi, M. (2011b). Work–Life Balance in Sweden: Working in a Flexible and Autonomous Manner. RIETI Discussion Paper Series 11-J-040. Tokyo: Research Institute of Economy, Trade and Industry (in Japanese).

Takeishi, E. (2011). 'Corporate and Workplace Challenges for Work–Life Balance', RIETI Discussion Paper Series 11-J-029. Research Institute of Economy, Trade and Industry. Tokyo: Bureau of Industrial and Labor Affairs (in Japanese).

Takeishi, E. (2012). Workplace Management that Facilitates the Realization of Work–Life Balance, in E. Takeishi (ed.) *Work–Life Balance in Japan as Seen from a Perspective of International Comparison*, pp. 147–82. Kyoto: Mineruva Press (in Japanese).

Tokyo Metropolitan Government Bureau of Industrial and Labour Affairs Employment Division (2007). *Survey of Companies on Implementation of EEOA and Childcare/Family Care Leave.* Tokyo: Tokyo Metropolitan Government Bureau of Industrial and Labour Affairs Employment Division (in Japanese).

Yamaguchi, K. (2009). *Waaku Raifu Baransu. Jissho to Seisaku Teigen* (*Work–life Balance: Empirical Proof and Policy Recommendations*). Tokyo: Nihonkeizaishinbun shuppansha.

Yoshizumi, K. and M. Takahashi (2003). Marital Power in Japan in Comparison to Sweden, in Carl le Grand and Toshiko Tsukaguchi-le Grand (eds), *Women in Japan and Sweden*, pp. 202–33. Stockholm: Almgvist and Wiksell International.

5

Agency freedom for worklife balance in Germany and Spain

Sonja Drobnič and Margarita León

Introduction

Changing job characteristics and employment relations as well as striking changes in the nature of the workforce, such as more dual-earner couples and rising numbers of working mothers with young children, have increased the likelihood that employed men and women have substantial household responsibilities in addition to their work responsibilities. Being both earner and carer has led to increased difficulties in balancing work and nonwork life. Empirical studies have revealed a number of negative consequences of high levels of work–home conflict for individuals, such as turnover, burnout, life stress and strain (Allen et al. 2000). Unsuccessful reconciliation is not only detrimental to individuals, but is seen as a probable cause of a number of social problems, including low and declining birthrates, ageing of society, lower productivity, and gender inequality. Worklife balance is a highly salient policy issue, and some see the integration of work and nonwork demands as one of the most critical challenges organizations, families, and individuals face today (Drobnič and Guillén 2011b).

In this chapter, we address the issue of work interfering with nonwork domains, in particular home responsibilities. Although many studies focus narrowly on the relationship between work and family, we support the broader view that although some employees may not have family-care responsibilities, this does not necessarily insulate them from other life stresses and pressures to integrate work and nonwork roles (Kossek and Lambert 2005). Also, we focus in particular on work interfering with home responsibilities. Early studies did not distinguish between different directions of the conflict between work and family/home. However, later research distinguished two directions of interference: work interfering with family/home and family/home interfering with work (Frone et al. 1992, 1997). Whereas the former occurs when paid work interferes with family/home responsibilities, the latter indicates that family/home responsibilities constrain the work sphere. However, the work–family/home interface was found to be asymmetrically permeable (Pleck 1977). Work as the stronger system interferes more often with home life than vice versa (Frone et al. 1992). In line with these findings, we focus on the interference of work into the private domain, and examine the role of family constellations in the successful management of the interface between work and home. In particular, we examine how work–home interference is related to the presence of a partner and children of different ages in an employee's household, and address gender differences in this respect.

Two major theoretical frameworks provide the basis to systematize and interpret our findings. The first one is the resources–demands approach, which is the most widely used framework in research on work and family. It juxtaposes the demands and resources in the domains of work and private life. High demands in one or the other domain can contribute to difficulties in performing roles in both life domains, while resources can facilitate role performance (Demerouti et al. 2001). This is a useful conceptual model for distinguishing the direction and the type (positive vs. negative) of spillover between work and home. However, it disregards the role played by broader institutional and societal arrangements, which becomes particularly evident in a cross-national comparison.

The conceptual framework of Amartya Sen (1992, 2006) and the application of this framework to worklife balance (Hobson and Fahlén 2009; Hobson 2011 and Chapter 1 in this volume) introduces new perspectives and adds new dimensions to the analysis. The argument developed in detail by Hobson in the introductory chapter is that worklife balance (hereafter referred to as WLB) is a valuable functioning that enhances capabilities for attaining a better quality of life. In our analysis, we focus on the means and resources individuals have to achieve this functioning, which Sen refers to as a capability set. We contend that high-quality jobs generate capabilities that allow incumbents to achieve work–home balance, and reduce negative interference between work and home. However, Sen also argues that the capabilities framework should be context specific. Thus, a capability set for a successful balancing of work and home life does not only depend on individual resources but is nested in institutional settings. Institutional and societal resources as well as normative expectations have to be taken into account to better understand how job quality and household characteristics affect the interface between work and home life.

This idea precludes focusing on one single country because this would make it impossible to measure whether certain findings are specific to the settings of this country or whether they have a broader relevance. Instead, we follow the suggestion of van der Lippe and van Dijk (2002) to include individual data from different countries and to combine these analyses with in-depth information on the institutional background. Using data from several representative large-scale European surveys, we perform a detailed analysis of work to home interference among men and women in Germany and Spain. Both countries are often placed in the cluster of conservative welfare states, and both have experienced significant changes over time from a male-breadwinner to a dual-earner model. Nevertheless, they differ in some important characteristics, such as the proportion of part-time employment and the involvement of the state in social policies that ease striving for worklife balance. Although women's labour force participation rates are still comparatively low in both countries, the mechanisms that limit female participation in paid employment differ. Mandel (2009) suggests that familial constraints are the main obstacle for women's employment in conservative states such as Germany, but general gender conservatism plays an important role in Spain.

Three aspects of the 'context' within which a capability set for a successful reconciliation of work and home life can be generated are addressed in this chapter. To better understand and interpret the results of empirical analyses, we first examine the relationship between women's employment rates and the presence of children in the family in Germany and Spain in the years 2006 and 2011, and compare the female labour force participation rate with that in other European countries. Second, we briefly present the institutional characteristics and analyse public provision of worklife measures in Germany and Spain. Third, we examine survey data on attitudes towards employment of men and women in Germany, Spain, and other European countries. In particular, the notion of normative support for working parents is analysed. We are particularly interested in attitudes towards working mothers and in the existence and strength of double standards regarding full-time employment of parents with young children. Double standards imply that status characteristics, such as gender, become a basis for stricter standards for the lower status person (Foschi 2000). A double standard in our context means that men and women are evaluated differently when displaying the same behaviour, which is an indicator of the level of gender inequality in a society. Although some authors have argued that after decades of promoting work–family reconciliation with the aim of promoting gender equality, the gender-equality agenda now has a subordinate role in the European Union Social Model (Knijn and Smit 2009), we aim to empirically test whether gender differences in this respect can be found. In the framework of the capabilities approach, our aim is to assess potential gender differences in the agency freedom for worklife balance in Germany and Spain, and to identify the various elements and levels at which the individual's capabilities and agency can be generated or constrained.

Theoretical Framework

Resources–Demands Model

The theoretical frame most widely applied to the interface between work and home has been the resources–demands approach. This approach resonates with the theory of role strain (Goode 1960), according to which individuals have a finite amount of resources available that can be devoted to multiple roles in life. Goode argues that people may encounter difficulties in performing their roles because they do not have sufficient resources and energy. There are diverse sources of role strain. First, even when role demands are not onerous, difficult, or displeasing, they are required at particular times and places and can come into conflict with other roles. Second, all individuals take part in many different role relationships, each with somewhat different obligations that may require contradictory performances or conflicts of time, place, or resources. Third, norms associated with each role may be contradictory. The individual is thus likely to face a wide, distracting, and sometimes conflicting array of role obligations. If he/she conforms fully or adequately in one direction, fulfilment will be difficult in another. Goode argues that role strain difficulty in meeting given role demands is a ubiquitous phenomenon; the individual's total role obligations are generally over-demanding (Goode 1960: 485).

Work demands refer to 'physical, social, or organizational aspects of a job that require sustained physical or mental effort, and are therefore associated with certain physiological and psychological costs' (Demerouti et al. 2001: 501).When the role demands stemming from one domain (work or family) are incompatible with role demands stemming from another domain (family or work), the result is work–family conflict that can be time-based, strain-based, or behaviour based (Greenhaus and Beutell 1985). Along similar lines, Voydanoff (2005a, b) distinguishes time-based demands, strain-based demands, and boundary-spanning job demands. Whereas time-based work demands are related to negative work–family outcomes through a process of resource drain or scarcity, strain-based work demands work through processes of psychological spillover between domains. Time-based work demands may include long working hours, overtime, and organizational time expectations. Examples of strain-based demands are work overload, work pressure, work distress, and job insecurity. Several work demands were found to be linked to higher levels of work–home conflict and lower levels of satisfaction with work–home balance (Frone et al. 1997; Voydanoff 2005a, b; Scherer and Steiber 2007; Valcour 2007; Schieman et al. 2009; Steiber 2009; Beham and Drobnič 2010; den Dulk et al. 2011).

Although the research has been dominated by a conflict perspective, multiple life roles can also generate social and economic resources and thus can be beneficial for individuals and their wellbeing, as suggested by the enhancement arguments (Sieber 1974; Marks 1977). Recently, work–family scholars have shifted their attention from work–family/home conflict to positive aspects of the work–home interface. However, comparative research on work–home conflict (Crompton and Lyonette 2006; Scherer and Steiber 2007; Drobnič and Guillén 2011b) suggests that in Europe this persists despite increasing awareness of the problem and the introduction of worklife policies. Thus, we focus on negative work–home interference in this study.

While the resources–demands perspective is a useful conceptual model for distinguishing the direction and type (positive vs. negative) of spillover between the domains of work and home, it is less clear why certain job characteristics are differentially perceived as resources or stressors by employees, and what the roles of broader institutional and societal arrangements actually are. Schieman et al. (2009) focus on social statuses and dimensions of stratification, such as age, gender, race, marital and parental status, and also contend that the ways in which work-related resources and demands influence these patterns is not well understood. Cross-country comparisons consistently reveal significant differences that cannot be explained within the resources–demands framework. Furthermore, the model insufficiently addresses the question of agency.

Capability Approach

To overcome these limitations of the resources–demands model, we incorporate in the analysis the capability approach developed by Amartya Sen, which adds new perspectives and dimensions to our understanding of the WLB. The capability approach is a broad normative framework for the assessment of individual wellbeing and social arrangements, the design of policies, and proposals for social change (Robeyns 2005). A key assumption is that the 'worklife balance' and the avoidance of work–home interference is a valuable goal that increases individuals' wellbeing. Sen (1992, 2006) explores wellbeing in terms of a person's ability to do valuable acts or reach valuable states of being. In his theory, '*[F]unctionings* represent parts of the state of a person—in particular the various things that he or she manages to do or be in leading a life. The *capability* of a person reflects the alternative combinations of functionings the person can achieve, and from which he or she can choose one collection' (Sen 2006: 31). The distinction between achieved functionings and capabilities is between the realized and the possible, between outcomes and possibilities, between achievements on the one hand, and freedoms or valuable options from which one can choose on the other (Robeyns 2005).

The capability approach thus focuses on what people are effectively able to do or to be and considers freedom to choose an important component of wellbeing. A person's capability set reflects the freedom to lead 'different types of lives' or the freedom to live in a particular way, and is defined in the space of functionings. This approach thus captures potentials for change, while analysing an individual's functionings. Further, to assess a person's capability set, the broader environmental and societal context has to be taken into account to understand which societal resources can be translated into agency and capability, and how individuals differ in their ability to achieve valuable functionings.

Hobson (2011) systematically applied Sen's capability set for a research design on work–family balance, distinguishing between individual, institutional, and societal/community resources, and developed it further in Chapter 1 in this volume. We build on this design, combining the individual-level analysis of work–home interference experienced by employees, with societal and institutional level analysis, including the cultural/normative framework within which individual men and women make choices and manage their lives. One aspect that is particularly relevant in the context of work–home conflict is agency inequality in terms of gender (Korpi 2000). Thus, we will specifically address the aspects of agency and the agency and capabilities gap that are likely to be decisive with respect to gender.

We first present selected outcomes of the analyses of work–home conflict in Germany and Spain based on European survey data, and interpret the results in the light of resources–demands as well as the capabilities perspectives. This section is largely based on comprehensive analyses conducted and presented in detail in Drobnič and Guillén (2011a). We then turn to the German and Spanish institutional contexts, and comparison with other European societies in terms of the level of female employment as well as cultural expectations related to reconciliation of work and family. In this way, we aim to assess the gender gap in agency inequality.

Survey Data, Hypotheses, and Methods

Data for the individual-level analysis come from various European data surveys that include information on work–home interference. The first data set is the *European Quality of Life Survey* (EQLS), conducted in 2003 on behalf of the European Foundation for the Improvement of Living and Working Conditions (EQLS 2003). The European Quality of Life Survey examines a range of issues, such as employment, income, education, housing, family, health, WLB, life satisfaction, and perceived quality of society. The survey covers 28 countries; we only analyse employed populations in Germany and Spain.

The second data set comes from the second round of the *European Social Survey* (ESS2) (ESS 2004), a social survey designed to chart and explain the interaction between Europe's changing institutions and the attitudes, beliefs, and behaviour patterns of its diverse populations. In the second round, a module on family, work, wellbeing, and WLB was included, which allows us to examine work–home interference. However, the measures of work–home interference as used in ESS2 have recently come under scrutiny. The items that set out to measure conflict between work and home have been criticized for being only poorly related to household conditions (Pichler 2009). Following this critique, we include the third round of the European Social Survey (ESS3) (ESS 2006) in the analysis, which measures *satisfaction* with the amount of time devoted to work and family rather than the level of interference. By using three different surveys with varying operationalizations of work–home interference, we aim at providing robust estimates of the relationship between working conditions, household conditions, and work–home interface.

In all three surveys, we analyse respondents who are employed and for whom we have data on their working conditions, family-related variables, and socio-demographic characteristics. In EQLS, the dependent variable is a constructed binary variable that captures time-related and strain-related difficulties in successfully combining work and home responsibilities. Our outcome measure is based on responses to the following items (response categories: several times a week, several times a month, several times a year, less often/rarely, never): 'I have come home from work too tired to do some of the household jobs which need to be done', and 'It has been difficult for me to fulfil my family responsibilities because of the amount of time I spend on the job'. To disentangle serious incidents of work–home interference from occasional occurrences, the variable is coded 1 if at least one of the two problems is reported *several times a week*.

In the ESS2 data, the binary dependent variable is based on four items: 'How often do you keep worrying about work problems when you are not working?', 'How often do you feel too tired after work to enjoy the things you would like to do at home?', 'How often do you find that your job prevents you from giving the time you want to your partner or family?', 'How often do you find that your partner or family gets fed up with the pressure of your job'? Response choices are 'never', 'hardly ever', 'sometimes', 'often', 'always'. Work–home interference is coded 1 if respondents claim that they face *at least one* of the four problems *always* or *two or more* of the four problems *often*. Finally, the outcome variable in ESS3 is based on the question 'How satisfied are you with the balance between the time you spend on your paid work and the time you spend on other aspects of your life?', ranging on an 11-point scale from extremely dissatisfied to extremely satisfied. This indicator does not measure the frequency of perceived interference between work and home, but the satisfaction with the achieved balance between work and nonwork aspects of life. Scholars in the work–family research tradition contend that satisfaction with work–family balance captures perceptual or affective reactions to an unspecified level of balance rather than the level of balance itself (Greenhaus et al. 2003). Similarly, our measurement can be understood as individuals' assessments of an adequate amount of resources to effectively respond to the demands of their work and nonwork roles.

Independent variables used in the analyses of all three surveys include various indicators for time-related and strain-related job demands as well as resources that have the potential to enhance respondents' capabilities. The significance of time-related demands is closely related to the family context. The time strategies of individuals depend not only on time demands of their jobs but also on demands in the home and family. For the family/home domain, we include information on partners and children. Not only the presence of a partner in the household is considered but also information on the partner's employment status and, in ESS, whether the partner commonly has long working hours (actual length including overtime) of 40 hours a week or more. Since family care responsibilities depend to a large extent on the age of children, we distinguish between preschool children (under 6 years of age), younger school-aged children (age 6–12), and older children (13–17 years). The reference group is grown-up children or no children.

A detailed list and information on the construction of composite variables, as well as descriptive statistics for dependent and independent variables from all three surveys, can be found in Drobnič and Guillén (2011a), where the impact of work characteristics and the quality of jobs on work–home tensions is analysed. However, the focus of the present chapter is not primarily on job-related demands and resources. Rather, we aim to highlight the role that domestic demands and resources play in the experience of work–home conflict.

We hypothesize that the presence of both a partner and children in the household may have an important impact on the experience of work–home interference for employees. A partner can take over part of the household tasks and caring responsibilities, and ease the work–home conflict. Particularly if children are present in the household, couples have better chances for WLB than employed single parents. A partner's employment may have the opposite effect, however. On the one hand, added income is a valuable resource and should have a positive impact on WLB. On the other hand, the partner's employment makes him/her unavailable in the household. Thus, all other things being equal, very long working hours of a partner is a constraint that is expected to increase work–home interference for employed respondents and decrease their satisfaction with WLB. Children, with the possible exception of teenage children who require less direct parental involvement and may provide help with household chores, are hypothesized to increase time demands in the family/home sphere. Children in the household require parents' time and they increase the demand for housework. They generate responsibilities that can create competing demands and time binds for individuals in competing roles, particularly for women. We thus hypothesize a higher work–home conflict and lower satisfaction with WLB for parents compared to employees without children. We expect the effect of children to be stronger for women.

Driven by the measurement scale of response variables, we use logistic regression for estimating the model of work–home interference using the EQLS and ESS2 data, and report results as odds ratios. The response variable in ESS3 is treated as a continuous variable and the method is ordinary least squares regression. To assess the institutional and societal-level impacts, as well as gender-related differences, we perform the analyses separately for Spanish women, Spanish men, German women, and German men.

Work–Life Interference: Results

Selected results of the regression analyses on the EQLS data for German men and women as well as Spanish men and women are reported in Table 5.1. Only the coefficients for variables that describe the family/household context are included in the table. Although the small number of cases in subgroups limits the statistical power to detect significant effects, the overall picture is surprising nevertheless. We do not find a single statistically significant effect of a partner and children in this analysis even though several coefficients for job characteristics reached a significant level, as is evident in the full report of the estimated model (Drobnič and Guillén 2011a: 245). Neither the coefficients referring to the partner nor to children in the household are significant at the conventional level. Estimates from ESS2, which are based on larger samples, indicate that partnered German men experience significantly less work–home interference than men without a partner (Table 5.2). For Spanish men, a partner's employment increases the odds of work–home conflict but, if the partner works long hours, this is associated with less interference. Both German and Spanish women have lower odds of experiencing work–home

Table 5.1 Family context and work–home interference: binary logistic regression models, odds ratios, EQLS 2003

	German men	German women	Spanish men	Spanish women
Partner	0.71	1.08	1.23	2.18
Partner employed	1.33	0.21	0.60	0.53
Child <6 yrs.	2.57	n.e.	1.06	1.05
Child 6–12 yrs.	1.63	0.74	1.22	1.21
Child 13–17 yrs.	0.78	0.73	0.90	1.52
N	179	189	197	147
Pseudo R^2	0.15	0.31	0.17	0.15

Notes: * $p < 0.1$, ** $p < 0.05$, *** $p < 0.01$; n.e.= estimate not possible due to insufficient data. Age, education (college/no college), working hours, commuting time, stressful job, time pressure, health risk, job insecurity, job influence/control, good career prospects, and pay are controlled.

Table 5.2 Family context and work–home interference: binary logistic regression models, odds ratios, ESS2

	German men	German women	Spanish men	Spanish women
Partner	0.37**	1.52	1.62	1.92
Partner employed	1.27	0.26***	2.23*	0.21*
Partner empl. ≥40h	1.26	2.02*	0.31**	1.00
Child < 6 yrs.	1.90	0.86	0.56	2.20
Child 6–12 yrs.	0.84	1.07	0.97	1.40
Child 13–17 yrs.	1.23	1.58	0.88	1.12
N	460	414	368	259
Pseudo R^2	0.226	0.189	0.147	0.150

Notes: * $p < 0.1$, ** $p < 0.05$, *** $p < 0.01$. Age, education (college/no college), working hours, commuting time, working hard, time pressure, health risk, job insecurity, job control, and good career prospects are controlled.

interference if they have a partner in paid employment. However, if their partners work long hours, German women's odds of experiencing work–life conflict double compared to women whose partners are employed but work less than 40 hours a week. Concerning the satisfaction with WLB, the only significant result shows that Spanish men with employed wives are less satisfied than those whose wives are not employed (Table 5.3).

Finally, we do not find any statistically significant impact of parental status on work–home interference. Regardless of whether there are children of various ages in the household or not, we find no systematic association with work–home interference or satisfaction with WLB, and have to reject the study hypotheses. Although it is perfectly plausible that the work-to-home interference is primarily associated with work-related demands and resources, the fact that family responsibilities and household demands seem not to be relevant for

Table 5.3 Family context and satisfaction with the balance between paid work and other aspects of life: OLS regression (unstandardized coefficients), ESS3

	German men	German women	Spanish men	Spanish women
Partner	-0.01	0.25	-0.11	0.32
Partner employed	-0.07	-0.54	-0.70***	-0.58
Partner empl. ≥40h	-0.10	0.14	0.34	0.15
Child <6 yrs.	-0.31	-0.10	0.14	-0.01
Child 6–12 yrs.	-0.30	-0.16	0.32	-0.29
Child 13–17 yrs.	0.01	0.05	-0.16	-0.19
Constant	4.77***	4.34***	2.98***	3.89***
N	675	505	531	379
Adj. R^2	0.211	0.180	0.304	0.266

Notes: * $p < 0.1$, ** $p < 0.05$, *** $p < 0.01$. Age, education (college/no college), working hours, stressful job, job insecurity, job control/influence, interesting job, appropriate pay, and supervisor status are controlled.

the tensions employees experience at the work–home interface is nevertheless surprising. In view of the 'double burden' hypothesis there is a danger of role overload and increased stress for individuals with multiple roles, and a potential role conflict between care for children and participation in the labour market (Bratberg et al. 2002). This is particularly true for women, who often face a second shift at home. However, we could not find statistically significant support for this hypothesis in any of the three large-scale surveys used in the analyses.

Are these results at odds with research findings in other survey studies of work–family conflict? The evidence in the literature is inconclusive. Some studies suggest that the presence of children (of various ages) in the household is associated with higher levels of work–home interference (Winslow 2005; Gallie and Russell 2009), while others observed no effect (Schieman et al. 2009). McGinnity and Calvert (2009) found a significant effect of the presence of children on work–life conflict of professional workers in seven European countries, but this effect disappeared when working conditions such as weekly hours, unsocial hours, or job pressure were controlled. Our results are thus not exceptional, but there are indications that successful balancing between raising children and being in paid employment may depend on different contexts and can vary across specific groups of employees.

In different national contexts the degree of work–family support and resources may vary considerably. Germany and Spain are considered conservative welfare states with a distinctive gender division of labour and strong remnants of the breadwinner family model. Public childcare provision, especially for very young children, is low in cross-national comparison and individuals lack societal and organizational resources for WLB. Given these characteristics, one would expect that particularly employed women, who are generally responsible for housework and childcare, would face severe difficulties in combining work and home/family. It is thus unexpected that we find no effect of children on work–home interference for German and Spanish women, and this outcome is difficult to understand within the resources–demands framework.

From the capabilities perspective, however, these results point to the divide between functionings and capabilities, between what individuals do and how this relates to alternative possibilities they face given the economic, social, and normative constraints in a given society. This framework allows us to reformulate the research questions and focus not only on the WLB of employed men and women but deliberate the outcomes in terms of capabilities. As Hobson points out in the introductory chapter, the capabilities framework, when applied across different institutional and normative contexts, provides a lens for understanding the mechanisms that lie behind the agency inequalities for participating in different spheres of life. In our study, this framework leads us to question which social processes and mechanisms might have led to the observed 'non-association' between children and work–home conflict. So we ask not only whether the presence of children has an impact on WLB of employees, but also whether the presence of children has an impact on participating in both spheres of work and family in the first place.

Female Employment Rate and Children

In Sen's capability approach, the emphasis is not only on how human beings actually function but also on their having the capability to function in ways they find valuable. Individuals' wellbeing is analysed through an examination of their capability sets, understood as their ability to maximize their potential functionings, as well as the agency they possess. Agency primarily refers to an individual's role as a member of society, with the ability to participate in socio-economic and public life. From this perspective, differences in labour force participation rates indicate basic agency inequality and call for a focus on gender. 'In debates on gendered agency inequality, it is necessary to recognize that behind the distinctions between paid and unpaid work, between the public and the private spheres, looms the fact that the labour force is the arena for the major socioeconomic stratification processes in modern societies, processes where agency is crucial' (Korpi 2000: 139). Thus, the integration of the sphere of work into one's life is an achievement that precedes the WLB as assessed in our analyses presented above. The question we address is whether care obligations in the family interfere with the labour force participation of women in Germany and Spain, as well as other European countries for which we have data from the Labour Force Surveys.

Research has shown that having children remarkably diminishes the chances of women entering or staying in the labour market. Burchardt (2010) shows how resources, including time as well as human and social capital, interact with responsibilities to produce a range of feasible time allocations. One of her findings is that having more or younger children—as well as being lone mother—is associated with having a small capability set defined in terms of the level and range of combinations of disposable income and free time that can be achieved. Table 5.4 displays the employment rate of women in 19 European countries aged 25–49, that is, in the life phase in which family obligations are likely to be most intense. The data refer to 2006, which corresponds to the year the European Social Survey ESS3 was carried out. Further, we include data for 2011, which is the last year for which the data are currently available, to assess the recent changes in the European labour markets.

Comparing women without children and those with one child, two children, and three or more children, in Germany and Spain in 2006, reveals that with every child the likelihood of a mother being in paid employment decreases. While more than 82% of childless German women are employed, this rate drops by ten percentage points for women with one child. Among women with three or more children, the majority (52%) is outside paid employment. A similar pattern is observed in Spain albeit at somewhat lower levels of employment (about seven percentage points), except for women with the largest families, where the drop in participation rate is less pronounced than in Germany (Table 5.4, column 4). It has to be noted, however, that most employed mothers in Spain work full-time, while part-time employment is the prevailing form of employment of German women with young children.

A similar pattern of decreasing employment rate as the number of children increases is found in most other European countries (Table 5.4). In contrast, as Eurostat data show, among men in the same age group 25–49, men with two children have the highest employment rate in both Germany and Spain. Criteria such as gender and parental status thus play an important role in selection into employment. Paradoxically, this selectivity leads to the consequence that low participation of women in paid work is associated with relatively favourable attainments for those who do enter the labour market (Mandel 2009).

In 2011, female employment in Germany increased in all subgroups but the pattern remained the same. In Spain, too, we observe that each additional child is associated with a lower employment rate. However, the general increasing trend of labour force participation over time, as seen in Germany, is not evident. Of all subgroups, childless women are still most likely to be employed; however, their employment rate declined considerably in the five

Table 5.4 Employment rate of women aged 25–49, by country and number of children

	2006				2011			
Country	0 children	1	2	3+	0 children	1	2	3+
Austria	83.6	80.1	72.3	57.9	85.6	83.1	76.8	60.4
Belgium	75.8	75.9	76.3	58.0	78.0	76.1	79.7	60.3
Bulgaria	77.3	75.2	70.8	36.6	74.6	76.1	69.1	36.0
Cyprus	82.4	76.6	76.2	63.3	82.5	75.9	79.6	67.2
Germany	82.2	71.5	65.4	47.9	85.6	77.9	71.0	54.9
Denmark	:	:	:	:	77.5	80.6	86.8	82.0
Estonia	85.6	83.4	76.2	64.0	81.6	75.2	69.9	57.2
Spain	75.0	64.7	58.1	50.3	70.2	62.7	60.3	48.4
Finland	81.8	78.7	80.9	66.5	82.0	77.5	80.8	66.6
France	80.4	78.2	74.4	54.5	79.6	78.5	78.4	58.1
UK	85.6	75.5	71.0	47.9	83.9	75.3	70.7	46.3
Hungary	79.2	66.5	66.4	39.1	79.0	64.5	62.9	38.0
Ireland	84.4	69.0	61.0	50.2	79.6	67.1	59.2	47.7
Netherlands	85.1	75.3	76.5	65.1	84.6	79.5	80.5	69.4
Poland	74.1	69.6	66.9	57.0	78.6	73.6	70.7	59.3
Portugal	76.2	78.0	77.5	65.8	76.5	77.9	74.9	63.8
Sweden	:	:	:	:	81.5	80.7	86.6	82.9
Slovenia	79.0	84.3	87.2	84.7	79.1	83.4	87.4	79.2
Slovakia	79.3	70.1	69.6	52.2	77.2	66.9	68.3	52.6

Source: Eurostat <http://epp.eurostat.ec.europa.eu/portal/page/portal/employment_unemployment_lfs/data/database>.

years covered by our data. It would appear that childless women, who are in general younger, are most likely to be affected by constraints and difficulties typical of the Spanish labour market in the period of a serious economic crisis. These data demonstrate vividly how gendered care obligations on the one hand, and the institutional and economic context on the other, generate agency inequality and constrain women's participation in the labour market.

Not only employment rates, but also the extent to which children, and the probable impact of the financial crisis on the labour markets, matter, differs between the countries. However, only in Belgium, Denmark, Portugal, Sweden, and Slovenia do employment rates of mothers surpass those of childless women in some cases (Table 5.4). To better understand the normative and institutional frameworks for the development of agency inequality, we will address these two aspects in the following sections.

Normative Contexts for Agency Inequality

Not only economic and social but also normative constraints and cultural norms may limit individuals' agency (Budig et al. 2012). In particular, gendered agency inequalities are reflected in normative barriers that shape the scope of alternatives men and women in given normative/institutional contexts perceive as 'possible'. Hobson (Chapter 1 in this volume) elaborates on Sen's approach to choice and agency: the choice made is bound up with what the 'real' opportunities to choose are. The capabilities approach leads us to question what individuals would actually prefer if they had the capabilities to choose among additional alternative paths or if they lived in a society with different norms towards gender roles. A definite answer to such a counterfactual question is not possible, but much cross-national comparative research suggests that the societal contexts matter for choices and these choices are constrained along gender lines.

To assess the normative barriers for simultaneously combining paid work and family care in Germany and Spain, we perform an analysis of survey data on attitudes towards employment of men and women when young children are involved. Negative attitudes toward women's employment among men as well as among women can be expected to be of relevance for women's choices concerning paid work. Data come from the third round of the European Social Survey which included a module 'The Timing of Life: The Organization of the Life Course in Europe' in 2006. This module assessed normative views on the life course and events that mark the transition from one life stage to another. Among other issues, the respondents were also asked: 'Using this card, how much do you approve or disapprove if a woman/a man has a full-time job while she/he has children aged under 3?', with the following categories: strongly disapprove, disapprove, neither approve nor disapprove, approve, strongly approve. In addition to asking the respondent's opinion, the survey solicited beliefs about social norms in that society: 'Apart from your own feelings, how do you think most people would react if a woman/a man they knew well...had a full-time job while she/he had children aged under 3?', with the following categories: most people would openly disapprove, most people would secretly disapprove, most people would not mind either way, most people would approve. The module used the split-ballot design. Two versions of the questionnaire—one referring to women and one referring to men—were randomly given to the ESS respondents to assess whether double standards along gender lines operate in European societies and whether gender is a basis for stricter standards for one group.

Table 5.5 indeed shows that negative attitudes towards women's employment differ radically from attitudes towards men's employment in the same life situation, but we also find considerable cross-country variation. In Germany, 42% of respondents disapprove or strongly disapprove if a mother with a child aged under 3 is employed full-time (Table 5.5). The perception of negative societal attitudes toward women's employment is even higher. Over

Table 5.5 Respondents' attitudes towards an employed woman/man with a full-time job while children are aged under 3

	Disapproval of a full-time working woman, percentages			Disapproval of a full-time working man, percentages		
Country	Disapprove or strongly disapprove	Believe most people would openly disapprove	Believe most people would secretly disapprove	Disapprove or strongly disapprove	Believe most people would openly disapprove	Believe most people would secretly disapprove
Austria	55.3	22.7	41.8	14.1	5.3	8.0
Belgium	25.2	4.7	21.0	4.3	1.7	4.5
Bulgaria	45.3	13.9	18.7	14.7	4.8	6.4
Switzerland	57.3	13.2	53.0	13.2	2.8	11.3
Cyprus	13.3	3.9	24.0	4.5	0.8	7.2
Germany	42.0	11.0	45.2	8.2	2.3	9.1
Denmark	14.9	1.5	9.1	2.2	0.1	2.4
Estonia	54.1	6.8	31.0	7.7	2.1	3.9
Spain	22.4	7.3	22.9	9.0	3.5	10.3
Finland	13.2	3.1	15.3	2.3	0.8	4.2
France	31.3	6.8	21.8	7.0	1.5	7.4
UK	39.6	6.6	37.4	3.3	1.1	4.0
Hungary	45.6	16.6	26.6	4.2	1.9	6.1
Ireland	24.7	5.7	19.0	5.1	1.2	3.6
Netherlands	51.8	16.0	48.3	8.5	2.2	8.6
Norway	15.0	1.3	11.0	4.2	0.5	4.0
Poland	29.0	4.1	18.8	4.7	1.2	5.2
Portugal	17.5	4.5	17.5	7.5	1.7	11.1
Russian Fed.	52.5	13.6	41.0	8.3	2.6	10.9
Sweden	20.3	4.0	22.2	10.7	2.0	8.5
Slovenia	29.4	4.9	19.5	12.7	3.0	12.2
Slovakia	45.0	11.6	33.3	8.7	2.8	9.8
Ukraine	57.5	22.2	32.7	12.1	5.1	5.4
Total	35.8	9.3	28.7	7.7	2.2	7.3

Source: European Social Survey 2006 (ESS3), split ballot, own calculations.

45% of respondents believe that most people would secretly (although not openly) disapprove of such an arrangement. Interestingly, such disapproval is less common in Spain. Less than one-quarter of respondents express their own negative attitudes or hold beliefs about the incidence of such norms in Spanish society. This places Germany among the countries that still clearly accentuates a highly 'traditional' set of expectations and norms around motherhood and care. Spain is in this respect placed among the middle-range countries in terms of gendered norms. Germany and Spain—as well as all other countries in the ESS3 survey—reveal double standards in terms of normative constraints and demonstrate a considerable gender gap in agency inequality.

Labour Market Contexts in Germany and Spain

Germany and Spain are both considered conservative welfare states, although the deviation of Spain and other more familialistic southern European countries from the typical conservative model in their patterns of care provision and gendered outcomes has been noted repeatedly (Mingione 1995; Guillén 2010; Guillén and León 2011). Both the German and the Spanish welfare state share similarities in the way and degree to which national social policies influence gender relations and the position of women as wives, mothers, or workers (Lewis 1992). Nevertheless, in both countries there has been a remarkable increase in women's educational level, especially for the younger cohorts, and women's employment increased significantly by the mid 2000s. Over a period of two decades (1987–2007), Spanish levels of female illiteracy dropped from 8% in 1987 to 3% in 2007, while the percentage of women aged 16 and older with tertiary education increased from 6% to 16% (Salido 2011: 190). In the context of low levels of state support to families with children, increasing education importantly contributed to higher female participation in paid employment. Mandel (2009) stresses higher levels of education as a particularly significant factor for female employment in Spain, while motherhood and familial constraints are more important in explaining women's employment levels in Germany. Nevertheless, data show that among Spanish women in the last 20 years, employment growth was also evident among the less educated. This trend is partly explained by the growth of opportunities in the Spanish labour market during the period of economic expansion, even for low skilled jobs. There has also been a change in the pattern of participation, with more women, especially the younger cohorts, staying in employment for longer and with shorter breaks (Salido 2011).

However, regardless of shifting gender norms and the increased propensity of mothers to enter employment, these changes cannot be translated into factual behaviour and expand individual agency if people face difficulties and obstacles in entering the labour market or finding a good job. The Spanish labour market is characterized by a very high proportion of fixed-term contracts, together with very low levels of secure part-time employment (Ibáñez 2011), which limit the genuine opportunities and agency of working women. The Spanish labour market has stood out since the early 1990s for having the highest rates of temporary employment of all the OECD countries (Polavieja 2006). In 2010, 25% of Spanish employees had a fixed-term contract, against a level of 14% for the EU15 average. The German level is slightly below the EU average, but the proportion of fixed-term contracts among new contracts has been increasing rapidly in the 2000s. Currently, every second new employment contract is a fixed-term contract and more women than men are affected by temporary employment (Hohendanner 2012). Another rapidly spreading form of 'atypical employment' in Germany is temporary-agency work. In such cases, the employee signs a contract with a temporary agency but the work is performed for the user company. The temporary agency is thus the employer that hires out its workers to the user company on a temporary basis.

Atypical forms of employment increase job insecurity, which has an effect on fertility levels. Fertility postponement among Spanish and German women, particularly among well-educated women with good career prospects, is well documented. The onset of the economic recession in 2007 has further exacerbated economic uncertainty and job instability, and affected family dynamics. The structural features of the labour market, much aggravated by the crisis, impose severe restrictions to WLB for large parts of the population, especially young people and women.

Work–Family Policies and the Crisis

Since the 1990s, various work–family policies have been implemented in Spain with the aim of facilitating reconciliation of work and family and enabling individuals to achieve worklife balance. However, these measures have been to a large extent eroded since the beginning of the economic crisis, especially by the austerity measures implemented since 2010.

The first piece of legislation explicitly addressing policies for the reconciliation of work and family life was introduced in 1999. This legislation was mainly the transposition of the EC 1992 Directive on Maternity Protection and the EC 1996 Directive on Parental Leave. The 1999 Act improved protection of expectant and breastfeeding working mothers by allowing time off work and guaranteeing job return. As for parental leave, fathers could take-up to 10 weeks of the mother's total leave of 16 weeks. In 2003, the conservative government introduced a new subsidy for working mothers with children under 3, consisting of monthly payment of 100 Euros. This measure is currently still in effect. In 2007, the socialist government introduced new measures with a focus on gender equality rather than the family. A paid paternity leave of 15 days at 100% salary replacement rate was introduced as an exclusive right of fathers. It was envisaged that paternity leave would progressively increase to four months by 2013. However, in 2011, as part of wider budgetary cuts, paternity leave was left unpaid. Further, a 'baby cheque' worth 2,500 Euros (3,500 Euros for families with three or more children), introduced as a lump sum for every new baby or adopted child with the sole requisite of a two-year residence permit, was cancelled at the beginning of 2011.

In terms of childcare, there is good public provision for 3 to 6 year-olds in Spain. However, for younger children the situation is very different. Cover rates are low and there is a very high degree of regional variation (León 2007). The programme Educa3, which was introduced in 2008 with the aim to increase the availability and improve the quality of childcare for ages 0–3, was discontinued in April 2012 as part of overall expenditure cuts in welfare benefits.

In the context of the shortage of public policies and state support, family solidarity has always played an important role in Southern European welfare states. The SHARE survey revealed that the frequency with which grandparents look after their grandchildren on a daily basis is higher in Spain (as well as Italy and Greece) than in other European countries (Albertini et al. 2007: 326). But the crisis is stretching the solidarity of the extended family even further. Recent reports on the effects of the crisis in Spain show how extended family networks are to a large extent shouldering the consequences of the crisis for many families. According to Laparra and Pérez Eransus (2012), 7.8% of all Spanish households in which all active members are unemployed have a 65+ year old living in the household. These percentage points doubled since 2007 and are up to 7 points above those in other countries such as the UK, France, or Denmark. The same study shows that retired people are the only social group that has not lost purchasing power during the crisis. Pensions of the elderly become an important stable monetary resource in a situation where the average income has dropped dramatically.

Germany has not experienced such a severe crisis. It has in effect expanded some social policy measures. Since the beginning of the 2000s, there has been considerable policy change in areas affecting WLB. Reforms of parental leave, parental benefits, and childcare were introduced in order to encourage the continuity of women's employment in the labour market as well as to improve childcare provision and early education. As Leitner (2010: 464) argues, this policy reform, framed within the new paradigm of a 'sustainable family policy', was directed at various simultaneous goals: to increase employability, expand childcare, foster gender equality, and increase the birth rate. Many of the policy initiatives undertaken during this period were the result of vivid political debates, where the Nordic countries with high fertility rates and high female participation in the labour market were taken as a role model (Spiess and Wrohlich 2008). In broad terms, the reforms introduced since the beginning of the 2000s can be understood as reforms that should enable WLB based on employment continuity rather than long breaks from employment.

The aim behind a set of parental leave reforms since 2000 was to encourage the combination of parenting with employment by offering incentives for parents, especially mothers, to quickly return to work. However, the lack of institutional childcare has been an important restriction on parents' choices. The reform of 2007 implied a paradigm shift with regard to German family policy, which previously promoted the male-breadwinner family model. Parents can take 14 months of parental leave, with a wage-dependent parental benefit (Elterngeld) that equals 67% of previous monthly net income, with an upper limit of 1,800 Euros. The benefit is universally available to all parents, including formerly non-employed parents who are entitled to the minimum benefit of 300 Euros. Parents can share their months of parental leave between them; however, following the 'use-it-or-lose-it' system, two months are reserved for the other parent, which significantly increased fathers' usage of parental leave (Reich 2011).

This is not the only significant discontinuity with Germany's institutional and cultural paths. Currently, there are attempts to expand care for children under the age of 3. In 2013, parents will acquire a legal right to childcare for children aged 1–3. The main aim behind the planned expansion of childcare facilities is to enable mothers' employment and a better balance between work and family life. This path towards policies sustaining the dual-earner/dual-carer model has, nevertheless, not been free of tensions. Leitner (2010: 464) argues that the resistance, especially by the Bavarian branch of the Christian Democrats, explains why the new childcare policy still contains elements of the traditional male-breadwinner model. The intra-party consent has been 'bought' by a political compromise and includes the new measure that parents who do not make use of the new right to publically funded childcare receive a childcare allowance of 100 Euros monthly until the child's third birthday. Thus, policies include elements that support both the traditional breadwinner and the dual-earner model.

Conclusion

This study is built around a paradoxical finding that emerged from the analyses of three different high-quality large-scale European surveys, conducted between 2003 and 2006, in which the level of interference between work and home, as well as the satisfaction with the balance in dividing time between work and other aspects of life in Germany and Spain, were analysed (Drobnič and Guillén 2011a). Indicators for job-related demands and resources as well as home-related demands and resources were considered in the analyses to test hypotheses derived from the resources–demands model. While job-related characteristics in most cases exhibited the expected impact on work–home conflict, in line with the resources–demands approach, a surprising result was that the presence of children of various ages in the household was not associated with work–home interference. Within the framework of resources–demands theory, it is reasonable to expect that the presence of preschool and school-aged children in the home increases demand for care and housework. Augmented demands and engagement in the family sphere imply that time and energy available for market work decreases and contributes to work–home conflict, particularly for women who primarily take responsibility for family work and often face a second shift at home. The outcome that children are not associated with the work–home interference cannot be explained within the resources–demands model.

The capabilities approach allows us to go beyond the explanatory frame of resources and demands. The strength of this approach is to draw into a predominantly individual focus on job characteristics and resources, the settings, the cultural normative frames, and the social stratification in which men and women work and live. In our analysis, the capabilities approach broadens our perspective when interpreting the association between family responsibilities/demands and work–home interference. Although mothers (and fathers) who are employed do not experience significantly higher levels of work–family/home tensions than non-parents, the focus on the agency and capabilities gap and overall wellbeing leads us to address this association within the broader country contexts.

By focusing on agency inequalities, understanding of the *selection* process into employment becomes crucial. As Mandel (2009) demonstrates, in the conservative welfare states, low participation of women in paid work is associated with relatively favourable attainments for those who do enter the labour market. This is something of a surprise for societies with a conservative tradition. Only a relatively select group of women—and in our case mothers—is able to enter an economy dependent on highly-committed male labour that is not adapted to women and mothers and does not offer them preferential terms of employment (Mandel 2009: 703).

In Germany and Spain, children are still an important obstacle in female employment, as evident from the labour force participation rates for women with and without children (Table 5.4). Women who anticipate high work–life conflict are less likely to be employed in the first place or they 'resolve' the conflict by not having children. In this respect, the situation in Germany and Spain resonates with low fertility in many other European countries, where women without children are often highly educated and have substantial resources. Our study also shows how constraints and opportunities in the labour market, as well as policy measures, exert an impact on selection into employment. The current economic crisis in Spain has had a devastating effect on general employment levels and female employment in particular. Such critical periods may decisively shape the agency inequalities along gender and other lines.

Not only the factual difficulties that employed women with children may face, but also the lack of societal support for worklife balance and restrictions in the labour market play a role in the employment decisions of women. Additionally, cultural expectations and normative prescriptions provide a framework within which the scope of alternatives is shaped. Employment and children are rarely seen as incompatible roles for men (Table 5.5). In contrast, women in Germany and Spain—as well as in many other European countries—face negative attitudes and disapproval when combining work and family roles. The institutional and normative contexts thus importantly curtail women's agency freedom for simultaneously balancing employment and family. This occurs at a level of capabilities and remains obscured when only the observed functionings are being examined.

Bibliography

Albertini, M., M. Kohli, and C. Vogel (2007). Intergenerational Transfers of Time and Money in European families: Common Patterns—Different Regimes? *Journal of European Social Policy*, 17(4):319–34.

Allen, T.D., D.E.L. Herst, C.S. Bruck, and M. Sutton (2000). Consequences Associated with Work-to-Family Conflict: A Review and Agenda for Future Research. *Journal of Occupational Health Psychology*, 5:278–308.

Beham, B. and S. Drobnič (2010). Satisfaction with Work–Family Balance among German Office Workers. *Journal of Managerial Psychology*, 25(6):669–89.

Bratberg, E., S-Å. Dahl, and A. Erling Risa (2002). 'The Double Burden': Do Combinations of Career and Family Obligations Increase Sickness Absence among Women? *European Sociological Review*, 18(2):233–49.

Budig, M.J., J. Misra, and I. Boeckmann (2012). The Motherhood Penalty in Cross-National Perspective: The Importance of Work–Family Policies and Cultural Attitudes. *Social Politics: International Studies in Gender, State and Society*, 19(2):163–93.

Burchardt, T. (2010). Time, Income and Substantive Freedom: A Capability Approach. *Time and Society*, 19(3):318–44.

Crompton, R. and C. Lyonette (2006). Work-Life 'Balance' in Europe. *Acta Sociologica*, 49:379–93.

Demerouti, E., A.B. Bakker, F. Nachreiner, and W.B. Schaufeli (2001). The Job Demands-Resources Model of Burnout. *Journal of Applied Psychology*, 86(3):499–512.

den Dulk, L., M. Bäck-Wiklund, S. Lewis, and D. Redai (2011). Quality of Life and Work in a Changing Europe. A Theoretical Framework, In M. Bäck-Wiklund, T. van der Lippe, L. den Dulk, and A. van Doorne-Huiskes (eds), *Quality of Life and Work in Europe: Theory, Practice, and Policy*, pp. 17–31. Basingstoke: Palgrave Macmillan.

Drobnič, S. and A.M. Guillén (2011a). Tensions Between Work and Home: Job Quality and Working Conditions in the Institutional Contexts of Germany and Spain. *Social Politics: International Studies in Gender, State and Society*, 18(2):232–68.

Drobnič, S. and A.M. Guillén (2011b) (eds), *Work–Life Balance in Europe: The Role of Job Quality*. Basingstoke: Palgrave Macmillan.

ESS (2004). European Social Survey Round 2 Data (2004). Data File Edition 3.1. Norwegian Social Science Data Services, Norway—Data Archive and Distributor of ESS Data.

ESS (2006). European Social Survey Round 3 Data (2006). Data File Edition 3.2. Norwegian Social Science Data Services, Norway—Data Archive and Distributor of ESS Data.

EQLS (2003). European Foundation for the Improvement of Living and Working Conditions and Wissenschaftszentrum Berlin für Sozialforschung. European Quality of Life Survey, 2003 [computer file]. Colchester, Essex: UK Data Archive [distributor], February 2006. SN: 5260.

Foschi, M. (2000). Double Standards for Competence: Theory and Research. *Annual Review of Sociology*, 26:21–42.

Frone, M.R., M. Russell, M.L. Cooper (1992). Antecedents and Outcomes of Work–family Conflict: Testing a Model of the Work–family Interface. *Journal of Applied Psychology*, 77:65–78.

Frone, M.R., J.K. Yardley, and K.S. Markel (1997). Developing and Testing an Integrative Model of the Work–Family Interface. *Journal of Vocational Behavior*, 50:145–67.

Gallie, D. and H. Russell (2009). Work–Family Conflict and Working Conditions in Western Europe. *Social Indicators Research*, 93:445–67.

Goode, W.J. (1960). A Theory of Role Strain. *American Sociological Review*, 25(4):483–96.

Greenhaus, J.H. and N.J. Beutell (1985). Sources of Conflict between Work and Family Roles. *Academy of Management Review*, 10(1):76–88.

Greenhaus, J.H., K.M. Collins, and J.D. Shaw (2003). The Relation Between Work–Family Balance and Quality of Life. *Journal of Vocational Behavior*, 63:510–31.

Guillén, A.M. (2010). Defrosting the Spanish Welfare State: The Weight of Conservative Components, in B. Palier (ed.), *A Long Good Bye to Bismarck: The Politics of Welfare Reforms in Continental Europe*. Amsterdam: Amsterdam University Press.

Guillén, A.M. and M. León (2011) (eds), *The Spanish Welfare State in the European Context*. Surrey and Burlington: Ashgate.

Hobson, B. (2011). The Agency Gap in Work–Life Balance: Applying Sen's Capabilities Framework Within European Contexts. *Social Politics: International Studies in Gender, State and Society*, 18(2):148–67.

Hobson, B. and S. Fahlén (2009). Competing Scenarios for European Fathers: Applying Sen's Capabilities and Agency Framework to Work–Family Balance. *The Annals of the American Academy of Political and Social Science*, 624:214.

Hohendanner, C. (2012). Befristete Arbeitsverhältnisse. Auch Mann trägt kurz. *IAB-Forum*, Nr. 1, 62–67.

Ibáñez, Z. (2011). Part-time Employment in Spain: A Victim of the 'Temporality Culture' and a Lagging Implementation, in Guillén, A.M. and M. León (eds), *The Spanish Welfare State in the European Context*, pp. 165–86. Surrey and Burlington: Ashgate.

Knijn, T. and A. Smit (2009). Investing, Facilitating, or Individualizing the Reconciliation of Work and Family Life: Three Paradigms and Ambivalent Policies. *Social Politics: International Studies in Gender, State and Society*, 16:484–518.

Korpi, W. (2000). Faces of Inequality: Gender, Class, and Patterns of Inequalities in Different Types of Welfare States. *Social Politics: International Studies in Gender, State and Society*, 7(2):127–91.

Kossek, E.E. and S.J. Lambert (2005). 'Work–Family Scholarship': Voice and Context, in E.E. Kossek and S.J. Lambert (eds), *Work and Life Integration: Organizational, Cultural and Individual Perspectives*, pp. 3–16. Mahwah, NJ: Lawrence Earlbaum Associates.

Laparra, M. and B. Pérez Eransus (2012) (eds), *Crisis y fractura social en Europa. Causas y efectos en España.* Barcelona: Obra Social La Caixa.

Leitner, S. (2010) Germany Outpaces Austria in Childcare Policy: The Historical Contingencies of 'Conservative' Childcare Policy. *Journal of European Social Policy,* 20(5):456–67.

León, M. (2007). Speeding Up or Holding Back? Institutional Factors in the Development of Childcare Provision in Spain. *European Societies,* 9(3):315–37.

Lewis, J. (1992). Gender and the Development of Welfare Regimes. *Journal of European Social Policy,* 2(3):131–52.

Mandel, H. (2009). Configurations of Gender Inequality: The Consequences of Ideology and Public Policy. *The British Journal of Sociology,* 60(4):693–719.

Marks, S.R. (1977). Multiple Roles and Role Strain: Some Notes on Human Energy, Time and Commitment. *American Sociological Review,* 42:921–36.

McGinnity, F. and E. Calvert (2009). Work–Life Conflict and Social Inequality in Western Europe. *Social Indicators Research,* 93:489–508.

Mingione, E. (1995). Labour Market Segmentation and Informal Work in Southern Europe. *European Urban and Regional Studies,* 2(2):121–43.

Pichler, F. (2009). Determinants of Work–Life Balance. Shortcomings in the Contemporary Measurement of WLB in Large-scale Surveys. *Social Indicators Research,* 92:449–69.

Pleck, J.H. (1977). The Work–Family Role System. *Social Problems,* 24:417–27.

Reich, N. (2011). Predictors of Fathers' Use of Parental Leave in Germany. *Population Review,* 50(2): 1–22.

Polavieja, J.G. (2006). The Incidence of Temporary Employment in Advanced Economies: Why is Spain Different? *European Sociological Review,* 22(1):61–78.

Robeyns, I. (2005). The Capability Approach: A Theoretical Survey. *Journal of Human Development,* 6(1):93–114.

Salido, O. (2011). Female Employment and Policies for Balancing Work and Family Life in Spain, in Guillén and León (eds), *The Spanish Welfare State in the European Context,* pp. 187–208. Surrey and Burlington: Ashgate.

Scherer, S. and N. Steiber (2007). Work and Family in Conflict? The Impact of Work Demands on Family Life, in D. Gallie (eds), *Employment Regimes and the Quality of Work,* pp. 137–78. Oxford: Oxford University Press.

Schieman, S., M.A. Milkie, and P. Glavin (2009). When Work Interferes with Life: Work-Nonwork Intrerference and the Influence of Work-Related Demands and Resources. *American Sociological Review,* 74:966–88.

Sen, A. (1992). *Inequality Re-examined.* Oxford: Oxford University Press.

Sen, A. (2006). Capability and Well-being, in M. Nussbaum and A. Sen (eds), *The Quality of Life,* pp. 30–53. Oxford: Oxford University Press.

Sieber, S. (1974). Toward a Theory of Role Accumulation. *American Sociological Review,* 39:567–78.

Spiess, C.K. and K. Wrohlich (2008). The Parental Leave Benefit Reform in Germany: Costs and Labour Market Outcomes of Moving towards the Nordic Model. *Population Research and Policy Review,* 27:575–91.

Steiber, N. (2009). Reported Levels of Time-based and Strain-based Conflict Between Work and Family Roles in Europe: A Multilevel Approach. *Social Indicators Research*, 93(3):469–88.

Valcour, M. (2007). Work-based Resources as Moderators of the Relationship Between Work Hours and Satisfaction with Work–Family Balance. *Journal of Applied Psychology*, 92(6):1512–23.

van der Lippe, T. and L. van Dijk (2002). Comparative Research on Women's Employment. *Annual Review of Sociology*, 28:221–41.

Voydanoff, P. (2005a). Toward a Conceptualization of Perceived Work–family Fit and Balance: A Demands and Resources Approach. *Journal of Marriage and Family*, 67: 822–36.

Voydanoff, P. (2005b). Work Demands and Work-to-Family and Family-to-Work Conflict: Direct and Indirect Relationships'. *Journal of Family Issues*, 26(6):707–26.

Winslow, S. (2005). Work–Family Conflict, Gender and Parenthood, 1977-1997. *Journal of Family Issues*, 26:727–55.

Part II

The Firm Level and the Agency and Capabilities Gap: Policies, Managers, and Work Organization

6

Workplace worklife balance support from a capabilities perspective

Laura den Dulk, Sandra Groeneveld, and Bram Peper

Introduction

This chapter focuses on workplace worklife balance (hereafter WLB) support across different European countries and presents new findings from a capabilities perspective. Work organizational cultures vary across countries and among workplaces regarding the degree and nature of the worklife balance support offered to working parents. WLB policies are mediated, translated, and sometimes initiated at the firm level. Hence, workplaces affect capabilities for agency freedom to achieve WLB. This chapter confronts a key dimension of the volume: the relation between institutional contexts and workplace support.

Individual capabilities to find a satisfactory WLB are shaped at various levels of society: the state, the workplace, and the household (see Introduction in this volume). This chapter looks at the laws and policies developed in different European countries to reconcile paid work with caring tasks (leave, childcare, and flexible work arrangements) along with the supportive measures developed within firms and organizations. Hence, we consider two institutional factors that affect agency for WLB: public provisions developed by national governments, and policies and arrangements developed by organizations.

Work–family researchers increasingly point out the need to broaden the scope of research in order to shed light on the interactions between public policies at the country level, human resource practices and policies at the organizational level, and employees' needs and expectations at the individual level (Poelmans 2005; Kossek et al. 2010). Cross-national research is needed to capture a multilayered approach. Although there is a growing body of cross-national research on WLB experiences taking up this challenge (i.e. Lyness and Brumit Kropf 2005; Lewis et al. 2009; Ollier-Malaterre 2009; Abendroth and den Dulk 2011; den Dulk et al. 2012; Nilsen et al. 2012), most cross-national research focuses either on national policies (see for instance Gornick and Meyer 2003; Moss 2012) or on individual WLB experiences (i.e. Poelmans et al. 2003; Spector et al. 2007) and seldom includes the workplace level, while most research focusing on the workplace level are single country studies often conducted in the USA or the UK (see den Dulk and Peper 2009 for a review). There are a few notable exceptions, however, which will be discussed below.

In this chapter we look at workplace support for working parents in relation to country-level public policy. Does extensive public policy encourage employers to develop workplace support or inhibit them? Is it the other way round that the near absence of public policies tends to stimulate a tradition of corporate welfare (Lewis 1997)? These are relevant questions. Having WLB policies both at the state level and within the workplace increases the agency of working parents to make claims at work for WLB. When organizations supplement or extend public provisions they signal that they are willing to support employees to balance work and family demands. Research has pointed out the important role of organizations for implementing WLB policies and that without supportive organizational cultures many employees do not exercise their right to use the existing possibilities (Thompson et al. 1999; Allen 2001; see also other chapters in this volume). Formal entitlements are translated within organizations into claims where requests to use policies are granted or denied. Hence, organizations are conversion sites for WLB capabilities.

Unfortunately, with the available data we were not able to fully analyse how institutional resources at state and workplace level are converted into agency. To fully analyse the conversion of public WLB policies, detailed data on workplace organizational culture is needed. Other chapters in Part Two of this volume take up this issue and offer in-depth investigations of the way organizational culture plays out, shaping or distorting agency and capabilities for WLB in the workplace context. The data analysed in this chapter on workplace support is restricted to public policies and organizational policy practices. However, the cross-national nature of our research allows us to shed light on variations in WLB support, taking into consideration both the level and nature of workplace policies and public provisions at the national level. The central question addressed is: in what contexts—taking into account both workplace and state support—do working parents have most agency and capabilities to achieve WLB?

To answer this question, first we investigate the degree of workplace support in different national contexts across Europe. Since we drew on the *Establishment Survey on Working time and Work–Life Balance* 2004–05

(ESWT), which was conducted in 21 European countries, we were not able to include the Japanese case in this analysis. We then turn to a discussion of how workplace support interacts with state support. A cluster analysis using data from the ESWT survey is presented in the following section, in which we examine whether and to what extent high scores on state policies and different indicators of workplace support cluster. We also investigate what type of organization offers the most capabilities for working parents, looking at country, sector, size, and proportion of women in the workforce. In the conclusion, we present our findings and elaborate on the relevance of cross-national research on WLB support when approaching WLB from a capabilities perspective.

Workplace Worklife Balance Support

Organizations can influence the capabilities and agency freedom of employees to balance work and personal life in various ways. They may offer formal and informal workplace worklife arrangements, such as (enhanced) leave entitlements, childcare support, or flexible work arrangements—such as teleworking, compressed work week, and reduction of working hours (den Dulk 2001; Poelmans et al. 2003; Appelbaum et al. 2005; Kossek 2005; Ollier-Malaterre 2009). Here, a distinction can be made between workplace childcare and enhanced leave arrangements on the one hand, which enable working parents to combine work and family life, and flexible work arrangements, which are not restricted to employees with children (Lee and Kim 2010; den Dulk et al. 2012). Childcare provisions give the possibility of outsourcing care during time at work and allow parents to stay in employment. Leave entitlements, such as parental leave, enable parents to temporarily stay home with young children and not lose their job. Flexible work arrangements allow employees to adapt working hours or place of work to responsibilities outside work, for instance to work from home in case of a sick child or other family member. In addition, organizations may offer supportive arrangements like professional and personal counselling and worklife balance management training (Bardoel et al. 1999; den Dulk 2001). It is important to make this distinction between types of worklife policies and arrangements because research indicates that organizations in different countries not only vary regarding the number of policies introduced but also with respect to the type of policies. Den Dulk and colleagues (2012) show, for instance, that organizations in the UK and conservative welfare states such as the Netherlands, Germany, Austria, and Belgium offer the most workplace childcare and leave arrangements, while organizations in Scandinavian countries have the most extensive flexible work arrangements. Supportive arrangements like counselling and support groups are reported in particular by workplaces in liberal welfare states where individual responsibility is a central value, such as the USA and the UK, and are less common in organizations operating in other welfare state regimes (den Dulk 2001).

Most studies simply count the number of arrangements present in organizations, and it then becomes clear that public sector and other large organizations take the lead (Goodstein 1994; den Dulk 2001; Evans 2001; OECD 2001; Appelbaum et al. 2005; den Dulk et al. 2010). This is true of almost all European countries (den Dulk et al. 2012). Importantly, the proportion of women in the workforce has been found to be associated with the degree of support offered by the organization (Poelmans et al. 2003; Remery et al. 2003; Lee and Kim 2010), although not all studies confirm this finding (Ingram and Simons 1995; den Dulk 2001; den Dulk et al. 2010). Ingram and Simons (1995) suggest that the skill level of the female workforce might be a significant mediator here, that is whether or not they are easy to replace. Alternatively, when the proportion of women working in the organization is very high, high (potential) utilization costs may be a reason for organizations not to invest in WLB support. Hence, there may be a cut-off point after which the proportion of women no longer has a positive effect. In other words, the relationship between the proportion of female employees and WLB support might actually be curvilinear (den Dulk 2001; den Dulk and Groeneveld 2012).

Simply introducing WLB policies and arrangements is not enough to create a supportive organization, however. Worklife policy needs to be integrated into an organizational culture that is concerned about the responsibilities of employees outside of work. Having a worklife policy in place is a visible indication of the organization's intention to support its employees in balancing work and family, but is not always easy to put into practice. Shared standards, values, and assumptions shape the 'unwritten rules' that determine how the work is done and how people should behave within the organization. When the standards and values within the organization conflict with utilization of worklife policies, employees capabilities to make claims is seriously impeded (Thompson et al. 1999) and they need to seek relief elsewhere. Research indicates that the emotional support of colleagues and managers is at least as important for reducing conflicts and tensions between work demands and care tasks at home as any practical support in the form of a worklife policy (Behson 2005). However, emotional support alone is insufficient. Abendroth and den Dulk (2011) found in their cross-national study among service workers that instrumental support and emotional support are complementary and that both are needed to find a satisfactory balance between paid work and personal life.

Workplace Worklife Balance Support in the Context of State Support

Research discussed in the previous section on WLB support indicates that not only are there differences in the number and nature of the worklife policies adopted by organizations according to such organizational characteristics as size, sector, and workforce, but these also exist across countries. Cross-national differences in workplace support emphasize the need to study how workplace support relates to the national context in which the organizations operate. This multilevel approach is not only vital to understanding differences between organizations, but also for assessing the capabilities of working parents. A relevant question for agency and capability to achieve WLB is whether, in a context of limited public provisions, organizations step in and develop additional policies and arrangements.

Chapter 2 discussed state policies aimed at enhancing people's WLB across 11 European countries. This overview clearly indicated differences in the level and nature of state policies, despite the existence of various EU directives. Countries vary with respect to leave arrangements, public daycare services, and legislation regarding flexible work arrangements. In some countries the emphasis is on long-term leave arrangements for care of small children, while other governments stimulate part-time work to enable parents to balance work with childcare. Policies are more advanced and generous in some countries than others. Scandinavian and post-socialist countries, for instance, are known for their relatively generous statutory leave policies and public childcare, while in the Netherlands and Germany more recently introduced state support is relatively modest.

It is important to consider how policies are structured and formulated and how they are embedded in the larger societal context. Hobson and colleagues, for instance, show that although Sweden and Hungary both have generous parental leave systems (see Table 6.1) the way this plays out for working parents differs. In Hungary, despite the long and relatively well-compensated parental leave (36 months), take-up among women in employment remains low due to precarious labour market conditions. In addition, the long parental leave reinforces traditional gender roles as it assumes that the mother is the one to take leave. Swedish parental leave, in contrast, is characterized by a strong incentive for fathers to take leave and high flexibility in take-up (see Chapter 3 in this volume). Table 6.1 offers an overview of the different policy measures in 21 European countries.

Differences in state policies across countries have inspired many scholars to develop welfare state classifications in order to compare different policy models and their impact (e.g. Esping-Andersen 1990; Sainsbury 1996; Korpi 2000). Based upon the work of Esping-Andersen (1990, 1999) and Blossfeld and

Table 6.1 State support in 21 European countries, statutory leave and flexible work arrangements, 2012, and children in formal childcare, 2008

Country by welfare regime	Maternity leave	Paternity leave	Parental leave	Childcare % children in formal care 2008 0–2	3–5	Right to reduce hours
Social democratic regime						
Denmark	**18** weeks***	**2** weeks***	**32** weeks***	65.7	91.5	–
Finland[1]	**17.5** weeks***	3–4 weeks***	**158** working days***	28.6	74.2	Until the end of 2nd year at school**
Sweden	7[2] weeks***	**2** weeks***	**480** days***	46.7	91.1	Until the child is 8*
Conservative regime						
Austria	**16** weeks***	–	**24** months**	12.1	77.6	Until child is 7*
Belgium	**15** weeks***	**2** weeks***	**4** months per parent**	48.4	99.4	–
France	**16** weeks***	**2** weeks***	**36** months**	42.0	99.9	–
Germany	**14** weeks***	–	**36** months***	17.8	92.7	–
Luxembourg	**16** weeks***	**2** days[3]***	**6** months per parent**	38.6	85.9	–
Netherlands	**16** weeks***	**2** days***	**26** weeks per parent**	55.9	67.1	All employees*
Liberal regime						
Ireland	**42** weeks**	–	**14** weeks per parent*	30.8	56.4	–
UK	**52** weeks**	**2** weeks**	**13** weeks per parent*	40.8	92.7	–
Mediterranean regime						
Cyprus	**16** weeks***	–	**3** months per parent*	32.7	73.4	–
Greece	**17** weeks***	**2** days***	**4** months per parent*	15.7	46.6	Until child is 2.5 or 4***
Italy	**20** weeks***	–	**10** or 11 months**	29.2	97.4	Until the child is 6
Portugal	17[2] weeks***	**20** days***	**3** months per parent**	47.4	79.2	Until the child is 12*
Spain	**16** weeks***	**3** weeks***	**36** months*	37.5	98.5	Until the child is 8*
Post-socialist regime						
Czech Republic	**28** weeks***	–	**36** months**	2,2	91,5	–
Hungary	**24** weeks***	**5** days***	**36** months[4]***	8,8	87,1	–
Latvia	**19** weeks	**10** days***	**36** months***	8,1	73,5	Until the child is 1 (only mothers)
Poland	**24** weeks***	**2** weeks***	**36** months**	7,9	47,3	–
Slovenia	**15** weeks***	**13** weeks**	**37** weeks***	33,8	77,5	Until the child is 3**

Notes: * statutory entitlement but unpaid; ** statutory entitlement paid but either at a low flat rate or earning related at less than 66% of earnings or not universal; *** statutory entitlement paid for all or part of the duration to all parents at 66% of earnings or more (Moss 2012).

[1] In Finland 6 working days per week are calculated in leave arrangements.
[2] In Portugal and Sweden legislation does not refer to maternity leave but the leave is part of parental leave. In Portugal paternity leave is also mentioned under parental leave in the legislation.
[3] Luxembourg: in legislation no mention of paternity leave but fathers can use another type of leave at the time of the birth of a child. Greece: paternity leave is paid by the employer but public sector employees do not get paid.
[4] In Hungary there are two types of parental leave: a higher and lower paid leave: first two years 70% of earnings, third year flat rate payment (Anxo et al. 2007; Moss 2012).

Source: Moss (2012), International Review of Leave Policies and Related Research 2012; OECD (2011), OECD Family Database, except for Latvia and Cyprus (source for leave arrangements: Anxo et al. 2007).

Drobnič (2001), five different welfare state regimes can be distinguished in Europe: the social-democratic welfare state regime, the conservative regime, the Mediterranean regime, the post-socialist regime, and the liberal regime. Esping-Andersen describes the dominant character of the welfare package in each country in terms of the role of the state, of the family, and of the market, and this classification offers a way of investigating how institutional context influences the level and nature of the WLB support offered by the state and by workplaces (den Dulk 2001).

This classification of welfare state regimes has been challenged and debated in the literature. Most importantly, Esping-Andersen's original typology of three welfare state regimes—the social democratic, the conservative, and the liberal—was criticized for not paying enough attention to gender, the role of the family, and unpaid work (Lewis 1992; Orloff 1993; Plantenga and van Doorne-Huiskes 1993; Sainsbury 1996; Korpi 2000) and, in a revised typology, two additional regime types were added: the Mediterranean and the post-socialist. The Mediterranean regime consists of South European countries characterized by few public worklife policies that support dual-earner families and that also lack support for the traditional breadwinner family as is the case in many conservative regimes such as Germany and Austria (Antonnen and Sipila 1996). The post-socialist regime represents a fifth cluster. According to Ferrarini (2006), using Korpi's family policy models as a starting point, post-socialist countries combine high levels of both traditional and dual-earner support. During the communist era, women's labour market participation was higher than in most West European countries and was supported by extensive public childcare and long parental leaves. Less attention was paid, on the other hand, to the division of unpaid work at home, which has remained rather traditional (Blossfeld and Drobnič 2001; Tang and Cousins 2005; Nilsen et al. 2012). Today, although post-socialist countries share a common background and legacy, they show very different developments. Some, like Slovenia (see Chapter 9 in this volume), have moved in the direction of the social democratic welfare states, while others have more leaned towards the conservative regime pattern, cutting financial compensation during leaves and reducing public childcare services, and giving policy support to the traditional family, as is the case in Poland (Ferrarini and Sjöberg 2010).

Despite the fact that post-socialist countries seem to be developing in different directions, they are still treated as having a common regime or model (Ferrarini 2006; den Dulk et al. 2010, 2012; Ferrarini and Sjöberg 2010; Boye 2011). Several West European countries, on the other hand, are a hybrid form or mix of different welfare state regimes. The Netherlands, for instance, is seen as an ambiguous case because it combines the traditional family support characteristic of the conservative regime with several universal social policies that are more in line with the social democratic welfare regime (Sainsbury 1996). Moreover, within the conservative regime, some countries place more emphasis on the role of the state (France, Belgium) while others rely more on employers and the family in combination with modest state support (the Netherlands, Germany). In addition, neoliberal trends in these countries in relation to the restructuring of the welfare state has led to a stronger emphasis on the role of the market; that is worklife policies offered by employers (den Dulk et al. 2012).

However, despite its limitations and the criticism against it, the classification remains a fruitful analytical tool to compare the levels of state and workplace WLB support across countries. According to Gornick and Meyer (2003), classifications that incorporate gender show large similarities to Esping-Andersen's typology, suggesting that 'the welfare state principles underlying these clusters are highly correlated with those that shape family policy' (2003: 23). In social democratic welfare states there is a strong commitment to gender equality, while in the conservative and Mediterranean regimes this is less prevalent, resulting in lower levels of dual-earner support. Table 6.1 shows that social democratic countries—like Sweden, Finland, and Denmark—are characterized by long, well-compensated leaves and high childcare coverage in all age groups. The Mediterranean countries (Greece, Italy, Cyprus, Portugal, and Spain) have shorter and/or lower compensated parental leave as well as low enrolment of children less than 3 years of age in formal childcare. The level of state support present in Japan (not included in Table 6.1) is similar to that of the Mediterranean countries (see Chapter 4 in this volume). In the liberal welfare state regime, men and women are treated as equal despite differences in caring responsibilities, and WLB support is mainly left to market forces and treated as an individual, private responsibility (Plantenga and Van Doorne-Huiskes 1993). Ireland and the UK, which most closely represent the liberal welfare state in Europe, have long maternity leave of which the greater part is unpaid, short unpaid parental leave, and limited public childcare (see Table 6.1). The question is whether workplaces are indeed taking an active role in this regime type given the emphasis on market forces. The post-socialist countries combine a tradition of state dual-earner support, although support has declined in many instances since the transition, and less attention has been paid towards gender equality as in countries representing the social democratic regime (Pascall and Manning 2000; Kocourková 2002). Moreover, the transition to a market economy has often been accompanied by new experiences of job insecurity and unemployment, which may limit expectations of workplace support. So, what is the relationship between state policies, the wider welfare state context, and workplace WLB support?

Different arguments abound. First, based on institutional theory (DiMaggio and Powell 1983; Scott 1995), it is put forward that public provisions indicate a strong government commitment to WLB and tend to create normative and coercive pressure on organizations to develop additional support (Dobbin and Sutton 1998). According to this argument, the more state support in a country for WLB, the more such support offered by organizations (den Dulk 2001; Poelmans and Sahibzada 2004); and the more state support, the stronger the sense of entitlement of employees to WLB (Lewis and Smithson 2001).

On the other hand, based on economic arguments or the so-called business case, it has been argued that the presence of public policies makes it less likely that employers develop their own additional provisions as it makes no sense for organizations to duplicate existing policies. Rather, it is the absence of public provisions that stimulates organizations to develop policies that gain them a competitive edge over other employers in the recruitment and retention of talented workers. This business case may in particular be strong when the labour market is tight and organizations need to compete for valuable personnel (den Dulk et al. 2010).

Based on the business case argument, we can expect some organizations to step in and offer WLB support when there is only limited state support for working parents. However, the strength of the business case is likely to depend on the organization's specific conditions and characteristics, such as the proportion of female workers or whether the organization is experiencing difficulties recruiting and retaining personnel. According to this argument, variation in workplace support is particularly high in countries where there is little regulation and little state support (den Dulk et al. 2012). So far, research indeed indicates that when public provisions are very limited there are large variations in workplace support along the lines of organizational conditions, with some organizations offering a large number of workplace policies while in other workplaces support for the worklife balance is mainly absent (den Dulk 2001; den Dulk et al. 2012). However, workplace support varies across different types of organizations even in countries with modest public worklife policies (den Dulk et al. 2012). In fact, variations in workplace support are greater *within* countries than *between* them (den Dulk et al. 2010, 2012; den Dulk and Groeneveld 2012).

Den Dulk et al. (2013) argue that not only does the degree to which economic arguments matter differ across different types of organizations, but so also the impact of institutional pressures. For instance, being a public or a private sector organization is a relevant factor affecting economic considerations as well as the amount of institutional pressure experienced. Public organizations are more in the public eye and are more likely to be evaluated according to government standards and norms, while in private sector companies profit-related arguments tend to be more important. Some public sector organizations are even required to execute government policies, and governments that stimulate employers to offer WLB support create normative pressure in public organizations to conform (Goodstein 1994; Ingram and Simons 1995; den Dulk 2001; den Dulk and Groeneveld 2012).

Large organizations, like public sector organizations, are very visible in society, making them sensitive to institutional pressure to be supportive (Goodstein 1994). However, economies of scale also make the introduction of WLB support relatively cheaper per employee in large organizations compared with smaller ones. The proportion of women in the organization is another relevant factor (Poelmans et al. 2003; Remery et al. 2003). Organizations with a substantial proportion of women (up to a certain point) may benefit more from the effects of WLB support in terms of productivity gains, less absenteeism and turnover than male dominated organizations, since women still bear the largest burden of care responsibilities (Goodstein 1994). A large share of women in the organization can also result in more requests for WLB support, increasing normative pressure to adopt workplace worklife arrangements.

In addition, trade unions can pressure organizations to adopt worklife policies that support employee needs. Whether this is a factor affecting the development of support at the organizational, sector, or national level is not yet clear. Powerful unions are able to influence management's decisions about employee benefits, but may also choose to raise the issue at the bargaining table at sector or national level, leading to the development of public provisions rather than specific workplace support. In particular in the conservative, corporatist regime and in the social democratic regime, unions are important actors operating not only at the company level but at the sector and national level as well (Ollier-Malaterre 2009; Yerkes and Tijdens 2010). Yerkes and Tijdens (2010), in their study on collective agreements in the Netherlands, show that collective bargaining may compensate for a lack of state provisions through collective agreements that offer high protection for part-time work and childcare support but also respond to state policies once they are developed. This suggests a positive relation between state policies and collective agreements.

However, research has also pointed out that unions, as traditionally male dominated institutions, tend not to place worklife issues high on the bargaining agenda (Hantrais and Acker 2005; Haas and Hwang 2013). US research in the 1990s found a negative relation between unionization and workplace worklife balance support (Auerbach 1990; Glass and Fujimoto 1995). In Europe, the (relative) level of unionization in an organization was found to be positively related to the adoption of workplace childcare and leave support, but not to the adoption of flexible work arrangements (Anxo et al. 2007; den Dulk et al. 2012). 'Flexibility has been seen by unions as a management tool to increase flexibility of labour rather than improve the conditions for employees' (Ravenswood and Markry 2011: 489), which may explain the reluctance among unions to support the introduction of flexible work arrangements. However, unions are not only important partners regarding the adoption of state and workplace WLB support but also for increasing employee awareness of existing policies and entitlements (Ravenswood and Markey 2011; Haas and Hwang 2013).

In this section we discussed the existing research on workplace support in the context of state support. However, our focus is not on this relationship per se. Our main interest here is to know where the most support can be found for working parents' capabilities, taking state support as well as organizational support into account. In what contexts do working parents have most capabilities to achieve WLB?

Identifying High Capability Contexts

To examine contexts in which working parents have the most capabilities to achieve WLB, we analysed *Establishment Survey on Working Time and Work–Life Balance 2004–2005* (ESWT) data collected on behalf of the European Foundation for the Improvement of Living and Working Conditions. The ESWT is the only representative data set that offers information on various types of workplace worklife policies in different European countries. Unfortunately, the latest Establishment survey conducted in 2009–10 does not contain data on childcare support and extra leave arrangements, and only limited information on flexible work arrangements. Therefore the ESWT survey conducted in 2004–05 was the most suitable data set to investigate the level and nature of workplace policies in relation to state support within Europe. In total 21 European member states and 21,031 organizations with ten or more employees participated in the project.

Following the capabilities perspective in this chapter we conducted a cluster analysis on the ESWT data set to identify organizational settings that are homogeneous with respect to the capabilities of employees to achieve a good worklife balance. Following the assumption that employees have the most capabilities in a work setting where both state and organizational WLB support are high, the clustering was based on three variables: leave and childcare policies, flexible work arrangements, and state support.

Within the ESWT survey, leave and childcare policies at the workplace were measured by including the following items: (1) allowing employees to use parental leave during the last three years; (2) long-term leave to take care of ill family members; (3) workplace crèche; (4) other forms of childcare support; and (5) support for domestic work (cleaning or shopping services). We gave a score of 1 for each policy as well as for letting employees use parental leave. The score for leave/childcare support within the workplace ranged between zero and five policies offered.

HR managers were asked whether the following flexible work policies were offered by their organization: (1) allowing part-time work according to employee wishes; (2) the possibility of changing from full-time to part-time employment for skilled work; (3) the possibility of changing from full-time to part-time employment for unskilled work; (4) flexible working hours; and (5) working time account (the possibility of saving hours amounting to a full day off). These are all employee-friendly forms of flexibility where the needs of employees are central rather than the needs of the organization, which is generally the case with employer-led flexible work practices (Fleetwood 2007). We gave a score of 1 for each policy the organization offered, except for the possibility for skilled and unskilled employees to change working hours where we gave each 0.5 (to give this policy a similar weight as the other policies). Thus the score for flexible work arrangements at the workplace ranged from 0 to 4 policies offered.

The variable 'state support' is based on the level of state support in 2004–05, when the data on workplace support were collected. The score representing the level of state support in 2004/05 is based on three components of worklife support as discussed earlier: public childcare provisions, parental leave arrangements, and the right to reduce working hours. We rated each country per component on a 4-point scale (high state support (4) to low state support (1)). We rated state support for childcare as high (4) when it generated high capabilities for working parents, that is included the right to a childcare place and high enrolment of children, both under 3 and older; as medium-high (3) when there was substantial enrolment (more than 30%) of children under 3 and older, indicating that parents in most cases were able to use public childcare if they wished to do so, but without a formal entitlement to childcare places (for instance, France and Belgium); as medium-low (2) when there was low coverage of the young age group, but substantial enrolment among children older than 3; and as low (1) when there was very limited public childcare for all age groups.

Regarding parental leave provisions, we took into account length of leave, payment, and leave for fathers, since these are all important conditions affecting the agency and capabilities of mothers and fathers to actually take-up leave (see also Chapter 2). We rated state support for leave as high (4) when it consisted of long, generously compensated leaves, including paternity leave and/or a specific 'daddy quota' for fathers; as medium-high (3) for long leave and leave for fathers, but with more minimal financial compensation; as medium-low support (2) for shorter leave periods, more unpaid leave, and/or the absence of specific leave for fathers; and as low (1) to indicate both the absence of parental and paternity leave.

Regarding flexible work arrangements, we focused on state regulations concerning the possibility of adjusting one's working hours in order to care for dependents or meet other responsibilities. We rated state support for flexible work arrangements as high (4) to refer to the entitlement for all workers to extend or reduce working hours (as is the case in the Netherlands); as medium-high (3) to indicate the presence of an entitlement for working parents to reduce working hours when they have young children (for instance Sweden); as medium-low (2) to indicate a right to *request* reduction of working hours; and as low (1) to reflect the absence of a specific entitlement for workers or only regulations that stimulate employers. All three scores were summated. The state support scores thus ranged from 3 (low) to 12 (high). We used the two-step clustering procedure in SPSS, which is particularly useful for large data sets. This involves a first step of assigning cases to pre-clusters and a second step of hierarchical clustering of the pre-clusters. We arrived at a two-cluster solution that fit the data reasonably well and that could be meaningfully interpreted. The average silhouette width, a measure of cluster cohesion and separation, was 0.5, which means that the clustering of organizations could be considered reasonable. The two-cluster solution distinguishes one cluster of organizations with a high level of capabilities for working parents (high score on all three types of support) from a cluster with limited capabilities (organizations that score low on state and the two types of workplace support). Within the high capabilities cluster, organizations had on average two flexible work arrangements and almost three leave/childcare policies, with the level of state support 8.4. In contrast, organizations in the low capability cluster had on average less than one flexible work arrangement and around one leave/childcare arrangement. State support was also lower in this cluster (7.2).

When considering the division of organizations across countries and welfare state regimes, Figure 6.1 shows that almost all organizations in the social

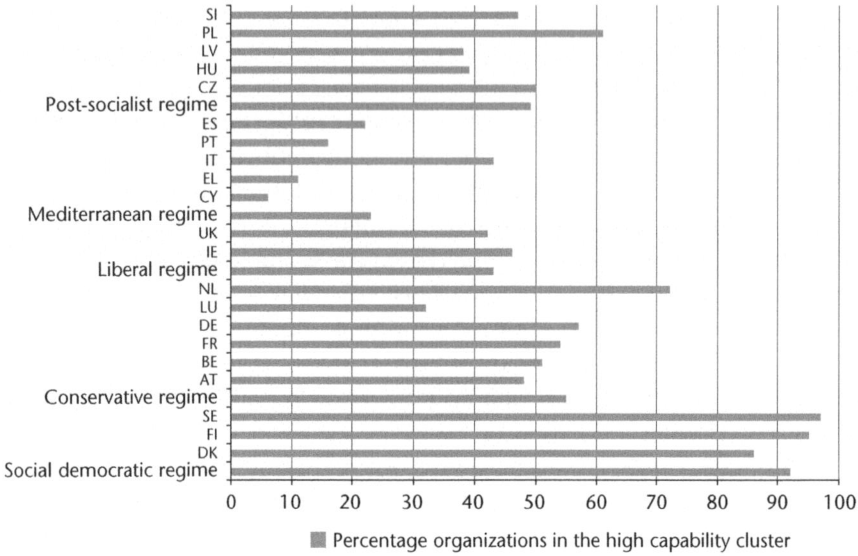

AT=Austria	EL=Greece	IE=Ireland	PL=Poland
BE=Belgium	ES=Spain	IT=Italy	PT=Portugal
CY=Cyprus	FI=Finland	LU=Luxembourg	SE=Sweden
CZ=Czech Republic	FR=France	LV=Latvia	SI=Slovenia
DE=Germany	HU=Hungary	NL=Netherlands	UK=United Kingdom
DK=Denmark			

Figure 6.1 Percentage of organizations in the high capabilities cluster

democratic regime (92%) are located in the high capability cluster. In contrast, the majority of organizations in the Mediterranean regime are found in the low capability cluster (77%). In the liberal regime, 43% of organizations are in the high capability cluster, compared with 55% in the conservative regime and 49% in the post-socialist regime. A Chi-square test showed that the differences between regime types are statistically significant. Nevertheless, differences between countries within regime types are also there to be seen. Within the conservative regime, Dutch organizations stand out with a relatively high score on state support because of the right of all workers to reduce or extend working hours, and a relatively high score on workplace arrangements regarding childcare and leave.

Figures 6.2 and 6.3 present the percentage of organizations belonging in the high capabilities cluster by sector, size, and proportion of female employees. Public sector organizations fall relatively more often in the high capability cluster (65%) compared with private sector organizations (45%). The extent

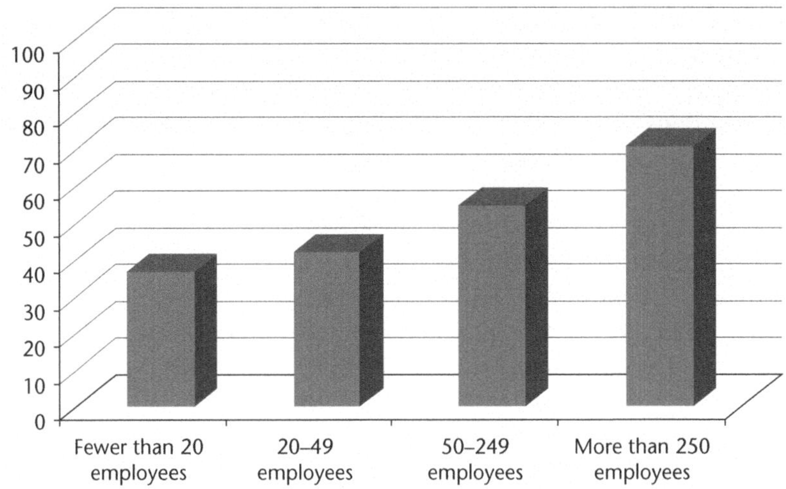

Figure 6.2 Percentage of organizations in the high capabilities cluster by size

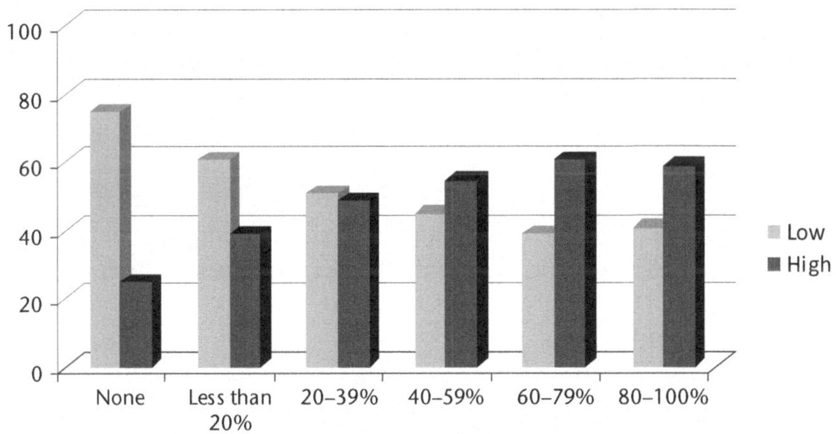

Figure 6.3 Percentage of organizations in the low and high capabilities cluster by proportion of women

to which employees have capabilities to achieve a good worklife balance is positively associated with the size of the organization. Finally, a relationship can be observed between capabilities and the proportion of women in an organization; with a workforce of up to 80% women, capabilities increase with the share of women in the organization. All observed differences are statistically significant.

To check whether the associations between organizational characteristics and the two clusters hold when conducting multivariate analysis we performed logistic regression analyses, using cluster as the dependent variable. This analysis confirms that employees living in social democratic welfare states, who are employed in the public sector, in large organizations, and in organizations with a relatively large share of female employees, experience the highest capabilities (findings not shown).

Conclusions and Discussion

Existing research tends to concentrate on the number of worklife policies adopted by organizations in relation to the public provisions present in a country. However, few studies look into the accumulation of state and workplace support and none so far have taken a capabilities approach. This chapter applied a capabilities approach (as shown in Figure 1.1, Introduction) to examine in what countries and workplace contexts working parents have the most capabilities and agency freedoms to achieve a WLB. Taking into account both state and workplace policy support, we found that employees working in public sector organizations, large organizations, organizations with a large proportion of women (up to 80%), and organizations operating in social democratic welfare states (Sweden, Finland, and Denmark) have the most capabilities in terms of policy measures. This finding confirms existing research showing that size, being public sector, and proportion of women (up to a certain level) are positively associated with the adoption of worklife policies and arrangements. Research also shows that the generous level of public policies for working parents in social democratic welfare states such as Sweden, Denmark, and Finland is closely followed by some of the post-socialist countries.

The capabilities approach clearly revealed some of the gaps in the existing research. First, most research simply looks at the number of policies offered either by the state or by organizations. This shows that organizations differ in the number of policies they have within and across countries (Goodstein 1994; Ingram and Simons 1995; den Dulk 2001; Poelmans et al. 2003; Remery et al. 2003; den Dulk et al. 2010). Although relevant, this does not tell us much about the capabilities of working parents. It is important to take into account how workplace policies are structured and formulated, and how they are embedded in the organizational and larger societal context. For instance, how do policies at different levels complement each other? Organizations can supplement public provisions by enhancing existing state policies (for instance by offering longer leave or increasing financial compensation) or complement public provisions by offering *different types* of policies, such as flexible working hours or a working time account. Supplementing existing provisions signals that the organization considers WLB an important topic that they are willing to support, which is an important conversion factor. However, the introduction of *different types* of policies, that is, complementation of public provisions by adopting policies and arrangements not offered by national government, should significantly increase the capabilities of working parents since it increases the number of options parents can choose from. Hence, research that investigates the relation between state and workplace policies should take into account the types of policies introduced and not only the number of policies. The first attempts that do take into account the types of policies introduced indicate that in the social democratic regime, in which the state takes a large share of the responsibility for supporting WLB, organizations tend to offer less support although they do not completely withdraw. Rather, they complement public provisions in those areas in which state support is less salient, such as flexible work arrangements (den Dulk et al. 2012).

Second, despite the fact that research indicates that it is important to investigate the interaction between state and workplace policies for the capabilities of working parents, cross-national data sets that allow such an examination are limited. Currently, the ESTW data collected in 2004–05 is the most suitable data set in Europe. The latest Establishment survey conducted in 2009–10 focuses on different topics and does not repeat the questions on different types of WLB policies. Also, other cross-national data sets, such as the Cranfield Network on Comparative Human Resource Management Survey (CRANET), which collects data at the organizational level, vary their survey questions and in recent years have tended to pay less attention to leave and childcare support issues. Consequently, despite the fact that WLB support is a dynamic, changing policy area in which many developments are to be witnessed, we lack data to map trends and developments regarding different types of workplace support and their interaction with state support.

Third, we need to monitor not only the development of workplace support in relation to public provisions, but also to collect detailed information on how public and workplace provisions are converted into capabilities and agency freedom to achieve a WLB. Data are needed about eligibility conditions and actual take-up both at the national level and within organizations. So far, information on these two issues is both limited across and within countries, making cross-national comparisons and comparisons between different groups of employees impossible (Moss 2012).

Finally, data are needed on existing workplace organizational cultures, to know whether the organizational culture conflicts or supports the take-up of policies (Thompson et al. 1999; see also other chapters in the volume). Currently, the ESTW 2004–05 contains one question only hinting at organization culture and that is whether the organization considers the WLB of its employees an organizational task (see Chapter 7 in this volume). This is a very limited indicator and might more reflect the attitude of the HR manager who answered the survey than describe the culture itself. Future research needs to try and incorporate a more extensive measure of organizational culture.

The following chapters address some of the gaps indicated. The chapter by Fagan and Walthery (Chapter 7) discusses flexible work arrangements in terms of eligibility criteria across countries and workplaces, and shows to what extent employees in diverse organization and country contexts are able to adapt their working hours from full-time to part-time or the other way round. Chapters 8 and 9 show how work-intensification trends prevent employees from taking up policies. More specifically, Chapter 8 focuses on the managerial discourse in organizations and its effect on the capabilities of working parents to make claims for WLB.

This chapter has shown that state and workplace policy support interact and that there is inequality in the capabilities of working parents to balance work and family life both between countries and in firms within them. Thus, inequality in access to worklife balance support is dependent on where people live and work.

Bibliography

Abendroth, A. and L. den Dulk (2011). Work–Life Balance Support in Europe: The Impact of the State, Workplace and Family Support on Work–Life Balance Satisfaction. *Work, Employment & Society*, 25(2):234–56.

Allen, T.D. (2001), Family Supportive Work Environments: The Role of Organizational Perceptions. *Journal of Vocational Behavior*, 58:414–35.

Antonnen, A., and J. Sipilä (1996). European Social Care Services: Is it Possible to Identify Models? *Journal of European Social Policy*, 6:87–100.

Anxo, D., C. Fagan, M. Smith, M.T. Letablier, and C. Perraudin (2007). *Parental Leave in European Companies*. Dublin: European Foundation for the Improvement of Living and Working Conditions.

Appelbaum, E., T. Bailey, P. Berg, and A. Kalleberg (2005). Organizations and the Intersection of Work and Family: A Comparative Perspective, in S. Ackroyd, R. Batt, P. Thompson, and P. Tolbert (eds), *The Oxford Handbook of Work and Organizations*, pp. 52–73. Oxford/New York. Oxford University Press.

Auerbach, J.D. (1990). Employer Supported Childcare as a Women-Responsive Policy. *Journal of Family Issues*, 11:384–400.

Bardoel, A.E., P. Tharenou, and S.A. Moss (1999). Organizational Predictors of Work–Family Practices. *Asia Pacific Journal of Human Resources*, 38(3):31–49.

Behson, S.J. (2005). The Relative Contribution of Formal and Informal Organizational Work–Family Support. *Journal of Vocational Behavior*, 66:487–500.

Blossfeld, H.P. and S. Drobnič (2001). *Careers of Couples in Contemporary Societies. From Male Breadwinner to Dual Earner Families*. Oxford: Oxford University Press.

Boye, K. (2011). Work and Well-being in a Comparative Perspective: The Role of Family Policy. *European Sociological Review*, 27(1):16–30.

DiMaggio, P.J. and W.W. Powell (1983). The Iron Cage Revisited: Institutional Isomorphism and Collective Rationality in Organizational Fields. *American Sociological Review*, 48:147–60.

Dobbin, F. and R. Sutton (1998). The Strength of a Weak State: The Rights Revolution and the Rise of Human Resources Management Divisions. *American Journal of Sociology*, 104(2):441–76.

Dulk, L. den (2001). *Work–Family Arrangements in Organizations: A Cross-national Study in the Netherlands, Italy, the United Kingdom and Sweden*. Amsterdam: Rozenberg.

Dulk, L. den and B. Peper (2009). *Managing Work–Life Policies in the European Workplace: Explorations for Future Research*. RECWOWE working paper 0409, RECWOWE Publication, Dissemination and Dialogue Centre: Edinburgh.

Dulk, L. den., P. Peters, E. Poutsma, and P.E.M. Ligthart (2010). The Extended Business Case for Childcare and Leave Arrangements in Western and Eastern Europe. *Baltic Journal of Management*, 4(2):156–84.

Dulk, L. den, P. Peters, and E. Poutsma (2012). Variations in Adoption of Workplace Work–Family Arrangements in Europe: The Influence of Welfare-state Regime and Organizational Characteristics. *International Journal of Human Resource Management*, 23(13):2785–808.

Dulk, L. den and S. Groeneveld (2012). Work–Life Balance Support in the Public Sector in Europe. *Review of Public Personnel Administration*, Online publication <http://dx.doi.org/10.1177/0734371X12449024>.

Dulk, L. den, S. Groeneveld, A. Ollier-Malaterre, and M. Valcour (2013). National Context in Work-life Research: A Multi-level Cross-national Analysis of the Adoption of Work-life Policies by Employers in Europe. *European Management Journal*, Online publication: <http://dx.doi.org/10.1016/j.emj.2013.04.010>.

Esping-Andersen, G. (1990). *The Three Worlds of Welfare Capitalism*. Cambridge: Polity Press.

Esping-Andersen, G. (1999). *Social Foundations of Postindustrial Economies*. New York: Oxford University Press.

Evans, J.M. (2001). *Firms' Contribution to the Reconciliation between Work and Family Life*, No. 48, OECD, Paris.

Ferrarini, T. (2006). *Families, States and Labour Markets: Institutions, Causes and Consequences of Family Policy in Post-war Welfare States*. Cheltenham: Edward Elgar Publishing.

Ferrarini, T. and O. Sjöberg (2010). Social Policy and Health: Transition Countries in a Comparative Perspective. *International Journal of Social Welfare*, 19:S60–S88.

Fleetwood, S. (2007). Why Work–Life Balance Now? *International Journal Human Resource Management*, 18(3):387–400.

Glass, J.L. and T. Fujimoto (1995). Employers Characteristics and the Provision of Family Responsive Policies. *Work and Occupation*, 22(4):380–411.

Goodstein, J.D. (1994). Institutional Pressure and Strategic Responsiveness: Employer Involvement in Work–Family Issues. *Academy of management Journal*, 37:350–82.

Gornick, J.C. and M.K. Meyers (2003). *Families that Work: Policies for Reconciling Parenthood and Employment*. New York: Russell Sage Foundation.

Haas, L. and P. Hwang (2013). Trade Union Support for Fathers' Use of Work–family Benefits: Lessons from Sweden. *Community, Work and Family*, 16(1):46–67.

Hantrais, L. and P. Ackers (2005). Women's Choices in Europe: Striking the Work–Life Balance. *European Journal of Industrial Relations*, 11:197–212.

Ingram, P. and T. Simons (1995). Institutional and Resource Dependence Determinants of Responsiveness to Work–family Issues. *Academy of Management Journal*, 38:1466–82.

Kocourková, J. (2002). Leave Arrangements and Childcare Services in Central Europe: Policies and Practices Before and After the Transition. *Community, Work and Family*, 5(3):301–18.

Korpi, W. (2000). Faces of Inequality: Gender, Class, and Patterns of Inequalities in Different Types of Welfare States. *Social Politics*, 7(2):127–91.

Kossek, E.E. (2005). Workplace Policies and Practices to Support Work and Families, in S. Bianchi, L. Casper, and R. King (eds), *Work, Family, Health, and Well-Being*, pp. 97–116. Hillsdale: Erlbaum Press.

Kossek, E.E., S. Lewis, and L. Hammer (2010). Work–Life Initiatives and Organizational Change: Overcoming Mixed Messages to Move from the Margin to the Mainstream. *Human Relations*, 63:1–17.

Lee, B.H. and J.S. Kim (2010). Is Family-Friendly Management Good for Firms? The Diffusion and Performance of Family-Friendly Workplaces in South Korea. *Journal of Industrial Relations*, 52:459–75.

Lewis, J. (1992). Gender and the Development of Welfare Regimes. *Journal of European Social Policy*, 2:159–73.

Lewis, S. (1997). An International Perspective on Work–Family Issues, in S. Parasurama and J.H. Greenhaus (eds), *Integrating Work and Family Challenges and Choices for a Changing World*, pp. 91–103. Westport: Quorum Books.

Lewis S., J. Brannen, and A. Nilsen (2009) (eds), *Work, Families and Organisations in Transition: European Perspectives*. The Policy Press: Bristol.

Lewis, S. and L. Smithson (2001). Sense of Entitlement to Support for the Reconciliation of Employment and Family Life. *Human Relations*, 54:1455–81.

Lyness, K.S. and M. Brumit Kropf (2005). The Relationships of National Gender Equality and Organizational Support with Work–Family Balance: A Study of European Managers. *Human Relations*, 58(1):33–60.

Moss, P. (2012) (ed.). *International Review of Leave Policies and Related Research 2012*. International Network on Leave Policies and Research. London: Institute of Education, University of London.

Nilsen, A., J. Brannen, and S. Lewis (2012). *Transition to Parenthood in Europe. A Comparative Life Course Perspective*. Bristol: The Policy Press.

OECD. (2001). Balancing Work and Family Life: Helping Parents into Paid Employment. *OECD Employment Outlook*, pp. 29–166. Paris: OECD.

Ollier-Malaterre, A. (2009). Organizational Work–Life Initiatives: Context Matters. France Compared to the UK and the US. *Community, Work & Family*, 12(2):159–78.

Orloff, A.S. (1993). Gender and the Social Rights of Citizenship, the Comparative Analysis of Gender Relations and Welfare States. *American Sociological Review*, 58:303–28.

Pascall, G. and N. Manning (2000). Gender and Social Policy: Comparing Welfare States in Central and Eastern Europe and the Former Soviet Union. *Journal of European Social Policy*, 10(3):240–66.

Plantenga, J. and A. van Doorne-Huiskes (1993). Verschillen in arbeidsparticipatie van vrouwen in Europa, de rol van verzorgingsstaten. *Tijdschrift voor Arbeidsvraagstukken*, 9(1):51–65.

Poelmans, S.A.Y., N. Chinchilla, and P. Cardona (2003). The Adoption of Family-Friendly HRM Policies: Competing for Scarce Resources in the Labor Market. *International Journal of Manpower*, 24(2):128–47.

Poelmans, S.A.Y., P.E. Spector, C.L. Cooper, T.D. Allen, M. O'Driscoll, and J.L. Sanchez (2003). A Cross-national Comparative Study of Work/Family Demands and Resources. *International Journal of Cross-Cultural Management*, 3:275–88.

Poelmans S.A.Y. and K. Sahibzada (2004). A Multi-level Model for Studying the Context and Impact of Work–Family Policies and Culture in Organizations. *Human Resource Management Review*, 14:409–31.

Poelmans, S.A.Y. (2005). *Work and Family: An International Research Perspective*. New Jersey: Lawrence Erlbaum Associates.

Ravenswood, K. and R. Markey (2011). The Role of Unions in Achieving a Family-Friendly Workplace. *Journal of Industrial Relations*, 53:486–503.

Remery, C., A. van Doorne-Huiskes, and J. Schippers (2003). Family-Friendly Policies in The Netherlands: The Tripartite Involvement, *Personnel Review*, 32(4):456–73.

Sainsbury, S. (1996). *Gender, Equality and Welfare States*. Cambridge: Cambridge University Press.

Scott, W.R. (1995). *Institutions and Organizations*. Thousand Oaks: Sage Publications.

Spector, P.E., T.D. Allen, S. Poelmans, L.M. Lapierre, et al. (2007). Cross-national Differences in Relationships of Work Demands, Job Satisfaction and Turnover Intentions with Work–Family Conflict. *Personnel Psychology*, 60: 805–35.

Tang, N. and C. Cousins (2005). Working Time, Gender and Family: An East-West European Comparison. *Gender, Work and Organization*, 12: 527–50.

Thompson, C.A., L.L. Beauvais, and K.S. Lyness (1999). When Work–Family Benefits are not Enough: The Influence of Work-family Culture on Benefit Utilization, Organizational Attachment, and Work–Family Conflict. *Journal of Vocational Behavior*, 54:392–415.

Yerkes, M. and K. Tijdens (2010). Social Risk Protection in Collective Agreements: Evidence from the Netherlands. *European Journal of Industrial Relations*, 16: 369–82.

7

Working time capabilities at the workplace: individual adjustment options between full-time and part-time working in European firms[1]

Colette Fagan and Pierre Walthery

Introduction

Part-time employment has increased in many European labour markets. While the rate of part-time work varies nationally, the common and dominant feature is that the majority of part-time workers are women, which stems from gender inequalities in family roles. In most countries the main reason women take part-time employment is that it is one way of balancing the time demands of employment with responsibilities for housework and providing care for children and elders. Women are also employed part-time for other reasons—on an involuntary basis because they could not find full-time employment, or they are students, or suffer ill-health—but in every country they are more likely than men to take part-time employment because of family care responsibilities. The rate of part-time working for men has been rising but the pattern of engagement remains gendered. Male part-time employment is concentrated among students and older workers approaching retirement, and is rarely due to care responsibilities during the core working years.

While some emphasize that the opportunity for part-time employment can enhance work–family balance, others argue that it perpetuates gender inequalities in employment and at home. In the 'individualized choice' camp are those who consider the gendered pattern of part-time employment to be largely unproblematic. Here are the neoclassical economists who contend that the decision to work part-time is a labour market choice that takes into account individual human capital and time-use preferences, often within a household decision-making process where the gendered division of labour is presented as a rational and efficient form of specialization (Becker 1981). In support of this interpretation, attention is drawn to the regular empirical finding that proportionately fewer women than men report that their part-time work is involuntary due to being unable to secure a full-time job. A similar explanatory emphasis on individual choice is made in Hakim's (2000) sociological preference theory: in modern liberal societies women are able to choose between a family-oriented or career-oriented lifestyle and if family-oriented they are more likely to choose part-time employment or labour market exits rather than a full-time continuous employment trajectory.

The 'constrained choice' camp deploy a more structural account of why women engage in part-time employment; influenced *inter alia* by feminist perspectives on gender relations and labour market segmentation theory (see for example, O'Reilly and Fagan 1998; McRae 2003; Duncan 2006; Perrons et al. 2006). Within this perspective there is more emphasis on the constrained nature of women's choices and the poor quality of many of the part-time jobs on offer: part-time work is chosen in a context where work–family reconciliation options are limited by gender inequalities within the family and shortfalls in public care services. Furthermore, questions about working time preferences reveal a more nuanced picture than identifying voluntary and involuntary part-timers: in industrialized countries sizeable proportions of women employed part-time want to work longer part-time hours or to switch to full-time arrangements (Fagan 2004).

There is less contention about the quality of part-time jobs than the reasons why women work part-time. Part-time jobs are disproportionately concentrated in the lower-skilled, low-paid parts of the economy. Where part-time employment exists in higher status jobs it is concentrated in the lower career grades of feminized professions (Blossfeld and Hakim 1997; O'Reilly and Fagan 1998; Burchell et al. 2007). Thus, in its current form, part-time employment for women tends to fuel gender segregated employment patterns and the gender wage gap (Rubery 2005; Smith 2005; Plantenga and Remery 2010). Women who work part-time rather than full-time are frequently penalized for making this decision: some in terms of downward mobility into a poorer quality job with lower rates of pay, and others by becoming stuck at lower career grades because full-time working is expected at higher grades (e.g. Crompton and Birkelund 2000). This penalty is more severe in some countries than others. For example, in the UK the average hourly pay of part-timers is substantially lower than that for full-timers, but this is not the case in the Netherlands (Yerkes and Visser 2006). Furthermore, in the UK a period of part-time work has a negative impact on the subsequent trajectory of employment and earnings progression—a so-called scarring effect—even for those who have subsequently moved into full-time employment (Francesconi and Gosling 2005).

Thus, part-time employment can be a means for individuals to increase their so-called 'worklife balance' but at the cost of reduced earnings and more limited options for advancement in the labour market, and where a spell of part-time work can reduce opportunities for moving into full-time employment at a later stage in the working life. Both strands of this 'choice' and 'constraint' debate are reflected in the European Commission's employment policy initiated by the Lisbon Summit. Part-time work is promoted as a work–family reconciliation measure and means of integrating more women into employment while also being an input for innovation in work organization and production systems (CEC 2003, 2004). Yet, in resonance with the constrained choice perspective, there is also mention of the need to improve the quality of part-time work by diversifying the range of jobs in which it is available, integrating part-time work into social protection arrangements, and increasing childcare to widen reconciliation options (CEC 2006, 2007). This policy approach to part-time employment is retained in the 'Europe 2020' employment strategy and associated guidelines (European Commission 2010; Council of the European Union 2010). This is in tune with the growing awareness of the need for a life course perspective in policy design in order to support transitions between non-employment, part-time and full-time working at different stages across the working life to accommodate caring responsibilities, periods of further education, and training as part of the 'lifelong learning' agenda; and a more gradual and later transition to retirement to contribute to a reformed financing of pension systems (O'Reilly et al. 2000; Anxo et al. 2007a, b; Schmid 2008).

Employees' capabilities to make transitions between full-time and part-time working arrangements are enhanced if there is scope to negotiate an individual adjustment between full-time and part-time working hours at their workplace. Such negotiations may also provide a lever for opening up options for part-time working in different occupations or at higher grades and thus contribute to diversifying the range of jobs in which part-time work occurs. Whether such adjustments are feasible depends on employers' policies and practices towards part-time work. The employer may have a formal policy or a *de facto* practice that enables individual adjustments between full-time and part-time working, perhaps as a result of collective bargaining or to redress recruitment and retention problems. The employers' response will depend on operational needs, such as whether there are skill shortages to redress, vacancies to fill, or workforce cuts to be made. In some countries the employer is operating in a legal framework that provides employees with a 'right to request' a reduction to part-time hours, and more rarely a right to request an increase to full-time hours, and the employer is obliged to consider this request.

In this chapter we focus on the policy implemented at the organizational level by employers, using a working time capability framework to guide the analysis. We assess what proportions of European firms operate different types of policy, ranging from 'full reversibility' between full-time and part-time working for all employees through to no adjustments for anyone, and the firm-level characteristics associated with each type of policy. The results reveal marked variation in employer policy across countries and within countries. We argue that state policy clearly matters but that the type of policy operated by employers is also shaped by firm-level characteristics, and other situational features also impact on the social conversion factors that shape an individual's working time capability. The sector, establishment size, presence of a trade union, and gender and skill composition of the workforce all have a significant influence on whether employers permit individual-level working time adjustments. The firm's organizational working time practices and culture towards safeguarding worklife balance (hereafter referred to as WLB) have an additional and independent effect, as do broader aspects of working time scheduling in place. The implications of these results are discussed in the concluding section.

Part-Time Work and Working Time Capabilities in European Countries

A working time capability framework (Lee and McCann 2006) helps advance the debate about choice and constraint in relation to part-time work because it focuses on analysing the feasible options from which an individual can select when determining their working time arrangements: what is genuinely possible rather than what may be possible in principle from the abstract concept of individual free choice. Lee and McCann draw on Sen's (1999) concept of capability, which expresses this in terms of the substantive freedom of an individual to choose between feasible alternative functionings—or ways of doing things; in other words the real options open to them—which are shaped by the social conversion factors of institutions and social norms. Hence, in the capabilities framework, a mother who works part-time because this is the only way in which she can earn a living and raise her children is in a different position to a mother who has selected part-time employment from a range of feasible working time and childcare arrangements. As Lee and McCann (2006: 67–68) note, the capability framework differs from mainstream economics and preference theory in two important ways. Whereas mainstream economics and preference theory concentrate on the labour supply outcome as a 'choice', the capabilities approach foregrounds the options from which this choice was selected. It is concerned with 'the opportunities given to workers to choose and change their working time so as to improve the quality of their lives' (Lee and McCann, 2006: 67). Second, the capability framework does not assume that the labour market adjusts effectively to ensure a correspondence is reached between actual and preferred hours of work. Instead, the focus on conversion factors suggests that the individual capacity set for many people is much smaller than that assumed in the utility-maximizing language of mainstream economics. Finally, the capability framework is a means for embedding a life course perspective into employment and social policy debates because of the focus it brings to the social conversion factors—the social institutions and norms—that enable individuals to move between different working time arrangements as circumstances and preferences change.

At a fundamental level, an individual's capability to secure part-time employment will be affected by whether this form of employment is already widespread practice in the labour market. In some countries, part-time employment is a common undertaking for women, particularly those with care responsibilities, while in others full-time employment is the norm for women. The amount and quality of part-time employment varies across countries and this has emerged historically due to the interplay of state policy in relation to employment and welfare systems, the actions and negotiations of employers and unions, and cultural differences in the organization of family life and gender roles or the 'gender regime' (O'Reilly and Fagan 1998).

A key issue from a capability perspective is whether there are social conversion factors in place that enable employees to make an individual adjustment between full-time and part-time hours while remaining with their employer in the same or similar job; and if there is scope to reverse this adjustment at a later stage (Fagan 1999; Anxo et al. 2007c). In such conditions employees can switch to part-time hours without searching the labour market for a part-time position. This provides some protection against occupational downgrading and has the potential to widen the range and quality of jobs in which part-time working can be secured. Such options enhance employees' capabilities to balance care responsibilities with employment, which is particularly relevant for women given they do most of the care, but such policies also increase men's capabilities to make adjustments as a means of becoming more involved in care responsibilities. For example, the introduction of the legal 'right to request' reduced or flexible hours in the UK has resulted in fathers using this new social right to negotiate such adjustments with their employers, even if the proportion of fathers who make use of this right is lower than the take-up by mothers and few fathers request part-time arrangements in contrast to mothers (Fagan et al. 2006). Policies that enhance the capability for individuals to make smooth transitions between full-time and part-time hours are also likely to become of growing importance as part of the policy agenda for prolonging the working life of older workers, and for helping to create more stable pathways into full-time employment for young people who enter the labour market via a part-time position.

Individual capabilities to adjust working hours are shaped at multiple levels of society: through state policies, through policies and practices devised at the workplace, and at the household level. The *state's regulatory framework* plays a key role in shaping national working time arrangements; particularly the number of hours worked by full-timers, but also the development and organization of part-time employment (Bosch et al. 1994; Rubery et al. 1998; Messenger 2004). State policies also have a major impact on the availability, quality, and affordability of childcare and eldercare services, which shapes the working time decisions of women with care responsibilities.

Statutory provisions for individual-level adjustments to working hours vary. In quite a few European countries the statutory parental leave scheme provides eligible parents with a right to work reduced or part-time hours until the child reaches a given age (typically between 3 and 6 years old). In a few countries there is an employee right to request an individual adjustment to working hours (see Fagan and Walthery 2007; Kamerman and Moss 2009; Plantenga and Remery 2010). The detail, efficacy, and usage of these provisions vary across countries in important ways; here we highlight some key examples. In Sweden, the comprehensive parental leave scheme includes options for part-time employment and in addition parents have a right to reduce their working hours until their child starts school. The Dutch legislation provides all employees with the right to request a switch to part-time or full-time hours, thus permitting individuals to move from full-time to part-time and back to full-time at a later stage, or what is termed 'full reversibility'. Variations on this right to request, which give a weaker entitlement and are narrower in scope, exist in Germany and the UK. In Germany the employee right to request is only for a reduction from full-time to part-time working hours; while in the UK the right to request is for part-time or flexible working hours, is restricted to employees with dependent children or adult care responsibilities, and the legal redress is much weaker than in the Dutch system (Fagan et al. 2006). A different approach is taken in the Belgian statutory time credit and career break scheme, which provides some employees with opportunities to switch to part-time hours.

Within the national framework the policy and practices devised at the *organizational (employer) level* are pivotal for shaping individuals' capabilities to adjust their working hours. Some employers may not comply fully in implementing statutory requirements; others may operate a policy which enhances employees' statutory rights. Collective bargaining arrangements are also important. For example, the majority of employees are covered by collective agreements in the Nordic countries, Belgium, the Netherlands, Austria, and Germany, and where bargaining on working time is well-developed. In contrast, less than a quarter of employees are covered by collective bargaining in the UK, Hungary, and the Baltic States (Visser 2011; OECD 2012).

Sector- and firm-level cross-national studies show that the working time practices of a firm are shaped both by the 'country' effect of national policies and the 'sector' effect of operating requirements, market conditions, and collective agreements (e.g. Rubery et al. 1998; Bosch and Lehndorff 2005; Anxo et al. 2007c). There are three main reasons why employers create part-time jobs: as 'secondary worker', 'optimal staffing', or 'accommodation' strategies (O'Reilly and Fagan 1998; Allart and Bellman 2005). The first two are when part-time jobs are created mainly for operational reasons of flexibility; either to obtain cheap and flexible labour (a segmented secondary workers strategy) or to provide a more efficient way of covering extended operating hours or workload variations across the day or week (optimal staffing strategy). The third accommodation strategy is where part-time employment is part of a recruitment and retention strategy of promoting WLB or work–family reconciliation in response to the preferences or availability of employees (e.g. parents, older workers, student labour). Policies that give employees rights to request adjustments to their working-hours can be expected to nurture an accommodation emphasis in a firms' policy towards part-time working, but adjustments may also be feasible under the other two strategies.

Whether the right to request is a statutory entitlement or a voluntary workplace policy, the ability of an employee to convert this 'right' into a 'claim' will be influenced by the employers' judgement of their individual characteristics. An employee is more likely to have their request accepted if they have sought after skills, or are considered to be hard working or otherwise deserving, for example because of loyal service or gender stereotypical assumptions about men and women's family responsibilities.

Hence, the organizational working time culture created by regulations, policy, norms, and habitual practice is the setting in which an individual's working time capability is formed in articulation with the individual's household-level circumstances (material resources, norms and values, personal relationships and negotiations, etc.). A growing body of qualitative case study research has explored the meaning and role of organizational culture for employees' working time; including employees' decisions about whether to request reduced or part-time arrangements (see Lewis 1997, 2003; Crompton 2006; den Dulk and Spenkelink 2009; Chapter 6, this volume). Here, we use a European survey of companies to explore which types of firms permit individual employees to make adjustments between full-time and part-time working, including proxy measures for some aspects of organizational culture. We explore this from the perspective of the employer because the policy in place at the organizational level is one of the important social conversion factors that sets the environment, shaping whether employees feel able to request an adjustment, the type of negotiation that occurs between the employee and their line manager (and co-workers), and the outcome.

Research Questions and Data

Given that employers' policies at the organizational level are one important social conversion factor for enhancing employees' capabilities for negotiating an individual adjustment between full-time and part-time hours, we address three questions in our analysis. First, in Europe, what policies do employers operate with regard to individual-level adjustments between full-time and part-time working? Second, can this variation in employer policy be attributed to specific firm-level characteristics? We are particularly interested in exploring the influence of the organizational culture with regard to part-time work and 'worklife balance', collective representation by a trade union or works council, and whether the firm has been increasing or contracting its workforce; the latter being a particularly topical concern for debates about firms' restructuring strategies in the current economic recession. Third, are comparable firms more likely to permit adjustments if they are located in countries where there is national legislation or policy that gives employees rights to request individual level adjustments?

We use the European Establishment Survey on Working Time, which was launched in 2004–05 by Eurofound in order to provide the first representative European survey of companies[2] (Bielenski and Riedmann 2005). This survey asked human resource managers what the current practices in place were for three scenarios:

- If a skilled full-time worker requested a transfer to part-time work.
- If a low-skilled or unskilled full-time worker requested a transfer to part-time work.
- For companies with part-timers in the workforce: if a part-time worker requested full-time work.

The response options for all three questions were:

- He or she usually gets an appropriate full-time/part-time job quickly.
- He or she has to wait for some time.
- It would be possible only exceptionally.
- There is practically no chance.
- Does not apply/has never happened.

A couple of question design limitations should be noted. Skilled jobs were defined as jobs requiring a university degree, an apprenticeship, or any specific training. Such a wide definition potentially raises response issues since it encompasses a large number of heterogeneous occupations that may be offered different adjustment options in a wide variety of contexts. Second, while the question specified that the work should be an appropriate job in the same establishment, unfortunately it does not differentiate between those organizations where the adjustment is made to the same or similar job position and those where the adjustment entails moving to a lower level position or other reduction in job quality (such as switching to a fixed-term contract or other forms of increased insecurity). So, as is often the case with secondary data analysis, we have to work without these data refinements and recall them when interpreting results. Finally, part-time work was defined as working time arrangements below the usual full-time level, so this captures a reduction relative to the full-time norm at the workplace rather than an absolute threshold.

European Employers' Policies on Individual Working Time Adjustments

The general expansion in the rate of part-time employment across Europe since the early 1980s means that this working arrangement is now used by many employers. In this survey of establishments with ten or more employees, nearly one-quarter (24%) had at least one-fifth of their workforce employed part-time, and overall two-thirds (64%) employed at least one part-time worker. Not surprisingly, organizations were more likely to have part-time employees if they were located in countries with a high overall incidence of part-time work in the economy, but multivariate analysis confirmed that firm-level characteristics were also salient: part-time working is more common where the organizational workforce contains a high proportion of women, in the public sector, in service activities, in large establishments, those with extended operating hours and those which operated flexi-time or working time accounts (Anxo et al. 2007c).

Table 7.1 Reversibility policies operated in European establishments

Number of reversibility options available immediately or after some time	Companies with part-time staff	All companies
No reversibility	22.8	41.8
Limited adjustment—one option	23.7	17.8
Partial adjustment—two options	25.4	22.1
Full reversibility between full-time and part-time hours for all employees	28.1	18.3
Total	100	58.2

Notes: weighted proportions of companies allowing one or more reversibility options between full-time and part-time work immediately or after some time.

Key to the reversibility options:

[a] Transfer from full-time to part-time working permitted for skilled employees;
[b] Transfer from full-time to part-time working permitted for unskilled/low-skilled employees;
[c] Transfer from part-time to full-time working permitted for all part-time employees.

Source: European Survey on Working Time 2005.

Table 7.1 shows the type of individual working time adjustment policies in European establishments according to whether one, two, or three types of adjustment are possible: a reduction from full-time to part-time hours for skilled staff; a similar reduction for unskilled staff; a move from part-time to full-time work available to all workers. Nearly one-fifth of all employers (18.3%) and just over a quarter of those that had some part-time staff (28.1%) permit *full reversibility*; namely the personnel manger reports that it is possible for any individual employee to request to change their working hours from either full-time to part-time, or part-time to full-time, and to secure this adjustment either quickly or after some time. This includes 9% of establishments that meet the tighter criteria of permitting such movements to be made quickly (Anxo et al. 2007c).[3]

There are other firms that do not operate a policy of full reversibility but permit a *limited adjustment* (one option) or a *partial adjustment* (two options); so that overall more than three-quarters of employers with part-timers, and 58% of all employers, operate either limited adjustment, partial adjustment, or full reversibility policies.

Of the employers with part-time staff that offered a limited adjustment, just under half permitted all part-time employees to move to full-time work (47%). This suggests a rather basic policy whereby employees can increase their hours when there is a vacancy or other increase in labour demand. The other firms that employed part-timers and offered a limited adjustment were fairly evenly divided between those that permit a move from full-time to part-time work restricted to one category of employees; either skilled or low-skilled employees. These different personnel approaches may be connected to factors such as compositional differences in the skill profile of their workforce or recruitment/retention problems that vary by skill level.

The most common form of partial adjustment was for employers with part-time staff to permit all full-time employees to switch to part-time hours (46%). However, just over a third (35%) offered full reversibility for skilled employees, while low-skilled employees could only move from part-time to full-time hours. This implies a personnel strategy that offers full reversibility targeted at retaining skilled staff. Conversely, nearly one-fifth (19%) offered full reversibility to their low-skilled employees but only permitted their skilled employees to move from part-time to full-time arrangements. This latter personnel policy may reflect skill shortages, so that while full reversibility is possible for low-skilled employees, part-time employment is discouraged among skilled employees.

Despite a general expansion across Europe, part-time employment remains more common in some countries than others (Anxo et al. 2007c; Plantenga and Remery 2010). These national labour market differences are built from different patterns of usage of part-timers in firms, which is illustrated with the establishment survey data in Figure 7.1. This shows pronounced national differences in the proportion of firms with part-timers in their workforce. On the left-hand side of the graph are ten countries where more than 60% of firms employed at least one part-timer in 2005; led by the Netherlands where nearly 90% of establishments employ part-timers. In another six countries, between 40–60% of firms employed at least one part-timer, declining to less than one-fifth of employers in Greece and Portugal. Typically part-time employees represent less than 20% of the establishment workforce in most companies across Europe. However, the left-hand side of the graph shows that the countries where part-time work is widespread across establishments also have a higher proportion of employers with at least one-fifth of their workforce employed part-time; particularly in the Netherlands, Sweden, Germany, and the UK. This is likely to denote human resources management strategies designed to use part-time working for large parts of the establishments' operations, which may include reversibility provisions.

Figure 7.2 elaborates on this issue by exploring whether employers enable individual employees to make adjustments between working full-time and part-time, using the categories developed in Table 7.1. As in Figure 7.1, the countries are ranked according to the proportion of firms which have at least one part-timer in their workforce. It suggests that, in general, employers are more likely to operate policies that permit some adjustments between full-time and part-time working in countries where part-time work is an established, familiar practice in the economy. The causality may run either way: where employers have started to use part-time arrangements this may

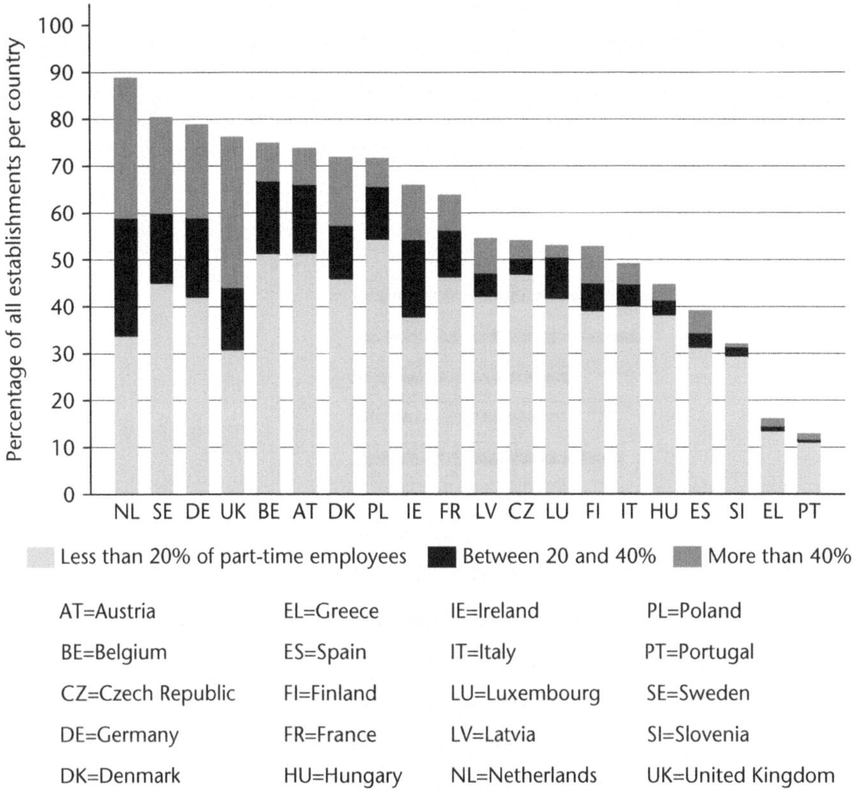

Figure 7.1 Prevalence of part-time work in European establishments in 2005

have stimulated the development of workplace policies to enable employees to adjust between full-time and part-time working; or the implementation of such policies may have nurtured an expansion of part-time arrangements. In the examples of the UK and the Netherlands, at least, the scope for individual employees to adjust between full-time and part-time working emerged in workplaces in advance of statutory provision, with the Dutch legislation stimulated by widespread collective negotiation on this topic (Yerkes and Visser 2006).

Figure 7.2 also illustrates the pronounced variations across European countries in the adjustment policy operated by employers, both between and within countries. It is particularly uncommon for employers to offer reversibility or other adjustments in five countries: Portugal, Greece, Hungary, Slovenia, and Cyprus. The figure suggests that state policy has some effect, as the countries with national policy frameworks that have established rights for employees to request an adjustment to part-time hours—Sweden, the Netherlands, the UK, Germany, and Belgium as discussed above—have more

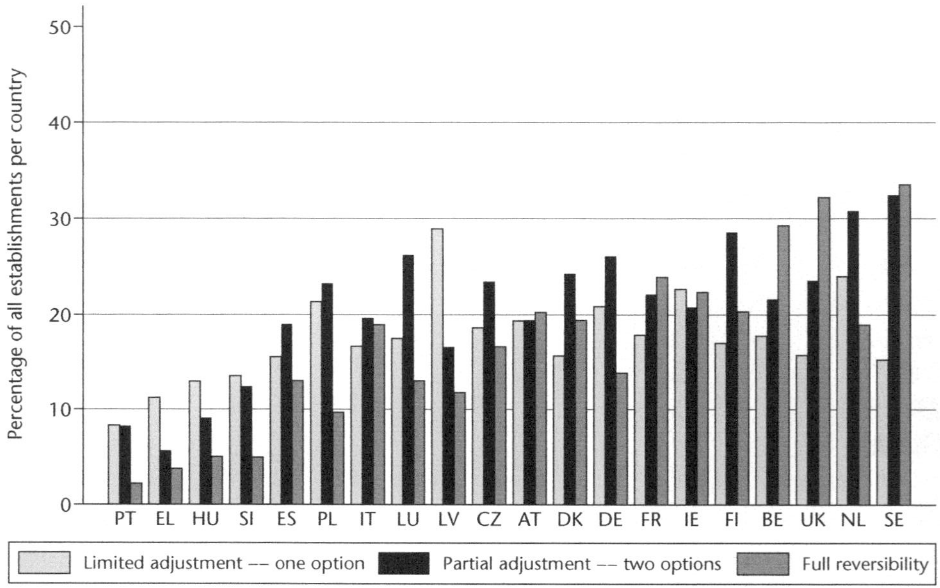

AT=Austria
BE=Belgium
CZ=Czech Republic
DE=Germany
DK=Denmark
EL=Greece
ES=Spain
FI=Finland
FR=France
HU=Hungary
IE=Ireland
IT=Italy
LU=Luxembourg
LV=Latvia
NL=Netherlands
PL=Poland
PT=Portugal
SE=Sweden
SI=Slovenia
UK=United Kingdom

Figure 7.2 Prevalence of working time reversibility in European establishments

firms operating some form of reversibility policy than is the case for many of the other countries shown. Thus, full reversibility is most common in firms in Sweden, the UK, and Belgium. However, while the Netherlands has legislation that permits full reversibility, the proportion of employers that report this as possible is lower. Furthermore, there is variation in what is offered by firms within each national context, whether it is Greece, France, or Germany, for example, which indicates that factors other than legislation or the prevalence of part-time working in the economy are also at play.

The exploratory analysis in this section has demonstrated the variation in the extent and type of individual working time adjustment policies operating in firms. While some relationship with the national policy framework can be discerned, the relationship is not straightforward for other characteristics and situational conditions also shape employers' policy and behaviour. This is explored in the next step in the analysis.

Which Type of Individual Working Time Adjustment Policy is Operated by Which Employers?

To advance our understanding of which types of organizations offer which options for working time adjustments to their employees to enhance their working time capabilities, we must bring additional variables into the picture that we suspect influence employers' behaviour; namely other features of the organization and its workforce. The first step is to identify a limited number of discrete profiles capturing the most typical policies on adjustments between full-time and part-time working operated by firms, by building four variables. Three variables that were explained in Section 2 measure whether the employer permits: (a) their skilled employees to move from full-time to part-time working; (b) their low-skilled employees to move from full-time to part-time working; and (c) their employees to transfer from part-time to full-time working. These variables have three response categories: the move is granted quickly or after some time, it is granted only in exceptional situations, or it is never granted. To this we add a fourth derived variable: a count of how many of these three options are offered 'quickly or after some time' by the employer.

We focus on those companies which employ part-time staff[4] and we use Latent Class Analysis (see Fagan and Walthery 2011: technical annex) to summarize and reduce the permutations to a limited number of typical policies. Table 7.2 shows the relationship—conditional probabilities—between the five latent classes and the observed variables. These are the most common patterns of association between the type and number of reversibility options available in our sample of companies and confirmed that the LCA model

Table 7.2 Conditional probabilities of the five class LCA model

	No reversibility	Full reversibility	Some reversibility	Skilled full reversibility	Part-time to full-time
Class size[a]	24.5	27.4	22.2	15.2	10.7
Observed variable 1: Transfer from full-time to part-time work permitted for skilled employees[b]					
Quickly or after some time	–	1	.25	.6	1
Exceptionally	.36	–	.34	.2	–
No chance	.64	–	.41	.2	–
Observed variable 2: Transfer from full-time to part-time work permitted for unskilled/low-skilled employees					
Quickly or after some time	–	1	.56	1	–
Exceptionally	.50	–	.29	–	.61
No chance	.50	–	.15	–	.39
Observed variable 3: Transfer from part-time to full-time working permitted for all part-time employees					
Quickly or after some time	–	1	1	–	–
Exceptionally	.36	–	–	.19	.42
No chance	.64	–	–	.81	.58
Observed variable 4: Number of moves allowed immediately or after some time					
0 Nil	1	–	–	–	–
1 Limited	–	–	.26	.43	1
2 Partial	–	–	.74	.57	–
3 Full	–	1	–	–	–

[a] Class size (percentage of all companies of at least 10 employees with part-time staff)

[b] Probability for observations in each category of the four observed variables to belong to one of the latent classes, ranging from 0 to 1.

Source: European Survey on Working Time 2005.

selected the most typical categories of reversibility identified in the discussion of Table 7.1.

One-quarter of establishments with part-timers fall into the *no reversibility* class, which comprises organizations where individual working time adjustments are not generally available (a probability equal to 0 of granting any type of reversibility immediately or after some time, and a probability equal to 1 of granting no such options). Only in exceptional cases are individual-level adjustments permitted, and the most probably exceptional case would be a move for a skilled employee from full-time to part-time hours. The *full reversibility* class accounts for 27% of the establishments and comprises organizations which allow adjustments between full-time and part-time working in either direction 'quickly or after sometime' for both skilled and low-skilled employees (probability equal to one for each variable).

Just over one-fifth of employers with part-time staff are in the *some reversibility* class. They generally allow their employees to reduce their working time from full-time to part-time (always in the case of their unskilled workforce; often in the case of skilled employees). There is some scope for part-time employees to switch to full-time arrangements, but the probability of this being available on an unrestricted basis is much lower than in the other classes (0.25). This predominance of the full-time to part-time adjustment for this class echoes the earlier descriptive results shown in Table 7.1.

Employers in the *skilled full reversibility* class—about 15% of the sample—only permit a reduction from full-time to part-time hours for their skilled employees. The majority of these companies also permit a move from part-time to full-time working for all employees (p=.62). Overall, employers in this class are slightly less likely to allow partial reversibility (p=.57) than employers in the 'some reversibility' class (p=.74).

The *part-time to full-time* class is the smallest (11% of the cases). These employers allow their employees to increase their working time from part-time to full-time hours. In exceptional circumstances a move from full-time to part-time may be allowed; and this is more likely for skilled staff (the probability is equal to.61 against.41 for low skilled staff). This confirms our results, discussed above, which identified this type of reversibility as the most common among companies offering only one option (see Section 3).

Now that four typical patterns of reversibility have been unearthed—five when the no reversibility class is taken into account—we can analyse the extent to which these are associated with the variables of interest.

Our key concern is whether the type of adjustment option made available to employees is associated with other features of employers' working time policy that can be considered as 'conversion factors' by creating a supportive workplace environment that enhances the capability of individual employees to improve their WLB. Four indicators were available to capture this aspect of the organization's working time arrangements: '*management agrees that supporting work–life balance is a duty of the company*' (measured by an attitude question), the *main reason part-time working was introduced* was to meet employee needs rather than employer needs for more flexible operating practices, *part-time schedules are flexible* rather than fixed to daily/weekly schedules and *flexi-time or other time banking accounts* exist as another means of creating an environment that enables individuals to vary their working hours. We judge that these indicators provide a reasonable handle on whether managerial attitudes and policies promote a 'worklife balance culture' that supports individual-level adjustments; although ideally the survey would have probed in more depth on other dimensions, such as the key role of line managers as 'gate keepers' in the implementation of organizational policy (see for example Lewis 2003; Crompton 2006; den Dulk and Spenkelink 2009).

It is plausible that the extent and form of individual adjustment options between full-time and part-time working might be affected by the firm's operating requirements for staffing associated with its production processes. We included a measure of complexity and predictability of workflow rhythm (over the day, week, and year) to see whether this was conducive to the firm offering some types of adjustment rather than others. Similarly, a measure of staffing level trends was included with the expectation that if the company had contracted or grown its staff in recent years then this would also impact on the types of adjustment options in place; for example, movement from part-time to full-time hours is likely to be easier during periods of growth rather than contraction.

The firms' working time practices and culture—including any policy position concerning WLB responsibilities—is likely to be shaped by the gender and skill composition of the workforce and whether employees have collective representation by a union or works council. Given that the majority of part-time employees are women with family care responsibilities for children and elders, it is likely that firms with a sizeable proportion of women in their employ may face more demands for working time adjustments between full-time and part-time hours. The skill profile may also be important; the recruitment and retention of skilled workers can be a catalyst for the development of flexible working time options and this may extend to offering reversibility adjustments. Collective representation may advance reversibility options at the firm level.

Given the results of our preliminary analysis a control variable was introduced for sector, differentiating between the public sector, private service sector, and other industry (manufacturing, extraction, construction, and transport). We controlled for establishment size, since larger establishments are often assumed to have more leeway to allow for flexible working time arrangements. Finally, we also introduced dummy variables for those countries discussed in Section 1 where national law or policy makes provision to enable individuals to request an adjustment to their working hours, which have more extensive coverage than the options that exist in some statutory parental leave arrangements; namely Belgium, Germany, the Netherlands, Sweden, and the UK. We did this to explore whether the effect of state policy could still be discerned once the firms' characteristics and policies were taken into account. Other variables were left out of the model for operational reasons: in order not to overload the model with too many parameters or because their explanatory power was limited in relation to the reversibility issue and because their effect can hide other interesting associations.

Table 7.3 presents the results of the multinomial logit model that measures the odds of companies belonging to one of the reversibility rather than no reversibility latent classes given each independent variable.[5]

The first point to note is that the type of individual-level adjustments deemed feasible by the manager were influenced by two structural factors: the

Table 7.3 Multinomial logistic regression relative risk ratios of the reversibility latent class model[a]

Latent class (base: 'no reversibility' class)	1. Full reversibility	2. Skilled full reversibility	3. Some reversibility	4. Part-time to full-time
Class size.[b] (No reversibility =24.5%)	27.4	15.2	22.2	10.7
Management agrees that promoting worklife balance is a duty of the company	**1.46*****	**1.32***	*1.23+*	1.08
Neither agrees nor disagree *(Base: Management disagrees)*	**1.40****	0.92	**1.28***	1.22
Reason the firm introduced part-time work:				
To meet employees' WLB needs	**4.14*****	**3.01*****	**1.46****	**2.89*****
To meet the needs of both employer and employees	**2.22*****	**1.98*****	1.23	**1.37***
Don't know (*Base: to meet employers' operating needs only)*	**0.62***	0.83	**0.65***	0.96
Presence of flexi-time or other time banking arrangements	**1.31****	1.05	**1.32****	0.90
Part-time work schedules are flexible	**1.33***	1.29	**1.47****	1.00
Workflow rhythm unpredictable	0.87	0.96	0.93	0.91
complex (yearly, weekly, and daily variations) (*Base: Workflow rhythm is predictable: yearly, weekly, OR daily fluctuation)*	**1.44****	1.35+	1.27+	1.07
Sector: Private sector service activities	1.23+	1.09	0.94	0.98
Public sector (*Base: industry i.e. extraction, manufacturing, construction + transport)*	**1.37****	**1.66****	1.05	**0.58****
Establishment size: 10–19 employees	**0.14*****	**0.52****	**0.49*****	**0.41*****
Size: 20–49 employees	**0.20*****	0.71	**0.65***	**0.46****
Size: 50–99 employees	**0.29*****	0.95	0.86	**0.50****
Size: 100–499 employees *(Base: 500+ employees)*	**0.41*****	0.78	0.73	**0.62***
Collective representation—union/works council present	**1.29***	1.03	1.30*	0.85
Gender profile: between 20 and 60% staff are female	**1.64*****	1.31+	**1.73*****	1.03
More than 60% staff are female *(Base: less than 20%)*	**2.44*****	**2.20*****	**2.58*****	1.04
Skill profile of workforce: 100% skilled	**0.52*****	**3.51*****	**0.38*****	1.05
Between 60–99% are skilled	0.89	**1.62****	**0.77***	0.96
Between 20–59% are skilled *(Base: less than 20% skilled)*	0.96	1.19	**0.71***	1.01
Staffing level trends—decreased recently	**0.59*****	0.93	1.07	0.70*

Latent class (base: 'no reversibility' class)	1. Full reversibility	2. Skilled full reversibility	3. Some reversibility	4. Part-time to full-time
Staffing level has been stable (*Base: increased recently)*	**0.64*****	0.92	**0.80***	**0.58*****
Countries with working time adjustment regulation				
1. Belgium	**1.95*****	**2.53*****	1.90**	**1.16**
2. Germany	**0.54*****	**1.59****	1.03	**0.63****
3. Netherlands	**0.64***	**2.38*****	0.91	0.88
4. Sweden	**2.29*****	**2.66*****	**2.05*****	1.23
5. UK (Base: all other EU-21 countries)	**1.38***	**1.63****	1.06	0.87

Notes: A relative change in probability for observations to belong to Latent Class 1, 2, 3, or 4 (rather than the 'No reversibility' class) given the characteristics listed in the table. Odds greater than one denote an increase in the probability to be in a latent class, odds smaller than one denote a decrease. b Percentage of all establishments with at least 10 employees and employing part-time staff; Significant + at.1 * at .05 ** at .01 *** at .001. Unweighted sample: 12,314 establishments in the EU21.

sector the organization operated in and, to a lesser extent, the establishment size. Policies for full or skilled reversibility were more likely to exist in public sector organizations. Conversely, public sector organizations were significantly less likely to have a policy that only permitted part-time to full-time adjustment. Private sector service companies were also 1.23 times more likely to offer full reversibility than other private sector companies operating in manufacturing, extraction, construction, or transport; and the size of the effect is not much lower than that for public sector—although this only holds at the 0.1 significance level. These results indicate that, in the EU as a whole, the service sector—primarily the public sector—is leading developments in individual-level working time adjustments. This may be due to a combination of contextual factors; for example in most countries the public sector may be more sheltered from market pressures than the private sector and has been more directly exposed to government-led initiatives to promote WLB policies as part of wider equal opportunities action plans.

Large establishments (500+ employees) have a higher probability of offering full reversibility or permitting part-time employees to switch to full-time hours than medium- or small-size ones. Conversely, small establishments (fewer than 20 employees) were much less likely to offer any type of reversibility than medium or large establishments. Part of the explanation for the size effect may be that a larger workforce provides more opportunities to accommodate individual-level adjustments as part of general personnel policies to manage turnover and other fluctuations in staffing levels through internal and external recruitment.

The presence of a trade union (or works council) affects workplace policy: unionized establishments are 1.3 times more likely to have a policy of full or some reversibility, but their presence does not influence whether the employer operates a policy of skilled full reversibility. In the case of the part-time to full-time class, although not significant, the coefficient is negative, which hints at the possibility that collective organization may encourage employers to adopt a different reversibility policy to this one.

The gender and skill profile of the workforce is salient. Given that part-time working is still largely a preserve of women, and that adjustment policies are most likely to be taken up by women and set up with them in mind, it is not very surprising to find that firms with a high proportion of women in their workforce are more than twice as likely to offer full, some, or skilled reversibility. The skill level of the firms' employees exerts a weaker effect than gender overall. A policy of full reversibility restricted to skilled employees (skilled full reversibility) is more probable in firms if they have a high proportion of employees who are skilled: they are 1.6 to 3 times more likely compared to firms where less than 20% of the workforce is skilled. Conversely, a policy of full or some reversibility is less probable if the firm has a large proportion of skilled employees. We did not find any evidence of a specific interaction between the skills and gender profile of the workforce, for when the latter was introduced into the model the coefficients were not affected. Neither the gender nor the skills profile of the firm's workforce influences the probability that a firm only offers a part-time to full-time adjustment.

The analysis confirms the key question addressed in this chapter: the firm's organizational working time practices and culture towards safeguarding WLB have a significant influence on the availability of individual-level working time adjustments, over and above the other firm and workforce characteristics controlled in the model. All four types of adjustment analysed here were more likely in firms where the managers stated that the reason part-time work was introduced was mainly to meet the needs of their employees; and full or skilled full reversibility options were also more likely where the rationale was to meet a combination of employer and employee needs. In particular employers were three to four times more likely to operate full or skilled reversibility where employee needs was the rationale, compared to those establishments where part-time work had been introduced to meet the needs of management. Management attitude had an additional independent effect: if management agreed that it was their duty to support the WLB of their employees, they were more likely to report that a policy of full reversibility was in operation. Even where managerial attitude was ambivalent about it being their duty, they were more likely to offer full reversibility than managers who disagreed. A supportive managerial attitude also had a weaker but still significant effect on the probability that employers offered some or skilled reversibility.

The broader context of work scheduling in the workplace also influenced the type of adjustments that were deemed feasible by employers. Establishments which operated flexi-time or other time banking schemes—which are other working time options that enhance the capabilities of employees for securing work–family balance—were more likely to belong to the class that offered full or some reversibility. Similarly, establishments had an increased probability of offering individual working time adjustments when part-time work was managed flexibly rather than via fixed schedules; where fixed schedules might indicate company- rather than employee-driven working time flexibility policies. Full reversibility, and to a lesser extent 'skilled' or 'some' reversibility', was more likely in workplaces where the workflow rhythm is complex (weekly, daily, and seasonal variations). Workflow rhythm did not have a significant influence on the probability of an employer offering only the marginal move from part-time to full-time working.

Finally trends in staffing levels also impacted on the type of policy being operated. Employers were less likely to offer full reversibility or the option to move from part-time to full-time working if their workforce was contracting or stable. Having a stable workforce also reduced the likelihood that the employer operated some reversibility or full-time to part-time adjustments. This could indicate the existence of leaner working time arrangements that make it difficult for line supervisors to accommodate individual requests for working time adjustments. Interestingly, the probability that an employer operated full reversibility policies restricted to skilled employees was not affected by trends in staffing levels.

Turning now to the country effects, we can see that establishments in Sweden and Belgium are markedly more likely to offer full, skilled full, or some reversibility than similar firms in the other European countries in the analysis. This also applies to a lesser extent for firms in the UK with regard to full and skilled full reversibility. Firms in the Netherlands and Germany are more likely to offer full reversibility to skilled employees than comparable firms elsewhere, but are actually less likely to grant full reversibility to the whole of their workforce. The German legal framework also appears to make firms less likely to operate the limited part-time to full-time adjustment. As already discussed in Section 1, these five countries have legislation or national policies that grant employees some rights to request individual adjustments to their working hours, but there are important differences in the detail of the provisions. The results from this analysis suggest that these state-level policies have an important regulatory effect on the type of policy developed and implemented by employers, which is apparent even when relevant establishment-level characteristics are taken into account. Conversely, that establishment-level characteristics remain significant indicates that the implementation of state-level provision is shaped in important ways at the organizational level of the workplace.

Reversibility Profiles

Leaving aside the effect of national-level policy on firm practices, which we have just discussed, we can now summarize the main establishment-level findings and draw a more precise picture of what type of organization operates each type of reversibility in comparison with organizations that employ part-timers but offer no reversibility. In other words: what type of firm enhances the working time capability of all their employees by offering either full reversibility or the less extensive version permitted under 'some reversibility'; or targets full reversibility on their skilled employees; or limits the adjustments employees can make to one of moving from part-time to full-time hours?

FULL REVERSIBILITY ORGANIZATIONS

These organizations have a workforce containing high proportions of women and low-skilled employees who are likely to be unionized. They are likely to be large public sector or private service establishments where the workflow tends to be complex. Part-time work was introduced at least partly with the employee needs in mind; there are other policies in place that enhance the capability of individual employees to improve their WLB, such as flexi-time; together with a managerial sense of duty towards promoting WLB. Full reversibility is less likely if staffing levels are stable or falling than rising.

SOME REVERSIBILITY ORGANIZATIONS

These organizations generally allow adjustments from full-time to part-time working with some scope for moves from part-time to full-time arrangements.

The workforce profile is similar to that for full reversibility organizations: high proportions of women and low-skilled employees who are likely to be unionized. There are also similarities in WLB policies: part-time work was introduced at least partly with the employee needs in mind and there are other policies in place that enhance the capability of individual employees to improve their WLB, such as flexi-time. The adoption of some reversibility is also associated with a managerial sense of duty towards promoting WLB, although the significance of managerial attitudes is weaker than for the full reversibility policy.

Again, like the organizations offering full reversibility, some reversibility organizations are likely to have a complex workflow rhythm. Yet the probability of this type of policy being operated is not affected by whether they are located in the public sector, private services, or other industry sectors. Small and medium size establishments (fewer than 50 employees) are less likely to make this kind of arrangement than larger ones.

A policy of some reversibility is less likely where staffing levels have been stable. Recall that the most feasible adjustment under this policy is a move from full-time to part-time hours (Table 7.2). It may be that in a situation of expansion and recruitment, or the turbulence of downsizing, there is more scope for staff to make some adjustments than in a situation of stability.

SKILLED FULL REVERSIBILITY ORGANIZATIONS

These organizations operate a policy of full reversibility for skilled employees while other employees can generally only move from part-time to full-time arrangements.

These organizations are also likely to have a higher proportion of women in their workforce, but unlike the full reversibility and some reversibility organizations, the workforce is likely to be highly skilled. Collective representation does not increase the probability that an organization adopts this type of policy, presumably because union bargaining agendas focus on extending full or some reversibility to all employees rather than focusing on benefits for skilled employees. These organizations are more likely to be public sector organizations and to have a complex workflow rhythm. Establishment size is not a discerning feature except that very small ones (fewer than 20 employees) are significantly less likely to operate this type of policy.

Like the full reversibility model, this type of organization introduced part-time work with the needs of employees in mind and there is a managerial sense of duty towards promoting WLB. However, there is no association between this type of policy and the availability of flexi-time or other time banking arrangements to enable individuals to vary their working time; although there is a significant positive association with part-time work schedules being flexible rather than fixed.

Trends in staffing levels have no impact on the probability that an organization operates a policy of skilled reversibility. This suggests that in these organizations the retention of their skilled staff is at the core of their business model, justifying any additional costs incurred in operating this policy regardless of any change in staffing levels (and where any changes in staffing levels may be focused on the small proportion of low/unskilled employees in their employment).

PART-TIME TO FULL-TIME ORGANIZATIONS

This is the smallest class of organizations, accounting for 11% of organizations with part-timers in their workforce, and it is the narrowest form of adjustment policy considered in the analysis. Only in exceptional circumstances can part-timers move to full-time arrangements.

In sharp contrast to the other three types, the probability that an organization operates this type of policy is unrelated to the gender, skill level, or collective representation of their workforce. The organizations are likely to be very large establishments (500 or more employees) in the private sector; the odds are similar for private services and the rest of the private sector (extraction, manufacturing, construction, and transport), and the complexity of the workflow rhythm is not relevant either. Organizations are more likely to have adopted this policy if part-time work was introduced to meet the needs of employees, but the managerial attitude towards WLB duties is not influential. Whether or not the organization offers flexi-time or time banking is also irrelevant.

Taken together, this suggests that this narrow type of adjustment policy emerges as a pragmatic response, whereby part-timers can move into full-time arrangements when such vacancies arise through turnover or expansion. This is congruent with the finding that organizations are more likely to offer this form of reversibility rather than no reversibility if staff levels have been rising.

Developments in Part-time Work

What has happened to employers' use of part-time working with the 2007/08 onset of economic recession and the subsequent job losses and deterioration in real wages across Europe? The EuroFound's second establishment survey in 2009 provides some indication of trends in employers' use of part-time work since the onset of the recession.

It reveals an increase in the proportion of companies that employ part-timers and an increased intensity of part-time working within companies compared to the situation in 2005 (Figure 7.3). This suggests firms are using part-time work as one working time adjustment to manoeuvre during the recession. Unfortunately, the questions about employer's provisions for their employees to switch between full-time and part-time working were not repeated in the 2009 survey so it is not possible to gauge whether this working time capability has been enhanced, but this seems unlikely for two reasons. First, there have been no significant legal reforms to enhance employees' capabilities to request individual working time adjustments changes in the countries of study (OECD 2012). Second, Labour Force Survey data shows full-time jobs are being lost and the increased rate of part-time working includes an expansion in involuntary part-time work by men and women unable to obtain full-time employment (Smith 2009). This latter form of part-time work is about avoiding unemployment rather than enhancing working time capabilities and the reconciliation of work–family balance. It may be that some

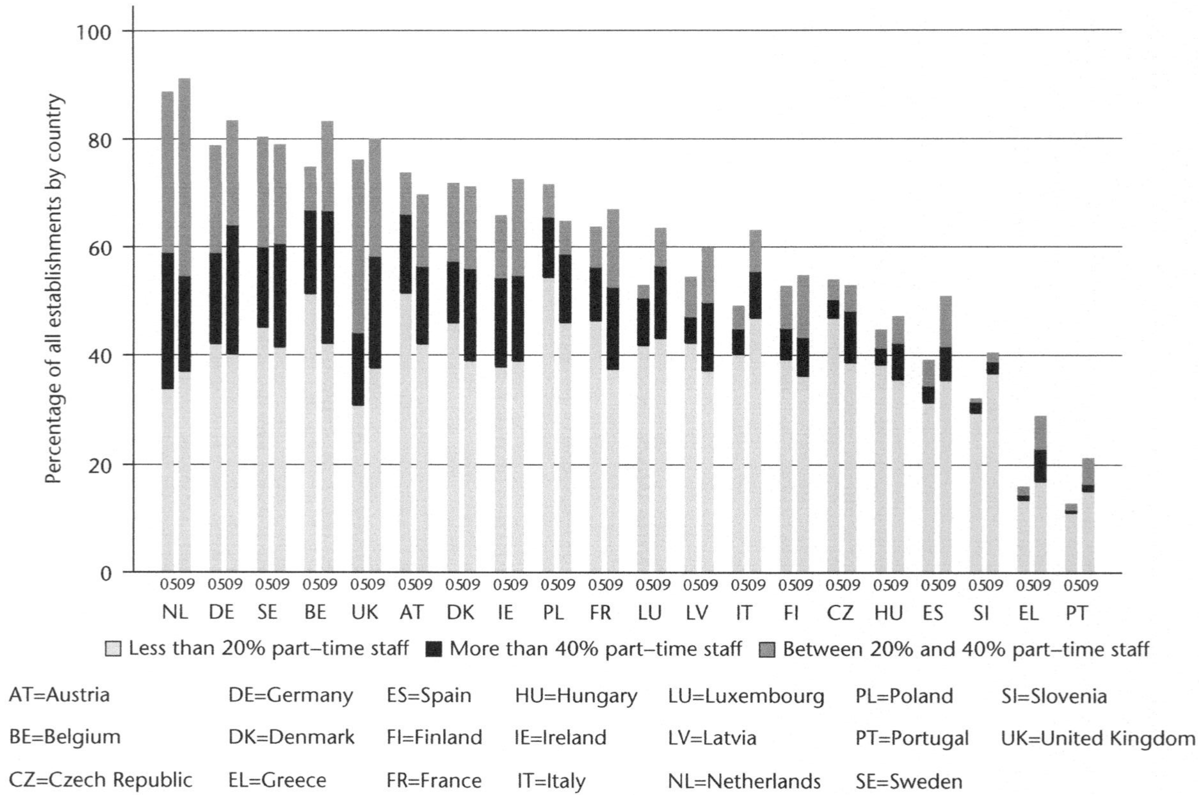

Figure 7.3 Proportion of part-time employees in European establishments: trends, 2005–09

employers are enhancing their employees' working time capabilities through alternative policies. For example, across the 20 countries in this study the proportion of firms that give some employees the possibility to adapt their daily start and finishing times[6] increased from 48% in 2005 to 57% by 2009. Just over 70% of these firms made this provision available to at least one-fifth of their workforce in 2009, as in 2005.

The increase in firms' use of part-time working is particularly noticeable in countries where part-time work is still comparatively low, such as Greece, Portugal, Spain, and Slovenia. A marked increase was also noticeable in Italy and, to a lesser extent, Belgium and Ireland. By contrast, Poland and Austria were the only countries with a modest decrease in the propensity for companies to use part-time staff. In a few countries where the overall proportion of companies employing part-time workers did not change very much, the trend appears to be an increase in the proportion of firms with 20% or more of their workforce employed part-time; this was the case in Germany, Sweden, Austria, Denmark, France, and Finland.

Further inspection of the data revealed that the expansion of part-time work was greatest in the service sectors, with the notable exception of health and education where the rate of part-time working was already high at the start of the period. The most marked increase was in transport, and there was significant growth in business and financial services. By contrast there was little increase in industry or construction companies. The expansion of part-time work was most pronounced in small- and medium-size firms, there was no significant increase in the usage of part-timers in larger companies.

Conclusions

Following Sen's capability framework, we have argued that employers' policies in place at the workplace are one of the key social conversion factors that shape the capability set and functionings of individual employees. In this chapter we have explored organizations' policies towards employees making individual adjustments between full-time and part-time hours. Where such transitions are possible, this helps to redress some of the career progression penalties associated with part-time work as it enables the current occupational position to be broadly maintained if moving from full-time to part-time hours. If there is a full reversibility option this provides a route back to full-time employment, thus widening the range of working time options open to the individual at different stages in their working life.

We have shown that across Europe there is marked variation in whether employers operate a policy of full reversibility, skilled full reversibility, some reversibility, part-time to full-time adjustments, or no reversibility to their employees. In a large number of establishments these adjustments are not possible. One-quarter of European firms that employ part-timers do not permit such adjustments. Another quarter do not have part-timers in their workforce, which suggest that such adjustments are not common practice in their workplace either. It is rarely easy to move from part-time to full-time hours. Yet, more positively, around a quarter of firms with part-timers permit full reversibility, another fifth permit some reversibility, and a smaller proportion permit skilled full reversibility or part-time to full-time adjustments. These results suggest that the capability that an individual employee has to adjust their hours varies markedly according to their workplace setting and is very constrained in many workplaces.

State policy clearly matters, for firms are more likely to permit such adjustments where they are legal requirements or where other national policy tools are in place. For example, in this analysis once firm-level characteristics are taken into account, we find that full reversibility is more likely to be found in some of the countries with generalized 'right to request' laws or government policy than in other European countries where the employee 'right to request' policy does not exist or is a limited one contained within the parental leave scheme. Yet, firm-level characteristics and other situational features also impact on the social conversion factors that shape an individual's working time capability. This underscores that the implementation of state-level provision is shaped in important ways at the organizational level of the workplace. The sector, establishment size, presence of a trade union, gender, and skill composition of the workforce all had a significant influence on whether employers permitted individual-level working time adjustments. The firm's organizational working time practices and culture towards safeguarding WLB had an additional and independent effect, as did broader aspects of working time scheduling in place.

Finally, if the workforce was contracting in size or was stable, employers were less likely to offer full reversibility or options to move from part-time to full-time working. The significant negative effect of staffing reductions in most cases does not bode well for the current period of economic recession and restructuring. If firms are shedding jobs then, while it may be possible to secure reductions from full-time to part-time hours in some settings, curtailment of reversibility policies can be expected in practice. What is clear from the available establishment-level time series is that the use of part-time work is spreading across a larger proportion of establishments, and becoming more widespread within establishments; but that it remains largely focused in the service sector while the male-dominated industry and construction sectors remain organized around full-time employment.

The focus in our analysis has been on the accounts of employers about their policies. This is clearly an important part of the picture for researching individuals' capabilities, but of course the employee voice has not been captured in this analysis. Some reassurance can be taken from the fact that in companies whether trade union representatives were present, their account was similar to the employers' account, although they tended to be more conservative about what was offered by the employer. It is entirely feasible that an employer reports that something is possible and part of company policy while their employees remain ignorant of the policy, or reluctant to use it because they foresee obstacles or penalties, such as line manager resistance or being sidelined for promotion. We should also remember that employees in the same workplace covered by the same policy will still have different capabilities; for example, it may be more socially acceptable for women than for men to reduce their hours to manage care responsibilities. Whether and how employees make use of a policy will also depend on other contextual factors; including other aspects of the working time policy at the workplace—how long full-time hours are, whether flexi-time and other ways of adjusting working time arrangements are in place—and resources and infrastructure that can be accessed beyond the workplace, including the availability of affordable and good quality childcare alternatives. So employer policy is only one part of the picture, but it is one of the important social conversion factors shaping the individual's capability set, and the individual's capability to make working time adjustments is likely to be enhanced in firms that operate policies which permit such adjustments than in those firms that offer more limited or no such adjustments.

Notes

1. We are grateful to Dr Nick Shryane of the University of Manchester, for his technical advice on the development of the Latent Class Analysis in this paper; to participants in the RECWOWE Network of Excellence for their comments on earlier versions of this paper presented in workshops at the annual RECWOWE conference, and to the anonymous reviewers of our article published in *Social Politics*. This is an extended version of our article: Colette Fagan and Pierre Walthery (2011) 'Individual Working Time Adjustments between Full-time and Part-time Working in European Firms' *Social Politics,* 18(2).
2. It is a stratified random sample survey clustered in a number of countries carried out in 2004–2005 in the EU25 member states minus Malta, Estonia, Lithuania, and Slovakia. The reference population is about 2.7 million companies employing more than 9 employees in the EU21 countries covering all economic sectors except agriculture, fishing, and hunting, extraterritorial organizations, and private households (NACE classification). As a result, while the survey is representative of this population, it is not of economic sectors, since small companies are unevenly spread among them. The sample comprises 21,031 establishments across the public and private sector. For each establishment one interview was carried out with

the personnel manager and one with a formal employee representative from the same establishment (union shop stewards, works councils) where such representation existed. In total an employee representative was interviewed for 5,232 of the establishments (Bielenski and Riedmann 2005). In this chapter we only use the sample of personnel managers.

3. We use a wider measure here to include adjustments that were permitted either 'quickly' or 'after some time' to capture the diversity of situations in which requests for adjustments may arise, such as smaller companies where, for operational reasons, a move cannot be granted immediately, irrespective of how supportive of worklife balance issues the employer might be.
4. This decision was taken for three reasons: exploratory analysis showed that companies whose manager declared that they did not have any part-time employees would have to be recoded as 'Never' in the variable measuring the presence of moves from part-time to full-time. This would inflate the weight of the 'No reversibility' latent class (cf. below) at the cost of more detailed and precise analysis of reversibility classes. Furthermore, keeping variables measuring the reasons for introducing part-time work or the way it is managed within the company would have proven difficult—and dropping them would have significantly weakened part of our analytical framework.
5. The value of the sample/size adjusted BIC parameter is the lowest observed among all models tested stepwise which indicates the best relative fit; in any case a very significant improvement over the empty model. Entropy remains close to the value observed in the empty model—.996. Similarly the *P* value of the modified Likelihood ratio test was not altered by the introduction of independent variables.
6. The survey question asked about 'the possibility for employees to adapt—within certain limits—the time when they begin or finish their daily work according to their personal needs or wishes'.

Bibliography

Allart, P. and L. Bellmann (2005). Employers' Demand for Part-time Workers: Incidence and Motives in Germany and the Netherlands, in M. Ramioul, U. Huws, and A. Bollen (eds), *Measuring the Information Society*, pp. 3–18. Leuven, Belgium: Higher Institute for Labour Studies (HIVA).

Anxo D., C. Fagan, I. Cebrián, and G. Moreno. (2007a). Patterns of Labour Market Integration in Europe—A Life Course Perspective on Time Policies. *Socio-Economic Review*, 5(2):233–60.

Anxo D., C. Erhel, and J. Schipper (2007b) (eds), *Labour Market Transitions and Time Adjustment of the Life Course*. Amsterdam: Dutch University Press.

Anxo, D., C. Fagan, M.T. Letablier, C. Perraudin, and M. Smith (2007c). *Part-Time Work in European Companies*, Luxembourg: Office for Official Publications of the European Communities.

Becker, G. (1981). *A Treatise on the Family*. Cambridge, MA: Harvard University Press.

Bielenski, H. and A. Riedmann (2005). Establishment Survey on Working Time and Work–Life Balance in 21 EU Member States. Technical Report: Methodology, Questionnaire Development and Fieldwork. Dublin: European Foundation for the Improvement of Living and Working Conditions.

Burchell, B., C. Fagan, C. O'Brien, and M. Smith; for the European Foundation (2007). *Working Conditions in the European Union: The Gender Perspective*. Luxembourg: Office for Official Publications of the European Communities.

Blossfeld, H-P. and C. Hakim (1997) (eds), *Between Equalisation and Marginalisation*. Oxford: Oxford University Press.

Bosch, G. and S. Lehndorff (2005) (eds), *Working in the Service Sector—A Tale from Different Worlds*. Routledge: London and New York.

Bosch, G., P. Dawkins, and F. Michon (1994). *Times are Changing: Working Time in 14 Industrialised Countries*. Geneva: Institute for International Labour Studies.

Celeux, G. and G. Soromenho (1996). An Entropy Criterion for Assessing the Number of Clusters in a Mixture Model. *Journal of Classification*, 13(2):195–212.

Commission of the European Communities (CEC) (2003). *Jobs, Jobs, Jobs: Creating More Employment in Europe*. Report of the Employment Taskforce, headed by Wim Kok. Brussels: Commission of the European Communities.

CEC (2006). Green Paper. Modernising Labour Law to Meet the Challenges of the 21th Century. Com(2006) 708 final. Brussels: Commission of the European Communities.

CEC (2007). *Towards Common Principles of Flexicurity 6*. 16201/07 Brussels: Commission of the European Communities, December.

Council of the European Union (2010). Proposal for a Council Decision on Guidelines for the Employment Policies of the Member States: Part II of the Europe 2020 Integrated Guidelines SOC 414, 10907/10, Brussels: Commission of the European Communities, June 9.

Crompton, R. and G.E. Birkelund (2000). Employment and Caring in British and Norwegian Banking: An Exploration Through Individual Careers. *Work, Employment and Society*, 14:331.

Crompton, R. (2006). *Employment and the Family: The Reconfiguration of Work and Family Life in Contemporary Societies*. Cambridge: Cambridge University Press.

Dulk, den L. and S. Spenkelink (2009). Dutch Employers and the Work–Life Balance: Attitudes, Policies and Practices. FP6 Network of Excellence RECWOWE, Work Package 02—Working paper contribution to D02.12.

Dulk, den L., B. Peper, N.Č. Sadar, S. Lewis, J. Smithson, and A. van Doorne-Huiskes (2011). Work, Family and Managerial Attitudes and Practices in the European Workplace: Comparing Dutch, British and Slovenian Financial Sector Managers. *Social Politics*, 18(2):300–29.

Duncan, S. (2006). Mothers' Work–Life Balance: Individualized Preferences or Cultural Construction? in D. Perrons, C. Fagan, L. McDowell, K. Ray, and K. Ward (eds), *Gender Divisions and Working Time in the New Economy*, pp. 127–47. Cheltenham: Edward Elgar.

European Commission (2004). Facing the Challenge—The Lisbon Strategy for Growth and Employment. Report from the High Level Group chaired by Wim Kok. Luxembourg: Office for Official Publications of the European Communities.

European Commission (2010). Europe 2020—A European Strategy for Smart, Sustainable and Inclusive Growth COM (2010) 2020, Brussels, 3.3.2010.

Fagan, C. and P. Walthery (2007). The Role and Effectiveness of Time Policies for Reconciliation of Care Responsibilities, in OECD (ed.), *Modernising Social Policy for the New life Course*, pp. 75–116. Paris: OECD.

Fagan, C. and P. Walthery (2011). Individual Working-Time Adjustments between Full-time and Part-time Working in European Firms. *Social Politics*, 10(2):269–99.

Fagan, C., A. Hegewisch, and J. Pillinger (2006). Out of Time—Why Britain Needs a New Approach to Working-Time Flexibility. Research report for the Trades Union Congress <http//:www.tuc.org.uk>.

Fagan, C. (1999). Developing the Concept of Lifetime Working Hours: The Potential Role of Part-time Work, in R. Hoffman and J-Y. Boulin (eds), *New Paths in Working Time Policy*, pp. 51–74. Brussels: European Trade Union Institute.

Fagan, C. (2004). Gender and Working-time in Industrialised Countries: Practices and Preferences, in J. Messenger (ed.), *Working Time and Workers' Preferences in Industrialized Countries*. London and New York: Routledge.

Francesconi, M. and A. Gosling (2005). Career Paths of Part-Time Workers. *Labour Market Trends,* 113:272.

Hagenaars J. and A. McCutcheon (2002) (eds), *Applied Latent Class Analysis*. Dordrecht: Kluwer.

Haki, C. (2000). *Work-Lifestyle Choices in the 21st Century: Preference Theory*. Oxford: Oxford University Press.

Kamerman, S. and P. Moss (2009) (eds), *The Politics of Parental Leave Policies—Children, Parenting, Gender and the Labour Market.* Bristol: Policy Press.

Lee, S. and D. McCann (2006). Working Time Capability: Towards Realizing Individual Choice, in J-Y. Boulin, M. Lallement, J. Messenger, and F. Michon (eds), *Decent Working Time—Trends, New Issues*, pp. 65–92. Geneva: International Labour Office.

Lewis, S. (2003). Flexible Work Arrangements: Implementation, Outcomes and Management, in C.L. Cooper and I.T. Robertson (eds), *International Review of Industrial and Organizational Psychology*, pp. 1–28. New York: John Wiley & Sons, Ltd.

Lewis, S. (1997). Family-Friendly Employment Policies a Route to Changing Organizational Culture or Playing Around at the Margins? *Gender, Work and Organization*, 4(1):13–23.

Messenger, J. (2004) (ed.). *Working Time and Workers' Preferences in Industrialized Countries*. London and New York: Routledge.

McCutcheon, A.C. (1987). *Latent Class Analysis*. London: Sage Publications.

McRae, S. (2003). Constraints and Choices in Mothers' Employment Careers: A Consideration of Hakim's Preference Theory. *British Journal of Sociology*, 54(3), 317–38.

OECD (2012). How Good is Part-time Work? *Employment Outlook 2012*, ch. 4. Paris: OECD.

O'Reilly, J and C. Fagan (1998) (eds), *Part-Time Prospects: An International Comparison of Part-Time Work in Europe, North America and the Pacific Rim*. London: Routledge.

O'Reilly, J., I. Cebrián, and M. Lallement (2000) (eds), *Working-Time Changes—Social Integration Through Transitional Labour Markets*. Cheltenham: Edward Elgar.

Perrons, D., C. Fagan, L. McDowell, K. Ray, and K. Ward (2006) (eds), *Gender Divisions and Working Time in the New Economy*. Cheltenham: Edward Elgar.

Plantenga, J. and C. Remery (2010). *Flexible Working Time Arrangements and Gender Equality—A Comparative Review of Thirty European Countries*. Luxembourg: Official Publications of the European Communities.

Raftery, A.E. (1995) Bayesian Model Selection in Social Research. *Sociological Methodology*, 25:111–63.

Rubery, J. (2005). The Shaping of Work and Working Time in the Service Sector: A Segmentation Approach, in G. Bosch and S. Lehndorff (eds), *Working in the Service Sector—A Tale From Different Worlds*. London and New York: Routledge.

Rubery, J., M. Smith, and C. Fagan (1998). National Working-Time Regimes and Equal Opportunities. *Feminist Economics*, 4(1):71–101.

Schmid, G. (2008). *Full Employment in Europe: Managing Labour Market Transitions and Risks*. Cheltenham: Edward Elgar.

Schwarz, R. (1978). Estimating the Dimension of a Model. *Annals of Statistics*, 6(2):461–4.

Sen, A. (1999). *Development as Freedom*. Oxford: Oxford University Press.

Smith, M. (2005). The Incidence of New Forms of Employment in Service Activities, in G. Bosch and S. Lehndorff (eds), *Working in the Service Sector—A Tale From Different Worlds*. London and New York: Routledge.

Smith, M. (2009). Gender Equality and Recession. Analysis note financed by and prepared for the the European Commission, Directorate-General for Employment, Social Affairs and Equal Opportunities <http://ec.europa.eu/social/BlobServlet?docId=2839&langId=en> [2013.18.06].

Visser (2011). Database on Institutional Characteristics of Trade Unions, Wage Setting, State Intervention and Social Pacts in 34 countries between1960 and 2010, Amsterdam Institute for Advanced Labour Studies (AIAS), University of Amsterdam, Amsterdam.

Yerkes, M., and J. Visser (2006). Women's Preferences or Delineated Policies? The Development of Part-time Work in the Netherlands, the UK and Germany, in J.Y. Boulin, M. Lallement, J. Messenger, and F. Michon (eds), *Decent Working Time, New Trends, New Issues*, pp. 235–62. Geneva: ILO.

8

Capabilities for worklife balance: managerial attitudes and employee practices in the Dutch, British, and Slovenian banking sector[1]

Bram Peper, Laura den Dulk, Nevenka Černigoj Sadar, Suzan Lewis, Janet Smithson, and Anneke van Doorne-Huiskes

Introduction

Do employees have the capabilities to reconcile increasing job pressure with expanding demands from the private domain? Increasingly among couples both partners are working, partly because of economic need, but also because of the wish to express themselves through work. Over recent decades growing attention has been paid to the reconciliation of employment with the needs of personal life. National governments, workplace organizers, and individual employers have introduced worklife policies and regulations, including reduction of working hours and flexible work and leave arrangements. In practice, however, employees do not always utilize policies and arrangements (Anderson et al. 2002; Eaton 2003; Lewis 2003). These inequalities in agency occur not only within national policy contexts—with varying care services, benefit levels, and through gendered, working time norms—but also at the workplace level.

Scholars have shown the importance of an organizational culture that is open to worklife issues for creating an environment positive to employee claims for worklife balance (hereafter WLB) (Thompson et al. 1999; Lewis 2003; den Dulk and Peper 2007). Organizational culture plays a key role in working parents' sense of entitlement to make claims (see Introduction and Chapter 3 in this volume), defined by Lewis as 'a set of beliefs and feelings that enable individuals to voice and make visible their needs to modify traditional structures at work and beyond' (Lewis 1996: 1). Within the organizational culture of a firm, managers have a crucial role in creating a sense of entitlement by seeing to the conversion of WLB policies into worklife practices. For it is at the workplace and work-organizational level that formal worklife policies are converted into entitlements and claims, where requests are granted or denied (Lewis 2003).

Sen's (1999) capabilities approach provides a framework for capturing the multilevel processes that embed individual agency into specific institutional/normative settings. Research at the firm level and the implementation of policies through managerial practices add another dimension to the agency and capabilities gap in WLB. Considering the capabilities of clients in social welfare systems, Bonvin and Farvaque (2003), in their study of government agencies, highlight the importance of the implementation of policies through local actors, although the mediation and translation of policies may enhance or weaken the agency and capabilities of individuals.

Few researchers have examined the factors that shape the practical implementation of worklife policies as part of the multilayer dynamics influencing the impact of policies in specific contexts. We view these dynamics from two vantage points: the managers' perspective and the employees' experiences. By studying managerial attitudes and practices concerning worklife policies in a cross-national perspective, we investigate how institutional factors influence the potential capabilities of workers for a better WLB within specific organizational contexts. We focus on the role of managers not only as implementers of policies and work organizational culture, but also as translators, mediators, and interpreters of the discursive rationales for promoting or denying claims for WLB. Looking from the employee perspective, we analyse the impact of managers' attitudes on employee capabilities. This analytical approach, which focuses on structural and cultural constraints within firms, permits interesting comparisons across countries and/or firms concerning the capabilities of employees.

In this chapter we explore the role of managers' attitudes towards, and responses to, worklife policies, along with the experiences of working parents in financial organizations in three countries: the Netherlands, the UK, and Slovenia, representing three different European welfare state contexts. The UK approximates a liberal welfare state with minimal state regulation and emphasis on the business case for worklife policies, while the Netherlands is often placed in the conservative welfare regime type, with moderate statutory worklife policies, but with a stronger regulatory framework of legislation and stronger collective agreements than the UK. Slovenia, on the other hand, is of the post-socialist context, with a strong tradition of state support for reconciling work and family, but at the same time a liberal market economy with little regulation (for a more elaborate description of the three countries, see Chapters 6 and 9 of this volume).

This chapter examines the phase after worklife policies have been adopted, which can be at the national level through statutory provisions, or at the organizational level through collective agreements and company policies. The broader institutional context can be seen as a frame within which managers' attitudes towards work–family issues develop and worklife policy decisions are mediated. In turn, managerial behaviour generates either institutional constraints upon, or support for, individual WLB. Managers play an important role because worklife policies, whether statutory or organizational, often contain an element of manager discretion. Hence, they may encourage or restrain the implementation of policies. The introduction of performance-related Human Relations Management (HRM) practices and the general trend toward decentralization—in which HRM practices have devolved to line managers—have made the role of managers even more important (Wise and Bond 2003). However, line managers often work long hours, and are less likely to use worklife policies than non-managerial employees (Poelmans and Beham 2005; den Dulk and Peper 2007). Hence, managers are seldom role models in policy utilization and are often seen as gate keepers to the take-up of policies.

We pose two general questions in this chapter: how do managers respond to worklife policies in practice in three organizations across national contexts? And, what is the effect of managerial discourses on the capabilities of employees? The three different countries function as the wider social policy context. To analyse the interplay between managerial discourses on worklife issues, and the capabilities of employees to make use of worklife policies, we incorporate both the managerial and the employee perspective. The managers' perspective is theoretically informed by the research on managerial discourses of disruption and dependency in the work organizational literature (Powell and Mainiero 1999; Klein et al. 2000). The employee perspective is shaped by the capabilities of employees to use policies that allow them to combine employment with family responsibilities, and their agency to make claims for them, as reflected in their subjective experiential sense of entitlement (Chapter 3 in this volume). This chapter consists of two main sections; Section 1 consists of discussion of managerial and employee perspectives, the research design and methods, and a detailed presentation of our three cases. In Section 2 we turn to the data and analysis of managerial discourses and employee perceptions and experiences. We conclude by discussing the implications of our research for employee capabilities and WLB.

A Manager's Perspective: Dependency and Disruption

Most research on the management of worklife policies has been conducted in the US, UK, or Canada (den Dulk and Peper 2009), all considered liberal welfare regimes (see Chapter 6). The focus on these country cases tends to emphasize the business case as the dominant management rationale, which assumes considerable scope for managerial discretion. Given this context, two theories of management decision-making have emerged: one on the potential disruptiveness and the other on dependency considerations that can result from implementing WLB policies (Powell and Mainiero 1999; Klein et al. 2000). According to the disruptiveness hypothesis, managers consider granting a request for a WLB policy based upon whether it will disrupt the work of the department. Powell and Maniero (1999) argue that managers are rewarded primarily for the results achieved in their work units, rather than for demonstrating sensitivity to the WLB of their employees. Hence, managers may be unwilling to grant requests that they believe will disrupt the conduct of work. Klein et al. (2000), on the other hand, stress the importance of dependency considerations and assume that managers 'cherish' the human capital in their department. Managers depend on the input of their employees and want to motivate and retain employees who make a major contribution to the performance of the department or work unit. In their study of attorneys who request to work part-time, Klein et al. found that managers' attitudes were more positive when the attorneys in question performed well, would be difficult to replace, had strong organizational connections, and threatened to leave if their requests were denied. In earlier research, we found a third management discourse when we analysed management interviews. For managers, providing support for working parents can also be a 'right thing to do'. Managers operate on the delicate balance between meeting organizational output targets and being a good supervisor to their subordinates. This discourse is considered to be a moral or ethical discourse (den Dulk et al. 2011).

Managerial discourses can be understood as the rationales for accepting or refusing WLB claims by managers; skill and dependency, as well as disruption (rationales) are connected to employee capabilities. On the one hand, the lack of resources for replacing staff on leave creates disruption and weakens the possibility of managers supporting the use of worklife policies by their employees, even when policies have a statutory basis or when managers are inclined to be supportive (dependency or moral argument). On the other hand, this reduction in managers' capabilities will also have a profound impact on capabilities of working parents. The ethical argument, however, reaches beyond the more practical influence of disruption and dependency discourses. The ethical discourse addresses the feeling that managers have that they should consider the needs of their employees. The ethical discourse will enhance employees' sense of entitlement, since they will feel morally supported by their managers in their need to combine work and family care.

In our focus on managers, we examine whether these considerations also play a role in managerial attitudes towards worklife policies in firms in different European societies with their own institutional contexts, which differ from the US context in that WLB policies are more institutionalized at national and EU level.

Comparative research on the effects of managerial attitudes on employee experiences with WLB policies falls short when considering the multidimensional factors shaping the implementation of such policies. For example, managers are mostly studied as bounded by their specific organizational context. Organizational case study research emphasizes how managerial behaviour shapes and is shaped by the organizational culture. A manager's response to WLB policies is influenced not only by official policy, but also by the 'unwritten rules' of their organization (Perlow 1995; Lewis 1997). However, organizational cultures do not exist in a vacuum, but develop in relation to national cultural and policy contexts. By analysing similar organizational case studies across different national contexts, the influence of institutional factors may come to the fore.

At the national level, legislation and policy debates may produce a social climate in which employers and managers are expected to show support for the combining of work with personal life (den Dulk 2001). Managers are expected to be more positive toward policy utilization in national contexts with extensive statutory work–family provisions such as Slovenia, where they have little scope to deny them, than managers in contexts of limited state support, as is the case in the UK and the Netherlands. In both countries, statutory provisions as well as formal organizational policies contain provisions for line managerial discretion, so that managers in both countries can decline a request to reduce working hours on the basis of business needs (see Table 6.1 in Chapter 6 of this volume), although the scope for managerial discretion is greater in the UK than in the Netherlands, where the right to reduce working hours is embedded in a wider framework of working time policies. Moreover, the right to request flexible working hours is restricted to working parents and caregivers in the UK, but not in the Netherlands (Fagan et al. 2006; Chapters 6 and 7 in this volume). Consequently, in the Dutch context, an employee's sense of entitlement is likely to be stronger as there are moral and legal pressures on managers to grant WLB claims.

An Employee Perspective: Sense of Entitlement

The capability approach, focused on the agency of employees to combine work and family needs, can be considered to include multiple layers. Capabilities includes a layer of room to manoeuvre where the national context, the organizational context, and managerial decisions operate. This room to manoeuvre will often be implicit or tacit for employees. In our research we focus on the 'sense of entitlement' perspective of employees, that is, the extent to which employees feel empowered to utilize existing worklife policies (Lewis 1996). The sense of entitlement is the experienced and expected agency of employees. Low expectations of the employer regarding worklife issues lead to a restricted sense of entitlement and to a low level of utilization. Greater sense of entitlement leads to greater demand for worklife arrangements and therefore to more utilization of such arrangements (Lewis 1996; see also Lewis and Smithson 2001; Herman and Lewis 2012).

When looking at the actual use of worklife policies by employees, some employees may experience a greater sense of entitlement depending on their situation both at home and at work (den Dulk and Peper 2007). Working parents with young children may express more of a sense of entitlement to WLB than younger or older employees who do not have family commitments. However, there are differences even within the category of working parents. There are several factors that are important for an employee's sense of entitlement: gender, the socio-political context, and the organizational culture (Lewis and Smithson 2001; Herman and Lewis 2012). Based on the sense of entitlement perspective, Lewis (1996) suggests that individuals often behave in accordance with traditional gender roles. Mothers who do not opt out of employment may feel more entitled to make claims for WLB to combine employment with family responsibilities than fathers at workplaces, for as role theory assumes, men are expected to reduce their involvement in childcare in favour of their career. However, modern fathers may feel that they too should have possibilities to utilize worklife policies (Hobson and Fahlén 2009; and Chapter 3). Clearly, gendered norms continue to operate at workplaces and men's sense of entitlement to WLB varies across societal institutional contexts and within firms. The sense of entitlement is gendered, as well as the managerial discourses. This is especially the case in the disruption discourse, where maternity and parental leave are considered to disrupt the work process for a relatively long period (see also den Dulk and De Ruijter 2008). We are interested in the interplay between managerial discourses on worklife issues, and the experienced capabilities of employees to use WLB policies.

Research Design and Methods

The perspectives and behaviours of managers and employees need to be understood within multiple, intersecting layers of context (Smith and Meiksins

1995; Nilsen et al. 2012). Therefore a multiple case-study approach was used to explore the practices of managers on WLB policies and the influence of these managerial perspectives on the perceptions and experiences of their employees. We selected cases within the same sector but in different national welfare state contexts in order to illuminate how processes at different layers of context intersect and are reflected in decisions relating to worklife policies. A case-oriented comparative method enables us to address the complexity in analysing worklife issues in organizations in the three different countries (Ragin 1987; Crompton 2001).

A common difficulty with this approach, however, is the problem of commensurability (Crompton and Lyonette 2006). We addressed this issue by working in a cross-national research team, comprised of members from the countries being studied. This has enabled us to reflect on the meaning of concepts before and during data collection and throughout the analysis. The in-depth description of the organizational environments helped us to highlight contextual factors impinging on the different organizations. Our aim was twofold: (1) to explore how national institutional features and specific organizational circumstances provide a context for understanding managers' perspectives on worklife policies; and (2) to analyse how this multilayered contextual strategy is reflected in the agency and capabilities of employees for WLB. Our rich qualitative study does not assume that there is a direct causal relation between the impact of these influences and claims of employees (which would require quantitative data). Rather, we seek to show the interplay between the managerial discourses and the capabilities of employees for shaping their WLB.

We collected qualitative data in three financial organizations, in the UK, the Netherlands, and Slovenia, as part of an EU funded research programme called the Transitions Project. Data were collected at BIC, a large Dutch banking and insurance company; at PEAK, a British insurance company; and at SAVA, a Slovenian bank (see Table 8.1). The financial sector is often known for its favourable working conditions for WLB (Fagan and Walthery Chapter 7 of this volume) and as such is not representative of all sectors and workplaces. Finance tends to be a sector with employees who have a relatively high education, of which a high proportion are women. Studying managers in this context may reveal how gender plays a role in managerial discourses. Gendered assumptions can also be found in the perceptions and experiences of the employees. The proportion of female employees varied between the cases, in BIC 37% of the employees were female, in PEAK 50%, and at SAVA 76%. BIC and PEAK offer worklife policies above the national average, while SAVA offers statutory policies. Most workers are highly skilled, and part-time work is common, except for employees at SAVA.

Table 8.1 Overview of selected cases

	BIC	PEAK	SAVA
Country	*The Netherlands*	*UK*	*Slovenia*
Industry	*Banking and insurance*	*Insurance*	*Banking*
Work force	*30,000*	*4,500*	*1,000*
Worklife policies	*Above national average*	*Above national average*	*Only statutory*
Organizational change	*Merger & restructuring*	*Merger & restructuring*	*Privatization & changing market, restructuring*
Work intensification	*Yes*	*Yes*	*Yes*
Line manager more responsible for HR policies	*Yes, downsized HR*	*Yes, move from HR policy to culture change*	*Yes*
Formal/informal culture	*Formal, but consensus based*	*Informal trust based*	*Formal, in some units informal culture*
% female employees	*37 %*	*50% (estimate)*	*76%*
Skills of most workers	*High*	*High*	*Medium/High*
Part-time work	*Usual*	*Usual*	*Unusual*
Trade Union participation	*Low*	*High*	*Low*

In all cases the managers were interviewed individually; the employees—all working parents—participated in focus groups. Analysis of company documents provided contextual background for the managers' interviews and focus groups. Six managers were interviewed at PEAK, including supervisors, HRM, and department managers, most of them parents. Seven managers were interviewed at SAVA: two men and five women including two directors, three departmental managers, an HRM manager, and a supervisor who was also a trade union representative. All except the HRM manager were parents. At BIC eight managers were interviewed including directors, team managers, project managers, the HRM manager, and product/account managers. Most managers had children. Eighteen focus groups were conducted, ranging between four and eight focus groups per case study. The total number of participants consisted of 85 people; 24 at PEAK, 32 at BIC, and 29 at SAVA. The participants were predominantly highly educated (see Table 8.1). Almost all of those recruited for the focus groups were in white-collar or professional jobs. The UK and Dutch companies had significant numbers of part-time employees in the focus groups. See Tables 8.2 and 8.3 for an overview.

The semi-structured interviews typically lasted about one hour. The focus groups lasted one to two hours. Both interviews and focus groups took place during office hours and were recorded and transcribed. The manager interviews and the employee focus groups were based on a jointly developed interview guide, structured for comparability between the countries, although the respondents were given space to expand on the topics.

Table 8.2 Summary of manager interviews and focus groups

	Number of managers interviews	Number of focus groups (total members)	Focus group size (2, 3–4, 5+)	Number of mixed-sex focus groups	Whether manager present at focus group
PEAK	6	6 (24)	1, 3, 2	4/6	5/6
BIC	8	4 (32)	0, 1, 3	4/4	0/4
SAVA	7	8 (29)	0, 6, 2	4/8	0/4

Table 8.3 Summary of characteristics of employees in focus groups

	No. in FGs	No in PT work	No. aged 40+	No. with a child 11+	No. fathers	No. lone parents	No. in agency work	Education level Deg, US, C
PEAK	24	6/24	4/24	2/24	10/24	3/24	0/24	12 3 9
BIC	32	23/32	2/32	0/32	12/32	0/32	0/32	14 17 1
SAVA	29	2/29 *	4/29	5/29	7/29	0/29	0/29	16 12 1

* In SAVA 2 people worked 6 hours per day

Code: PT—part-time

Deg—degree

US—upper school education

C—compulsory education

FG—focus group

Three Cases: Context, Discourses, and Practices

BIC, the Dutch company, has a reputation for good working conditions and flexibility. PEAK, the UK company, was attempting to forge a new workplace culture based on flexibility and trust following recent mergers and acquisitions. Many PEAK employees felt that the new culture gave more power to managers. SAVA, the Slovenian company, mostly adhered to labour laws and had care-leave policies in place. All three organizations were undergoing a process of change, adapting to the demands of the global economy. For SAVA, this process was intensified by the transition to a market economy with privatization and the restructuring of public businesses formerly managed by workers. Both the Dutch company BIC and UK PEAK were undergoing mergers and restructuring that produced changes within them, where some departments disappeared while others remained fairly stable. In SAVA, the restructuring created greater work intensity for some departments, especially the IT department. PEAK has witnessed many redundancies; this was less true at BIC and SAVA. In all three organizations, employees and managers experienced work intensification. Slovenian organizations have been affected by the same processes found across Europe, such as an intense market globalization and liberalization, but they also faced changes in the political system, in the economy, and in technology, as well as the effects of EU membership.

Line managers were responsible for the implementation of human resource policies, including worklife policies. However, in Slovenia, with a tradition of representative decision making and well-developed public worklife policies, HR managers paid relatively little attention to work–family issues. WLB issues are considered to be a private matter for the employee and not something the organization should pay extra attention to. Work–family issues had a higher profile in BIC and PEAK, as they were part of organizational policies.

Working conditions in the three financial firms were generally good compared with the national average in their country at the time of the study. All offered part-time work and flexible start and end times. BIC followed the collective agreement in the Dutch banking sector regarding a 36-hour work-week and permitted different work schedules, such as a compressed work-week (for example working nine hours for four days). These sector specific work arrangements were used by around one-third of BIC employees at the time of the research. A compressed work-week was particularly popular with male employees, while women typically worked part-time. The high percentage of women working part-time all over the Netherlands is well documented (Visser 2002), whereby women with higher education often choose a four-day work-week, while those with lower educations choose a short work-week of three days or even less. At SAVA, parents with young children could work part-time until the child was 3, following a 2003 Law on Labor Relations. In practice, this was almost the only form of part-time work. Utilization of part-time work schedules was low at SAVA, following the pattern at most firms in the country (see Kanjuo Mrčela and Černigoj Sadar in Chapter 9 of this volume). At BIC and PEAK, part-time work was more common. All three organizations offered sick leave, maternity leave, parental leave, short-term care leave, and emergency leave. Data from SAVA and BIC showed that mainly women used these different types of leave; male workers rarely used leave arrangements. Data from PEAK on use of these leave policies were not available. At SAVA, as is normal in Slovenia, a relatively long parental leave of 37 weeks is widely used by women (Rener et al. 2005), but rarely by men. At national level, about 1–2% of men take parental leave (Office for Equal Opportunity 2007) although they have full rights to use it and are 100% compensated. At SAVA, not a single interviewee or focus group participant mentioned the father taking parental leave. In the Netherlands, all employed women take maternity leave, but the use of parental leave is much lower (27%) (Portegijs et al. 2004). Maternity leave is fully compensated, but parental leave is compensated at 70% and in the public sector only for the first

13 weeks. At BIC use of parental leave was below the national average: 10% of workers used parental leave in 2003. Most leave arrangements in the three case studies had a statutory basis (see Table 6.1 in Chapter 6), although these arrangements were unpaid in the UK. BIC supplemented the Dutch Parental Leave Act with extra time and had an annual budget of 0.5% of the total gross amount spent on salaries for childcare. PEAK had recently closed a crèche but provided childcare vouchers.

Framing of Worklife Policies in Three Organizations

In all three cases, most managers were aware of their key role for policy implementation. The managers at BIC accepted a larger employers' role in a context in which employers' organizations, trade unions, and individual organizations were viewed as important actors for developing tailor-made facilities to meet the needs of employers and employees. The BIC managers presented their organization as decent and caring with good policies for working parents, but they expected employees also to consider the needs of the organization. At PEAK, worklife policies were connected to a rhetoric of mutual flexibility and trust. There was a strategic move to develop a distinctive people-focused culture, based on trust, mutual flexibility, and self-management at all levels of the newly merged company. The emphasis on a less hierarchical structure and greater team and individual autonomy was the primary reason given for a shift from formal to informal flexi-time, that is, from a clocking-in system to a more 'contemporary' trust-based approach rooted in good management and on good working relationships. This shift at PEAK towards a more informal approach increased managerial discretion to a larger degree than in our other two cases. At BIC and SAVA, worklife policies were framed as entitlements and formal policies. In all three cases, most managers were aware of their key role for policy implementation. They made decisions on leaves, short-term absences, and overtime and assessed effectiveness.

Managers noted that women requested WLB policies more often than men. Worklife issues were mainly seen as work–family issues, and were framed as women's issues in all three cases. This reflects a motherhood culture in which women are viewed as the primary caretakers of children (Morgan 2006). The traditionally strong male-breadwinner ideology in the Netherlands has persisted despite the dramatic increase in female employment, and is reflected in the dominance of the one-and-a-half earner family in which the mother works part-time and the father full-time. There are more mixed attitudes towards the importance of motherhood in relation to work and care in the UK, but ideals of motherhood still underlie most worklife policies (Kremer 2007). Slovenia has a longstanding dual-breadwinner culture, but caring work is still mainly expected of women. Managers reported that the use of worklife policies contains a *tacit understanding of the tradeoff* that career trajectories will be affected if one decides to work part-time or take long-term leave. Worklife policies are framed as gender neutral and have existed in Slovenia for decades, but are predominantly used by women. Gendered norms at PEAK and BIC limited men's capabilities to use worklife policies and often limited a women's career development. In contrast, as part-time work was a relatively new arrangement at SAVA, possible career consequences were rarely discussed, but opportunities to reduce working hours remained limited. Like the fathers in Hobson and Fahlén's study (2009), men in these three firms had weak agency and capabilities to reduce working hours.

In the following section we present some of the key discourses emerging in each organization. After analysing the managerial discourses, we turn to the focus group data and consider the following questions: do employees discuss or express the influence of the(se) discourse(s) on their own capabilities for using WLB policies? Do employees discuss or express the influence of the(se) discourse(s) on the organizational (worklife) culture? And, do these managerial discourses enable or hamper employees' capabilities?

Three Managerial Discourses

In analysing the manager interviews, three different discourses as described above emerged to varying degrees across the three cases: a disruption discourse justifying restricted use of worklife policies, which was particularly apparent among all middle managers; dependency considerations, expressed particularly among PEAK managers; and an ethical discourse in which managers considered support for working parents as the 'morally right thing to do', which arose among BIC and SAVA managers. In the following we will elaborate on these managerial discourses in each of the three cases and summarize the similarities and differences between them.

PEAK: The UK Case

At PEAK, where the business argument prevailed, managers drew on both dependency and disruption discourses. They discussed the potential disruptiveness of WLB arrangements in relation to operational needs, and about planning difficulties and the struggle to meet competing demands of employees and their department goals.

> One of my temporary managers asked for part-time a few months ago. I didn't refuse her the part-time hours. I said what we'd have to do is find a replacement

> for the day that she wasn't here, but the day she wanted off was the Friday and that I couldn't accommodate because I've got other managers that are off on Fridays.... she specifically wanted Friday off and I had to refuse that...we've just offered her another position, where she can actually have Friday off if she wants. (PEAK, female manager, two adult children)

This woman manager found a strategy for accommodating the needs of a temporary member of staff, albeit in a less interesting position. Managers who resisted flexibility at PEAK often drew on a *disruption* argument. While official entitlement to flexible working policies is available for most employees, the reality depends on how managers perceive their department's operational needs. For example, the need for people to service phones throughout working hours was viewed as a rationale for set hours. Departments that did not have a public interface had more flexible hours, and staff in sales departments could usually work from home at least some of the time.

Based on dependency theory, Klein et al. (2000) argue that employees who are most difficult to replace and on whom the manager 'depends' for departmental performance, have the most power in negotiations and are most likely to have requests to use WLB policies granted, even if this causes disruption. Managerial discourses at PEAK emphasized *dependency*, in keeping with national discussions of the business case and the company rhetoric promoting flexibility, trust, and empowerment. The discursive rationale for WLB polices was that employers depended on their workforce and therefore needed to 'keep them happy' by meeting their flexibility needs.

> in becoming more business focused what they've done is focus on the employees and asked them: you know what you want, what can we do for you? And, no, people no longer want to work well...a percentage of people no longer want to work just 9 to 5.... (PEAK, female manager, two children)

Not all PEAK managers considered themselves a part of the 'new style'; within the organization were more autocratic 'old style' managers who did not accept the business case for supporting work–family needs. The discourse of the new culture and management style emphasized the dependency argument, while for the old-style managers the disruption argument was used as a reason for not implementing flexibility and trust, despite the drive for work organizational culture change. All managers interviewed presented themselves as 'new style' managers, emphasizing the focus on trust and mutual responsibility and concern for the wellbeing of their employees.

> I don't monitor the number of hours everybody does each week...that may be done in other departments, but from my perspective, as long as...we've maintained our service quotas each week then...people who want to leave early, five,

> four, three o'clock, then they leave early, it's no problem...but equally, people can volunteer to do extra hours just to catch up. So it's a bit of give and take now...I don't see any point in monitoring how many hours people do because we have trust there. (PEAK, male senior manager, one child)

Thus the business case discourse in UK policy was reflected in both disruption discourses for some managers and dependency for others. The dependency discourse has more potential to promote agency to reconcile work and family, particularly for the valued workers, but this could result in an agency and capabilities gap for the less valued, that is, agency inequalities for those on whom managers are less dependent. Moreover, inconsistencies between the two styles of management reduced opportunity structures for employees overall to exercise agency in their planning.

BIC: The Dutch Case

At BIC, both disruption and dependency discourses emerged, and we also found evidence of the ethical discourse. When employees were denied flexibility, as in PEAK, this was based on a *disruption* argument, reflecting the agency and capabilities gap between formal entitlements and daily practices. This difference is due to the way managers perceive the operational needs of their departments. BIC managers also differentiated between employees. They found part-time work in more senior roles more disruptive than among assistants. Moreover, when managers addressed the issue of part-time work, it was often linked to implicit gendered assumptions.

> No problem for assistants. But it becomes pretty difficult for employees with a higher position. If you get a woman who wants to work 2.5 days, you would have to find another woman who also wants to work 2.5 days. And precisely on the other days too, because men don't work part-time. That would really become very awkward. I wouldn't know how to deal with that. (BIC, female project manager, no children)

Managers also spoke of the ramifications of agreeing to a request for flexible working hours for social cohesion and solidarity in their groups.

> I think there is some sense of injustice.... It's difficult to sell to the rest of the team that someone who already works part-time also takes extra leave. (BIC, male team manager, father of two children)

However, they recognized that these difficulties were not a consequence of worklife policies per se, but were because resources for replacement were rarely available and the workload often remained the same, increasing work pressures for all.

> I lose hours, and don´t get any replacement. It doesn´t lead to a new vacancy, and therefore it means an extra burden for the rest of the team. (BIC, male team manager, father of two children)

The dependency discourse was less prominent, although some managers did argue that WLB policies that benefited employees would benefit the overall organization.

> If people are feeling comfortable because of a good work–life balance it will benefit the company. (BIC, male team manager, no children)

We have made an analytical distinction between the dependency and the disruption arguments. However, in practice managers may consider both types of arguments simultaneously. Managers wanted to grant leave requests to hard-working employees, yet at the same time these were the employees that would be missed the most during their absence.

> I find it more difficult to grant a hard-working employee that request, compared to someone who works less hard, because I won't miss the latter as much when he starts working part-time. On the other hand, someone who works very hard should be granted that request. So, it's a little ambiguous. But I'll grant the request faster to the hard working employee, although it will damage my business. (BIC, male manager, no children)

This more complex view of dependency suggests that at BIC it was less salient and explicit in the work-organizational culture than in PEAK.

A third discourse also emerged in BIC. For many managers, operating the delicate balance between meeting organizational output targets and being a good supervisor supporting working parents (mothers) was experienced as the 'right thing to do'. Several managers explicitly mentioned that private issues prevailed above work, particularly for new parents, or in a crisis.

> You know, if someone has a child, first you get pregnancy leave and afterwards parental leave. And that is also necessary, because so much changes in the lives of that someone and his family. It's logical that you must regain that balance. Therefore I find parental leave in this also a completely logical consequence. (BIC, male director, no children)

The management discourse at BIC on WLB privileged motherhood, which could increase tensions at the workplace between mothers and others who are childless. BIC managers talked about mothers needing to attend to emergencies at home and noted if there were many mothers in the department that this could create resentment, especially if childless employees had to take over the work. Nevertheless, support for combining work and childcare and the capabilities of mothers to make claims for care was embedded in the corporatist nature of the Dutch welfare state, which emphasizes a role for the employer as well as the state to support it. Moreover, Dutch society places high value on parental care at home. The moral discourse was also intertwined with dependency considerations, in which managers argued that people should be able to attend to their personal problems in order to be effective at work.

> They get the time they need. If an employee has a problem in his or her private life, work will suffer too. Some will use work as a distraction, which is also a possibility. Sometimes, choosing for their private life will help people to get a better overview of the work they are doing here. (BIC, male director, no children)

SAVA: The Slovenian Case

In the Slovenian context of well-established statutory worklife leave policies, but with little experience of other flexible or part-time work arrangements, managers at SAVA regarded part-time work or a temporary leave of absence as problematic. On the other hand, short-term leave or occasionally working from home were considered less disruptive than long-term parental leave, as the latter required finding a suitable replacement. Finding replacements for people on parental leave could be difficult given financial constraints, but was managed. Within the firm, there was an emerging discourse on the disruptiveness surrounding part-time work. Managers anticipated implementation difficulties, partly related to unchallenged assumptions about the organization of work. In much the same way as expressed by managers in BIC and PEAK, they saw problems in terms of replacement and intensification of work for team members linked to a tight labour force.

> First of all I would have a talk with this parent to point out that the nature of work in the front office makes it impossible...that I as manager could not burden the other workers for the other part of his/her working day. (SAVA, female manager, aged 55, mother of one child)

Although managers did mention disruptiveness arguments when discussing several forms of leave or flexible work, at SAVA, in contrast to PEAK and BIC, this seldom led to actual denials of an employee's request, especially when it related to statutory provisions. Nevertheless, employees often had to accept a different position within the organization or reduced career opportunities.

> employees are by law entitled to it (part-time work)—so there's not much to discuss. Another matter is where to place this employee. One (part-timer) per unit could be managed. But when there are two or more we need to find some other job position in another unit of the bank. (SAVA, female manager, mother of two children)

SAVA managers were generally positive about the use of leave in relation to childcare, despite potential disruptiveness. Still, they indicated problems if several parents were on leave in one department, again because of lack of replacements.

> Now we have six or eight on parental leave in our branch and only two are being replaced, not the rest of them, because as a rule there is no replacement for parental leave. Their colleagues have to do more of course... they are being overburdened.... (SAVA, female executive director, mother of one adult child)

Dependency discourse was rare at SAVA, although a minority recognized that worklife policies could benefit the organization.

> If you fulfil their needs in one way or another, they will give back to you. My opinion is that everybody could work less.... You can't force people on the basis of formal rules or law to work more. It's more positive to motivate people and get their cooperation. (SAVA, female network manager, two children in secondary school)

The human resource manager at SAVA indicated that it was difficult to find suitable people for some key positions, but she mentioned only financial stimulus/benefits used in recruitment. In contrast to other departments, in IT there was a high level of flexibility in terms of time and space and a fine example of good teamwork, but even here the male manager did not put forward a dependency argument; that some workers are more valued than others. The moral discourse was the dominant discourse among the managers at SAVA. Managers said that they should care for people.

> We all approve if we only see the chance to do so. We also know, together with co-workers, that anybody could find himself in such a situation—I think we always have found agreement. (SAVA, female network manager, mother of two children)

This was in particular true for relatively 'old' policy measures, like maternity and parental leave. The long tradition of statutory maternity and parental leave had an impact on other decisions regarding flexibility in terms of time and space, but mainly for mothers. This was in tune with the prevailing attitudes of managers and the public discourse about the gendered division of parental tasks. Fathers rarely took parental leave. Moreover, breastfeeding was strongly encouraged and the combination of maternity and parental leave gave women the opportunity to breastfeed for a longer period of time. Similar findings were found in a study of seven organizations in Slovenia (Kanjuo Mrčela and Černigoj Sadar 2007). However, the tight staffing levels in the newly privatized firm often precluded replacements for those on leave, which created disruption issues, reducing the capabilities of managers to support parents and potentially undermining parents' (mothers') capabilities to use entitlements without negative career consequences.

Managerial Discourses Across Cases

In all three cases, disruption and dependency discourses were invoked to justify negative and positive responses respectively to requests for WLB. The disruption discourse was strongest in BIC and PEAK, despite the fact that both companies offered additional worklife policies beyond the national legislation. Disruption was an emerging discourse in SAVA in relation to increasing work intensification and staff shortages following the transition to a market economy. Perceived operational needs were paramount in this discourse in all of the companies, as managers grappled with relatively new provisions, high work intensification, and low organizational support, particularly in lean workforces. Historical tradition and current employment norms collided in SAVA regarding newly introduced legislation on part-time work and the perceived disruptive effects on work organization. Managers lacked experience in organizing and coordinating part-time jobs, in contrast to their British and Dutch counterparts for whom part-time employment was very common. However, SAVA managers were less likely to openly deny requests as a consequence of disruption arguments, since in the Slovenian context there was less room for discretion.

Managers in all three cases also voiced general dependency considerations, arguing that a good WLB created a committed and productive workforce. Dependency discourse was most dominant in PEAK, where a business rationale supported a move from formal HR worklife policies to an informal culture of employee autonomy. The PEAK management rhetoric of dependency was often undermined in practice by disruption concerns, however. At SAVA and BIC dependency considerations were not expressed openly, and when visible they seem to be more linked to ethical considerations; WLB policies supporting workers' needs as well as retaining a skilled and experienced workforce.

In practice, it appears that managers considered both disruption and dependency arguments. The use of these apparently competing and contradictory discourses may reflect the issues and conflicts that managers face, in general applicability to all the cases, in reconciling goals of supporting employees to balance work and family life with the operational needs to sustain productivity and effectiveness in the globally competitive finance sector. Globalization trends may have reduced managers' freedom of action and capabilities to support employees, even when mandated or predisposed toward WLB claims. Managers, not only in the liberal UK context, but also in the corporatist Dutch and post-socialist Slovenian contexts, may be moving closer to their counterparts in the USA, where disruption and dependency considerations were initially promoted. Nonetheless, the resonance on the moral discourse in these firms suggests that local cultural and institutional factors also make a difference. Thus, the moral discourse expressed by BIC managers may be related to the Dutch valuing of more personal time and parental care at home, while at SAVA this discourse appears embedded in a long history of entitlements to reconcile work and personal life. In PEAK there was a strong discourse about 'trust' and employees being 'genuine'—moral categories invoked by the managers. Yet the discourse of moral expectation and norms focused on workplace moral values, rather than on the ethics of valuing people's nonworking time or their family lives. Finally, underlying the discourses of managers on WLB policies in all three cases were deeply embedded gendered assumptions reflecting wider societal contexts.

Working Parents' Capabilities and the Impact of Managerial Discourses

The three managerial discourses are an analytical construction, made after our analysis of the interviews. We had no explicit questions on these discourses in the focus groups. Therefore, we assume that these discursive rationales are implicit, when considering the subjective experienced capabilities of working parents to combine work and family care.

British Employees

There was a strong discourse by PEAK managers on the new style of management, in which individual flexibility is encouraged, a strategy that is supposed to increase capabilities for WLB; but the focus group participants were far more ambivalent than their managers about the positive effects of this strategy. The change from formal regulations to informal arrangements was portrayed by managers as permitting more autonomy, but from the working parents' perspective it placed greater pressure on team relations and on inexperienced supervisors. The new UK parental leave restrictions are more restrictive than in many EU countries, and the PEAK organization has added further restrictions that are certainly against the spirit of the law and probably illegal. For example, we were told that parents have to take all of their annual leave before they can take parental leave. The (unpaid) leave has to be applied for in week blocks, 28 days in advance, and the manager has to approve the leave for that period. Parents spoke about limits on how and when they were 'allowed' to use the leave rather than as an entitlement:

> I thought about asking for it because I have a childminder, and obviously she's entitled to holiday, and that's 4 weeks' holiday a year, so I thought about doing that. The problem is, she took a week in February, a week in May, a week in August and she's due a week in a couple of week's time. So I have to make other

> arrangements at that time. But of course they won't allow me to use it at the beginning of the year, because I've not used my holidays up, it seems, and then they won't allow me to use it for my holidays.

Parents, both fathers and mothers, mentioned feeling guilty about asking for parental leave, clearly tending to have little sense of entitlement:

> I think, I'd feel really guilty asking for some unpaid leave with all my colleagues and my manager not having children and they're very understanding but, to turn around and say 'Oh by the way, I want the summer off'...for 4 weeks, you know. (mother)

There is also some inflexibility in being able to book the two weeks' paid paternity leave that the company offers, and in booking maternity leaves:

> I think it's a lot harder to arrange though isn't it paternity leave, we're finding that, I know my finishing date unless anything happens before that, then that's when I finish, whereas with paternity leave it's hit and miss really isn't it, they don't quite know when they're gonna be taking that time, so.... (father)

Feelings of guilt at taking more leave than non-parents are particularly noteworthy as the discussions are in the context of talking about how non-parents can also, under company regulations, apply for unpaid leave each year. For unexpected family needs or crises, parental leave is unsuitable, as it needs to be approved a month in advance. The company offers leave for emergency family reasons, at the discretion of the managers. Employees are often not clear about the regulations governing this. The ambiguity about what counts as a real emergency, mentioned earlier, is reflected in pay issues for emergency childcare leave. There is resentment about being docked pay for time off for sick children:

> It is annoying because I never take time off sick for myself but I had to take time off a couple of years ago for one of my children being sent home from school and I was told I had two shorter days holiday. That really naffed me off.

The importance for expectant parents of having understanding managers was highlighted in the focus groups. Women managers, and managers who had young children themselves, were seen as particularly sympathetic. Women in male dominated teams and with male supervisors reported less understanding and more stress than women with female supervisors. Women spoke about confidence loss during maternity leave. Losses in both confidence and skills during maternity leave can be reduced by supportive managers and team environments as well as the possibility of keeping in touch with developments while on leave. As with other practices, an employee's perception that the manager is understanding and supportive tends to increase their commitment to the organization.

The use of managerial discretion and inconsistency in the application of policies across departments was also a source of frustration.

> I don't think there's consistency across the company, anyway, across departments... our manager's under the impression that the supervisor's position is 9 to 5, which isn't in our contract, and she's made you feel bad if you asked to go early which isn't what flexible working's all about. (expectant mother)

The downside of the changes linked to 'modern' ways of working is that if employees, and managers, are not satisfied with the changes, this can be interpreted as an inability to fit into a modern, well-functioning organization. Focus group participants described differences in the ways in which the drive for flexibility was interpreted, and appeared more concerned about inconsistencies than the managers. Few of the refusals of flexible or part-time work have been official requests using the new legislation. People were reluctant to use this as they worried it would give the wrong impression. If they thought the company would not agree they felt it unwise to risk their image. They also felt that the company deliberately did not communicate some of its policies well, so people would not request them. Some employees expressed discomfort at having to use official procedures to push for flexible working rights: 'I probably wouldn't, I'm not that kind of person'.

The organization had venues for encouraging workplace solidarity and better communication. The PEAK employees we interviewed did not interpret these initiatives in relation to dependency rationales—keeping the workforce happy. They perceived these bonding exercises as placatory gestures rather than actually looking after the employees, specifically losing the perks they really cared about (like the workplace nursery, etc.). Employees tended to be cynical about the organizational discourse of looking after employees. They found discrepancies between the perceptions of managers that policies were communicated well and the understanding of employees that sometimes they were low-key or hidden. A downside of the organizational changes linked to more 'modern' ways of working was that if employees, and managers, were not satisfied with the changes, they could be seen as not fitting into a modern, evolving organization.

Dutch Employees

BIC can be characterized as an organization with a wide variety of WLB policies, according to both the managers we interviewed and the employees in the focus groups. However, the implementation of policies varied widely between departments and between managers. Employees noted that organizational culture still plays an important role in the way policies were implemented. In some cases, it was even more important how each specific team dealt with the policies.

> Now look, there are arrangements they have to apply, like parental leave, that is a legal right, but no, a lot of things are not part of the culture. It is dependent on the team. (mother, aged 37)

Formally, everybody is entitled to existing policies; informally, there can be career consequences for the employees who actually use them. The tradeoff for using the policies can be a loss of career opportunities. In addition, there is no structural solution for a temporary replacement within the organization. The manager and team of the employee who uses leave, or works part-time, will suffer from an increase in work pressure. This is because the workload is not adjusted when there is a fluctuation in available workers. Much is left to the work floor to find a solution for people on leave or who reduce their working hours.

> You cannot replace somebody in no time. That is a problem your colleagues will have to solve. That's the way it works. (father, aged 33)

Employees have to deal with the extra workload themselves when colleagues are on leave. Managers have a discretionary space for granting requests, but no structural possibilities to replace absent employees, which means that the remaining employees need to rearrange things amongst themselves. For the managers, disruption is not a rationale for denying claims per se, but disruption affects the capabilities for worklife balance among other employees, who have to pick up the burden of the extra workload.

In general, all workers seem to be able to get requests granted, but in some cases it took considerable effort and involved openly opposing their manager's decision. Although policies formally have to be granted to each employee, sometimes the manager's unwillingness can cause irritation and stress.

> Yes, also in my case he came with his tail between his legs one and half week before I went on leave. But it has cost you so much energy and aggravation. (mother, aged 38)

Despite the absence of a culture of long hours, employees are experiencing an increase in their workload. Employees working part-time, or reducing their working hours, make a point of mentioning that their workload is increasing. Moreover, some managers expect people to be available at all times, without respecting actual working hours. Instead of looking at the output, some managers still think being present at the workplace is vital. In regard to this issue of presenteeism, we found that BIC allows its employees to reduce hours for

WLB but, at the same time, BIC does not promote flexible work situations. For instance, BIC does not hire part-time workers, as noted by a respondent.

> Yes, but the BIC policy varies in that respect. There are part-timers working in the company, but part-timers are never hired. Vacancies for job positions are seldom offered part-time, always full-time. (mother, aged 37)

Though managers differ in their responses to requests from their employees, for the most part, if an employee makes a strong claim, she or he will see the request honoured. Most respondents think it not difficult to make arrangements to meet WLB needs. Therefore most employees are quite satisfied with the arrangements at BIC.

> My personal situation is reasonably okay. I have reasonably flexible working hours, as long as I do my job. My husband has exactly the same. So, you can do a lot and then it doesn't matter if you have to work longer sometimes. And childcare is not at all a problem for us. (mother, aged 39)

The good policies at BIC are attributed to the dependence of organizational needs on the labour market. Most policies are recent, and recent years can be characterized as a time period in which employers made significant efforts to attract employees. WLB policies are one of these instruments, and some think these policies will decrease during the contemporary economic downturn.

> But let us be honest, as soon as there is an economic hype, they will do everything to keep you, but as soon as things go down, budgets are reduced, outputs increase. Things are different then. That's the way it is. (father, aged 36)

Our focus group gave the overall impression that employees are generally satisfied with the possibilities at BIC, although they expressed some dissatisfaction, which can be traced to two sources. First, BIC is not always clear in the way it deploys its policies. For instance, it is possible to work part-time, but internal job offers never contain part-time jobs. Second, and most importantly, managers differ in the way they grant employee requests. This discretionary component can lead to feelings of unfairness by employees, and the discretionary power can affect employees' sense of entitlement to claim WLB policies, and lead them to question whether the capabilities for enhancing WLB, promoted in Dutch policy and discourse, are as pervasive as one imagines.

Slovenian Employees

At SAVA, 76% of the employees are female and the generous parental leave is viewed as problematic for the work organization and the extra workload it imposes on other employees. The long care leaves also lead to social and gender differentiation in recruitment and promotion processes. The statutory public policies supporting care leave during times of financial crisis when some organizations have no resources to implement them, decrease the capability options for managers as well as for employees.

Management and employees both agreed that the intensification of work and the communication gap between various levels in the organization are the most prevalent problems in SAVA. Another concern voiced by employees is the inflexibility of working hours and the vaguely defined, but often rigid, organizational policies. Both employees and managers attributed these problems to the merger with another bank, which has led to an intensification of the workload.

> we have to do 70% of orders... (more). Before I had 30% to do all day, now I have 100%, and that is too much for me (mother, aged 33)

Employees often report that they come home feeling very tired and also share the opinion of managers that, despite improved IT support, the decrease in labour force means more work for those that remain.

Given that the public policies in place were regarded as quite generous from the employer's point of view, no special or additional organizational policies existed in the company for working parents. The long tradition of fully paid maternity and parental leave in Slovenia was taken for granted by managers as well as by parents. All mothers in the company used their maternity leave. Although parental leave was created to increase equal opportunity for men to participate in care and parental life, in practice it is viewed exclusively as a women's prerogative.

Because of the difficulty of getting short-term replacements, parents reported that they did not get support from management when they had to care for a sick child. They usually looked for other options, such as help from relatives, working overtime, or using vacation days. Receiving support is often discretionary and dependent upon the manager and, as one employee reported, that can go either way.

> It depends on what kind of person your superior is. You can apply for sick leave if you have a sick child at home and you can be criticized for not getting all your work done. Though my experience was positive. (mother, aged 33)

In an extreme, negative case, taking advantage of sick leave resulted in feelings of guilt and a loss of self-worth.

> When I was on a sick leave for a week, because both of them were sick, I had a really bad feeling when going back to work on Monday, one sick leave after another.... How can I be trusted at all? .... (mother, aged 33)

There are also quite a few barriers to the implementation of the law on working time. In general, parents are poorly informed regarding new legislation and constant changes in the legislation in all fields make it difficult keep up to date. Parents' needs are neglected and, when a request is granted, management sees it as an exception.

> Then one day I heard it on TV. And when I mentioned it to them, they said: 'Your request will be granted but don't talk about it...if the word gets about, somebody else might want it, too'. Even the employers themselves don't have enough information although they should be the ones to keep us informed. As I said, I heard only bits and pieces really, what it could bring along and all that. (mother, aged 39)

Although the employees were aware of the part-time option given by law, they still did not view it as their right and were concerned about the opinion of the employer:

> Now there is a possibility to work part-time after a maternity leave, if the employer allows. Again there is this thing: if the employer allows. (mother, aged 40)

Although a moral discourse was reported frequently by managers, some employees found that it was not always implemented:

> When you ask them, you are told your request will be granted (e.g. more flexible working hours) but then they make you wait for six months and still nothing comes out of it. (mother, aged 34)

SAVA had no explicit policy to enhance the capabilities of employees for a better WLB. There is no recognition that care for one's family could also be SAVA's responsibility. Both management and employees think that worklife policies are not an organizational matter.

> Parenthood is an employee's personal thing. (mother, aged 33)

> We are not accustomed to it and then one does not even expect it. (mother, aged 34)

Some employees take a critical attitude towards the employer point of view:

> If you look from the economic point of view...it does not matter to him (the employer) that you are a parent. He expects you to work, he pays for it, he expects results. That's why there are tendencies in the organization to employ men mostly, because they do not take maternity leave. (father, aged 26)

The disruption discourse, in combination with the belief that worklife issues are not an organizational responsibility, undermines employees' sense of entitlement to exercise rights for a WLB. This sense that family matters are not the responsibility of the firm is reflected in lower expectations, as seen in this employee's recognition that at SAVA, management is unresponsive to claims made by employees for shorter and flexible working hours. Yet the same father did praise the company for the good conditions of work regarding other aspects of the work process.

> The work itself is very good; the job is also very good, only the working time involved is curtailing the free time I could devote to my child. Because I come home relatively late—at 6 pm. (father, aged 26)

Informal practices can offset, at least to some extent, the lack of organizational support. Solidarity in small teams is high. In teams, and even sometimes in departments, employees created a good climate through frequent and supportive communications. Employees resolved everyday problems related to worklife reconciliation quicker when looking for support from their superiors. Informal practices created a social capital, which enhanced the development of capabilities for WLB.

SAVA assures its employees decent material wellbeing, that is a decent regular wage, a permanent work contract, and social security benefits (health and unemployment insurance, pension, etc.). In case of serious financial problems, SAVA helps employees solve them. All this has positive impacts on the working capabilities of parents. The constraints on the agency of employees from achieving WLB were: (1) organizational rigidity in implementing recent public provisions related to working hours; (2) the gendered norms regarding the use of leave; and (3) the extra workload for remaining employees when a colleague was on leave.

Working Parents Capabilities Across Cases

The capabilities of working parents to combine work and care are not explicitly influenced by the three management discourses. However, implicitly these discourses play a role in the way working parents view their (im)possibilities to achieve a WLB. The disruptiveness discourse seems to have the most negative impact on the capabilities and sense of entitlement of employees to make claims for, or use, WLB policies. This discourse has been influenced by the organizations' economic position, reflected in the employee discussions about increasing work intensification, mergers, new management, and job pressure. There was little evidence in the focus groups that employees felt that the organization was dependent upon retaining their employees and was willing to grant requests for that reason only. However, some employees at PEAK and some managers at SAVA mentioned extras for employees who were in demand. The moral discourse is understood by employees as increasing agency and capabilities. At BIC, managers and working parents considered that offering reasonable worklife policies was a decent thing to do, and also beneficial for the organization. At SAVA, care of material wellbeing and social security was seen as the main task of the organization, though there was little evidence that the organization was concerned about worklife imbalance, and quality of life aspects were ignored. At PEAK, the moral discourse held little sway in an organization in which the business case attitude to WLB policies was most prominent.

Conclusions

There is a body of research that focuses on the variations in WLB across welfare regimes (Crompton and Lyonette 2006; Gornick and Meyres 2003; Cousins and Tang 2004); but in the research on WLB, comparative studies of work organizational cultures across societies are lacking. Recently, growing attention has been paid to workplace organizational cultures and variations across institutional/societal contexts (Van der Lippe and Peters 2007; Lewis et al. 2009). Managerial support for WLB policies is crucial for shaping employees' capabilities to utilize them. WLB policies, whether statutory or organizational, are implemented in specific workplaces, which are themselves located in shifting global and national contexts. Previous research demonstrates the crucial role of managers (Lewis 1997; Wise and Bond 2003; Maxwell 2005; den Dulk and De Ruijter 2008). Our findings contribute to the worklife policy literature by situating managers simultaneously within specific workplace and national layers of context. We have investigated how financial sector managers frame the utilization of worklife policies in organizations in different welfare states. Research in the USA identifies disruption and dependency considerations as influencing managers' decision-making. Our findings show that these considerations were also important in these European case studies. A further management discourse also emerged—the moral case. Despite differences in dominant discourses in the three cases, a manager's capabilities to manoeuvre and negotiate WLB policies for their employees were restricted by resource issues and subsequent disruption concerns in the current competitive global context.

We have compared specific organizations and cannot make definitive inferences about cross-national differences from this qualitative multiple case study design; nor was that our intention. Nevertheless, the study has revealed the ways in which layers of context—workplace, national, and global—combine to shape the discourse of managers about worklife policies. At the same time we analysed the often implicit effect of these discourses on the sense of entitlement of their employees. Work and family processes are not static. The findings reveal some of the complex and dynamic processes whereby managers in these organizations in three European contexts make sense of the often competing demands from employees and the pressures from those above them in their organization. Organizational context is the most important layer of context for understanding the perspectives of managers and the experiences of employees, although these are also shaped by national and even global layers. National, historical policy and normative contexts underpin some of the variations in the processes observed in the three organizations, while global factors, including competition and subsequent intensification of work, may account for more of the convergence regarding the agency and capabilities for WLB (Smithson et al. 2012). To understand the agency and capabilities gap in the WLB of employees, our case study shows the importance of a multilayered perspective. This gap cannot be solely attributed to the relationship between the employee and the manager, nor solely to the relationship between the employee and the organization. The agency and capabilities gap is the result of the interplay between managerial discourses, which are coloured by the organizational and the national context, and the sense of entitlement of the employees. As our cases shown, these interplays work out differently in the three organizations.

The differences and similarities in the perspectives of managers, and the barriers they face in supporting parents, are important aspects in the overall context shaping an employee's capabilities to utilize policies. Seen from the individual employee, the agency and capabilities gap is revealed at the cognitive level through sense of entitlement to make claims for WLB at the workplace (Lewis and Smithson 2001; Hobson and Fahlén 2009). Previous research suggests that a sense of entitlement to work–family support varies across welfare states, as seen in the comparative studies in this volume, which show that gender equality discourses and longstanding WLB policies can foster a sense of entitlement to make claims for a WLB (see Chapter 3 in this volume), as is the case in the Nordic countries. We also suggest that an individual sense of entitlement can exist when there is a strong business case discourse. Our results reveal that both the dependency and the moral discourse can enhance agency to reconcile work and personal life (Lewis and Smithson 2001), although in the former only the most valued workers have greater agency to make claims, and moral arguments (as in the Slovenian case) may be overridden by organizational rigidity. The disruption discourse, which is more related to structural resources, may be associated with reduced capabilities to utilize and benefit from worklife policies.

Aspects of capabilities, including a sense of entitlement and freedoms to determine how to use time, are highly gendered (Robeyns 2003; Cornelius and Skinner 2008). This is also reflected in our findings; gender blindness in many of the policies and official organizational discourses, and obscure, gendered, managerial and employee practices and beliefs. In all three cases, worklife issues were viewed by managers as primarily women's issues, and were also experienced that way by working parents. This gendered dimension that runs throughout the data suggests that men's capabilities for utilizing policies is likely to remain low in all of the cases, reinforcing and reproducing gendered inequalities and limiting agency for women and men in relation to work and family (Hobson and Fahlén 2009).

The contemporary global economic crisis will affect the capabilities of working parents even more. Managers' room for manoeuvre will decrease. Therefore, comparative studies of the work organizational and managerial level remain important for understanding the WLB of employees. The use of a multilayered perspective on the capabilities of employees and the interplay with managerial discourses can provide new insights for understanding employees' WLB issues and the agency and capabilities gap they experience. Managers, on the other hand, are not just implementers of organizational policies; they are also mediators of the dominant discourses, thereby setting the tone and climate through which the capabilities of employees are given shape. Nevertheless, the capabilities of managers to grant requests are also bound by work organizational cultures and the dominance of the business case. This is particularly clear in the current global crisis of the neoliberal economies, where managers as well as employees are busy trying to survive the recession.

Note

1. This work was supported by the fifth framework programme of the European Union (Transitions project SERD-2002-00075).

Bibliography

Anderson, S. E., B.S. Coffey, and R.T. Byerly (2002). Formal Organizational Initiatives and Informal Workplace Practices: Links to Work–Family Conflict and Job-related outcomes. *Journal of Management*, 28(6):787–810.

Bonvin, J-M. and N. Farvaque (2003). Towards a Capability-Friendly Social Policy: The Role of Local Implementing Agencies. Paper presented at the VHI Conference Transforming Unjust Structures, Cambridge, 26–7 June.

Černigoj Sadar, N. (2009). Old Rights in New Times: The Experience of Parents in a Slovenian Organisation, in S. Lewis, J. Brannen, and A. Nilsen (eds), *Work, Families and Organisations in Transition. European Perspectives*. Bristol: Policy Press.

Cornelius, N. and D. Skinner (2008). The Careers of Senior Men and Women—A Capabilities Theory Perspective. *British Journal of Management*, 19:141–49.

Cousins, C. and N. Tang (2004). Working Time and Work and Family Conflict in the Netherlands, Sweden and the UK. *Work, Employment and Society*, 18(3):531–49.

Crompton, R. (2001). Gender, Comparative Research and Biographical Matching. *European Societies*, 3(2):167–90.

Crompton, R. and C. Lyonette (2006). Some Issues in Cross-national Comparative Research Methods: A Comparison of Attitudes to Promotion, and Women's Employment, in Britain and Portugal. *Work, Employment and Society*, 20:403–14.

Dulk, L. den (2001). *Work-family Arrangements in Organisations: A Cross-national Study in the Netherlands, Italy, the United Kingdom and Sweden*. Amsterdam: Rozenberg Publishers.

Dulk, L. den and B. Peper (2007). Working Parents' Use of Worklife Policies. *Sociologia, problemas e práticas*, 53:51–70.

Dulk, L. den and B. Peper (2009). Managing Worklife Policies in the European Workplace: Explorations for Future Research. RECWOWE Working Papers, REC-WP 04/09, <http://www.socialpolicy.ed.ac.uk/recwowepudisc/working_papers/working_paper_04__09>.

Dulk, L. den and J. de Ruijter (2008). Managing Worklife Policies: Disruptive Versus Dependency Arguments: Explaining Managerial Attitudes Towards Employee Utilization of Worklife Policies. *International Journal Human Resource Management*, 19(7):1224–38.

Dulk, L. den, A. Peper, N.Č. Sadar, S. Lewis, J. Smithson, and J. van Doorne-Huiskes (2011). Work Family and Managerial Attitudes and Practices in the European Workplace: Comparing Dutch, British and Slovenian Financial Sector Managers. *Social Politics*, 18(2):300–29.

Eaton, S.C. (2003). If You Can Use Them: Flexibility Policies, Organizational Commitment, and Perceived Performance. *Industrial Relations*, 42(2):145–67.

Employment in Europe (2009). Employment in Europe 2009. Luxembourg: Employment and Social Affairs, European Commission.

Esping-Andersen, G. (1999). *Social Foundations of Postindustrial Economies*. New York: Oxford University Press.

Fagan, C., A. Hegewisch, and J. Pillinger (2006). Out of Time. Why Britain Needs a New Approach to Working-Time Flexibility. TUC Research Paper. London: Trade Union Congress.

Fagan C. and P. Walthery (2011) Firm Characteristics, Organizational Culture and Reversible Working-time Adjustments in European Companies. *Social Politics*, 18(2):269–99.

Gornick, J.C. and M.C. Meyers (2003). *Families that Work: Policies for Reconciling Parenthood and Employment*. New York: Russell Sage Foundation.

Herman, C. and S. Lewis (2012). Entitled to a Sustainable Career? Motherhood in Science, Engineering, and Technology. *Journal of Social Issues*, 68(4):767–89. doi: 10.1111/j.1540-4560.2012.01775.x.

Hobson, B. and S. Fahlén (2009). Competing Scenarios for European Fathers: Applying Sen's Capabilities and Agency Framework to Work–Family Balance. *The ANNALS of the American Academy Political and Social Sciences*, 624:214–33.

Kanjuo Mrčela, A. and N. Černigoj Sadar (2007) (eds), *Delo in družina: s partnerstvom do družini prijaznega delovnega okolja* [Work and Family: With Partnership towards Family-Friendly Work Condition]. Ljubljana: Fakulteta za družbene vede.

Klein, K.J., L.M. Berman, and M.W. Dickson (2000). May I Work Part-time? An Exploration of Predicted Employer Responses to Employee Requests for Part-time Work. *Journal of Vocational Behaviour*, 57:85–101.

Kremer, M. (2007). *How Welfare States Care: Culture, Gender and Citizenship in Europe*. Amsterdam: Amsterdam University Press.

Lewis, S. (1996). Rethinking Employment: An Organizational Culture Change Framework, in S. Lewis and J. Lewis (eds), *The Work-Family Challenge: Rethinking Employment*, pp. 1–19. London: Sage.

Lewis, S. (1997). Family Friendly Organizational Policies: A Route to Organizational Change or Playing in the Margins. *Gender, Work and Organization*, 4:13–23.

Lewis, S. (2003). Flexible Work Arrangements: Implementation, Outcomes and Management, in C.L. Cooper and I.T. Robertson (eds), *International Review of Industrial and Organizational Psychology*, pp. 1–28. New York: John Wiley & Sons, Ltd.

Lewis, S. and L. den Dulk (2008). Parents' Experiences of Flexible Work Arrangements in Changing European Workplaces: A Multi-layer Contextual Approach. *Sociological Problems,* IL-II:5–28.

Lewis, S. and J. Smithson (2001). Sense of Entitlement to Support for the Reconciliation of Employment and Family Life. *Human Relations,* 54(11):1455–81.

Lewis, S., J. Brannen, and A. Nilsen (2009). *Work, Families and Organisations in Transition: European Perspectives*. Bristol: Policy Press.

Lippe, T. v. d., and P. Peters (2007). *Competing Claims in Work and Family Life*. Cheltenham, UK: Edward Elgar.

Maxwell, G.A. (2005). Checks and Balances: The Role of Managers in Worklife Balance Policies and Practices. *Journal of Retailing and Consumer Services*, 12:179–89.

Morgan, K.J. (2006). *Working Mothers and the Welfare State: Religion and the Politics of Work-Family Policies in Western Europe and the United States*. Stanford: Stanford University Press.

Nilsen, A., J. Brannen, and S. Lewis (2012) *Transitions to Parenthood in Europe: A Comparative Life Course Perspective*. Bristol: Policy Press.

Office for Equal Opportunities (2007) Očetje v Sloveniji [Fathers in Slovenia]. Office for Equal Opportunities: Ljubljana.

Perlow, L.A. (1995). Putting the Work Back into Work/Family. *Group and Organization Management*, 20:227–39.

Peper, B., L. den Dulk, and A. van Doorne-Huiskes (2009). Work–Family Policies in a Contradictory Culture: A Dutch Financial Sector Corporation, in S. Lewis, J. Brannen, and A. Nilsen (eds), *Work, Families and Organisations in Transition: European Perspectives*, pp. 113–28. Bristol: Policy Press.

Poelmans, S. and B. Beham (2005). A Conceptual Model of Antecedents and Consequences of Managerial Worklife Policy Allowance Decisions. Paper presented at the Inaugural Conference of the International Center of Work and Family, July 7–9, Barcelona, Spain.

Portegijs, W., A. Boelens, and L. Olsthoorn (2004). *Emancipatiemonitor 2004*. The Hague: Sociaal Cultureel Planbureau and Centraal Bureau voor de statistiek.

Powell, G.N. and L.A. Mainiero (1999). Managerial Decision Making Regarding Alternative Work Arrangements. *Journal of Occupational and Organizational Psychology*, 72:41–56.

Ragin, C. (1987).*The Comparative Method: Moving Beyond Qualitative and Quantitative Strategies*. Berkeley: University of California Press.

Rener, T., A. Švab, T. Žakelj, and Ž. Humar (2005). *Perspektive novega očetovstva v Sloveniji* (Perpective of New Fatherhood in Slovenia) Urad za enake možnosti: Research report. <http://www.uem.gov.si/fileadmin/uem.gov.si/pageuploads/Ocetovstvo_porocilo.pdf>.

Robeyns, I. (2003). Sen's Capability Approach and Gender Inequality: Selecting Relevant Capabilities. *Feminist Economics*, 9(2/3):61–92.

Sen, A. (1999). *Development as Freedom*. Oxford: Oxford University Press.

Smith, C. and P. Meikins (1995). System, Society and Dominance Effects in Cross-National Organisational Analysis. *Work, Employment & Society*, 9(2):241–67.

Smithson, J. and S. Lewis, S. (2005). *Report on National Debates on the Reconciliation of Family and Employment*. Manchester: RIHSC <http://www.workliferesearch.org/transitions>.

Smithson, J., S. Lewis, S. Kovacheva, L. den Dulk, A. Peper, and A. van Doorne-Huiskes (2012). Supports and Contraints for Parents: A Gendered Cross-national Perspective, in A. Nilsen, J. Brannen, and S. Lewis (eds), *Transitions to Parenthood in Europe: A Comparative Life Course Perspective*, pp. 89–105. Bristol: Policy Press.

Thompson, C.A., L.L. Beauvais, and K.S. Lyness (1999). When Work–Family Benefits are not Enough: The Influence of Work–Family Culture on Benefit Utilization, Organizational Attachment, and Work–Family Conflict. *Journal of Vocational Behavior,* 54:392–415.

Visser, J. (2002). The First Part-time Economy of the World—A Model to be Followed? *Journal of European Social Policy*, 12(1):23–41.

Wise, S. and S. Bond (2003). Worklife Policy: Does It Do Exactly What It Says on the Tin? *Women in Management Review*, 18(1/2):20–31.

9

Capabilities for worklife balance in the context of increasing work intensity and precariousness in the service sector and the IT industry in a transitional economy

Aleksandra Kanjuo Mrčela and Nevenka Černigoj Sadar

Introduction

Over the past two decades Slovenia has shifted from one economic and social system to another, as other post-socialist societies did; but compared with the other transition countries in Central East Europe, Slovenia is seen as a success story and therefore provides a perfect case study from which to view the agency and capabilities gap in worklife balance (hereafter WLB). Since the mid 1970s, unlike other Central Eastern European countries, both indirect and direct social policy measures have been in place for working parents and these continued even after the transition. This was enabled through a combination of factors: the economy was in comparatively good condition, the transitional model was based on gradual changes and social dialogue, and there was strong support for gender equality from different social actors, notably the women's movement, academics, and governmental bodies such as the Equal Opportunities Office. Yet the Slovenian case is paradoxical, since there is a vast agency and capabilities gap between the policies and the practice. In this chapter we analyse this gap within the multilayered framework of Sen's capability set as applied to WLB, viewing agency inequalities in terms of normative institutional constraints, structural features of labour markets, and with a specific focus on work organizational culture within three different sectors: retail, health, and IT.

The capabilities approach allows us to better understand the main tensions underlying agency and capabilities in Slovenia by identifying:

- the gap between existing rights of parents and their sense of entitlement to WLB;
- the gap between relative gender equality in paid work and gender inequality in parenting;
- the gap between public social policies and internal practices and cultures in organizations tuned to responding to competitive market pressures, creating differences between stated norms and actual practices.

The aim of this chapter is to understand how variations across different sectors within the same institutional and normative societal environment shape micro-level perceptions of risks, individual agency, and actual practices. The chapter is divided into three parts. First, we present the changing context of work, using statistical data and research results on Slovenian labour market characteristics and the work experiences of young people. We then provide an overview of three organizational settings in three separate sectors, followed by an in-depth analysis of qualitative data gathered within these organizations, which are a retail company, a department of a large public health organization, and an IT company. In the concluding section we reflect upon the cases presented and underline how our analysis of similarities and differences between the sectors contribute to an understanding of the capabilities of parents to achieve WLB in Slovenia.

The Changing Context of Work and Parenting in Slovenia

Although the changes in the Slovenian economy were viewed positively after the transition to a market economy, from the beginning of this century the economic situation and the conditions of work have worsened as a result of privatization, restructuring, and competitive pressure from international markets (Svetlik 2006; Kanjuo Mrčela and Ignjatović 2006). In order to increase business efficiency under the impact of the global economy, work organizations responded with de-standardization of employment and work practices (more fixed-term employment, functional flexibility, and place and time flexibility). These economic strictures and drastic structural changes within firms have meant that the social rights related to parenthood, taken for granted in socialist times, have begun to be questioned.

Part-time work is less common in Slovenia than in other EU countries, yet the share of workers with temporary (fixed-term) employment contracts, most common among women and young workers, is above the EU-27 average and has almost doubled in the last two decades (Ignjatović 2009) (see Figure 9.1). Further, while on average the gender gap among workers with temporary contracts is decreasing in the EU-27, it is increasing in Slovenia. The share of part-timers increased from the last quarter of 2007 for both women and men, but the gender gap remained stable. According to the SORS (2009a) data, the share of women in Slovenia working part-time (11.4%) in the last quarter of 2008 was higher than the share of men (7.3%). In Slovenia 28.6% of employees have access to flexi-time (European Commission 2009).

Over the last few years, the total unemployment rate in Slovenia has stayed below the EU average, reaching 4.4% in 2008, but young people in Slovenia are more often affected by involuntary job flexibility, which results in increased financial risks and an overall decline in quality of work, quality of life, and general wellbeing. In 2004, more than one-third (37%) of young people aged 15 to 29 in employment were on part-time or fixed-term contracts (Kanjuo-Mrčela and Ignjatović 2006). In 2006, 78.5% of all job vacancies in Slovenia were for fixed-term contracts (Ignjatović 2006).

Data from the Fourth European Working Conditions Survey (European Foundation 2007) confirmed the intensification of work in Slovenia. When compared with EU-27 averages regarding trends of flexibility and other dimensions of quality of work, conditions in Slovenia for WLB appear to be worsening. Between 2000 and 2005 the proportion of those working unsocial hours in the EU-27 decreased (shift work to 17%) or remained unchanged (working

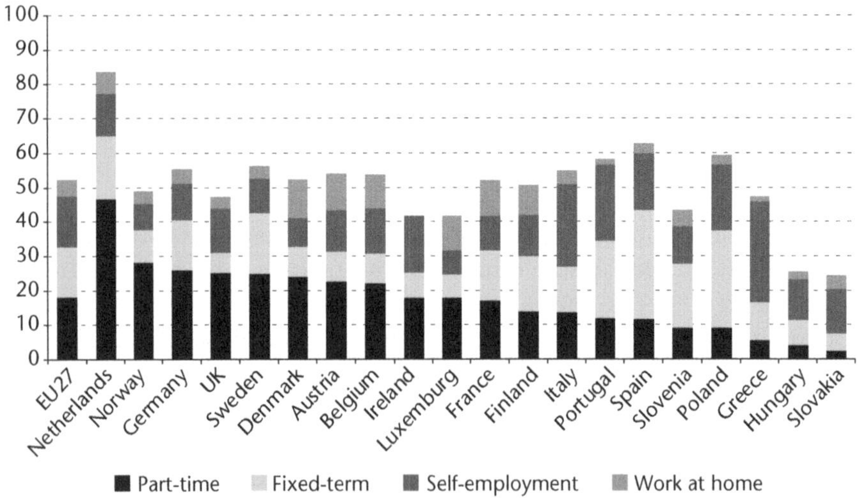

Figure 9.1 Flexible forms of employment in Slovenia and Europe in 2008*

* Suppose we consider the percentage of persons in employment in four flexible jobs in Slovenia and some other EU member states.

Source: Ignjatović (2009).

nights once a week or more to 19%; work on Sundays to 29%), while in Slovenia in all cases the levels are increasing (shift work to 30%; working nights once a week or more to 28%; work on Sundays to 33%). In the period analysed, the proportion of women working on Sundays rose by 13 percentage points as a result of a change in the opening hours of shops at weekends.

From 2000 to 2005 the number of working hours a week decreased slightly across the EU-27, while they actually increased slightly in Slovenia, to 43.6 for men and 41.9 for women in full-time employment. A 2005 survey of 882 young people (22 to 35 years of age) revealed high work intensity and low quality of work organization. On average, survey respondents worked 47 hours a week (including work at home, on business trips, etc. (Kanjuo Mrčela and Černigoj Sadar 2011)).

Thus it is not surprising that in Slovenia, employee evaluations of their working conditions were less positive than the EU-27 average; the proportion expressing satisfaction (72% in 2005) being about 10 percentage points lower than among the EU-27. Correspondingly, the proportion of workers dissatisfied with their WLB (26% in 2005) was 5 percentage points higher than in the EU-27.

Flexibility can increase individual choice and enable workers to more easily balance different activities/areas of life (work, family, leisure, political activities) and forms of work (paid work, housework, care work, voluntary work, learning). Nevertheless, it is important to understand the conditions under which 'real choices' can be made, particularly among those who have weaker capabilities—fewer resources, less power—to make meaningful decisions (Bradley et al. 2000) or, in other words, a 'bounded agency' (Hobson and Fahlen 2009). In Slovenia, flexibilization satisfies employers' needs rather than workers' demands or desires. By designing employment contracts and working arrangements in flexible modes employers have increased job precariousness. As a 2004 survey of 608 parents of children up to 7 years old shows, this has led to a forced adaptation among parents to the long working hours culture, where priority often is given to paid work when trying to balance this with parental obligations. Almost half of parents do not pick up their children from daycare themselves because of working obligations, and almost half (47%) of parents would like the kindergarten to be kept open after 4 pm (Kanjuo Mrčela and Černigoj Sadar 2011).

Results from the international research project CRANET (Kanjuo Mrčela and Ignjatović 2006) show that Slovenian organizations use family unfriendly forms of work and employment (unsocial hours of work, physically demanding work, fixed-term contracts, etc.) more than organizations in Western Europe or other transitional CEE countries. Flexibility is not a family-friendly form of work and employment in Slovenia, and it gives neither more autonomy nor employment security.

Our research has shown that flexibility—of labour markets and in firms/organizations—and the balancing of work and family life are intertwined, yet have tended to be analysed separately. The capability approach bridges the differences, suggesting that WLB is embedded in multilayered processes that involve individual, institutional, and societal resources. In our analysis we focus on the organizational level, but situate our respondents in specific normative and institutional contexts. We identify gender differences in agency inequalities for WLB and intersections of gender with other dimensions: age, education and skills, and parenting. We concentrate on how capabilities for achieving WLB are shaped by specific work settings and work organizational cultures.

Research Design

This study builds upon research concerning WLB issues of parents and potential parents carried out in Slovenia in 2004, 2005, and 2006, for which we used a combination of quantitative and qualitative research methods as presented in the article 'Social policies related to parenthood and capabilities of Slovenian parents' (Kanjuo Mrčela and Černigoj Sadar 2011). In this chapter we use original qualitative data obtained through focus groups with young people and interviews with management representatives in organizations in three different sectors, including one of the biggest Slovenian retail companies, a department of a large public health organization, and an IT subsidiary of a multinational corporation, which in our analysis we named 'Sun', 'Rainbow', and 'Star'.

This data was obtained from organizations in different sectors of the Slovenian economy in 2005 and 2006, when we conducted 14 focus groups with employees[1] and interviews with 7 managers[2] in 7 different Slovenian organizations[3] to gain a more focused insight into the situation of young (potential) parents in Slovenian organizations.

Focus groups were used because they allow participants to voice their own perspectives and raise or emphasize issues of importance to them, thereby enriching our knowledge of the problems analysed. A semi-structured focus-group guide was developed based on two survey questionnaires divided in five sections: (1) demography and employment data; (2) worklife balance experiences; (3) employment and work problems, and promotions connected to potential or actual parenthood; (4) organizational culture and WLB related practices at the present place of employment; (5) needs and wishes of participants to achieve WLB. Semi-structured interviews with managers covered the following: demographic data; data on employees in the organization (number, sex, education); existing programmes/policies regarding WLB (working time, leave, work organization); special programmes for parents of small children;

organizational culture and working practices; organizational changes and plans. Focus groups and interviews with managers were performed at the organizations' premises, audio-taped, transcribed, and thematically analysed.

Organizations and organizational cultures are among the most important factors influencing individual capabilities for WLB. Organizational cultures both reflect and shape managerial attitudes and practices (den Dulk and Peper 2007). They can enhance or inhibit the capabilities of individuals to exercise rights and utilize options for better balancing of paid work and private life. The organizational level is a crucial site for converting rights into claims, but organizations are also embedded in a wider structural context. In our analysis we pay attention to the characteristics of our three different sectors. We chose three organizations from these three sectors for in-depth analysis (Sun, private retail; Rainbow, public healthcare; and Star, international IT)[4] because their employees' experiences illustrate the general tensions between capabilities and WLB in Slovenian organizations, both private and public sector, and since they represent different feminized/masculinized workplaces and activities. At the same time, they allowed us to reveal how the structural features of the specific sector, organizational culture, and organization of work shape the capabilities and agency freedoms of workers in organizations of comparable size.

Our analysis revealed that differences at the structural, firm, and individual level shape specific features of capabilities of workers for WLB. This enabled us to grasp the different layers of meaning in the agency and capabilities gap: between existing rights of parents and their sense of entitlement for WLB; between acceptance of relative gender equality in paid work and gender inequality in parenting; and between public social policies and organizational practices characterized by differences between declared norms and practices.

At the structural level we paid attention to differences caused by the public and private status of companies and their market position, the prevalent type of employment contract (fixed and open-ended), and the gender and pay structure, within each sector. We established that market pressures and global competitiveness have the greatest impact on retail, but are also very important for IT. In both cases the competitive imperative weakens WLB capabilities. In healthcare, welfare state retrenchment undermines attempts to create a family-friendly workplace that allows employees to achieve even basic WLB standards and constrains the exercise of parental rights. Health and retail are both highly feminized and are also low-wage sectors with greater gender pay gaps. Retail is also characterized by low employment security. In the masculinized IT sector, capabilities for WLB are supported by higher employment security and considerably better wages.

At the organizational level we found differences in organization structure (flat versus steep organizational hierarchies). Work process characteristics and quality and conditions of work also varied, for example the length of working time, shift work, overtime, unsocial hours of work, time flexibility, space flexibility, and adequate/inadequate precision in definition of work tasks. Formal and informal rules were also dimensions that differed between our firms: how employees were rewarded and promoted, how work was organized in smaller or larger work units, and other aspects of organizational culture, often influenced by the role and attitude of managers regarding WLB. In all three organizations we interviewed either human resource managers or the middle line managers who performed the HR managerial role.

In a hierarchical, and less flexibly organized, environment (part of retail), employees felt less capable of claiming WLB compared with the flat organization of the IT company, where the flexible organization of work allowed for less strict boundaries between private life and work life. This was also true of the health sector, where work is spatially as well as symbolically separated from private life, as employees wear uniforms at work (see Nippert-Eng 1996). Formal organizational rules and respect for the legislative framework provide the basis for WLB, yet in all three organizations we found different informal aspects of the organizational culture operating that could result either in acceptance of the rules supporting WLB or work against them.

We also recognized that differences regarding individual characteristics and resources—gender, skills, and education, professional and non-professional status, support networks (family, parents and colleagues), and their combinations—influence the agency and capabilities gap in different ways and not always as expected. For example, while higher education is generally connected to more workplace autonomy, which is expected to enhance capabilities for WLB (Robeyns 2003 used education as capability dimension of gender equality), in the case of highly educated IT professionals it was also connected with self-pressures structured into the specific organizational culture of the competitive IT sector, thus reducing their capabilities for WLB (Drobnič and Guillén 2011 and Drobnič and León in this volume).

In short, the interconnectedness of the structural, firm level and the individual characteristics described above shape employees' capabilities to make claims for WLB. We use this multilayered lens in our analysis of the three companies. In the next section we consider each organization separately, underscoring how different workplace settings matter to capabilities for WLB.

WLB Capabilities Embedded in Three Workplace Settings

We present textured qualitative data that reveal how parents of young children cope with the demands of parenthood and paid work. We look at their experiences and the experiences of young people who are potential parents in the context of increased flexibility and worklife precariousness and how the latter affects agency inequalities for achieving WLB. Through our focus at the firm level, we seek to capture the different ways in which organizational cultures, the economic situation, and managers' attitudes and practices influence conditions for WLB.

Sun: Retail Sector

GENERAL CHARACTERISTICS OF THE RETAIL SECTOR

According to Labour Force Survey data, the commerce sector in Slovenia, with 117,000 employees in 2007, accounted for 12% of employment in the country's economy (Lužar 2011). While in the period between 2000 and 2007 the number of companies in commerce decreased (from 30,254 to 22,980), the number of employees increased by 15%. This trend of increased employment was especially evident among women in this sector, while men's employment decreased in the same period.

The retail sector in Slovenia has been characterized by the fast growth of private companies due to privatization of former socialist-run companies as well as the entrance of foreign commercial chains from 1991 (Rogelj 2004). Working conditions, which have always been hard (mentally and physically demanding work, shift work) have intensified due to increased competition. After a long and heated public debate regarding working hours in commerce, and in spite of strong opposition from trade unions and an important part of the politically-attuned civil society, many retail shops are now open on Sundays. The sector's rate of collective bargaining coverage is 100% and the social partners (two trade unions and three employer organizations) all evaluated sectoral social dialogue in 2009 as quite successful (Lužar 2011). The same analysis revealed the social partners' favourable evaluation of the commercial sector as a reliable employer. However, representatives of the sector's main trade union are also critical of the low wages within the sector and the huge differences in working conditions between different employers, some considered decent and others not, where laws and collective agreements are not carried out (Franca 2006). Analyses of working conditions have drawn attention to safety and health issues within the sector, confirming that retail has some of the highest numbers of accidents at work (Mrčela 2012). Wages in the retail sector are lower than the average wage in Slovenia, and differ considerably by gender. In 2006 the average gross earnings for men working in retail was 13,908 Euros and for women 11,917 Euros. Thus the difference per paid hour was almost 1 Euro (6.51 for men and 5.47 for women in October 2006; SORS 2009.)

SUN: MARKET PRESSURES, DECLARED NORMS, AND PRACTICES

Sun is one of the biggest Slovenian retail companies, employing around 9,000 persons at the time of our analysis (2006) of which 72% were women. The company is successful and nurses the ambition of becoming one of the leading retail chains for foodstuffs and household products in South-East Europe, where it has been expanding its business. Workplaces and working conditions vary considerably across this big retail enterprise, even though it is often presented and regarded as a good employer concerned with employees' wellbeing. We examined different types of employees in our analysis: those working in administration in company headquarters, those working in shops (salespersons and butchers), and those in security.

In their public presentations and in communications to employees, Sun places care of employees and their family life high on the agenda. However, despite this public portrayal, the organizational culture and actual working conditions are often family unfriendly. Yet employees do not hold the company responsible for their problems in achieving WLB, rather they view their situation as part of the low expectation for WLB in Slovenian workplaces and have adapted to this.[5] Public awareness of employers who are far worse certainly influences employees' level of tolerance of the gap between the official rhetoric and actual practice. Workers take a large part of the family unfriendliness at work (shift and weekend work) for granted because of the nature of the retail business and also because of the tendency to see WLB as a private problem. Such individualization as is present among parents generally constitutes an additional source of stress in the competitive world of Slovenian retail, where Sun is still seen as a case of good practice.

Sun's head of human resources pointed out the developed mechanisms of care for employee wellbeing that have been regularly evaluated as very good in annual surveys of employee satisfaction at work. However, his answers revealed that some aspects of the company's organizational practices and policies did not favour working parents and that there were obstacles to employees achieving WLB at Sun. According to the HR manager, Sun prioritizes employment of young, likable, and dynamic people who will please the customers. As the practice of employing young people is widespread in Slovenia, this is not a surprise in a customer-oriented company in which, in the HR manager's words,

> [the] aim is to have a younger structure of employees ... as young people are flexible ... dynamic, communicative ... A young woman without children gives more sophisticated and efficient work. (HR manager, 57)

In the year before our analysis, Sun took in around 200 new employees on mostly fixed-term contracts.

CAPABILITIES FOR WLB: FOCUS GROUP RESPONDENTS

Fixed-term contracts shift and weekend work are seen as serious problems among working parents, but are taken for granted by Sun employees, even though shift work often prevents people from being with their partners:

> When I am at work mornings we do see each other, as he comes home... around half past four, but when I am at work afternoons we don't see each other at all. I leave home around eleven, coming back at half past eight... then we have a little time together . . . . (female worker, 27)

> Yes, we work all the days of the week... now even Sundays... it is really hard during the week... but you can use Sundays, if you're not working. (male worker, 25)

However, some parents said that they actually liked to work in opposite shifts to their partners as it enables them to take turns caring for their children; as many cannot count on help from their own parents, they would otherwise have no way of caring for their children after the kindergartens close. Support from grandparents is also helpful and counted on when children are sick. Some parents reported the non-sympathetic company climate toward taking sick leave, so that employees feel forced to take help from parents/relatives instead of staying home with sick children. Here again is an example of how parents take obstacles to WLB upon themselves as private problems to be solved by the individual rather than viewing them as a company responsibility.

Low earnings mean that Sun employees rarely work part-time. Some mentioned that they dared not ask for part-time, as they are afraid that this could be taken as a sign of being less reliable and reduce their chances for a renewal of their contract. While shop working hours are fixed, in administration employees are permitted flexi-time (flexible arrival between 6 and 8 am and departure from 3 to 5 pm) where arrivals after 8 am or leaving before 3 pm are monitored and strictly sanctioned.

Our respondents highlighted the intensification of work caused by downsizing, both in terms of scope and pace. Besides working with customers, employees in shops now have additional tasks to perform (e.g. preparing the shop and filling shelves, closing checks, some cleaning). This means that they must stay at work longer, without being paid for their extra work. In hard economic times retail employees also have to deal with more shop-lifting, which they are expected to monitor and prevent. The amount of administrative work has also increased; as no new employees are being hired, those left have to pick up the slack. Moreover, parents on leave are not replaced. Instead, their work is distributed among others, which sometimes provoked negative reactions.

PRESENTEEISM: A GENDERED PROBLEM OF WORKING PARENTS

An aspect of organizational culture described by one manager is where employees who always are present at the workplace are respected and rewarded (financially and also by promotion). This existence of a long-hours culture with presenteeism, regardless of actual work results, has been confirmed in interviews with employees.

Sun-employed parents also reported being denied promotions and negative experiences when taking leave because of children. Given the traditional gender roles in Slovenian families, this mainly affected women, who have primary responsibility for all forms of care.

> When they found out that I was pregnant for the second time, they removed the proposal for my promotion... It has been three years since then... and now each time I have to go on sick leave because of the children, they look at me as if I've done something wrong, even though I've done all the work I'm supposed to do. (female worker, 33)

The pressures of the Sun organizational culture cause many of our respondents to give paid formal work priority over family obligations:

> Yes, you put work in first place most of the time. Everything else is in the background, the job is first! (male worker, 34)

For working mothers this was problematic.

> It is easier for men, I can't... put either one ahead of the other, especially not work above the children. What's the point of having children if they are to be secondary to the job... to me my children are more important than anything in life. I am trying of course to do my best at work... but I have to adjust to the kindergarten's opening hours... and take home a full briefcase of papers to work on in the evenings. (female worker, 33)

Traditional gendered parental roles create a gap between fathers' rights and their sense of entitlement to use them, along with a gap between the gender equality of the public sphere and the gender inequality in the private sphere. The well-developed Slovenian parental leave policies allow fathers to be on leave with their newborn children and to use paternal and (part of) parental leave as well as sick leave for childcare. However, our male respondents reported that using these rights is difficult because of negative responses at work:

> They gave me such looks... we were few and it was considered bad if you took these two days for childbirth let alone other leaves, so I did not use it... and I will not... only in case of serious illness, but usually the wife uses it. (male worker, 34)

Fathers took the 15 days of paid paternity leave (that are 100% reimbursed), but not the remaining two and a half months for which only social insurance based on the minimum wage is paid:

> We have not so high salaries that we can afford it…so it makes no sense to take it. (male worker, 32)

This reflects the fact that choices regarding leave and thus capabilities of men for WLB, besides being influenced and constrained by prevailing norms, are also constrained by financial considerations.

Both the organization of work and WLB practices of employees working in shops depend on agreements with bosses and co-workers that seem to work out well. Our respondents from sales departments were more satisfied with their possibilities of WLB then the professionals and administrative workers in the Sun headquarters. Administrative workers and professionals are expected to work until the job is completed and their presence is more strictly monitored than in the shops. In a precarious labour market, Sun pays their employees regularly; employees reported fears that it would be very difficult to find another, similar job and were clearly reluctant to express their feelings about the lack of WLB or otherwise complain about working conditions. Instead they find ways, private solutions, to adapt.

Rainbow: The Health Sector

GENERAL CHARACTERISTICS OF THE HEALTHCARE SECTOR

Most healthcare in Slovenia is carried out by state- or municipally-owned and publicly-funded providers (healthcare institutions, hospitals, and clinics) that employ more than 75% of the total healthcare workforce. At the end of 2008, there were about 42,000 employees in the sector, of which slightly more than 22,000 were qualified healthcare personnel (among them 13% men) with the largest share (almost 14,000) having secondary education. Employees in public sector healthcare receive salaries from the health insurance fund (Plachtej 2011). In this highly feminized sector (81.9% female employees in 2008) the gender pay gap is the widest compared with other sectors of the Slovenian labour market: in 2008 women earned only 69.3% of men's earnings (SORS 2008). In 2008, a new salary system (by collective agreement) was adopted for the entire public sector. Consequently there were significant pay rises for nurses working at intensive care units (up to 30%), and also for other professionals. In spite of these positive changes, however, it still has the widest gender pay gap of skilled workforce sectors.

One of the most important successes of the social dialogue concerning healthcare has been the inclusion of the issues of violence and stress within the collective agreement. However, there is still a gap between the documents and the reality of the working environment. Additionally, as the economic crisis has deepened, the social dialogue has almost disappeared (Plachtej

2011). The requirement to reduce public spending on health and therefore to cut the number of employees, on the one hand, and the shortage of staff, on the other, is causing additional stress for those employed in the sector.

WORK INTENSITY AND THE SHIFT TOWARD FAMILY (UN)FRIENDLY PRACTICES

Rainbow has over 200 employees and is part of one of the largest internationally known public healthcare organizations in Slovenia, employing at the time of our research around 7,000 persons. Most female nurses have secondary education and some even a university diploma. Male nurses (health technicians) are in a minority. Information about the organizational culture and company policies came mainly from our interview with the management representative, the head nurse (the equivalent of the HR managers who mediate WLB claims). She had held this position for ten years, had no caring obligations, and was actively engaged with WLB issues at her department, devoting almost 100 additional hours of overtime work per month to collecting information about problems in the department.

The head nurse acknowledged that the employer is not obliged to introduce additional benefits beyond statutory demands. She was convinced, however, that efforts to meet employee needs enhanced management–employee relations and decreased workforce turnover, allowing the work to be done better by qualified, committed, and responsible workers. Yet, as the intensive work demands in the healthcare sector are combined with workforce shortage, the head nurse reported that there are many impediments to implementing parent-friendly policies:

> The system of work in our organization is unfriendly towards parents... The intensity and the demands of work have increased in recent years. Flexible working hours no longer exist; we have a three shift work schedule. Due to work force shortages and high frequency of maternity/parental leave and sick leave we have a lot of overtime work . . . .

As is true of Sun, the head nurse reported that the hiring selection process favours young women without children. Women or men with children were evaluated as lacking work flexibility and being less adaptable.

All our participants but one had open-ended employment contracts. Most commuted to work (spending on average two hours on travel per day), which placed an additional burden on them on top of their very demanding work. Work conditions in Rainbow are best illustrated by the following notions that focus group participants associated with the word 'work': 'Sunday', 'holidays', 'night shift', 'whenever', 'hard', and 'obligation'.

Everybody in our focus groups agreed that the intensity of work has been increasing, and that the organization of work was changing as well, involving more administrative tasks than in the past. There were also an increasing number of patients with complicated simultaneous symptoms of illness in different body parts. At the same time, patients were increasingly aware of their rights and demanded a high quality service that was hard to provide with the limited personnel resources.

> Patients are more demanding...intensity and demands of work have increased...there is a lot of paper work...in the last five years a lot of mental conditions have appeared among employees...especially among the young ones, which shows that people are overburdened. (head nurse)

Nevertheless, employees also reported positive experiences, especially concerning the solidarity built through teamwork that makes it easier to cope with stress at work. Health technicians reported dissatisfaction regarding the very hierarchical work organization. Most nurses who get additional training in order to improve their wages wanted to change jobs and were looking for employment outside the health sector. Working parents were most critical of the conflicts around the organization of work.

THE AGENCY AND CAPABILITIES GAP: GENDERED NORMS, RIGHTS, AND PRACTICES

Parental leave entitlement and leave for care of sick children were mainly used by women. As the physically demanding work with patients requires a healthy worker, it often happened that future mothers took sick leave before taking maternity leave (which begins one month before delivery is due) because they were not able to perform all their job tasks and/or felt unwanted at work:

> The boss, not mine but the main one, said to me: 'Just go!' in a rather ugly manner. (female worker, 29)

Due to labour force shortages, problems also arise in taking regular annual leave. When employees take leave, the distribution of their workload becomes an organizational problem for their superiors and an additional burden on other employees.

> At the moment we get 14 days; that is mandatory by law.... Usually it is like this—one year one group gets leave during the high season, the next year the other group.... This is all written down.... But it happens that responsible persons mix it up a bit. (male worker, 32)

The results obtained from our focus groups confirmed the gaps between normative arrangements (based on legal documents and collective agreements) and the reality of working conditions at Rainbow.

Similar problems arise when a child falls ill; co-workers have to take over the work of the absent parent or must prolong their shift. Particularly in the case of frequent child illnesses combined with mother's illness, parents reported feelings of guilt:

> The little one was ill already during my parental leave. So when I was to start work again I had to take sick leave. Now my sick leave absence has become a bit prolonged. I don't know.... It's as if it's my fault that all this is happening. I'm afraid even before I telephone the company. That is stressful. (female worker, 31)

Our respondents also reported on a variety of negative experiences on returning from parental leave. We heard that in another department of the same healthcare organization, a mother lost her job because her employer refused to extend her contract. Another superior was not responsive to the needs of a breastfeeding mother, who had to work for 12 hours without a break and suffered a lot. Another mother was upset by the response of her superior regarding time arrangements after her return from parental leave. When the mother suggested a time table nobody was satisfied:

> It did not suit the boss, it did not suit the co-workers.... And then the message: 'I really don't care whether she has children!' (female worker, 31)

However, we also heard of positive experiences: one mother got promotion on returning from parental leave and fathers reported having no problems in taking their 15 days of paternity leave.

WORK ORGANIZATION: EFFECTS OF WLB AND QUALITY OF LIFE

Due to very unstable timetables, parents at Rainbow constantly had to negotiate childcare arrangements with their partner and members of their extended family. Some parents had partners that also worked in healthcare or worked three shifts, meaning the family rarely was together.

Even employees with no children had problems combining paid work and private life:

> In fact we only sleep together. (female worker, 32)

Another female worker (27), who was combining work with studies, did not see her partner more than two or three days a week. She and her partner accepted this situation because they both usually worked long hours. In cases like this the role of managers is very important; some respondents claimed to have managers who were responsive to their needs, others that they were not.

The acceptance of long hours of work, overtime work, work on Sundays, and so on, is related to higher/additional income. Only two men expressed negative attitudes towards work at unsocial hours and shift work. They said that there should be a ban on night work for all parents with preschool children and that mothers who return from parental leave should only work the morning shift. However, others did not agree with these suggestions. For most young employees the possibility of a choice regarding the division of childcare among parents is important and additional income essential. Our respondents thus reported that regular overtime is largely taken for granted in Rainbow (up to 30 hours per month are paid and for additional overtime work employees can get days off). Our respondents underlined the role of informal agreements that allow for flexibility and the chance to influence their work schedules, as these are considered to be as or more important than the number of working hours.

Although the head nurse was fairly responsive to parents' needs and sought to accommodate parents' to the extent that existing human resources and work processes would permit, the parents at Rainbow had only limited possibilities to determine their working time. They worked in shifts, often unsocial hours, and had long working days. Sometimes it seemed that they themselves made bad choices because they wanted to earn the extra money needed to settle their basic living conditions, or because they had no other option for managing their childcare. Such decisions clearly decreased the quality of their lives, particularly their relations with their partner and family. The embeddedness of these decisions in the economic situation of the health sector reflects the weak capabilities of parents to make better decisions. Although they still see WLB as their own private problem, some pointed out how solidarity within their workplace—helping each other—alleviated the problem to some extent. Yet dissatisfaction over the division of tasks and pay for work done indicates serious problems and could provoke further conflicts between employees with different levels of skill and education. For example, the fact that persons with middle-level education do tasks intended for the higher educated, while not being adequately paid for it.

In addition to time pressures, work in health organizations is psychologically and emotionally demanding. Employees do not take work tasks home with them, but often carry the emotional burdens of the day, and are not mentally able to switch off. As the head nurse was doing her best to be responsive to parents' needs, employee turnover was low at Rainbow. However, intentions to leave were expressed frequently, especially by young people. Most parents were actually looking for jobs outside the hospital because of the poor possibilities for WLB.

Star: A High Tech Company in the ICT Sector

GENERAL CHARACTERISTICS OF THE ICT SECTOR

According to Stanovnik et al. (2008), in 2003 there were 2,825 companies in the information and communication technology (ICT) sector in Slovenia (672 enterprises in ICT production and 2,153 enterprises providing ICT services) employing 24,670 people (11,812 workers in production and 12,858 workers in services). Compared to some other countries (e.g. with well-developed ICT environments, such as Finland, Sweden, the USA, or some transitional countries such as Hungary and Latvia) the Slovenian ICT sector is a less important part of the economy (Berce et al. 2010).

The ICT industry in Slovenia recorded a dynamic growth in the 1990s that slowed somewhat though did not stop in the first decade of the twenty-first century. Analysts estimated the level of investments in ICT to remain solid and sustained throughout the transition; ICT companies are mainly oriented to the domestic market, where a lack of ICT experts limits the further growth of the sector (Berce et al. 2010). The sector is characterized by dispersion, weak innovative activities, and orientation to market niches, the major part connected to multinationals. Production chains are very rare, mainly one-off events (Stanovnik et al. 2008). The majority of enterprises in the sector are micro companies.

Salaries in this sector (where women represent only 36.4% of the workforce) are higher than the Slovenia average (for both men and women); in 2008 women earned 82.9% of male earnings (SORS 2008).

Star is part of a multinational company that is a leader in the development and production of informational technology, employing more than 300,000 people worldwide. The company has been present in the Slovenian market for over 70 years, but the Slovene branch was only established in 1992. At the time of our analysis there were more than 100 employees (a figure that has more than doubled since), 70% of them men and all but one employed on open-ended contracts. There were also 30 students and other temporarily employed persons. The company is among the top four ICT companies in Slovenia regarding sales.

We planned and organized interviews in the company with the help of the HR director, who was interested in and supportive of the topic of our research, being a mother of two young children. This HR manager described Star employees as very responsible and committed. As employees are on average relatively young, they do not often take sick leave. She reckoned that they worked a lot and were satisfied with their working conditions and wages.

WORK COMMITMENT AND WORK CULTURE

To an outside observer Star is a closed virtual world, in which childless employees and a few parents are constantly present (in person or through the technologically possible connections) and have almost no time for anything other than being a Star employee.

A pleasant organizational climate, combined with high self and peer pressures concerning expected results and professional workforce standards, cause these employees to willingly subordinate private, family life to working life. Capabilities for WLB are thus diminished without these individuals noticing it, let alone fighting it.

Star employees show high commitment and acceptance of organizational values and principles. They see themselves as part of an international team that involves intensive work, long working hours, and flexible organization. They are highly motivated and prepared to work hard for a company that indeed provides a positive working environment. We found that the majority work long hours (50–60 hours a week on average), not expecting to be paid for their overtime work. The positive climate is created by good management practices, high work autonomy, employment security, and the sense of belonging to a big and successful international enterprise. In return, the employer expects high productivity and almost constant availability, by phone and e-mail.

These highly committed professionals took for granted the nature and increasing intensity of work.

> All of us here work like slaves, telephones are ringing all the time...even on Saturday, when a customer calls and says that their system stopped working, you can only say to your wife nicely that the shopping is off, postpone it for three hours...that happens...we have already postponed leaving on summer holidays. (male worker, 34)

> I have very high standards regarding my work; and the environment is such that work has to be done and it has to be done well...I think that we all work more than is needed and we do what we do well. (female worker, 38)

THE SPILLOVER EFFECT: WHEN WORK BECOMES HOME AND HOME BECOMES WORK

Employees prize the pleasant working environment in which they cooperate well with co-workers and build friendly relationships; some of them also socialize outside the workplace, although not many and not regularly. As hierarchical boundaries in team-organized work are not strong, many employees are on friendly terms with their superiors too. The friendly atmosphere and easy communication is encouraged by the open plan working environment. This sociability can inhibit some employees from concentrating on their tasks, so the work has to be finished after official working hours, at home. The work environment at Star resembles what Hochschild calls the 'new company town', where work becomes home and home becomes a less desirable place to be (Hochschild 2003). Some employees at Star, unlike those in Hochschild, are aware of the price they are paying for their enjoyment of pleasant, relaxed, long hours at work, namely the shading out of other parts of their lives. Still, only rarely do employees put clear limits on the amount of time and work they devote to the company. The only person among our respondents who seemed to be successful in this was also the only one who expressed reservations over the idea of organizing a company kindergarten with flexible working hours, an idea very much supported by other employees at Star. He understood that such a proposal for afternoon care for children at the company probably would lead to prolonged working hours for parents even beyond what they already were doing.

FLEXIBLE WORKING PRACTICES CAN HAVE BOTH POSITIVE AND NEGATIVE CONSEQUENCES FOR WLB

Employees used the opportunities offered for the flexible organization of work, namely space and time flexibility; although the HR manager did express the opinion that flexible working practices are sometimes bad for private lives. She herself had been considering the possibility of compressing her 40 working hours into four days per week; but as her workload would not be reduced, in four days of work she 'would not be able to even see my children and on the fifth day off they would be in school and in kindergarten' so she decided to stick with her regular five-day working week in order to prevent 'an even worse impact of my work on my family life'.

The possibilities of flexi-time, and working from home or elsewhere using IT, were regarded by employees with some ambivalence, as surely leading to an undesirable blurring of the boundaries between private and working life, so these flexible working practices were both welcomed and not so well liked, as seen in the employee responses below.

> There are no problems if you have to leave earlier during the week...you can come in on weekends. (male worker, 27)

> You would at least check your mails and respond to them when away from here...I do that every weekend. (female worker, 28)

> The work has to be done...it's your problem how much time it takes and when you do it. (female worker, 28)

> We have computers at home...even if on sick leave, the work process does not end. (male worker, 31)

Total flexibility in the organization of work, which can promote WLB, 'allows' employees to work unsocial hours, at weekends, and when they are sick.

Blurring of the boundary between employment and private life increases employees' productivity, but also has negative effects as work tends to colonize their home life. One respondent reported that she felt even more work pressure when working at home and tended to prolong her working day.

> Actually, when you are at home, you work more and longer, but still I always worry a bit that they think that I'm at home doing nothing. In fact, I get up at 7 am, sit by the computer in pyjamas, and around 10 put a jumper on.... (female worker, 33)

> ...and it happens that you are in the same pyjamas at 7 pm.... (male worker, 34)

> As a matter of fact, you do more at home...then at 8 pm when you put kids in bed, you check the mail, see what's come in since 4, to have it clean next day. (female worker, 38)

GENDERED CAPABILITIES FOR WLB

All respondents with children reported problems with WLB, but mothers expressed more difficulties than fathers. Employees of both genders agreed that mothers have a greater sense of entitlement to WLB claims for care leave, working times, and site of work flexibility than fathers. Many fathers at Star revealed a poor knowledge of their parental rights. Fathers also stressed that it is expected of men (especially in IT) to be present at the job, to make work a priority and to have partners who will take care of their children.

> I see that men of my generation who are employed in this industry don't have children...I'm about the only one...so it's normal that they call me at 7 pm and want to seriously discuss business. I say, hey guys, it's 7 o'clock, I'm putting the children to bed. That is the only time that I'm with my children. (male worker, 34)

> If a man takes sick leave because of a child, all the people are surprised: Why you? What's with your wife?

Mothers more than fathers tended to take advantage of work flexibility to reconcile work tasks with family responsibilities. Yet mothers often felt torn between work commitments and family:

> I can work from home—I go two days to the office and three days I work from home. The advantage of that is that I don't have to be two hours on the road, and I have the feeling that I am more with my son. On the other hand, there are no established working hours. That means that if the phone rings at 5 pm, you have to work...and it could also be at 6 or 7...sometimes you work as long as your brains allow you, but then you have to stop, when you're not physically able to continue.... (female worker, 33)

All reported 'double guilt' feelings; guilt towards the children when working long hours, and guilt about not being sufficiently committed to work when they were devoting time to their children. Those who were not yet parents expected WLB to be harder when they have a family and children, and hoped that their partners, parents, and family would be able to help them then. Respondents without children noticed gender differences in parental roles and different expectations on mothers and fathers, but planned to build their parenting on gender equality.

Our own results confirm previous research results on forms of masculine organizational cultures in modern organizations (Maddock and Parkin 1993), that women (mothers) are not discriminated against per se, but that the standard organization of work rewards persons who are completely work-centred and whose private/family responsibilities are taken care of by someone else. Employees at Star have full on-line access to company data during maternity/parental leave. Yet this kind of accommodation does not enhance capabilities for WLB and quality of life in a work-intense culture.

Star's employees are assumed to have no responsibilities outside the firm, use modern technology and in a friendly organizational environment shade out all other spheres beyond work. Yet, many individuals offer little resistance to this takeover of their lives.

Star employees expected work intensity in the competitive ICT sector to increase in the future. They did not see their employer as being responsible for the very hard time they were having in reconciling the different spheres of their lives. On the contrary, both the manager and the employees described the company as a good employer in general and especially concerning WLB. They reported that besides respecting the existing legislative framework, the company tries to contribute to better WLB by flexible organization of work and some special practices targeted toward parents ('Kids at work'—days of open company doors for employees' children). They felt that Star provides more benefits to parents then other employers. Employees also did not blame Star for lack of WLB, rather being critical of the state, which they claim does not do enough for young parents regarding housing, credits, and opening times of kindergartens.

Conclusions

Our analysis focused on agency inequalities and agency freedoms of women and men to realize WLB in three companies in different sectors of the transitional Slovenian economy. The analysis shows some differences and three main similarities in sets of capabilities in these three companies. Specific firm and sector level variations exist in all three cases: differences in ownership, in market position, and in organizational cultures influenced by gender, age, and the educational/professional structure of employment. However, in all three places, certain assumptions operate that shape the agency inequalities of WLB: the increasing dominance of paid work over other parts of life; the gendered and unequal division of roles and responsibilities in the public and in the private sphere, and the sense that WLB is the responsibility of the individual parents, not the company.

Our analysis provides insights into the wide agency and capabilities gap regarding WLB in Slovenia, an economy that has been seen as one of the most successful examples of a transitional economy among Central and Eastern European countries, and that even throughout the transition managed to retain its generous WLB policies. Yet the high level of precarious employment, the long working hours, and the work intensity built into the organizational culture, weaken capabilities and provide a lens on why policies in place at state level are not exercised.

In our analysis we focused on the organizational level and presented data on the agency and capabilities of working parents to make claims for WLB in the sectors of public health, private retail, and IT. By analysing collected data from focus groups and interviews with managers we captured both employer accounts and the voices of employees. The capabilities approach allowed us to better understand some of the processes that influence capabilities of parents for WLB; the gap between parents' rights and their sense of entitlement to WLB; the gap between acceptance of relative gender equality in paid work and gender inequality in parenting; the gap between public social policies and organizational practices that reflect the impact of competitive market pressures on organizational cultures, creating differences between declared norms and practices.

At the IT company affiliated to a huge multinational complex, flexible work arrangements translated into increased work intensity. This effect is confirmed by other cross-national studies that warn of the negative aspects of high job autonomy/control (see Drobnič and Guillen 2011). Our results are also in line with studies showing how decisions on the use of WLB provisions depend on foreseen penalties and obstacles (Fagan and Walthery in this volume). In the privately-owned retail company, precarious employment conditions and high competitiveness are the factors that constrain the capabilities of parents for WLB. In both retail and health, employees take limitations on WLB for granted, as being part of the nature of work (e.g. shift work or work in unsocial hours).

The reasons for accepting the long working hour culture differ in the three cases. In the IT environment this is a product of self and peer pressure, high quality standards, and a quite specific organizational culture where the relaxed work organization and pleasant open-plan office space make it easier to socialize than concentrate on work, which means that a lot may have to be done in what should have been 'spare time'. Well educated and well paid professionals know that they have to work until the work is done well, no matter how long it takes, and no matter where, so they dig in and do what they have to do. In healthcare, meeting the WLB demands of one employee often means longer hours of work for others, as the work with patients is demanding and the employees few. Every parent's leave causes additional work for colleagues. Young people employed in healthcare do not, however, mind additional work as the extra earnings improve their low wages. In retail the incentive is a combination of financial reasons—most important for the low paid employees in sales—along with a perception of long working hours as a necessary condition both for retaining the job in a precarious market and for getting promotion within the administration.

Different pressures from the business/organizational environment—business competition in IT and retail, and cutbacks in public spending on healthcare—cause greater work intensity and a lower sense of entitlement among parents to claim WLB rights.

Although all three organizations share the same social environment, characterized by the same norms on gender roles and gender equality, some specifics exist as to how gender influences actual capabilities for WLB that reflect sector differences (e.g. male-dominant IT with its masculine culture of long working hours and employees who depend on someone else to take care of their families). It is interesting to see how the organization/technology of organization-specific work allows for different positioning of boundaries between the private life/family and the public life/work domains. In health and retail parents can maintain strict boundaries between work and home, but in IT the boundaries are more blurred; yet 'choices' (decisions embedded in sets of capabilities) regarding WLB always prioritize public life/working: in health and retail parents 'choose' to be more at work than at home, while in IT parents can 'choose' to work at home.

Our analysis showed that in all three cases the capabilities of employed parents are limited by the interplay of obstacles embedded in prevailing presumptions about gender roles and the dominance of paid work over other spheres of life. By using capabilities as the framework to look beyond actual practices and analyse individual aspirations and the potential of a person to imagine alternative scenarios (Hobson et al. in this volume), our analysis has enabled us to capture the subjective experiential sides of capabilities. We showed that although parents regard family as very important and strive to reconcile it with working, everyday practices place family in second position, which is destructive to private as well as to public life. For women in Slovenia, the experience of time squeeze is the most intense, as women who have long working hours are still expected to take the main responsibility for care of the family.

Sen's capabilities and agency-centred approach provides the theoretical space for capturing gender inequalities and the growing divide between rising expectations and norms for men and women to become carers and earners, and the economic, social, and normative barriers that they encounter (Hobson Introduction in this volume). The gender differences revealed in our study are reflected in the motherhood privilege, as women face fewer constraints in claims for reconciling employment with family than men, but consequently experience the motherhood penalty in job recruitment and promotion.

The capability perspective, which provides 'a return to an integrated approach to economic and social development' in 'policy analysis as well as for understanding of general economic, political and social connections' (Sen 1999: 294–7), is useful for understanding the recent processes of change and development in the Slovenian economy and society. Changes in the Slovenian transitional economy have led to the dominance of paid work over other spheres of life, in contradiction to the legacies and expectations for WLB and quality of life that existed during the former regime. One can view these changes within the broader context of the restoration of a neo-liberal economy and unregulated capitalism. Arlie Hochschild (2003: 209) defined (American) capitalism as 'not simply an economic but a cultural system as well... [that] presents a challenge to local cultures, including the local culture of families' and is accompanied by 'the missing culture of resistance' of American working parents who accept the dominance of paid work over care work and family. The tacit acceptance of the dominance of paid work over other parts of life in Slovenia can be seen as a reflection of the restoration of capitalism as a successful cultural project—in Arlie Hochschild's terms—that does not provoke much resistance. The success of this cultural project in Slovenia is reflected in the agency inequalities among Slovenian parents and their inability to make claims for alternative ways of living and for achieving WLB. In Sen's terms, potential capabilities, rights, and policies are not converted into realized functionings[6] for WLB, wellbeing, and quality of life.

Appendix: Characteristics of Managers and Focus Groups in Three Organizations

Retail Company 'Sun'

Representative of management: Director of HRM department (7 years), man in his late 50s, married, two grown up children.

First focus group: three women and three men aged from 23 to 26 years—one working in marketing (tertiary education) and five in sales (secondary education); three participants have a temporary contract, three have a contract for an unlimited period; all but one have partners.

Second focus group: three women and two men aged from 27 to 35 years—one working in HRM department (tertiary education), the others have secondary education. All participants have one or two children: five of them have preschool children; one has a child aged 15 years.

Healthcare Organization 'Rainbow'

Representative of management: Chief nurse (more than ten years)—middle-aged woman, has no care obligations.

First focus group: five women and two men aged from 22 to 32 years—working as nurses or health technicians (all of them have secondary education). All of them but one have contracts for an unlimited period; three of them have no partners, the others have a partner or are cohabitating.

Second focus group: four women and two men aged from 27 to 31 years—working as nurses or health technicians (all have secondary education) and have contracts for an unlimited period. All but one are married and have children aged from under 1 to 7 years.

IT Company 'Star'

Representative of management: Director of HRM (1.5 years), married woman in her mid 30s with two children (7 and 4 years).

First focus group: three women and three men aged from 27 to 31 years in different jobs—two in support to users (tertiary education), one in marketing, and one as a sales manager (tertiary education), and two employed in administration (secondary education). All but one have contracts for an unlimited period. All have partners.

Second focus group: three women and three men aged from 31 to 38 years—two of them have leading positions (Master's degree), two are in administration (tertiary education), one is a sales manager, and one is an IT architect (both have tertiary education). All participants have contracts for an unlimited period. They are married, having one or two children aged from 1.6 to 14 years.

Notes

1. We had 70 participants from seven organizations in 14 focus groups (two per organization). Of these 43 were women and 27 men; 40 participants were without children and 30 were parents.
2. The seven managers were: three general managers (all three men), two human resource managers (one man and one woman), and two middle managers (one woman, one man).

3. The seven organizations pursued different activities and were of different sizes: small private catering organization, big private retail organization, middle-size private IT organization, big public healthcare organization, small private textile organization, middle-sized private hairdresser, and middle-size public administration organization.
4. Detailed characteristics of the managers and employees interviewed in focus groups in the three organizations are presented in the Appendix.
5. Sen makes this point in his discussions of poor conditions in developing countries. This is covered in the Introduction to this volume.
6. For an account of the implementation of Sen's capability and agency perspective in analysis of WLB, see Hobson, Introduction in this volume; Hobson and Fahlén 2009.

Bibliography

Berce, J. et al. (2010). *Merjenje raziskovalno-razvojnega potenciala na področju IKT v Sloveniji* [Measurement of ICT Research and Development Potential in Slovenia]. Ljubljana: FDV/IER.

Bradley, H., M. Erikckson, C. Stephonson, and S. Williams (2000). *Myths at Work*. Cambridge: Polity Press.

Černigoj Sadar, N. and P. Kersnik (2004). 'Analysis of Organisational Case Study: Slovenian Finance Sector'. National report for the EU Framework 5 funded study 'Gender, Parenthood and the Changing European workplace'. Ljubljana: Faculty of Social Sciences.

Černigoj Sadar, N. and P. Kersnik, et al. (2005). Transitions—Well-being Report. Report for the EU Framework 5 funded study 'Gender, Parenthood and the Changing European Workplace'. Manchester: Research Institute for Health and Social Change, Manchester Metropolitan University.

Drobnič, S. and A.M. Guillen Rodriguez (2011). Tensions Between Work and Home: Job Quality and Working Conditions in the Institutional Context of Germany and Spain. *Social Politics*, 18(2):232–68.

Dulk, L. den and B. Peper (2007). Working Parents' Use of Work–Life Policies. *Sociologia, problemas e practicas*, 53:51–70.

Dulk, L. den et al. (2011). Work, Family, and Managerial Attitudes and Practices in the European Workplace: Comparing Dutch, British, and Slovenian Financial Sector Managers. *Social Politics*, 18(2):300–29.

European Commission (2009). Indicators for Monitoring the Employment Guidelines Including Indicators for Additional Employment Analysis, 2009 Compendium (29 July).

European Foundation (2007). 4th European Working Conditions Survey. Dublin: European Foundation for the Improvement of Living and Working Conditions.

Franca, V. (2006). Intervju: Franci Lavrač, predsednik Sindikata delavcev trgovine Slovenije—Poklic prodajalca je povsem razvrednoten. [Interview with Franci

Lavrač, the President of the Trade Union of Workers in Commerce of Slovenia: Sales Occupation is Entirely Devalued]. Ljubljana: Finance.

Hobson, B. and S. Fahlén (2009). Applying Sen's Capabilities Framework within a European Context: Theoretical and Empirical Challenges. REC-WP 03/2009. Working Papers on Reconciliation of Work and Welfare in Europe. Edinburgh: RECWOWE Publication, Dissemination and Dialogue Center.

Hochschild, A.R. (2003). *The Commercialization of Intimate Life: Notes from Home and Work*. Berkley, CA: University of California Press.

Ignjatović, M. (2006). 'Flexicurity', Contribution to the EEO Autumn Review.

Ignjatović, M. (2009). Pre-NRP Assesment 2009 Slovenia. Unpublished manuscript.

Kanjuo Mrčela, A. and M. Ignjatović (2006). Unfriendly Flexibilisation of Work and Employment—The Need for Flexicurity, in I. Svetlik and B. Ilič (eds), *HRM's Contribution to Hard Work*, pp. 215–50. Bern: Peter Lang.

Kanjuo Mrčela, A. and N. Černigoj Sadar (2011). Social Policies Related to Parenthood and Capabilities of Slovenian Parents. *Social Politics*, 18(2):199–231.

Lužar, B. (2011). Representativeness of the European Social Partner Organisations: Commerce, Slovenia <http://www.eurofound.europa.eu/eiro/studies/tn1008018s/si1008011q.htm> [2012.6.15].

Maddock, S. and D. Parkin (1993). Gender Cultures: Women's Choices and Strategies at Work. *Women in Management Review*, 8(2):3–9.

Mrčela, M. (2012). EWCO CAR on Working Conditions in the Retail Sector <http://www.eurofound.europa.eu/ewco/studies/tn1109058s/si1109051q.htm> [2012.6.6].

Nippert-Eng, C.E. (1996). *Home and Work: Negotiating Boundaries through Everyday Life*. Chicago: University of Chicago Press.

Plachtej, B. (2011). Slovenia: Industrial Relations in the Health Care Sector. University of Ljubljana, Faculty of Social Sciences, Centre for Organisational and Human Resource Research <http://www.eurofoun.europa.eu/eiro/studies/tn1008022s/si1008021q.htm> [2012.6.15].

Robeyns, I. (2003). Sen's Capability Approach and Gender Inequality: Selecting Relevant Capabilities. *Feminist Economics*, 9(2/3):61–92.

Rogelj, J. (2004). Trgovinska dejavnost v Sloveniji pred in po vstopu v Evropsko unijo. [Commerce in Slovenia Before and After Entering EU]. Chamber of Commerce Symposia, Radenci, 8–10 November.

Sen, A. (1985). *Commodities and Capabilities*. Oxford: Oxford University Press.

Sen, A. (1992). *Inequality Reexamined*. Oxford: Oxford University Press.

Sen, A. (1995). Capabilities and Well-being, in M.C. Nussbaum and A. Sen (eds), *The Quality of Life*, pp. 30–53. Oxford: Clarendon Press.

Sen, A. (1999). *Development as Freedom*. New York: Oxford University Press.

SORS (2008). Structure of Earnings Survey <http://www.stat.si> [2012.10.10].

SORS (2009). Earnings (by the Structure of Earnings Survey), Slovenia, 2006—final data. Rapid reports. No. 30. Statistical Office Republic of Slovenia <http://www.stat.si> [2009.4.20].

SORS (2009a). Labour Force Survey Results, Slovenia, 4th quarter 2008, Rapid reports, No. 21 (20 April) Statistical Office Republic of Slovenia <http://www.stat.si> [2009.4.20].

Stanovnik, P. et al. (2008). Tehnološka predvidevanja in slovenske razvojne prioritete: končno poročilo- 2. faza [Technological Forecast and Slovenian Developmental Priorities: Final Research Report—Phase 2]. Ljubljana: Inštitut za ekonomska raziskovanja, Fakulteta za družbene vede; Koper: Fakulteta za management.

Svetlik, I. (2006). Introduction: Cracks in the Success Story, in I. Svetlik and B. Ilič (eds), *HRM's Contribution to Hard Work*, pp. 9–24. Bern: Peter Lang.

Walby, S. (2011). *The Future of Feminism*. London: Polity Press.

10

Conclusion

Barbara Hobson

This concluding chapter is not a summary of the findings in each chapter, but rather addresses how the capabilities framework and the conceptual tools we applied across our different studies have added new perspectives to the work-life balance research terrain (worklife balance hereafter WLB): for analysing the multidimensional aspects of WLB; and for theorizing agency in WLB. I highlight key points from our research that reveal the agency and capabilities gap in WLB. I also consider how the institutional sociological models we use, as well as our focus on the firm level in WLB, extend the conceptual borders of the capabilities framework. The chapter also identifies how gendering the models and frameworks in capabilities poses challenges for us and leaves unresolved dilemmas in our conceptual and empirical applications of choice and agency. Finally, the chapter ends with a discussion of some effects of the global financial crisis on WLB capabilities and takes up the question of the widening gap in agency and capabilities for WLB between European societies as well as the widening of inequalities between rich and poor nations that has emerged from the global care chain.

The Capabilities Framework and Worklife Balance

Over the last decades, there has been a plethora of WLB research and its effects on health, family life, gender equality, and other aspects of wellbeing and quality of life. This research has tended to focus on different aspects of worklife balance/imbalance; individual time stress and strain (Voydanoff 2005; Drobnič 2011); policies and welfare regimes (Lewis 2009; Strandh and Nordenmark 2009); and the firm or work organizational culture (van der Lippe and Peters 2007; Lewis et al. 2009). To this broad and amorphous research terrain, we bring Sen's capabilities framework, which has enabled us to analyse the interactions at these different levels—individual/household, the workplace, and the policy state level—as demonstrated in our model of capabilities and conversion factors (see the Introduction in this volume). Our core concept of the agency and capabilities gap in WLB confronts the reasons why rights and policy options are not utilized and the broader processes that limit possibilities for achieving WLB. The research in this book has shown how different institutional and normative contexts shape this gap and the potentialities for change.

All the countries included in this book have introduced policies for WLB; the EU has been the driver for many of these policies in Europe, setting minimal standards and guidelines. The Japanese government put into place many of the same policies concerning parental leave, care for others (sick leave), and rights to reduce hours. As our research shows, these policies pass through many filters before individuals have the possibility of utilizing them. Implementation, the standard concept employed to analyse policies, and their translation into different contextual settings, does not capture the complex processes shaping how rights and policies are converted into capabilities and agency freedoms for WLB.

Sen's multidimensional approach has provided us with a framework for analysing the agency and capabilities gap for WLB, which we adapted to our evaluative space and institutional approach, and applied in our nested model of capabilities and conversion factors. The cognitive dimensions that we introduce, the sense of entitlement to make claims and the scope of alternatives, are mechanisms that reveal variations in agency and agency inequalities in WLB. The scope of alternatives operationalized in qualitative and quantitative studies comprises both the scope of policies and the situated agency of working parents, as well as their perception of the possibilities to make claims for a better WLB. Our research demonstrates how the sense of entitlement is embedded in different layers of context: welfare regime configurations, work organizations and societal norms, and within individual lived lives.

Our research highlights the ways in which the firm level is a crucial site for mediating claims, for understanding the scope of alternatives deemed possible, and for the sense of entitlement to make claims. Fagan and Walthery (Chapter 7) take up the question of the right to reduce hours in firms' policies. The scope of alternatives for reducing hours ranges from none, to moves from part to full-time, or vice versa. Full reversibility provides the most possibilities for agency freedoms for WLB, a statutory right offered in only few countries. What firms offer does not always map onto statutory rights (policies are not implemented), although sometimes policies actually go beyond them.

The qualitative studies at the firm level captured the nuances in work organizational culture and the role of managers, revealing another contextual layer in the WLB claims. The study of commercial banking across three societies (Chapter 8), emphasized the salience of discursive frames and rationales (the business case and moral grounds) for granting claims for reduced hours and flexible working times. These were expected to influence the capabilities of individuals working in the firm, yet they did not necessarily predict what managers would do or how those working in the firm perceived the risks involved in making claims for WLB policies. This comparison of banks in three countries revealed that the firm level is just one layer of institutional context shaping capabilities for WLB, nested in national policy context. The Dutch bank appeared most family friendly, a reflection of the policies, politics, and discourse creating a sense of entitlement for WLB claims.

Throughout this book the question of the interplay between firm and state/ policy level was raised, explicitly or implicitly, in relationship to agency and capabilities for WLB and the extent to which the firm was a primary driver in agency or agency inequalities for WLB. This varied across societies, work sectors, and specific work organizations. The Slovenian study demonstrated the layers of context that shape both the sense of entitlement and perceived scope of alternatives for WLB in three firms in different sectors, considered to be good employers, but operating in highly competitive areas (IT and retail) and within a public sector that has undergone retrenchment and budget cuts.

Though we focus on specific WLB policies, our analyses of how institutional context matters reaches beyond actual policy implementation. The sense of entitlement and perceptions of the scope of alternatives for change are bound up with broader aspects of the economy and labour market structures, as is evident in the two CEE countries featured in this book, Hungary and Slovenia.

A weak sense of entitlement to make claims for WLB within firms was also disclosed in the perceptions about the role of the state in intervening or resolving tensions between employment and family. This was the case in CEE countries, where there are legacies of state control as well as a general attitude that these tensions in WLB are private issues. In Japan, there have been extensions in social policies for care and WLB since the 1990s; the firm is the gatekeeper in this developmental productivist state (Peng 2005).

Societal norms and cultural factors (the third circle in our model of capabilities and conversion factors in the introductory chapter) greatly influenced the sense of entitlement to claim rights at the workplace and within households. In most of our case studies, traditional notions of motherhood and care and fatherhood and breadwinning shaped practices; they placed limits on the agency freedoms for men's claims to be more engaged in family life and women's claims for a fairer division of unpaid work. The Swedish case, however, showed that normative pressures worked in another direction, in that fathers who did not take their parental leave felt defensive, and men in our survey expressed guilt over not doing more housework. Still, in their perceptions of the scope of alternatives for WLB, men in Stockholm voiced concerns about being left behind with regards to job promotion and over the loss of family income. In many respects, while the single male breadwinner model is on the wane, the male breadwinner as the primary earner is still in place for most dual-earner couples.

Gender is interwoven into the web and warp of WLB policies and the entitlement to claim them. Though all the policies we analysed are gender neutral in law, WLB policies associated with care are gender-coded in practice. Gender was a decisive factor in the sense of entitlement to make a claim for WLB and the likelihood that it would be granted at the firm level. This was true almost universally with respect to parental leave, the exception being Sweden, where men in both public and private sector jobs felt a strong sense of entitlement to exercise their rights; close to one-third reached parity in the share of leave. Our capabilities survey in Hungary showed that the persistence of traditional societal norms was so entrenched that parental leave for men was unimaginable. In Japan, a significant proportion did not even know that men were entitled to parental leave or other leave policies. Our studies confirm that the gender-coding of these policies produces streaming of women in the public sector, a deskilling of women who return to jobs after leave, and—in welfare states in which the laws against discrimination are not enforced—a lack of integration back into paid work.

More so than parental leave, claims for reducing hours, even when it is a right (Fagan 2004), are made almost exclusively by mothers, not fathers. As shown in Chapter 2, based on the European Social Survey, a significant number of men would reduce working hours even if this meant a loss in pay. Another evaluation from the Eurofound survey claimed that men wanted to reduce hours, but not work part-time (Anxo and Boulin 2006). Here, the Japanese case is suggestive, since part-time is not a matter of hours, but of status, a job without benefits or security—in short, a second class job. However, this is less true in European countries and varies across different welfare regimes (Fagan 2004); the conversion factors that we identify as relevant include specific laws on part-time thresholds for benefits and job protections; union coverage; and working time regulations.

Flexibility, the cornerstone of EU policy for WLB, encompasses multidimensional facets in different institutional contexts, as well as differences in situated agency that influence access to part-time jobs and flexi-time and the consequences of their use. For women in many countries, part-time work is the only way they can combine employment with family (Fagan 2004). Mothers in our Budapest sample longed for the possibility of finding jobs with reduced hours. Nevertheless, Fagan (2004) has acknowledged the double-edged sword inherent in part-time work for many women: that of becoming locked in to dead-end jobs. The research in this book underlines how different levels of resources and skills influence the conversion of policies into capabilities for WLB. Fagan and Walthery (Chapter 7), in their comparison of EU countries, show that within organizations highly skilled women are most likely to have the option of reversibility. The study of banks (Chapter 8) also makes the point that the highly skilled and highly educated, both men and women, viewed as indispensable in the firm (the business case), were in a much stronger position to claim reduced hours and flexibility. Still, the literature shows that professionals profit less from reduced working hours than non-professionals (Beham et al. 2012), and employees in their study of commercial banks voiced the tacit understanding of the tradeoff in career terms when they reduce working hours.

Flexibility in working hours, even when it is employee-driven, can be seen as two-sided coin. As Hobson et al. (Chapter 3) showed, flexibility is used extensively in Sweden, providing the opportunity for mothers and fathers to collect their children early from daycare. However, the widespread use of flexi-time did not necessarily lead to a shorter working day. Significant proportions of men in Sweden work more than 40 hours a week, as shown in Chapter 2. Flexi-time was presented as the hallmark of new management and the modern work organization that responds to employees' needs in the IT and bank sectors. These findings confirm research that a lack of boundaries and work intensity go hand and hand with autonomy and flexibility in the New Economy (Perrons et al. 2006; Drobnič and Gullíen 2011; see also Chapter 9). In our capabilities survey, less educated self-employed Hungarian women had the weakest agency and capabilities for WLB; flexibility in working hours existed alongside extremely precarious and unpredictable work situations.

Sen's capabilities approach provided us with a multidimensional framework that embeds individual agency into institutional normative settings; the highly contextualized studies across different regimes and within firms, with its focus on capabilities and conversion factors, extends the conceptual borders of WLB. The capabilities framework also offered a dynamic framework for WLB: by asking us to look beyond what individuals do, to consider what they would do if they had other alternatives.

Through the qualitative questionnaire that we tailored for a capabilities approach and applied in three cities (Stockholm, Budapest, and Osaka), and through the focus groups used in two studies, we explored the subjective experiential level of the agency gap in WLB. The capabilities perspective allowed us to tap into the agency and capabilities gap in making changes in the organization of time and the stress in everyday lives, as well as the gap between aspirations for change and possibilities for achieving a WLB. Our results indicate that there are tectonic plates moving beneath the surface: individuals challenging work organizational cultures; managers caught between pressures from above and below; full-time mothers expressing a need for alternatives to ease the time squeeze. Whereas mothers are most often the focus of WLB research, in our research men are also treated as subjects.

Across our countries, we found a desire among a generation of young fathers for WLB, even in institutional settings in which there had not been a strong presence of politics and discourse around WLB. In the Japanese case, where men exercised almost no rights for WLB and had the widest agency and capabilities gap for WLB, in a national survey more than 30% said that they would have liked to have taken parental leave (see Chapter 4). Reaching the subjective-experiential sides of WLB enabled us to contextualize the perceived constraints for WLB, revealing the different meanings of time poverty and economic pressure in societies with high and low expectations for WLB and wellbeing (shown in our comparative study of Sweden and Hungary). These insights offered perspectives on comparative subjective measures of worklife conflict and satisfaction with WLB, in which individuals with long working times and low job quality do not voice their dissatisfaction with their lot or view their situation in terms of worklife conflict; rather, these conditions are accepted as business as usual in a particular society or community.

The capabilities approach also provided conceptual leverage to interpret results from existing surveys that have been used to analyse worklife interference. In their comparative study of Germany and Spain, Drobnič and León (2011) were faced with the paradox of the presence of young children having had no effect on work–home conflict. The unobserved effects suggested a selection bias: mothers with greater individual resources and better networks could combine employment with family; other women resolved the conflict by either not having children or not being in paid employment. Both solutions reflect weak capabilities, a lack of institutional supports (childcare for children under 3), and bedrock traditional constructions of motherhood and care.

A central debate within WLB research revolves around whether it is possible to find measures—either subjective or objective—for WLB, a concept that is considered vague or lacking value for interpreting results or choices (Guest 2002; MacInnes 2006). Our purpose here has not been to construct a measure of the agency gap in WLB, but to reveal the multidimensional factors that facilitate or impede possibilities for achieving WLB and quality of life. Ours is a process-oriented approach that brings to the research terrain a dynamic and agency-centred framework in which we have asked different questions; not just what individuals do, but what their opportunities are to make other choices in WLB that would lead to a better quality of life.

New Perspectives and Challenges for the Capabilities Framework

Although the first wave of research on capabilities emerged in studies of development, over the last decades there has been a flowering of literature that engages with the capabilities framework in advanced capitalist societies. Applications of the capabilities framework with an empirical analytical research design have addressed poverty and social exclusion; disability (Burchardt 2004; Burchardt 2008); education (Otto and Zegler 2010); employment (Lessman 2012); and inequalities and discrimination (Evans et al. 2011). Empirical research on capabilities in an era of welfare state change and global competitiveness address not only employment concerns, but also those of employability and activation (Bonvin and Farvaque 2003; Salais and Villeneuve 2004; Dean et al. 2005). There are few studies with a sociological/institutional approach and research design (Korpi 2000; Bonvin and Farvaque 2003; Bifulco et al. 2010) and even fewer in that category in which gender is the main text rather than a subtext (Korpi 2000; Lewis and Guillari 2006). This book is the first to apply the capabilities approach to WLB within a multilevel framework, incorporating individual, institutional, and societal factors that comprise the capability set. Other innovations in our applications of Sen's framework include fine-grained contextualized comparative analysis in countries and in firms, and a qualitative survey specifically designed for our agency and capabilities approach.

All applications of the capabilities approach face the challenge of how to operationalize it in empirical studies. We have introduced new conceptual tools and levels of analysis. In our research, the sense of entitlement to make clams for WLB is not merely a question of formal laws or specific policies (Browne et al. 2004), but one of institutional embeddedness in the welfare regime and within the firm and work organizational culture, which are conversion factors in our analyses. From this perspective, our multidimensional model of capabilities goes beyond Lee and McCann's (2006) concept of working time capabilities. In our models, gender equality norms and discourse are also conversion factors underlying the sense of entitlement and self-efficacy to make claims for WLB and the possibilities of achieving them. We touch upon the role of social movements and political actors in promoting WLB policies and challenging gendered norms (in the discussion of the Swedish and Japanese cases), however more research, with a multidimensional approach, needs to be done on collective capabilities (Evans 2002).

Sen views subjective measures as a cognitive exercise in which individuals evaluate specific domains, such as family, work and economic situations, or more generally take stock of their lives and fulfilment of their goals. Again, the challenge is how to operationalize subjective dimensions into empirical research on capabilities and agency. Burchardt et al. (2012) use autonomy and control as their conceptual tools for assessing the cognitive level of capabilities across several domains, including WLB. They are interested in the ability of individuals to make decisions and their participation in decision-making. Our approach, in which institutional/cultural context is central and not an indirect effect on choice (Burchardt et al. 2011) necessitated other dimensions for assessing agency freedoms and agency inequalities in WLB. The scope of alternatives for making change to achieve a better WLB goes beyond taking stock of one's life situation. Rather our purpose is to identify how specific institutional/normative contexts not only shape subjective assessments of agency and choice, but also influence perceptions of what is possible or imaginable and how this is reflected in the sense of entitlement to make claims for rights for WLB in households and firms. These dimensions provided the conceptual tools for analysing and explaining the differences across and within societies.

Our approach builds upon the work of others who began addressing capabilities within the context of institutional frameworks and welfare regimes. In his article, 'Faces of Inequality', Korpi (2000) does not fully develop a model of capabilities, nor use many of the conceptual tools, but he paved the way for others in this book to consider welfare regime typologies and agency for gender equality. For him, participation in the labour force is a 'functioning' for gender equality, which not only determines the distribution of resources, but also how it affects women's self-perception, identity, and the scope for capabilities and freedom in different spheres of life. He concludes that welfare state shapes the patterns of agency inequalities—institutional contexts that support dual-earning couples are those most likely to reduce gendered agency inequality.

However, Korpi does not take into account the fact that the social quality of jobs may be poor with bad conditions and low wages (Drobnič and Gullién 2011). Seen from our evaluative space (WLB), women's employment in Korpi's typology is a capability, as it assumes there are policies that support a dual-earner family (see Korpi's typology, pp. 158–59). In our applications, we underscore how being able to participate in employment needs to be coupled to other capabilities for achieving WLB: such as being able to refuse extra or asocial hours and having rights and protections against discrimination for those taking care leave (see Chapter 3 and 4). One example of how capabilities and functioning often overlap is in having the possibility to find work in a family-friendly environment (often dependent upon individual and institutional factors) and actually having employment that supports other functionings, such as time for family, leisure, and self-development.

By incorporating the dimension of care into the capabilities framework, Lewis and Gulliari (2006) set the agenda for those of us who are seeking to go beyond employment in designing research for WLB and quality of life. Choice features prominently in Lewis' (2009) universe of the constraints that women face with diverse situations and work/care responsibilities. Men's capabilities and agency freedoms to choose to be carers and earners is a focus in this book, though men's care has not been addressed in the capabilities framework; men are often construed in WLB research in terms of obstructing women's choices

(Orloff 2009). Throughout our analyses of the cognitive level of agency and agency inequalities in WLB, choice is ever present, bounded by the choices of spouses/partners, work organizational cultures, and access to policies.

Challenges in Gendering Capabilities and WLB

Gendering the capabilities framework involved incorporating the relational sides of capabilities. This presented a conceptual challenge for us, given that the point of departure for conventional models applying the capabilities approach is the individual as the agent in converting means and resources. Iversen's (2003) article on power and dynamics in families identified this problem. However, our research indicates that bargaining models do not offer much leverage for understanding how gendered agency inequalities operate within families (Sen 1990; Agawarl 1997). Gendering capabilities embrace the relational aspects of agency. These interdependencies are encapsulated in our concept of situated agency, which provided analytical space for analysing agency inequalities in WLB at the household level. Most obvious is the fact that the WLB choices of one individual in the family can shape the agency/agency inequalities of the other. It is not just differences in income and resources that explain the differences in the sense of entitlement to make claims (Sen 1992). Gendered norms operate at this level, evident in some working mothers' lack of any sense of entitlement— even those working full-time—to make claims for more equal sharing of household tasks. This was highlighted in the Japanese, Hungarian, and Slovenian cases. Class and educational differences also shaped the intra-household dynamics, as shown in our comparative cases.

The sociological/institutional approach to WLB and capabilities emphasizes the nestedness of individual capabilities. Our research showed that the skill and human capital of mothers and fathers were resources for the sense of entitlement to make claims and the granting of them at the workplaces (seen in the discourses among managers; dependency/disruption rationale for WLB). However, in our models and throughout our analysis we have underscored the interactive effects in agency and structures: the classic sociological position (Giddens 1986; Sewell 1992).

Irresolvable Dilemmas: Choice and Adaptive Preferences

Choice in the capabilities framework poses challenge for all empirical studies. As discussed in the introductory chapter, choice is problematized as the counterfactual dilemma in capabilities research (Comim et al. 2008): how do we know what someone would choose? What are the alternative scenarios for choosing other ways of living? We sought to address this dilemma through questions relating to the perception and scope of alternatives. We found that not only what was viewed as possible, but also what was conceivable or imaginable, was deeply embedded in taken for granted norms that shaped choice and agency, and this was most apparent in countries with naturalized views of motherhood and fatherhood.

Returning to Sen's distinction between fasting and starving in terms of choice within the realm of WLB, one could make a similar comparison between the father who is a workaholic and the father who takes on two jobs to make ends meet. Yet even this example is not as clear-cut as it appears. In many workplaces and sectors, workaholism is the norm and those who do not keep up with high work demands and expectations for productivity are cast out. The financial sector and the IT company case studies presented in this book foster this intense competitiveness, which is internalized by those who work in these environments.

Women's and men's choices around caring and employment have generated many debates in WLB. The early feminist debates on women's choice revolved around the right not to care (Land and Rose 1985), reflected in women's lack of choice, embodied in the term 'compulsory altruism'. With the majority of mothers in Europe now in the labour market, the choice to care is uppermost in the minds of policy-makers and is displayed in the tensions of WLB practices: the choices around care can involve leaving the labour market for short or lengthy leaves, dropping out entirely, or returning to employment with reduced hours, in other words part-time work.

Here, we confront the black box of adaptive preferences: do the majority of mothers in Spain, Germany, and Hungary—case studies in this book—who leave the labour market for long periods, do so voluntarily? Although the majority of Japanese mothers drop out of employment after having children, national surveys reveal that most of them would not choose to stay out of the labour market. The model of women's capabilities for employment in Britain, proposed by Burchardt (2002), confronts the issue of voluntary and non-voluntary choice; after controlling for education and jobs, she concludes that even among those that are 'voluntary' leavers, adaptive preferences lie beneath the surface.

The applications of Sen's capabilities approach to childbearing also sheds some light on choice and constraints, since in many studies of fertility few women would choose to be childless (Fahlén and Oláh 2013; Pailhé and Solaz 2013). In Fahlén's (2013) study of birth intentions and Hobson and Oláh's (2006) analysis of women's childbearing in countries with the lowest fertility, choice is constrained and reflects the rising expectations for gender equality in the family and labour market among a generation of women living in societies where few policies enable women to reconcile family with employment (Hobson and Oláh 2006; Fahlén 2013). The result is childlessness or having fewer children than a woman would choose or would choose with real agency freedom.

The capabilities approach is unique in seeing freedom of choice as an essential ingredient of wellbeing (Lessman 2012), yet the capability set cannot be observed (Sen 1992: 52), only the option chosen. This brings us into territory beyond the capabilities framework: what are the consequences of choice over the life course. The high proportions of solo mothers who experience poverty after divorce (Millar 2001) bear out the potential consequences of 'choice' for those who leave employment after having children or who have weak and intermittent attachment to employment, such as short-term, part-time, or temporary work. The effects of long breaks from employment among our Budapest mothers reveal the difficulties of retaining the possibilities to find work. The effects of choices that can give rise to weak capabilities in later life need to be built into the framework of capabilities.

Ascertaining genuine choice in WLB is elusive. We have concentrated on agency inequalities and the barriers that stand in the way of agency freedoms to make choices; and in doing so have acknowledged that the dilemmas surrounding choice are not resolvable. Although several chapters in this book engage with what individuals would change and what they think would lead to a better WLB, our project lies closer to the analytical capabilities applications than the normative (Robeyns 2006). Within the capabilities paradigm, normative dimensions of capabilities are developed in assessment or evaluation of policies and practices and often offer recommendations for policy change. Within the current literature on WLB and gender equality, there are examples of similar normative exercises; most well known are the blueprints for change in the Real Utopias Project (Gornick and Meyers 2009).

Blueprints for Change

The Real Utopias Project has generated much debate in agenda-setting studies and their critics (Gornick and Meyers 2009). Most relevant to capabilities and WLB are those debates that address the question of choice, freedoms, and fairness in gender equality and how to design institutions for WLB policies that would lead toward a more equitable redistribution in caring and earning among mothers and fathers. Our research on capabilities and agency freedoms sheds light on these.

Gornick and Meyers' (2008) article put forward a blueprint for institutional design that would support an earner–carer society where gender symmetry was at the core. It would have to involve high levels of support for parental care and a shift in men's allocation of time from the labour market to the home. The Nordic countries come closest to the Real Utopia, as they have embraced some of the key policies, such as reduced working times; part-time work with job security; and non-transferable parental leave to create incentives for fathers and mothers to become more fully engaged in caregiving and earning. Although implementing policies that reshape the caring practices of parents and the allocation of time between men and women do not necessarily limit the choices available to men and women, Gornick and Meyers' blueprint for change has some non-transferable care leave equally shared, which would limit options of some mothers and fathers.

Brighouse and Wright (2009), also in the Real Utopia Project, take a more radical stand in suggesting policies that would make the use of the leave contingent upon the other partner using his share of care leave. Choice takes a back seat to gender equality and justice in their advocacy of strong gender egalitarianism.

Coming from the capabilities tradition, Gheaus and Robeyns' (2010) are critical of these blueprints for change, particularly Brighouse and Wright's model, since in promoting gender equality they sacrifice too much individual choice. Their proposal, the normative default option, in essence, recasts reserved father leave as the norm rather than the exception. Those who do not choose this option formally would have to opt out of the system. All these blueprints for change conceive of shared parental leave as transformative, which is not borne out by research (see Chapter 3). Also, within Gheus and Robyens' proposal, which is not presented as a real utopia but a viable option, there is a failure to understand that what appears reasonable and logical can, when applied in different societal contexts, be seen as untenable and coercive. They compare their proposal to another policy that has been successful in several societies, in which organ donorship is the default option. Obviously, these are not comparable, since fathers' and mothers' care leave is about lived lives. The studies in this book, as well as many others, reveal many contentions and complexities, even in societies where incentives for men to take care leave exist, such as the Nordic countries. In other countries with different policy legacies and gender politics, this would be much more difficult to put into place.

Other authors in the Real Utopias volume on gender equality (Ferree 2009; Orloff 2009) make a similar contextual argument against a blueprint for gender egalitarianism in caregiving and earning that could be applied across societies. Policy legacies and politics are crucial dimensions for understanding the emergence of the dual-earner dual-carer model in Nordic countries. The difficulties encountered in implementing existing policies—even when they are supported by EU law—reveal the importance of politics and path dependencies in policy choice. Nevertheless, our research suggests that incentive structures and laws can seed new norms and create a sense of entitlement to make claims, for WLB. Cross-national data show increases in men's use of parental leave in societies in which men's care leave is targeted (Ray et al. 2010).

Another contextual level that needs to be built into blueprints for gender equality is the firm and work organizational culture. The research in this book reveals the significant role of work organizational cultures for the sense of entitlement to make claims for WLB, or the lack thereof. Those who claim rights for WLB often face resistance and discrimination at workplaces, for instance, a loss of job, relocation to another job in the organization, or deskilling in the job offered.

A critique levelled at the Real Utopia's blueprint for gender egalitarianism in work and family is the failure to recognize diversities around women's choices regarding caring and earning (Ferree 2009; Orloff 2009). Yet in acknowledging diversities—that one size does not fit all—it is important to avoid reifying categorical or cultural difference (Fraser 2003).[1] There is a tendency in policy debates and some scholarship to presume that all immigrant and working class women hold traditional gendered norms regarding family and employment. Here, Sen's (2002) caution against reducing agency to group identity should be taken seriously in discussions of diversity and choice in WLB. The capabilities approach presupposes that the individual immigrant or working class woman might make other choices if she had the agency freedoms for alternatives. Our research suggests that an exclusive focus on cultural factors can shade out others; for example, it is important to consider the quality of jobs, the employment options, and the wages of less educated women. Neither immigrant women, nor men, are a unified category. In fact, one study of immigrant men and parental leave in Sweden showed a U curve; some immigrants took more leave than Swedish men; others took less (Duvander 2006).

Orloff (2009) has argued for openness in choice, while maintaining that policies that impede choice should be removed. This brings to the fore the question of which policies impede and for which women and for which men. Designing polices in WLB that provide effective choice for some often imply some curtailment of choice for others. Consider an example in our case studies, the three-year parental leave policy, which is often a flat rate benefit. This policy allows women the possibility of an extended leave, however, it can reinforce norms naturalizing the mother's role in childrearing, which can have the effect of circumscribing other women's choices to return to employment (see Chapters 3 and 5). Even though a long parental leave policy might be cast in gender neutral terms, the assumptions and norms that lie behind it can close off the possibility of men to choose to be more engaged in caregiving. Lack of affordable childcare does not necessarily impede resource-rich women, who can purchase services, from combining employment with family. The global crisis has afforded middle-class European women a new resource of migrant labour to resolve their worklife conflict. This brings a global dimension to the widening agency gap in WLB. In an era of welfare state retrenchment and deepening unemployment, policy choices framed in terms of increasing individual choice often result in expanding the range of choices for those with the most resources and narrowing the choices for those with fewest.

A Widening of the Agency and Capabilities Gap in WLB?

Much of the data for this book was collected either before the emergence of the global financial crisis in 2008 or just when the first ill winds began to blow (the Japanese qualitative survey began in 2009). In the following section, I combine some recent findings gleaned from published reports, with the insights and perspectives from the authors in this book on the effects of the financial crisis on WLB capabilities. Much of this is speculative since the full brunt of the crisis is still being felt and there is not much empirical research on its effects on subjective experiential aspects of everyday lives.

As the recent EU report on the impact of the global crisis on men and women and gender equality policies contends (Bettio et al. 2012), the global crisis has spawned many episodes of bank crises and recession that vary across countries, sectors, and between men and women within societies. Before the financial crisis had begun to penetrate the economies in most European societies, several of the case studies featured here—Spain, Slovenian, and Hungary—already displayed the salient characteristics associated with it: high levels of precarious work; intermittent employment; and unemployment (Chapters 3 and 9; Frey 2011). Temporary employment, however, has actually decreased in many countries because those holding these types of jobs are the first to be laid off (Bettio et al. 2012: 80–83).

Eurostat data reveal that, as of 2010, the financial crisis and the recession that followed has not adversely affected gender equality in many countries. In fact there appears to be a pattern of narrowing gender gaps in employment, unemployment, pay, and employment statuses (Bettio et al. 2102). Some negative changes are more pronounced for men, seen in the rate of unemployment and duration of unemployment. Segregation of women in the public service sector has somewhat sheltered them from unemployment and pay cuts (Bettio et al. 2102: 8). Men report that they have been more affected in having to accept cuts in pay. Some of the repercussions of the recession, in some countries, that specifically affect women involve the weakening of rights protecting mothers on maternity leave against discrimination. Women's integration into the labour market was above 65% in ten member states before the recession, but it is only at this level in six now (Bettio et al. 2102: 9).

Considering the agency and capabilities gap in WLB, it is logical to turn to WLB policy changes. Most obvious would be policies that have been eliminated or drastically cut, which does not seem to have happened yet. Instead, we are seeing a discontinuation of policies promised, but not implemented. In Spain, where effects of the crisis are felt intensely, and which has one of the highest levels of unemployment in the EU, the bite is visible in never-implemented WLB policies. For example, promised reforms for paid paternity leave to encourage fathers' care have not materialized, nor has the promise of increased availability in childcare. Furthermore, the care subsidy for those caring for elderly has been reduced by 15%, along with a loss of benefits and cutbacks in welfare. The reliance on family networks has increased not only with respect to care of grandchildren, but also providing support for their unemployed children (see Chapter 5).

In Slovenia, the recession hit somewhat later than in other countries, beginning in the first half of the 2009. Data from Eurostat for that year show that women were losing jobs to a lesser extent than men, since male-dominated sectors were affected first by the crisis; but on the other hand, fewer unemployed women were able to obtain a new job. There have been few changes in WLB policies. The compensation for parental leave was reduced from 100% to 90%. That change, considered to be temporary, will be in place until growth of the real GDP exceeds 2.5%. Also considered temporary is the cutting back of the fee subsidy for childcare for families with more than one child in preschool. (Parents who have two children used to pay only 30% of the costs.) This may not seem dramatic, but in a country with low birthrates, it is significant.

In addition to the gap between Eastern and Western Europe, revealed in research prior to the crisis, we find a widening gap between countries in which the economic crisis has not had a strong impact to date, such as Germany and Sweden. Clearly, there is a gap between Northern and Southern European countries in terms of the penetration of the crisis and recession into everyday lives. Neither Germany nor Sweden has seen reductions in WLB policies; on the contrary, there have been some extensions. For instance, in Germany, childcare and policy initiatives to expand the daddy months and to obtain a legal right for daycare places for children between the ages of 1 and 3 have been put forward. Sweden has retained its generous parental leave and there is some discussion about increasing the daddy months to three. Other incentives for fathers to take more leave remain, such as the equality tax bonus for families in which fathers take more than the two months leave reserved for them. Within these countries where the economic crisis appears to have less impact, it remains to be seen whether the sense of entitlement to make claims and the self-efficacy to defend WLB rights when they are denied, will be weakened in the current climate of insecure futures and in the absence of any clear indication that the recession in Europe will abate.

The Japanese case study suggests that long-term financial pressures in a country can produce paradoxical effects on WLB. The reduction in full-time guaranteed lifetime jobs has led to a questioning of the working time regime in the corporate world and the sacrifices it entails regarding men's involvement in family life. Dramatic rises in non-regular work among young men and women may be the drivers of change. Nevertheless, leaner work forces have translated into longer working hours and intense performance-based payment structures for those still holding permanent jobs (Taga 2011), a change that is also occurring in other countries with leaner work forces.

A significant change in the agency and capabilities gap is the growing inequality between rich and poor nations, which pre-dates the financial crisis (Lutz 2008; Williams 2012). The agency and capabilities gap in earning and caring has become global, captured in the global care chain (Hochschild 2001). Mothers from poorer countries in Africa and Asia as well as Eastern European countries resolve the tensions in WLB for some European women in richer countries, and more importantly take the pressure off governments to increase their social investment in care. Migrant care/domestic workers show some of the weakest capabilities for WLB both in terms of their inability to care for their own children and their everyday care/domestic employment, in which they lack protection and rights for decent working times and wages (Lutz 2008; Williams 2012).

Many countries provide subsidies for families to outsource domestic and care work, including Germany, Spain, and Sweden among those studied here. WLB is no longer merely a question of redistributive conflict in the family around the division of unpaid work, or the redistribution effects in welfare states when the costs of care are covered by state policies (Sainsbury 1996; Korpi 2000). The increased use of migrant labor for care/domestic work is a recent phenomenon in Europe compared to the USA. It reflects the widening agency and capabilities gap for WLB within European societies, since it is middle-class families who can afford their services. The discourses underpinning government subsidies for domestic/care work revolve around choice; they are also conjoined with a discourse on promoting gender equality so that some women can invest in their human capital and compete with men in careers. The implications of these shifts reflect greater agency inequalities among women for WLB. They signal the increasing role of the household in contracting care and domestic services for families with children and for their elderly parents built upon migrant cheap labour. Finally they raise the question of whether the ideological basis of WLB is on the wane, which encompasses not only promoting participation of both men and women in paid work, still prominent on the EU agenda, but also the sharing of caregiving and unpaid work.

Note

1. Ferree (2009) and Orloff (2009) are careful not to do this.

Bibliography

Agarwal, B. (1997). 'Bargaining' and Gender Relations: Within and Beyond the Household. *Feminist Economics*, 2(1):1–51.

Anxo, D. and J-Y. Boulin (2006). The Organization of Time over the Life Course: European Trends. *European Societies*, 8(2):319–41.

Beham, B., P. Präg, and S. Drobnič (2012). Who's got the Balance? A Study of Satisfaction with the Work–Family Balance among Part-Time Service Sector Employees in Five Western European Countries. *The International Journal of Human Resource Management*, 23(18):3725–41.

Bettio, F., M. Corsi, C. DiIpppolti et al. (2012). The Impact of the Economic Crisis on the Situation of Women and Men and on Gender Equality Policies. European Experts on Gender Equality (Enege), Instituto per la Ricerca Sociale. Brussels: European Commission.

Bifulco, L., R. Monteleone, C. Mozzana, and I. Rolfini (2010). A Social Theory for the Capability Approach: Conversion Factors, Capabilities and Education. Final Comparative Report: A Blue-Print of Capabilities for Work and Education. Collaborative Project.

Bonvin, J. M. and N. Farvaque (2003). Employability and Capability: The Role of Local Agencies in Implementing Social Policies. Paper presented at the Conference on the Capability Approach 'From Sustainable Development to Sustainable Freedom'. University of Pavia, September.

Brighouse, H. and E.O. Wright (2009). Strong Gender Egalitarianism, in J. Gornick and M. Meyers (eds), *Gender Equality: Transforming Families by Division of Labor*, pp. 79–62. New York: Verso Books.

Browne, J., S. Deakin, and F. Wilkinson (2004). Capabilities, Social Rights and European Market Integration, in R. Salais and R. Villeneuve (eds), *Europe and the Politics of Capabilities*, pp. 205–21. Cambridge: Cambridge University Press.

Burchardt, T. (2002). Constraint and Opportunity: Women's Employment in Britain. Paper prepared for Von Hugel Institute Conference, Cambridge, 9–10 September.

Burchardt, T. (2004). Capabilities and Disability: The Capabilities Framework and the Social Model of Disability. *Disabilities and Society*, 19(7):735–75.

Burchardt, T. (2008). Time and Income Poverty. Centre for Analysis of Social Exclusion, CASE report 57. London: London School of Economics.

Burchardt, T., M. Evans, H. Holder, and P. Vizard (2011). Identifying Inequalities in Autonomy Through the Equality Measurement Framework. Social Policy Association Conference, Lincoln, 5 July.

Burchardt, T., M. Evans, H. Holder, and P. Vizard (2012). Identifying Inequalities in Autonomy Through the Equality Measurement Framework. *Social Indicators Research*, 106(1):1–25.

Comim, F., M. Qizilbash, and S. Alkire (2008) (eds), *The Capability Approach: Concepts, Measures and Applications*. New York: Cambridge University Press.

Dean, H., J-M. Bonvin, P. Vielle, and N. Faraque (2005). Developing Capabilities and Rights in Welfare-to-Work Policies. *European Societies*, 7(1):3–26.

Drobnič, S. (2011). Introduction: Job Quality and Work–Life Balance, in S. Drobnič and A.M. Guillén (eds), *Work–Life Balance in Europe: The Role of Job Quality*, pp. 1–16. Basingstoke: Palgrave Macmillan.

Duvander, A.Z. and S. Eklund (2006). Utrikesfödda och svenskfödda föräldrars föräldrapenninganvändande [Foreign Born and Swedish Born Parents' Parental Leave Use], in de los Reyes (ed.), *Om välfärdens gränser och det villkorade medborgarskapet*, pp. 33–68. SOU 2006:37. Stockholm: Fritzes.

Ehrenreich, B. and A. Hochschild (2001) (eds), *Global Women*. New York: Metropolitan Books.

Evans, P. (2002). Collective Capabilities, Culture, and Amartya Sen's Development as Freedom. *Studies in Comparative International Development*, Summer 37(2):54–60.

Fagan, C. (2004). Gender and Working-time in Industrialized Countries: Practices and Preferences, in J. Messenger (ed.), *Finding the Balance: Working-Time and Workers' Needs and Preferences in Industrialized countries*, pp. 108–46. London: Routledge/ Institute for Labour Studies of the International Labour Organisation.

Fahlén, S. and L.Sz. Oláh (2013). Work and Childbearing Intentions in a Capability Perspective: Young Adult Women in Sweden, in L.Sz. Oláh and E. Frątczak (eds), *Childbearing Intentions, Female Employment and Reconciliation Policies in Modern Europe*. Basingstoke: Palgrave MacMillan.

Fahlén, S. (2013). Capabilities and Childbearing Intentions in Europe: The Association between Reconciliation Policies, Economic Uncertainties and Women's Fertility. *European Societies*: DOI:10.1080/14616696.2013.798018.

Ferree, M.R. (2009). An American Road Map: Framing Feminist Goals in a Liberal Landscape, in J. Gornick and M. Meyers (eds), *Gender Equality: Transforming Family Divisions of Labor*, pp. 283–315. New York: Verso.

Fraser, N. (2003). Rethinking Recognition: Overcoming Displacement and Reification in Cultural Politics, in B. Hobson (ed.), *Recogntion and Social Movements: Agency and Power*, pp. 21–34. Cambridge: Cambridge University Press.

Frey M. (2011). Nők és férfiak a munkaerőpiacon, különös tekintettel a válságkezelés hatásaira [Women and Men on the Labour Market—With Special Focus on the Effects of Crisis Management], in: I. Nagy and T. Pongrácz (eds), *Szerepváltozások. Jelentés a nők és a férfiak helyzetéről 2011* [Changing Roles: Report on the Situation of Women and Men in Hungary 2011], pp. 17–48. Budapest: TÁRKI Zrt.—Nemzeti Erőforrás Minisztérium.

Giddens, A. (1986). *The Constitution of Society*. Cambridge: Polity Press.

Guest, D.E. (2002). Perspectives on the Study of Work–Life Balance. *Social Science Information*, 42(2):255–79.

Gheaus, A. and I. Robeyns (2010). Equality Promoting Parental Leave. *Social Philosophy*, 42(2):173–91

Gornick, J. and M. Meyers (2008). Creating Gender Equality Societies: An Agenda for Reform. *Politics and Society*, 36(3):313–49.

Gornick, J. and M. Meyers (2009) (eds), *Gender Equality: Transforming Families by Division of Labor*, pp. 79–62. New York: Verso Books.

Hobson, B. and L.Sz. Oláh (2006). Birthstrikes? Agency and Capabilities in the Reconciliation of Employment and Family. *Journal of Marriage and the Family Review*, 39(3–4):197–227.

Hochschild, A.R. (2001). *The Time Bind: When Work Becomes Home and Home Becomes Work* (second edition). New York: Henry Holt.

Iversen, V. (2003). Intra-Household Inequality: A Challenge for the Capability Approach? *Feminist Economics*, 9:93–116.

Korpi, W. (2000). Faces of Inequality: Gender, Class, and Patterns of Inequalities in Different Types of Welfare States. *Social Politics*, 7(2):127–91.

Land, H. and H. Rose (1985). Compulsory Altruism for Some or an Altruistic Society for All? in P. Bean, J. Ferris and D. Whynes (eds), *In Defence of Welfare*, pp. 74–96. London: Tavistock.

Lee, S. and D. McCann (2006). Working Time Capability: Towards Realizing Individual Choice, in J-Y. Boulin, M. Lallement, J.C. Messenger, and F. Michon (eds), *Decent Working Time: New Trends; New Issues*, pp. 65–82. Geneva: International Labour Office.

Lessman, O. (2012). Applying the Capability Approach Empircally: An Overview with a Special Attention to Labor. *Management Review*, 23(2):98–118.

Lewis, J. (2009). *Work–Family Balance and Gender Policy*. Cheltenham: Edward Elgar.

Lewis, J. (2006). Work/Family Reconciliation, Equal Opportunities and Social Policies: The Interpretation of Policy Trajectories at the EU Level and the Meaning of Gender Equality. *Journal of European Public Policy*, 13(3):420–37.

Lewis, S., J. Brannen, and A. Nilsen (2009) (eds), *Work, Family and Organisations in Transition: A European Perspective*. Bristol: Policy Press

Lutz, H. (2008) (ed.). *Migration and Domestic Work: A European Perspective on a Global Theme*. Avebury: Ashgate.

MacInnes, J. (2006). Work–Life Balance in Europe: A Response to the Baby Bust or Reward for Baby Boomers? *European Societies*, 2(2):223–49.

Millar, J. and K. Rowlingson (2001) (eds), *Lone Parents, Employment and Social Policy: Cross-National Comparisons*. Bristol: Policy Press.

Orloff, A. (2009). Should Feminism Aim for Gender Symmetry? Why a Dual Earner Dual Carer Society is Not Every Feminist Utopia, in J. Gornick and M. Meyers (eds), *Gender Equality: Transforming Family Divisions of Labor*, pp. 129–60. New York: Verso.

Otto, H-U. and H. Ziegler (2010). Theoretical Framework and Methodology of Capability Acquisition—A Final Report. Final Comparative Report: A Blue-Print of Capabilities for Work and Education. Collaborative Project, WorkAble—Making Capabilities Work.

Pailhé, A. and A. Solaz (2013). Employment Instability and Childbearing Plans in a Child-Oriented Country, in L.Sz. Oláh and E. Frątczak (eds), *Childbearing Intentions, Female Employment and Reconciliation Policies in Modern Europe*. Basingstoke: Palgrave MacMillan.

Peng, I. (2005). New Politics of Welfare State in a Developmental Context: Explaining the 1990s Social Care Expansion in Japan, in H.-J. Kwon (ed.), *Transforming the Developmental Welfare State in East Asia*. London: Ashgate.

Perrons, D., C. Fagan, L. McDowell, K. Ray, and K. Ward (2006) (eds), *Gender Divisions and Working Time in the New Economy: Changing Patterns of Work, Care and Public Policy in Europe and North America*. Cheltenham: Edward Elgar.

Ray, R., J. C. Gornick, and J. Schmitt (2010). Who Cares? Assessing Generosity and Gender Equality in Parental Leave Policy Designs in 21 Countries. *Journal of European Social Policy*, 20(3):196–216.

Sainsbury, D. (1996). *Gender Equality and Welfare States*. Cambridge: Cambridge University Press.

Robeyns, I. (2006). The Capability Approach in Practice. *The Journal of Political Philosophy*, 14(3):351–76.

Salais, R. and R. Villeneuve (2004) (eds), *Europe and the Politics of Capabilities*. Cambridge: Cambridge University Press.

Sen, A. (1990). Gender and Cooperative Conflicts, in I. Tinker (ed.), *Persistent Inequalities: Women and World Development*, pp. 123–49. New York: Oxford University Press.

Sen, A. (1992). *Inequality Re-Examined*. Cambridge, MA: Harvard University Press

Sen, A. (2002). Response to Commentaries. *Studies of Comparative International Development*, 32(2):78–86.

Sewell, W. (1992). A Theory of Structure: Duality, Agency and Transformation. *AJS*, 98(1):1–29.

Strandh, M. and M. Nordenmark (2006). The Interference of Paid Work with Household Demands in Different Social Policy Contexts. *British Journal of Sociology*, 57(4):597–617.

Taga, F. (2011). Yuragu Roudou kankyo to Kazoku kihan—Salaryman no kako togenzai [Uncertain Work Environments and Family Norms—The Past and Present of Salaried Men] in F. Taga (ed.) *Yuragu Salaryman Seikatsu* [An Uncertain Salaried Man's Life], pp. 1–33. Kyoto: Minerva Press.

Van der Lippe, T. and P. Peters (2007). *Competing Claims in Work and Family Life*. Cheltenham: Edward Elgar.

Voydanoff, P. (2005). Work Demands and Work-to-Family and Family-to-Work Conflict: Direct and Indirect Relationships. *Journal of Family Issues*, 26(6):707–26.

Williams, F. (2012). Converging Variations in Migrant Care Work in Europe. *Journal of European Social Policy*, 22(4):363–76.

Index

Note: bold entries refer to figures or tables.

Index

The manufacturer's authorised representative in the EU for product safety is Oxford University Press España S.A. of El Parque Empresarial San Fernando de Henares, Avenida de Castilla, 2 - 28830 Madrid (www.oup.es/en or product.safety@oup.com). OUP España S.A. also acts as importer into Spain of products made by the manufacturer.
Printed and bound by CPI Group (UK) Ltd, Croydon, CR0 4YY
13/08/2025
01935911-0009